ELEMENT

MW01077864

Many social scientists want to explain why people do what they do. A barrier to constructing such explanations used to be a lack of information on the relationship between cognition and choice. Now, advances in cognitive science, economics, political science, and psychology have clarified this relationship. In *Elements of Reason*, 18 scholars from across the social sciences use these advances to uncover some of the cognitive foundations of social decision making. They answer tough questions about how people see and process information and provide new explanations of how basic human needs, the environment, and past experiences combine to affect human choices. *Elements of Reason* is written for a broad audience and can be read by anyone for whom "Why do people do what they do?" is an important question. It is the rare book that transforms abstract debates about rationality and reason into empirically relevant explanations of how people choose.

Arthur Lupia is Professor of Political Science at the University of California, San Diego. He is coauthor of *The Democratic Dilemma: Can Citizens Learn What They Need to Know?* (Cambridge University Press, 1998).

Mathew D. McCubbins is Professor of Political Science at the University of California, San Diego. He coauthored *The Democratic Dilemma: Can Citizens Learn What They Need to Know?* (Cambridge University Press, 1998).

Samuel L. Popkin is Professor of Political Science at the University of California, San Diego. He is the author of *The Reasoning Voter: Communication and Persuasion in Presidential Campaigns*.

Cambridge Studies in Political Psychology and Public Opinion

This series has been established in recognition of the growing sophistication in the resurgence of interest in political psychology and the study of public opinion. Its focus ranges from the kinds of mental processes that people employ when they think about democratic processes and make political choices to the nature and consequences of macro-level public opinion.

Some of the works draw on developments in cognitive and social psychology and relevant areas of philosophy. Appropriate subjects include the use of heuristics, the roles of core values and moral principles in political reasoning, the effects of expertise and sophistication, the roles of affect and emotion, and the nature of cognition and information processing. The emphasis is on systematic and rigorous empirical analysis, and a wide range of methodologies are appropriate: traditional surveys, experimental surveys, laboratory experiments, focus groups, and in-depth interviews, as well as others. These empirically oriented studies also consider normative implications for democratic politics generally.

Politics, not psychology, is the primary focus, and it is expected that most works will deal with mass publics and democratic politics, although work on nondemocratic publics is not excluded. Other works will examine traditional topics in public opinion research, as well as contribute to the growing literature on aggregate opinion and its role in democratic societies.

Other books in the series

Series list continues on page following the Index

ELEMENTS
OF
REASON

COGNITION, CHOICE, AND THE BOUNDS OF RATIONALITY

Edited by

ARTHUR LUPIA
University of California, San Diego

MATHEW D. MCCUBBINS
University of California, San Diego

SAMUEL L. POPKIN
University of California, San Diego

CAMBRIDGE
UNIVERSITY PRESS

PUBLISHED BY THE PRESS SYNDICATE OF THE UNIVERSITY OF CAMBRIDGE
The Pitt Building, Trumpington Street, Cambridge, United Kingdom

CAMBRIDGE UNIVERSITY PRESS
The Edinburgh Building, Cambridge CB2 2RU, UK
40 West 20th Street, New York, NY 10011-4211, USA
10 Stamford Road, Oakleigh, VIC 3166, Australia
Ruiz de Alarcón 13, 28014 Madrid, Spain
Dock House, The Water Front, Cape Town 8001, South Africa

http://www.cambridge.org

First published 2000

Printed in the United States of America

Typeface Sabon 10/12 pt.   *System* QuarkXPress [BTS]

A catalog record for this book is available from the British Library.

Library of Congress Cataloging in Publication Data
Elements of reason : cognition, choice, and the bounds of rationality / edited by Arthur
Lupia, Mathew D. McCubbins, Samuel L. Popkin.
p.   cm. – (Cambridge studies in political psychology and public opinion)
Includes bibliographical references and index.
ISBN 0-521-65329-0 (hb) – ISBN 0-521-65332-0 (pb)
1. Political psychology.   2. Reasoning (Psychology)   3. Political sociology.
4. Social choice.   I. Lupia, Arthur, 1964–   II. McCubbins, Mathew D. (Mathew
Daniel), 1956–   III. Popkin, Samuel L.   IV. Series.
JA74.5 .E434   2000
320'.01'9 – dc21   99–059174

ISBN   0 521 65329 0   hardback
ISBN   0 521 65332 0   paperback

Contents

Contents

Tables and Figures

Tables and Figures

Acknowledgments

Elements of Reason draws from the lessons of a wide array of scholarship to provide a cohesive and positive statement about human reasoning and political decision making. This project spanned six years from inception to publication and benefited from the input of dozens of scholars from political science, economics, psychology, cognitive science, and philosophy.

The essays here were first presented at a seminar series on reasoning and politics held at UCSD between 1994 and 1996. We thank the American Political Institutions Project, the Public Policy Research Project, and the Department of Political Science at UCSD for their support of these seminars.

We owe a great many debts of gratitude. We acknowledge the support of the National Science Foundation and its Political Science Program, through grant SBR-9422831. Dr. Lupia acknowledges a UCSD COR grant for partial support of the research reported here. This volume was begun while Dr. McCubbins was a fellow at the Center for Advanced Study in the Behavioral Sciences and was completed during Dr. Lupia's Center fellowship. The editors are grateful for the financial support for this fellowship, provided by the National Science Foundation, grant SBR-9022192.

We owe heartfelt thanks to several hardworking research assistants: Scott Basinger, Greg Bovitz, and Andrea Campbell. We are especially grateful for the hard work and keen insight of James Druckman.

Contributors

Arthur T. Denzau, *Claremont Graduate School*
Michael A. Dimock, *North Carolina State University*
Norman Frohlich, *University of Manitoba*
Shanto Iyengar, *Stanford University*
James H. Kuklinski, *University of Illinois at Urbana-Champaign*
Milton Lodge, *State University of New York at Stony Brook*
Arthur Lupia, *University of California, San Diego*
Mathew D. McCubbins, *University of California, San Diego*
Douglass C. North, *Washington University, St. Louis*
Joe Oppenheimer, *University of Maryland*
Samuel L. Popkin, *University of California, San Diego*
Paul J. Quirk, *University of Illinois at Urbana-Champaign*
Wendy M. Rahn, *University of Minnesota*
Paul M. Sniderman, *Stanford University*
Charles Taber, *State University of New York at Stony Brook*
Philip E. Tetlock, *Ohio State University*
Mark Turner, *University of Maryland*
Nicholas A. Valentino, *University of Michigan*

1

Beyond Rationality: Reason and the Study of Politics

ARTHUR LUPIA, MATHEW D. MCCUBBINS, AND SAMUEL L. POPKIN

A primary objective of social science is to explain *why people do what they do*. One of the great difficulties inherent in crafting such explanations is that we cannot observe the thoughts that precede a choice. As a result, social scientific explanations of individual behavior must be based on assumptions about the relationship between thinking and choosing – assumptions whose validity is not obvious.

In this volume, 18 scholars from a broad range of social scientific perspectives join together in an effort to craft better explanations of political behavior. Individually, each contributor argues that better explanations will come from paying closer attention to the relationship between thinking and choosing.

Collectively, our goal is to transform debates about the limits of rationality into more effective explanations of why people do what they do. Our attempt at such a transformation begins in this chapter, where we develop an alternative approach to the study of politics. Our approach combines *a single, empirically sensible definition of rationality* with *an aggressive pursuit of how people seek and process information*.

Our definition of rationality is motivated by the belief that scarcity is ubiquitous in political contexts. There are, for example, more ways to spend public funds than there are funds to spend, more ideas about what a society should do than there are opportunities for society to act, and so on. Time and energy are also scarce. As a result, people lack the time and energy to pursue all possible opportunities. Because scarcity is ubiquitous in political contexts, political actors must make choices.

To explain why people make certain choices, it is necessary to understand that *choice is the product of reason*, where reason is the human process of seeking, processing, and drawing inferences from information. People reason about how the consequences of various actions relate to

1

the satisfaction of their desires. This relationship between reason and choice is as true for the selfish or wealth-maximizing actors common to economic models as it is for the altruist who *chooses* to allocate scarce resources for the benefit of others. It is as true for people who think of themselves primarily in terms of cultural or group identities as it is for rugged individualists. Scarcity forces all people to make choices, and these choices are the product of reason.

Since reason is the antecedent of choice, limits in our understanding of reason shackle our ability to explain what people do. We argue that these shackles can be lifted. Indeed, the point of the volume is to identify *elements of reason,* the systematic components of the process by which humans seek and use information. Our main premise is that, whatever their motivations, people seek and process information about politics in predictable ways. The purpose of *Elements of Reason* is to clarify what these predictions might be.

The premise that people seek and process information about politics in predictable ways permeates the entire book. Each of our contributors defines an element of reason that should be incorporated into the study of politics. Collectively, these elements are supported by empirical discoveries from a broad range of perspectives. Cognitive scientists, economists, political scientists, and psychologists all contribute elements of reason to this volume. While these essays – described in greater detail at the end of this chapter – are not a comprehensive overview of the links between the social sciences and the study of the mind, each clarifies an important aspect of the relationship between thinking and choosing. They show that *reason* determines how the environment, the basic needs of the human organism, and past experiences combine to determine people's desires, and ultimately, their choices.

Our goal is to create a new understanding of how people reason. By applying these insights to the study of politics, we can better explain *why people do what they do.*

RATIONALITY AND THE IMPORTANCE OF LISTENING TO REASON

Many scholarly approaches to the study of politics rely on controversial or unspecified assumptions about the relationship between thinking and choosing. Political systems theories, group theories, elite theories, and prospect theories, for example, rely on vague or narrowly tailored assumptions about *how* people think about what they choose.

One well-known and particularly controversial approach to the study of politics operates on the premise that people are rational.[1] Unlike some other approaches to the study of politics, rational choice theories are seldom vague in their assumptions about how people think. One of the reasons that rational choice theories are so controversial, however, is that some of the best-known applications are perceived to rely on unrealistic assumptions. Complicating matters further is the fact that the term *rationality* means different things to different people. As a result, when people argue about the role of rationality in the study of politics, they are often arguing about very different concepts.

In this section, we use the controversy about rational choice theories to demonstrate that more careful attention to reason can help a broad range of scholars – regardless of whether they glorify or vilify rational choice theories – to craft better explanations of why people do what they do.

Rationality's Dueling Definitions

> Here the problem is first to see just what is meant by rationality. The term, as a recent writer noted, "has enjoyed a long history which has bequeathed to it a legacy of ambiguity and confusion. . . . Any man may be excused when he is puzzled by the question how he ought to use the word and particularly how he ought to use it in relation to human conduct and politics." Several meanings can be differentiated.
>
> – Berelson, Lasarsfeld, and McPhee
> 1954: 310

Rationality is a concept so central to human endeavor, so important, and yet so empirically elusive that it cannot help but be subject to a broad range of interpretations when used in everyday discourse. In scientific discourse, however, it is desirable for words to have precise meanings. The validity and soundness of scientific claims about causality, correlation, and truth depend critically on such precision. So, while it is not surprising that words such as rationality have multiple meanings in everyday discourse, when it comes to achieving scientific objectives, multiple meanings cause problems.

---

[1] The role of reason in rational choice theories is particularly relevant to the study of politics. Many of the best-known and most-cited scholarly tomes of the last two decades – including works on voting (Cain, Ferejohn, and Fiorina 1987), the U.S. Congress (Cox and McCubbins 1993; Kiewiet and McCubbins 1991; Krehbiel 1991; Rohde 1991; Shepsle 1978, 1979; Shepsle and Weingast 1981, 1995), political parties (Aldrich 1995), elections (Cox 1997; Enelow and Hinich 1985; Fiorina 1981; Hinich and Munger 1994; Popkin 1991), interest groups (Olson 1965; Ostrom 1990), international relations (Bueno de Mesquita and Lalman 1992; Powell 1990), and comparative politics (Bates 1989; Laver and Schofield 1990; Laver and Shepsle 1996) – are influenced by rational choice theories.

The *Oxford English Dictionary* (*OED*) is arguably the most authoritative and general source for determining the print-based origins of English words. The 1989 *OED* contains the following definitions of the word *rationality*.

1. The quality of possessing reason; the power of being able to exercise one's reason.
2. The fact of being based on, or agreeable to, reason. A rational or reasonable view, practice, etc.
3. The tendency to regard everything from a purely rational point of view.

This definition, while not multiplicitous, is not very informative. In each case, rationality is defined in terms of the words *rational* or *reason*. Consider *OED*'s definitions of the term *rational*.

1. Having the faculty of reasoning; endowed with reason.[2]
2. Exercising (or able to exercise) one's reason in proper manner; having sound judgment; sensible, sane.
3. Of, pertaining, or relating to reason.
4. Agreeable to reason; reasonable, sensible; not foolish, absurd, or extravagant.
5. Descriptive of methods of analysis and planning that make use of calculation to bring about a projected result, esp. in economic or social organization.

While we will discuss *reason* in greater detail below, the *OED* defines it[3] as

[2] Older uses of *rationality* in the *OED* are quite clear about rationality's dependence on reason. Consider, for example, usage from the year 1398: "the soule racional, in that he vsyth contemplacion, he hyghte *speculativus*"; from the year 1547: "the racionall sences consisteth in reason, the whiche doth make a man or woman a reasonable beaste"; and from the year 1615: "We determine that the Braine is the Pallace of the Rationall Soule." Note that these uses, unlike contemporary definitions, predate the advent of scientific revolution and originate from Europe – England, in particular. As a result, they were offered in historical contexts where men could employ reason, but it was sacrilege to assert that anyone but God could be omniscient. Hence, at the time of these uses of the term *rationality*, rationality and omniscience were clearly distinct concepts. A problem with many modern uses of the term *rationality*, by critics and proponents of rational choice theorists alike, is the belief that rationality implies omniscience (i.e., the belief that someone making a mistake is sufficient to judge them irrational). The rationality definition we advocate restores the separation between the two concepts. The confounding of omniscience and rationality has, in our opinion, severely impeded scientific progress, particularly in the last half century.
[3] We recite here the relevant definitions of the word, omitting irrelevant definitions, such as "A statement of some fact (real or alleged) employed as an argument to justify or condemn some act, prove or disprove some assertion, idea, or belief."

1. That intellectual power or faculty (usually regarded as characteristic of mankind but sometimes also attributed in a certain degree to the lower animals) which is ordinarily employed in adapting thought or action to some end; the guiding principle of the human mind in the process of thinking.
2. The ordinary thinking faculty of the human mind in a sound condition; sanity.

Many of the controversies concerning the social scientific usage of rationality are apparent in the definition of the word *rational*. Consider, for example, the *OED*'s characterizations of what rational behavior must not be. It must not be "foolish." It must not be "extravagant." In addition, it must be "sane." Yet these terms, each descriptive of behavior, complicate more than they clarify. Who is to judge what constitutes foolishness or extravagance? Even the meaning of sane behavior is subject to broad interpretation (e.g., Foucault 1965).

A consensus on the constitution of a scientifically useful rationality definition would ameliorate the problems caused by multiplicity of meaning. A consensus that rationality is wealth-maximizing behavior, or that a behavior is rational only if it is the same one that an omniscient calculator would choose, would help determine whether rationality is a useful basis for social scientific explanation. But no consensus has emerged, even within economics – the discipline with which rational choice explanations are most commonly associated. The present condition of the term *rationality* is that it has multiple personalities. Consider, for example, these contemporary definitions of the term:

1. "A decision is only rational if it is supported by the best reasons and achieves the best possible outcome in terms of all the goals."[4]
2. "Rational choice theory holds that choices among relevant goods involve comparing all goods against each other to make correct choices dictated by preference schedules."[5]
3. "The second basic assumption of positive economics is that people are rational in the sense that they have an objective and pursue it in a reasonably consistent fashion. When considering *persons*, economists assume that the objective being pursued is *utility maximization*; that is, people are assumed to strive toward the goal

---

[4] From Herbert A. Simon, "Rationality in Political Behavior," in *Political Psychology* 16 (1995): 48. Simon provides this definition as modern neoclassical economics' standard of rationality.

[5] From Robert E. Lane, "What Rational Choice Explains," in *Critical Review* 9 (1995): 110.

of making themselves as happy as they can (given their limited resources)."[6]

4. "We have assumed, in particular, that consumers always strive to obtain the greatest possible satisfaction from spending their incomes, and that businessmen always try to make the biggest profits they can."[7]

5. "Beyond requiring that the utility function is consistent, no specific content is specified for it. As far as economics is concerned, a utility function can assign as much or more utility to giving away goods as to consuming them; it can award as much utility (to me) for an increase in the living standard of an Indian peasant as it does for the same increase in my own living standard. *Rationality is orthogonal to selfishness* [emphasis added]."[8]

6. "A 'rational agent' in such a model is simply one who obeys certain axioms, and that is the end of it."[9]

7. "A key economic assumption is that individuals, in making choices, rationally select alternatives they perceive to be in their best interests. . . . This reliance on *rational self-interest* should not be viewed as blind materialism, pure selfishness, or greed. We all know people whose favorite radio station is WIIFM (What's In It For Me?), but for most of us self-interest often includes the welfare of our family, our friends, and perhaps the poor of the world."[10]

8. "[R]ational choice involves three optimizing operations. The action that is chosen must be optimal, given the desires and beliefs of the agent. The beliefs must be optimal, given the information available to the agent. The amount of resources allocated to the acquisition of information must be optimal . . ." (Elster 1999: 285).

9. "Virtually all human behavior is rational. People usually have reasons for what they do, and if asked, can opine what these reasons are" (Simon 1995: 48).

From an intellectual distance, it is possible to agree with all of these definitions – or at least to be offended by none of them. But for the purpose of scientific inquiry, the conflict inherent in these defi-

---

[6] From *Modern Labor Economics: Theory and Public Policy,* by Ronald G. Ehrenberg and Robert S. Smith, 6th ed. (Reading, MA: Addison-Wesley, 1997), p. 4.

[7] From *A Textbook of Economic Theory,* by Alfred W. Stonier and Douglas C. Hague, 4th ed. (New York: John Wiley & Sons, 1973), p. 657.

[8] Simon 1995: 48.

[9] From *Rationality, Allocation, and Reproduction,* by Vivian Walsh (Oxford: Clarendon Press, 1996), p. 3.

[10] From *Macroeconomics: A Contemporary Introduction,* by William A. McEachern, 3rd ed. (Cincinnati: College Division, South-Western Publishing Co., 1994), pp. 6–7.

nitions is detrimental. For example, someone who wants to explain political behavior may have to grapple with a question such as this: What will people do if forced to choose between obtaining the greatest possible satisfaction from spending their incomes, attempting to make the biggest profits they can, or considering the welfare of the poor of the world? Conventional notions of rationality give inconsistent guidance.[11]

If we can distill these many definitions of rationality into one that is sensible empirically and widely applicable, we can avoid much of the confusion currently associated with the concept of rationality and, as a result, craft better explanations of why people do what they do. We will now argue for such a definition. The basis of our argument is that there is at least one issue on which these many definitions of rationality agree. The issue is that people have reasons for the choices they make. That is, regardless of people's genetics or socialization, if they are able to make choices, then reasons will precede these choices. Therefore, we conclude that *a rational choice is one that is based on reasons, irrespective of what these reasons may be.*

Given the definition we offer, it may be the case that all of the choices we observe are rational. Of course, rational choice theorists have made this claim before, much to the delight of the approaches' critics.[12] In this case, however, such derision misses a fundamental point of the social scientific enterprise. If our collective scientific goal is to explain why people do what they do, then our task is to understand the reasons for the

[11] Ordeshook 1986 also articulated this problem in the introduction to his book *Game Theory and Political Theory*:

> The word "rational" is commonly used to summarize our assumptions about these choices. The meaning of this word has been the subject of a lively debate during the past 20 years and has given rise to considerable misunderstanding among the antagonists. Instead of entering this debate, we note that purposeful choice does not necessarily mean that people carefully and consciously list their alternative actions, map all the relevant or possible consequences of each act, estimate the probability of each consequence, and define precisely their preferences across all consequences. Thus, we cannot ignore habit, instinct, and the use of simple cues and heuristics to uncomplicate complex decisions. Indeed, one of the formal theorists' most important activities is to understand why various heuristics are reasonable responses to complex environments and to the costs of alternative modes of making decisions. The presumption of purposeful choice implies simply that, after taking account of people's perceptions, values, and beliefs, we can model their decisions by asserting that they act as if they make such calculations.

[12] The critics' delight stems from the idea that if we can conjure a rational explanation for all observed behaviors, then rational choice theories are post hoc and explain nothing. In our claim that all behavior is rational, our intent is to draw maximum attention to the fact that reason precedes choice and to the implication that explaining many choices is aided by understanding human reason.

choices they make. Whether we agree with these reasons or not, whether these reasons make sense to us or not, and whether we use the term *rationality* to describe the process by which these reasons are formed or not is irrelevant.[13] If we desire improved explanations of why people do what they do, then we must introduce greater clarity about the properties of human reason into our analyses.

STANDARD ECONOMIC RATIONALITY, BOUNDED RATIONALITY, AND ELEMENTS OF REASON

In the search for improved explanations of human behavior, scholars have offered many distinct definitions of *rationality*. The continuing battle over the meaning of rationality continues to produce many new and important insights (see, e.g., Rubenstein 1998 for a review). To clarify our plan for incorporating reason into the study of politics, however, we restrict our focus to two of the most common definitions of rationality. Both are often cited in debates about rational choice theory and distinguish themselves from the extant population of definitions because they are so well known.

The definitions are *standard economic rationality* (aka *homo economicus,* substantive rationality) and *bounded rationality*. Each definition is based on a distinct assumption about how people reason. In what follows, we will compare and contrast these two focal definitions to show why progress in the attempt to explain social behavior requires more advanced concepts of reason than most social scientists currently employ.

Standard Economic Rationality

The standard economic definition of rationality (also commonly employed in rational choice theories of politics) equates rational actors with omniscient calculators.[14] Consider, for example, the rationality definition in Kreps's (1990a) microeconomic theory text. Kreps's rational actor is omniscient with respect to the domain of choice. By his definition, rational actors know the consequences of all the actions available to them and choose the action whose consequences provide the highest benefit. Kreps defines a player as "not fully rational" when "she doesn't quite understand the full implications of her actions" (480).

---

[13] With respect to this goal, normative judgments about the quality of people's reasons, while appropriate in philosophical discourse or casual political conversation, are no substitute for a logically valid and empirically sound social scientific explanation of political or economic behavior.

[14] While there exist economic definitions of rationality that do not fit this description exactly, it is a reasonable description of many economic treatments.

8

While this definition of rationality is not completely realistic, it has been very useful in application. The unique success of contemporary microeconomic theory as an explanatory endeavor is a great testament to the standard definition's effectiveness. This success should also be no surprise, for in many of the cases that economists examine, interested audiences do not find controversial the assumption that people act "as if" they were omniscient calculators.

Standard economic rationality is not as widely accepted in political science. Many political scientists know that when you ask the typical political decision maker, be it a voter, a legislator, or a juror, a detailed question about a political matter, he or she often offers incorrect responses. Therefore, it is only natural that many political scientists are skeptical of explanations of political behavior that rely on the assumption that political actors act "as if" they are omniscient calculators. This characteristic of political decision making has led to heated debates in the discipline about the usefulness of rationality-based theories and proposed alternatives to standard economic rationality (see, e.g., *Critical Review* 9, no. 102, 1995).

Bounded Rationality

Herbert Simon argued that unlike *homo economicus,* people are not omniscient calculators – they do not do all of the calculations all of the time. Simon affected a generation of social scientists by introducing bounded rationality – a framework for explaining behavior that recognizes that human cognition is limited. His insight, so controversial at first and so obvious in retrospect, challenged scientists to consider a very different view of economic and political behavior.

The concept of bounded rationality found a receptive audience in political science. It is clear that political decision makers have limited ability to perceive and calculate. However, while bounded rationality seems like the perfect alternative to standard economic rationality, the literature growing out of this concept has had two serious shortcomings.

The first shortcoming is that bounded rationality is often incorrectly presumed to imply nonmaximizing or non-self-interested behavior. This presumption leads to a false polarization between bounded rationality and other rationality definitions. As Jensen and Meckling (1976: 307) observe:

Simon's work has often been misinterpreted as a denial of maximizing behavior, and misused, especially in the marketing and behavioral science literature. His later use of the term 'satisficing' (Simon 1959) has undoubtedly contributed to this confusion because it suggests rejection of maximizing behavior rather than maximization subject to costs of information and decision making.

Indeed, Simon (1995: 45) later admitted that "virtually all human behavior is rational. People usually have reasons for what they do."[15]

A second problem with the concept of bounded rationality as it is often interpreted is that it is underdefined. Simon forced scholars to recognize that people are limited in their ability to seek and process information. This was brilliant and valuable. Yet beyond that, Simon's bounded rationality offers little systematic guidance as to where the bounds of rationality are. Simon provides his most specific clues about these bounds when he discusses irrationality. Consider the following passage (1985: 297):

We may deem behavior irrational because, although it serves some particular impulse, it is inconsistent with other goals that we deem more important. We may deem it irrational because the actor is proceeding on incorrect facts or ignoring whole areas of relevant fact. We may deem it irrational because the actor has not drawn the correct conclusions from the facts. We may deem it irrational because the actor has failed to consider important alternative courses of action. If the action involves the future, as most action does, we may deem it irrational because we don't think the actor uses the best methods for forming expectations or for adapting to uncertainty. All of these forms of irrationality play important roles in the lives of every one of us, but I think it is misleading to call them irrationality. They are better viewed as forms of bounded rationality.

Of course, this directive is problematic in that it does not lend itself to better explanations of why people do what they do. For example, how would a scholar seeking to render a positive explanation (rather than a normative description) of political behavior determine "areas of relevant fact" or "important alternative courses of action." Is a voter who bases her choice on the endorsement of a political party or an interest group (such as the Sierra Club or the NRA) less "rational" than she would have been had she based her vote on a careful consideration of 100 candidate issue positions? If the answer to this question seems to be an obvious yes, then consider the fact that she may draw the same conclusion and have the same degree of certainty about the consequence of her choice

---

[15] The term *satisficing,* when employed post hoc, offers no clarity over and above that provided by standard definitions of rationality. This is why the many satisficing-based explanations of behavior that are unaccompanied by insights on the trade-offs and reasons that precede a decision to satisfice, or without evidence on the cognitive mechanisms that would activate a satisficing algorithm, have had no discernable impact in the fields of political science and economics. Indeed, we have encountered many scholars who interpret the possibility of satisficing as a license to throw away all of rational choice theory, including its focus on motivations and its logical rigor. This is nonsense. The idea that humans are limited cognitive entities, far from relieving scholars from the burden of rigorous analysis, requires us to apply the most reliable scientific methods we can muster to understanding the complex contours of human reason.

in both cases. What then would distinguish rational choice from irrational choice? *More importantly, how would such a distinction, if it could be made, help scholars explain why people do what they do?* The simple answer is that such a distinction would not be helpful. Of course, Simon realizes this. He concludes that it is impossible to generalize about the bounds of rationality as the following passage (1985: 297) indicates: "To understand and predict human behavior, we have to deal with the realities of human rationality; that is bounded rationality. There is nothing obvious about these boundaries; there is no way to predict, a priori, where they lie."

Why We Seek Elements of Reason

If our goal is to explain why people do what they do, then both the standard economic treatment of rationality and the common interpretation of bounded rationality are of limited applicability. Standard economic rationality assumes that rationality is merely the pursuit of objectives, given perfect information and unlimited information-processing capacity. But, in reality, omniscience is impossible. People never have *all* of the facts; further, even if an individual did have all of the facts, then cognitive limitations would often render him or her unable to perform the calculations necessary to deduce an optimal choice. So, from the perspective of explaining many political behaviors, standard economic rationality is either an impossible fantasy or a stylization, but not a realistic option.

The concept of bounded rationality tells us this much, but nothing more. Worse yet, the initial attractiveness of bounded rationality has led many observers to confound the fact that people are not omniscient calculators with the notion that their decisions are not the product of reason (e.g., analysts labeling as "irrational" those actions based on reasons they either disagree with or do not understand). This confusion has not only retarded debates about the applicability of rationality; it has hampered our discipline's ability to get on with the business of explaining why people do what they do. If a primary objective is to explain why people do what they do, we accomplish it more effectively by understanding how people reason. It is time to move beyond the heated, but fruitless, debate about whether people are rational and toward a scientific search for the elements of reason.

It is at this juncture that our efforts in *Elements of Reason* part ways with many extant rational choice theories and Simon's view of bounded rationality. We argue that human reason has systematic attributes and that social scientists should learn these properties and incorporate them into their explanations. We advocate an approach to the study of poli-

11

tics that combines the premise that people have reasons for what they do with the premise that our treatment of how people reason should be informed by modern scholarship about how cognition and affect affect information processing.

PLAN OF THE BOOK: BUILDING SIMON'S BRIDGE

Simon urged social scientists to think about the cognitive limits that underlie human behavior and to pursue what individual and collective actions are possible given those limits. At the same time, he proposed a bridge between the sciences of the mind and social sciences such as economics and political science. But in the 1950s and 1960s, the era in which Simon first advocated such a bridge, the tools for building it were not available.

At the time of Simon's initial challenge to standard economic rationality, the cognitive and neural sciences were in their infancy. Throughout the 1950s and 1960s, for example, psychology was still emerging from an era dominated by behaviorism and the belief that behavior can be explained without peering into the black box of the brain (Delgato and Midgley 1992). And cognitive science, as we know it today, did not exist. As a result, experimental evidence and theorizing on the contours of human reason were quite sparse.

In the years since Simon's initial contributions, the science of the mind has undergone great change. Advances in technology have allowed scholars ranging from psychology to biology to observe brain-behavior correspondences more accurately (e.g., Damasio 1994). Advances in computer technology have allowed for estimation and simulation procedures, such as neural networks, that allow evaluation of complex hypotheses about reasoning and behavior (e.g., see Churchland and Sejnowski 1991, Clark 1997, and Crick 1994 for reviews of progress in this field; see McCauley 1997 for current controversies). Moreover, advances in the technology of game theory, such as Harsanyi's (1967, 1968a, b) innovations regarding games with incomplete information, provide a window through which clear links between rationality and reason can be seen. Put another way, the scientific advances of the last four decades give us an opportunity that Simon did not have when he forged the concept of bounded rationality – the opportunity to build Simon's bridge.

In the chapters that follow, we take the next step in building that bridge and toward offering more effective explanations of why people do what they do. Like Simon, we proceed with the belief that an exhaustive brain-behavior mapping is an unrealistic goal. However, such a mapping is unnecessary for *improving* our ability to explain why people do what they do. Between a brain-behavior mapping and such widely used concepts as standard economic rationality and bounded rationality are other alternatives – explanations of behavior that incorporate well-established elements of reason and provide more precise inferences about why people do what they do. The chapters that follow represent the responses of scholars from different intellectual perspectives to the following challenge: help broad, scientific audiences understand elements of reason.

The chapters of the book are divided into two parts. The chapters in Part I describe *external* elements of reason. External elements of reason are incentive-altering forces outside the body, such as social norms and political institutions, that affect the collection and processing of information. In Part II, the focus switches to *internal* elements of reason. Internal elements of reason are brain-based factors inside the skin, such as affective states and prior knowledge, that have systematic effects on how individuals seek and process political information.

All chapters are unified in at least two respects. First, each chapter introduces a distinct element of reason. Second, each chapter challenges conventional wisdom. Common themes, such as "voters lack consistent attitudes" or "heuristics save the day," are eschewed in favor of more instructive explorations of the contours of human reason. As a result, each chapter points to a potentially important new direction in the study of political and economic behavior. Moreover, each chapter, in the way that it addresses the question at hand, reinforces our contention that advances in the social scientific explanation of reasoning and choice will depend less on whether people know what analysts thought they should have known and more on scientists' abilities to understand how people process the information they have.

Part I: External Elements of Reason

In the first three chapters of Part I, political institutions are the surprising source of elements of reason. We say surprising because the focus of the modern study of institutions has been on the way that institutions aggregate individual preferences into collective outcomes and on the way that institutions affect individuals' strategic considerations. In the chapters by Denzau and North, Lupia and McCubbins, and Sniderman, by contrast, the authors argue that institutions also affect what people do by structuring their choices and their beliefs.

In "Shared Mental Models: Ideologies and Institutions," Arthur Denzau and Douglass North argue that the "mental models that the mind creates and the institutions that individuals create are both essential to the way human beings structure their environment in their interactions with it." They motivate their arguments for greater attention to mental models by carefully differentiating cases in which the standard economic definition of rationality has succeeded and failed. They then suggest that replacing "the black box of the 'rationality' assumption used in economics and rational choice models" is the key to better explanations of many social behaviors.

The replacement they suggest is a theory of choice that recognizes the central role of shared mental models. The idea is that many social interactions, including most of those that we would recognize as political, require collective action. They continue that the evolution of collective endeavors will be shaped by the mental models (e.g., conceptualizations of what causes what in the world) that people share. They conclude that the types of uncertainty that social actors face and the types of institutional environments in which they interact constrain the set of mental models upon which collective action can be based. Denzau and North thus provide substantive insight into the determinants of economic and political development, as well as a methodological guide for incorporating cognitive limits into formal theories of choice.

Arthur Lupia and Mathew D. McCubbins's "The Institutional Foundations of Political Competence" continues the demonstration of how institutions affect reasoning. Their chapter focuses on communication. They begin with the premise that many political decision makers cannot learn what they need to know from direct experience (e.g., most people cannot experience the consequences of passing NAFTA or social security reform until after they are passed). As a result, many political decision makers must learn what they can from the testimony of others (voters from politicians and the media, juries from witnesses, legislators from bureaucrats, and so on). This reality implies that the types of decisions that people make depend on whom they choose to believe.

Lupia and McCubbins show how political institutions affect "who believes whom" by identifying conditions under which political institutions clarify others' incentives. They then draw on case studies, experiments, and formal modeling results to show when and how institutions allow people to make more effective decisions about whom to believe. Like the approach of Denzau and North, theirs blends the logical rigor of formal theory with insights about learning from the cognitive sciences. Lupia and McCubbins's research clarifies and amends extant explanations of when and how voters, jurors, and legislators learn what they need to know.

In "Taking Sides: A Fixed Choice Theory of Political Reasoning," Paul M. Sniderman argues that institutions affect reasoning by fixing certain choices. His argument is quite innovative in that it builds an institution-centered argument about politics from a social psychological perspective

– the usual projection from that perspective is an attempt to explain political behavior by focusing exclusively on citizen characteristics. Passages, such as the following, reveal the extent to which Sniderman's argument departs from the social psychological research tradition from which he hails:

> Initially, we asked how citizens effectively can simplify political choices so as to make them coherently. Putting the question this way led us, like virtually everyone else, to start the explanatory process by focusing on the characteristics of citizens. How much attention do they pay to politics? What do they know about it? What political ideas do they hold and how are they organized? Answer these questions, and we should be in a position to figure out how citizens make political choices. Or so it seemed then. Now, I am persuaded, we had the order of things wrong.

Throughout the chapter, Sniderman builds the foundations of a theoretical framework in which citizens "do not operate as decision makers in isolation from political institutions. If they are in a position to overcome their informational shortfalls by taking advantage of judgmental shortcuts, it is because public choices have been organized by political institutions in ways that lend themselves to these shortcuts." His argument clarifies the path to a way of thinking where psychological considerations of reason and the institutional structure of choice combine to produce more effective explanations of why people do what they do.

In the fourth through sixth chapters of Part I, public pressures generate external elements of reason. In the chapter by Frohlich and Oppenheimer, social norms are the public pressures that induce individuals to give up material gain for the benefit of anonymous strangers. For Iyengar and Valentino, campaign advertisements are the form of public pressure in question. In both chapters, clever experiments reveal systematic factors that determine how these public pressures affect reasoning and choice. In the chapter by Rahn, the source of pressure is public mood. Rahn uses data from several surveys to show how certain very public events (e.g., a war) lead entire populations to interpret new pieces of information in distinct ways.

The elements of reason in Norman Frohlich and Joe Oppenheimer's "How People Reason about Ethics" are social norms that induce self-interested individuals to engage in other-regarding behavior. Their chapter begins by alerting us to the fact that motives for altruistic behavior are hard to disentangle – selfish behavior and other-regarding behavior are often observationally equivalent. For example, if Joe helps Norm, it is hard to know whether Joe does it primarily for his own sake or primarily for the sake of Norm.

15

Because selfish and other-regarding behaviors are often difficult to disentangle, it can be hard to evaluate claims about the frequency or causes of other-regarding behavior. Frohlich and Oppenheimer have overcome some of these difficulties with a series of clever experiments. In their experiments, subjects have an opportunity to leave money for others. The donations are totally anonymous – the experiment is designed so that neither the experimenter nor the recipient can determine the source of any particular contribution. Their experiments reveal regular patterns in other-regarding behavior. In particular, they find that altruism is mediated by subjects' considerations of the unseen recipients' moral worthiness and by the personal costs of engaging in other-regarding behavior. Put another way, altruism in these experiments follows some simple, perhaps even economic, rules.

In Shanto Iyengar and Nicholas Valentino's "Who Says What: Source Credibility as a Mediator of Campaign Advertising," the source of public pressure is campaign advertisements, and the element of reason in question is the role of credibility in cue-based processing. A truth of modern politics is that some of the most important political communications are sent and received through the media. A particularly interesting class of such communications is the political advertisement – 30 to 60 seconds of carefully constructed prose and imagery. Although many ads are powerful, political advertisements vary in how effectively they build or reinforce support for the cause at hand.

Iyengar and Valentino offer a series of experiments that explain some of this variation. They focus on the relationship between a candidate's ideological background and his or her claims. Whereas successful candidates do not typically choose campaign themes on which they are not credible, the candidates in Iyengar and Valentino's experiments sometimes do. That is, they show that Democratic candidates suffer after airing advertisements on traditionally Republican issue areas and vice versa. The results are strong and emphasize how credibility is an essential part of effective campaigning in the television age.

Part I's final chapter is "Affect as Information: The Role of Public Mood in Political Reasoning." In it, Wendy Rahn challenges the common view that emotion only gets in the way of some proper or pure form of reason. She argues instead that certain types of emotional responses may actually help people process information more effectively. The element of reason upon which she focuses is public mood. Public mood is a type of time-dependent nationalism – a feeling that is good when your country wins a war or a major sporting event, a feeling that is bad following a national tragedy. Rahn then conducts several analyses in which she reveals a correspondence between variations in public mood and variations in opinion and behavior. Rahn also provides evidence that public mood acts as a filter through which other important types of information are received and interpreted. Her research suggests that public mood can have a very large influence on political judgment, and that such an influence, rather than interfering with cognition, can actually aid it.

Part II: Internal Elements of Reason

In Part II, the focus is on elements of reason that are housed within the skin. The first three chapters of Part II are attempts to construct general theoretical frameworks for understanding how people process information.

In James Kuklinski and Paul Quirk's "Reconsidering the Rational Public: Cognition, Heuristics, and Mass Opinion," the elements of reason in question are *heuristics* – common judgmental shortcuts that people use to draw complicated inferences from simple environmental cues. Kuklinski and Quirk's investigation starts at the point where psychological and political science treatments of heuristics part from one another. Kuklinski and Quirk remind us that psychologists view heuristic decision making as leading to inferior decisions. Political scientists, by contrast, have come to view heuristic decision making as therapeutic – leading people to make the same decisions that they would have made if better informed. This division suggests a middle ground – a set of conditions under which heuristics aid decision making and a set of conditions under which heuristics lead people to make different decisions than they would have made had they possessed greater amounts of political information.

Kuklinski and Quirk then set out to clarify the role of heuristics in political reason by stating and testing hypotheses about the benefits and drawbacks of heuristics usage. They review and compare results from a series of innovative experiments about heuristics that are distinctly political. These experiments document the fallacies that heuristic decision making can engender in important policy contexts. Together, their argument and experiments provide valuable clarification of the surprising ways in which common heuristics affect political choices.

In Milton Lodge and Charles Taber's "Three Steps toward a Theory of Motivated Political Reasoning," our attention is directed away from heuristics and toward an element of reason known as affective charge. In this chapter, as in previous ones, Lodge and Taber use theory and experiments to clarify how a common aspect of human cognition affects political choices.

Lodge and Taber's efforts extend exciting lines of research in psychology and cognitive science concerning the deep connections between cognition and affect. Whereas cognition and affect were once viewed as polar opposites in the context of understanding reason, an increasingly common view is that each is necessary for the proper functioning of the other. Lodge and Taber's research demonstrates this point in political contexts. They show how three factors ("hot cognition" – the hypothesis that people store feelings as well as facts about past events; "on-line processing" – the hypothesis that the interpretation of new information is affected by information or feelings that they already have; and a person's affective state at the time of processing) combine to lead people to interpret new pieces of political information in nonobvious ways. They show how feelings become information and are treated in the reasoning process as if they were objective facts.

Lodge and Taber's findings reinforce and extend the implications of the relationship between affect and reasoning suggested in the chapter by Wendy Rahn. Like Rahn's findings, those of Lodge and Taber suggest that affect and cognition are inextricably linked. Their unique contribution, however, is to offer us direct and controlled experimental observations of this link. In particular, we see affect leading people to have identifiable biases in the types of political information to which they will attend.

In Part II's third chapter, Samuel L. Popkin and Michael Dimock examine how prior knowledge affects the processing of new information. In "Knowledge, Trust, and International Reasoning," Popkin and Dimock show how the degree to which people's trust in government and in others corresponds to their interpretations of foreign affairs issues. They use surveys from the American National Election Study and the Times-Mirror polling organization to show that people who neither understand nor trust their own government are also suspicious of foreigners, apprehensive about international trade, and isolationist. These surveys form the basis for their ultimate, and more general, conclusion – that what people know about the political process and about political institutions have systematic effects on how they reason about new events in the political world. They conclude that prior knowledge of key political concepts provides people with a life raft and a compass with which they can survive and better navigate the turbulent and often complex seas of political debate.

The closing chapters of Part II draw our attention to the limits on the types of associations that political decision makers can and do draw. Knowing these limits is critical to many questions in political science. For example, understanding the conditions under which some political actors can get others to listen to and believe that an observable social phenomenon is associated with an unobservable political process is the key to winning elections and public policy debates. To supply us with elements of reason relevant to this question, we recruited a scholar with a background in social psychology, Philip E. Tetlock, and a scholar with a background in cognitive science, Mark Turner.

The starting point of Philip E. Tetlock's "Coping with Trade-Offs: Psychological Constraints and Political Implications" is that political interactions involve trade-offs. Economists typically treat people as able to engage in trade-off reasoning. Tetlock disagrees, arguing that "people are reluctant decision makers who do their damnedest to minimize cognitive effort, emotional dissonance, and moral ansgt by denying that important values conflict." So when faced with little motivation to make trade-offs, people refuse to do so. However, when they are motivated, Tetlock concludes that "[p]eople are best thought of not as cognitive misers but as cognitive managers who deploy mental resources strategically as a function of the perceived importance and tractability of the problem." Tetlock's chapter provides important clues about why people retain certain "core values," even in the face of evidence that the rationale for holding such values implies painful trade-offs.

The penultimate chapter of Part II is written by Mark Turner. Turner is a central figure in one of the most fundamental debates in cognitive science – the dynamics of concept formation and change. This debate matters to politics because the outcomes of familiar processes, such as persuasion, agenda setting, framing, and priming, depend on the conditions under which concepts do and do not change.

Where the standard view of cognitive operation once represented the mind as an inflexible serial calculator, Mark Turner's "Backstage Cognition in Reason and Choice" draws extensively from the modern view of the mind as a highly adaptable organ capable of drawing effective and complex inferences from relatively simple environmental stimuli. His argument reveals the often-obscure dynamics that differentiate persuasive claims from nonpersuasive ones. He considers, for example, the counterfactual claim that Hitler's influence would have been different if Churchill had been prime minister of England in 1938 instead of Chamberlain. He then shows us what an audience must know for such a claim to be effective in debate, as well as the situations in which analogous claims would be totally ineffective. While students of politics are quick to explain the effectiveness of rhetorical strategies by focusing exclusively on effective strategies, Turner's method of inference provides the foundation for a more systematic and useful approach.

CONCLUSION

The future success of political science depends on our discipline's ability to explain why people do what they do in political contexts. The chapters in *Elements of Reason* are the result of an intellectual challenge that we offered to scholars working in a number of academic disciplines. We challenged each contributor to help us understand and expand on why people do what they do. The product, though not a tightly bound theory of human behavior, clarifies the connections among exciting new ideas in several scientific disciplines.

Simon's bridge is worth building, but it will take a long time to build. Working with the contributors to *Elements of Reason* has given each of us, the editors, a clearer idea of how to contribute to its construction. We hope that it does the same for you.

PART I

External Elements of Reason

2

Shared Mental Models: Ideologies and Institutions
ARTHUR T. DENZAU AND DOUGLASS C. NORTH

The rational choice framework assumes that individuals know what is in their self-interest and make choices accordingly. Do they? When they go to the supermarket (in a developed country with a market economy), arguably they do: In such settings, they know, almost certainly, whether the choice would be beneficial, ex post. Indeed financial markets in the developed market economies (usually) possess the essential characteristics consistent with substantive rationality. However, the diverse performance of economies and polities both historically and contemporaneously argues against individuals really knowing their self-interest and acting accordingly. Instead people act in part upon the basis of myths, dogmas, ideologies, and "half-baked" theories.

Ideas matter; and the way that ideas are communicated among people is crucial to theories that will enable us to deal with strong uncertainty problems at the individual level.[1] For most of the interesting issues in political and economic markets, uncertainty, not risk, characterizes choice making. Under conditions of uncertainty, individuals' interpretation of their environment will reflect their learning. Individuals with common cultural backgrounds and experiences will share reasonably convergent mental models, ideologies, and institutions; and individuals with different learning experiences (both cultural and environmental) will have different theories (models, ideologies) to interpret their environment. Moreover, the information feedback from their choices is not sufficient to lead to convergence of competing interpretations of reality. In consequence, as Hahn (1987: 324) has pointed out, "there is a con-

This essay is reprinted with permission from *Kyklos* 47 (1994): 3–31, copyright © Helbing & Lichtenhahn.
[1] The literature on finite automata, starting with Aumann (1981), has taken a more formalist path to explore the implications of specific notions of bounded rationality (although some term this irrationality). This literature is compatible in certain ways with our argument, and can be supplemented by the communication of mental models notions developed here. For a comprehensive survey of this literature, See Binmore (1987, 1988) or Marks (1992).

tinuum of theories that agents can hold and act on without ever encountering events which lead them to change their theories."

In such cases, multiple equilibria will result. It is the argument of this essay that in order to understand decision making under such conditions of uncertainty, we must understand the relationships of the mental models that individuals construct to make sense out of the world around them, the ideologies that evolve from such constructions, and the institutions that develop in a society to order interpersonal relationships. Let us begin by defining each concept.

Following Holland et al. (1986: 12), we start with the presumption that "cognitive systems construct models of the problem space that are then mentally 'run' or manipulated to produce expectations about the environment."

For our purposes in this essay, ideologies are the shared framework of mental models that groups of individuals possess that provide both an interpretation of the environment and a prescription as to how that environment should be structured. As developed in North (1990: 3), institutions are the rules of the game of a society and consist of formal and informal constraints constructed to order interpersonal relationships. The mental models are the internal representations that individual cognitive systems create to interpret the environment; the institutions are the external (to the mind) mechanisms individuals create to structure and order the environment.

Some types of mental models are shared intersubjectively. If different individuals have similar models, they are better able to communicate and share their learning. Ideologies and institutions can then be viewed as classes of shared mental models. Our analysis in this essay is aimed at describing the more general set of shared models. The large body of work on cognitive science, especially the recent work on connectionism, can be used to analyze the features and dynamics of mental models, and thus of ideologies and institutions as well. But the social aspects of these models are of crucial importance in human society, and these cultural links are only now being explored in this literature (Hutchins and Hazlehurst 1992). These social features are modeled in this essay as necessitating communication that allows an individual's experiential learning to be based on a culturally provided set of categories and priors so that each person does not need to begin as a tabula rasa.

The mental models that the mind creates and the institutions that individuals create are both essential to the way human beings structure their environment in their interactions with it. An understanding of how such models evolve and the relationship among them is the single most important step that research in the social sciences can make to replace the black box of the "rationality" assumption used in economics and rational choice models. We need to develop a framework that will enable us to understand and model the shared mental constructs that guide choices and shape the evolution of political-economic systems and societies. What follows is an outline of how to go about this task.

THE CHOOSER FACING UNCERTAINTY

Neoclassical economics has evolved, especially since Marshall left the scene, into a series of applications of the constrained optimization model, under complete information. Von Neumann and Morgenstern, followed by Savage and others in the 1940s and early 1950s, extended the model to incomplete information, so that the chooser faces risk and chooses a lottery rather than a unique outcome. However, the overarching presumption is that the resulting choices always reflect substantive rationality. This approach has been under attack by a few economists, as well as other social scientists and philosophers, for decades; but there has been no serious alternative that incorporates the successful applications of the substantive rationality optimization model while still dealing in some productive manner with the shortcomings.

Friedman (1953: 19–23) provides one of the fundamental defenses for substantive rationality, as well as laying out its basic features (21): He considers

the economic hypothesis that under a wide range of circumstances individual firms behave as if they were seeking rationally to maximize their expected returns . . . and had full knowledge of the data needed to succeed in this attempt; as if, that is, they knew their relevant cost and demand functions.

Friedman states that it is unnecessary for the substantive rationality model to be a descriptive model, with the detailed implication true at the individual level. Rather, the model is supposed only to be applied empirically at the aggregated, or market, level. Even if we accept this justification and the philosophic approach behind it, there is still a problem for the substantive rationality paradigm: There are situations of societal decisions, or resource allocation, that substantive rationality models predict poorly, even at the market level. We believe that this is the situation now facing economics (and politics) in major areas of decisions, and that we must seriously consider the development of alternatives to applying substantive rationality in situations where it performs poorly.

The Conditions for Substantive Rationality

Before going further with this long march away from the neoclassical economist's behavioral assumption, we should further justify the need to take this divergent path. To do this, we first consider a question little asked in the economics literature: What characterizes the domain of application of the substantive rationality paradigm?

One way to answer this question is to consider a simple situation of choice in which substantive rationality models work well. Consider choice in competitive posted-price markets. In such a situation, the chooser need only choose the quantity to buy or sell, as the competitive environment makes the agent's situation relatively simple – the price can effectively be viewed as a parameter, and only the quantity need be chosen at this parametric price. The experimental literature, casual empiricism, and much empirical literature (at least on the demand side) have shown this approach to yield a good predictive model. Both proponents and critics typically acknowledge the power of the competitive behavior version of the substantive rationality paradigm in the appropriate domain of application. Even more widely studied, and found very successful, has been the experimental study of Double Auctions (DAs).

Recent work by Gode and Sunder (1992a, 1992b, 1993), however, raises important questions about why the substantial rationality approach is so successful in the DA setting. Gode and Sunder measure efficiency success by the percentage of the sum of potential buyer and seller rents (also termed consumer surplus and profits) that are realized. The first and second papers calculate the expected efficiency for several different types of exchange institutions, using traders they term Zero Intelligence (ZI). These traders "lack power to observe, remember, search, maximize, or seek profits." They summarize each case by the minimum of the expected efficiency.

In a sealed-bid auction, they find that the minimum efficiency for unconstrained ZI traders (ZI-U) is 0. If the bidders are constrained to make only bids that do not yield them losses on the proposed trade, these constrained (ZI-C) traders generate a minimum efficiency of 75%. Gode and Sunder (1992a cited in 1992b: 2) found that employing profit-motivated human traders instead of the ZI-C traders improved efficiency by 1%. They then compared their ZI-C traders when placed in two different versions of a standard experimental Double Auction. One auction allowed the bidders to accept bids and make contracts continuously, while the other mechanism first waited for all bidders to submit a bid before trying to clear any contracts. This difference in institution alone, with traders who do not respond at all to the differing strategic opportunities available, raises the minimum expected efficiency from 75% to 81%. The 6% improvement due to an institutional change, compared to the 1% improvement using human subjects, suggests that institutional features by themselves can be as important as rationality in generating efficient economic performance. The 81% minimum for one of the auction institutions even suggests that most efficiency gains in some resource allocation situations may be attributable to institutional details, independent of their effects on rational traders.[2]

Individual Chooser Attributes

What are the features of the choice environment that determine the success of the substantive rationality model in the posted-price case? We believe that the following are the most important, although further study of the experimental literature may require updating:

Complexity. How complex are the mental models required in order to make sensible choices given one's preferences and resources? This can best be judged by the similarity of the most appropriate models (so far as we now know) to what the chooser already knows. Analysis does not reduce the complex to the simple. Rather, it's a process by which we substitute a familiar complexity for one that we have found novel. The invisible-hand result is now obvious and intuitive, not because it is simple but because we are trained to see it when it may be present or useful. Thus, complexity and the frequency of similar choices may be related.

Motivation. This has two aspects. First, how important are the choice and the models underlying it to the individual? If the choice involves issues that are central to how the individual assesses herself and the world, and if the chooser is paying substantial attention to the situation, then learning may be much more rapid. Larger cognitive resources, in terms of both time and attention, are likely to be allocated to evaluating the choice and its effects. Second, to what extent does the individual believe that his own choice can affect the real outcomes? For example, the choice may be one that is actually made by some collective body, such as a committee. In such a case, the individual may realize that she cannot control the decision and therefore may devote less effort to finding a solution. On the other hand, the individual may perceive the situation as one that has carryover benefits to other such situations, and

---

[2] This may be the explanation for the results first noticed by Ledyard over a decade ago, and presented in seminars at that time, and which appear in Easley and Ledyard (1992). They study the individual decisions by participants in experimental double oral auctions, as Ledyard had found that they were not behaving as predicted by economic theory; i.e., they had apparently not learned the "right" model, even though the allocation results were very efficient (over 95% of the consumer and producer rents captured by the parties).

treat the learning as a capital investment with payoffs beyond the specific situation in which it is presented.

There is already experimental evidence of the existence of significant cognitive costs in learning to make decisions, *and of their capital investment nature*. Jamal and Sunder (1988) have found that when untrained subjects are involved in an auction experiment without being paid dollars for their accrued buyer and seller rents, the convergence to a competitive equilibrium price is slow and there is substantial variance even at the end of an auction period. Note that the efficiency achieved does not differ much whether the subjects are already trained, or not, but the Gode and Sunder work apparently provides an explanation for the high efficiency in the untrained auction experiments. When the same class of subjects are placed in the same institution, but know they are going to be paid, the convergence is much faster and variance much lower. In fact, once these subjects have gone through a paid session, and then are in an unpaid auction experiment with the same rules, the results are the same as if they were being paid. This strongly supports the idea that learning is irreversible.

Information (quality and frequency). How good is the information provided that would allow one to correct bad models? That feedback is essential to learning is suggested by the Jamal and Sunder experiments. The feedback needs to be in a form that makes its relevance to the mental models transparent, or complexity is increased further.

How often does the choice, or similar choices, occur in a situation in which feedback is provided? This problem is crucial in complex models. The basic problem is that the mappings we are trying to learn are usually multidimensional, possibly involving several dimensions in a complex, nonlinear relation. We only have a finite, often very small, data sample of real experiences from which to learn this mapping. This is not a simple statistical problem, especially when we start out not certain as to the relevant arguments involved in the mapping.

Easy Choices – Competitive Markets

In terms of the three criteria described, competitive markets provide a setting for easy choices:

Complexity. Minimal modeling is required for less complex situations. The institutions themselves may help reduce the complexity of the mental models that one must attempt to create. For example, behaving parametrically with respect to the market does not require building models of other agents. One need only decide how to maximize one's own utility.

28

Coursey and Mason (1987) found experimentally that people can maximize unknown functions in a few (5 to 10) choices if they are told the value of the function after each choice proposed.

Information. Having good information is essential to improving the mental models. Most of the information needed to make decisions is readily available in posted-price settings, and, due to the frequency of choices, there is a large enough sample to improve estimation of the necessary empirical relations. The consumer in a competitive market makes similar choices continually, and may be buying the same items continually. Even if the product is not being bought frequently, the choice is like many others, and protocols for dealing with such occasional choices have been developed and refined.

Motivation. Feedback is direct in some private goods markets; for search goods, the feedback is immediate. Even for experience goods, the feedback, while a bit less immediate, is reasonably quick. This holds nicely for private goods, but becomes more problematic for nonprivate goods, as suggested by Downs's idea of rational ignorance regarding publicly provided bundles of goods.

STRONG UNCERTAINTY, AND MORE COMPLEX PROBLEMS

Strong, or Knightian, uncertainty would occur when a chooser cannot be viewed as capable of having even subjective probability distribution functions defined over a set of possible outcomes. Such uncertainty is likely to occur when the chooser cannot even state a list of outcomes ranked in terms of their values. Without such a list, one cannot act as though the situation is one of Knightian risk or of Savage subjective probabilities. We believe that all people start out life in such a situation of strong uncertainty. Holland et al. argue that one needs to organize one's observations and learning into some sort of structure, one not already programmed at birth; we discuss some of the implications of such an approach to knowledge representation throughout this chapter.

If all choices were simple, were made frequently with substantial and rapid feedback, and involved substantial motivation, then substantive rationality would suffice for all purposes. It would be both a predictive and a descriptive model of equilibrium settings, and learning models based upon it could be used to describe the dynamics out of equilibrium.

But not all choices have all these characteristics. The choice may be made infrequently, sometimes only once in a lifetime. Without direct experience, information about potential outcomes may not be known or easily acquired. In these circumstances, substantive rationality may not be a good descriptive model. In some of these cases, however, the Gode and Sunder results suggest that the substantive rationality models can still be predictive even if rationality is actually irrelevant to the human behaviors involved.

Yet there are hard choices, made in institutional settings, that are not as conducive to efficiency as the Double Auction. These problems are now coming to the forefront in the social sciences. We have already developed an adequate framework for the easier problems in which the substantive rationality gives good results. But we have (for the most part implicitly) sometimes made the erroneous assumption that we can extend without explicit consideration the scope of the substantive rationality assumption to deal with the problems of ambiguity and uncertainty, which characterize most of the interesting issues in our research agenda and in public policy. Problems in political economy, economic development, and economic history, for example, all require an understanding of the mental models and ideologies that have guided choices. It is now time to refocus on the wide range of problems we have so far ignored that involve strong uncertainty.

Let's consider a likely candidate for being a hard choice. Suppose you are faced with accepting or rejecting a take-it-or-leave-it offer of 10 apples for $3 in a situation isolated from other potential apple sellers. Suppose further that you believe that the apples are of such a quality that you value them at more than $3. In order to increase your utility, however, you would like to acquire them at a lower price. You may wish to assess whether the seller is really willing to walk away if you reject the first offer, or would begin to bargain. You need to begin building a mental model of the seller, based on whatever information is available. Your past interactions, both with the seller and with other such vendors in similar situations, provide information for this construction. If you are purchasing 1,000 such bags, your motivation increases. Further, the situation may not be one of potential continual dealing. You must be able to assess this probability in order to best evaluate the risk that the apples are not what you expect them to be. All of these factors require, as Arthur (1992) suggests, the building of internal representations of the agents with whom one interacts.

An even harder choice would involve a game situation with a multiplicity of other agents. In such a situation, the likelihood that substantive rationality holds begins to dwindle more rapidly. The complexity of the situation increases dramatically, as is suggested by Kreps et al. (1982). Arthur (1992: 4) argues that the obvious flaws that would exist in one's mental models of other agents would make such decision situations not well defined, and thus the game becomes a situation in which the standard rational choice framework has no application and no results.

Another dimension of hard choices is involved in collective choices. Downs (1957: chap. 14) argued that the reduced ability of an individual to determine the decision also reduces the incentives to become informed about it. We argue that this also reduces the motivation to allocate cognitive resources to the building and improving of mental models.

In order to deal with the variation in the complexity of decision problems, Arthur (1992: 5) has introduced the idea of a problem complexity boundary. In dealing with problems less complex (Lindgren [1992] discusses the problem of a metric for this complexity) than this boundary, the substantive rationality approach is often a successful modeling approach, even if not all individuals would perform the problem analysis perfectly. The standard economic approach serves well with these problems. But with problems beyond the complexity boundary, Arthur argues effectively, the deductive rational procedure cannot be relied on. He claims that the level at which they can use it reliably and accurately is surprisingly modest. In spite of this, we are able to make decisions even in situations that are not well defined, and thus in which the rational procedure provides no clue as to how to proceed.[3]

In these situations, we must be using some procedure that differs fundamentally from the deductive rational procedure. But what is that procedure? How can people make choices when faced with complex problems in a situation of strong uncertainty? Holland et al., and Arthur (1992) argue that we must be employing some form of induction, enabling us to learn from the outcomes of our previous choices. To learn usefully by induction, an individual needs some sort of mental model with which to understand the implications of a chosen action, as well as needing some way to identify potentially useful actions and the possible outcomes of those actions. The very spaces for actions, outcomes, and reasonable strategies, as well as the mappings between them, may be objects of ignorance on the part of the individual.

If problem complexity is too great, possibly because of unreliable information as to the state of the world, then the substantive rationality results do not hold. Modeling such situations requires one to model the decision maker as building internal mental models to represent the world and to learn from that world in order to improve the resulting choices.

---

[3] The finite automata approach is one way to deal with ill-defined problems, but this literature does not necessarily produce substantive rationality results.

CHOICE AND STRONG UNCERTAINTY

Heiner (1983) presents a complementary argument in situations of uncertain choice. He argues that when there is a gap between an agent's competence and the difficulty of the decision problem to be solved (a C-D gap), the human agent constructs rules to restrict the flexibility of her own choices in such situations. This result can be derived using expected utility analysis once one incorporates a lack of reliability in interpreting environmental signals. By channeling choices into a smaller set of actions, an institution improves the ability to perceive the environment and to communicate. These benefits can then improve the ability of those involved in the institution to extract the potential gains from exchange or cooperation in production.

But that is not all that the agent does. Humans also construct explanations in the face of ambiguity and uncertainty and act upon them. Describing primitive societies, we call such explanations myths, dogmas, taboos. In our own society, we have religions, superstitions, and other belief structures to account for many aspects of the environment for which we do not possess or acquire the information to arrive at something like a scientific consensus. How do we account for belief in such ideologies and act upon them when they entail faith?

A partial answer may be derived from an experiment by a psychologist, Feldman (1959), in which subjects were shown sequences of 1's and 0's and were asked to predict which number would appear next. The subjects were quick to spot patterns in the sequence and to form hypotheses on the process generating the sequence. Using their models, they made predictions about which number would appear next when in fact the generation had been purely random.[4] It may be an evolutionarily superior survival trait to have explanations for inexplicable phenomena; or this effect may just be a by-product of the curiosity which helps make humans model builders. But whatever is the explanation, mental models and ideologies play a crucial role in choice making.

[4] The Feldman experiment is discussed in Arthur (1992: 12–13). Arthur's intention was to show how human decision makers discern patterns in the context of complicated and ill-defined problems. In fact, what Feldman is showing is that individuals see patterns where they don't exist. In the Feldman experiment as in life and science more generally, the models are underdetermined by the data. In other words, many models fit any finite data sequence, and data alone cannot judge among this multiplicity of "generalizations." Instead, one needs theory to generate hypotheses that can be tested, and impose constraints across sets of hypotheses involving different data, in order to perform inductions usefully.

LEARNING AND SHARED MENTAL MODELS

In order to deal with the issue of how the mind confronts complexity, we need first to step back and explore how learning occurs (Churchland 1989; Clark 1989; Holland et al. 1986). There are two conceptually distinct levels at which learning occurs, each with important implications for the effects of the learning. First, learning entails developing a structure by which to make sense out of the varied signals received by the senses. The initial architecture of the structure is genetic, but its subsequent development is a result of the experiences of the individual. This architecture can be thought of as generating an event space, which gets used to interpret the data provided by the world. The experiences can be classified into two kinds – those from the physical environment and those from the sociocultural linguistic environment (Hutchins and Hazlehurst 1992). The event space structure consists of categories – classifications that gradually evolve from earliest childhood on in order to organize our perceptions and keep track of our memory of analytic results and experiences. Building on these categories, we form mental models to explain and interpret the environment, typically in ways relevant to some goal(s) (Holland et al. 22). Both the categories and the mental models will evolve to reflect the feedback derived from new experiences – feedback that may strengthen and confirm our initial categories and models or that may lead to modifications: in short, learning. Thus, the event space may be continually redefined with experience, including contact with others' ideas.

Learning that preserves the categories and concepts intact, but that provides changed ideas about details and the applicability of the existing knowledge, is the second level of learning. Together, learning within a given set of concepts and learning that changes the structure of concepts and mental models suggest a widely known approach to the dynamics of learning, which we investigate further in the section "Dynamics of Mental Models and Institutions."[5]

It is at this juncture in the learning process that the learning of humans will diverge from that of other animals (such as the sea slug, which

---

[5] Randall Calvert has suggested a means of formalizing these ideas. The action-outcome mappings can be defined as $o = g(a|s)$, where a is an action, s an equivalence class of situations representing the state of the world as viewed by the agent. The function maps into the outcome, o, or a *pdf* over outcomes. The agent also values this outcome with a utility function, $u(o|s)$. In order to avoid problems with the notation as the event space changes, we collapse this into a mapping from actions into utility, $f(u|a,s)$. The learning process is represented by the evolution of the equivalence classes over the situation space, as well as a Bayesian learning involving a fixed situation space, in which only the mapping between actions and utility changes.

appears to be a favorite research subject of cognitive scientists) and certainly diverges from the computer analogy that dominated so much of early studies in artificial intelligence. The mind appears to order and reorder the mental models in successively more abstract form so that they become available to process information outside its special-purpose origins. The term used by Clark and Karmiloff-Smith (1994) to describe this process is *representational redescription.* The capacity to generalize, to reason from the particular to the general, and to use analogy are all a part of this redescription process.

At the individual level, the representational redescription is a reorganization of the categories and concepts and is a form of learning distinct from the parameter updating that is occurring in the "normal learning" phase. Once a useful set of categories and concepts has been acquired, the normal learning period is long, relative to the often sudden shifts in viewpoint that accompany representational redescriptions. The resulting dynamics are those of a punctuated equilibrium – a concept first used by Eldredge and Gould (1972) to describe their new theory of biological speciation.[6] We apply our own version of the punctuated equilibrium idea in the subsection "Changes in Mental Models as Punctuated Equilibria."

The world is too complex for a single individual to learn directly how it all works. The entire structure of the mental models is derived from the experiences of each individual – experiences that are specific to the local physical environment and the socio-cultural linguistic environment. According to Arthur (1992: 8), "it follows that if two people have been exposed to different experiences in the past, with resulting differences in the stock of conceptual representations they have formed, they may act on the same data differently."

In fact, no two individuals have exactly the same experiences, and accordingly, each individual has to some degree unique perceptions of the world. Their mental models would tend to diverge for this reason if there were not ongoing communication with other individuals with a similar cultural background.

One of the crucial tasks of human development is to replace the nearly tabula rasa situation at birth with one informed extensively by various forms of indirect learning. The vast diversity of human culture that anthropologists have discovered suggests the relevance of this claim. In

---

[6] If the event space does not undergo a representational redescription, then the dynamics are continuous. However, as note 3 notes, we are extremely unlikely ever to learn the true model, in the sense of assigning positive probability mass to it. It seems likely that there is always potential for learning more about the best event space in which to represent the world, and thus eventually the possibility for learning to result in a punctuation.

such a situation, learning other than direct must be providing the degree of similarity among its members that one finds within each human society. The cultural heritage provides a means of reducing the divergence in the mental models that people in a society have and also constitutes a means for the intergenerational transfer of unifying perceptions. We may think of culture as encapsulating the experiences of past generations of any particular cultural group. With the diversity of human experiences in different environments, there exists a wide variety of patterns of behavior and thought.

This learning can be called cultural learning, and what it provides in a premodern society is exactly the categories and concepts that enable members of that society to organize their experiences and be able to communicate with others about them. Cultural learning in premodern societies provided not only a means of internal communication but also shared explanations for phenomena outside of the immediate experience of the members of the society in the form of religions, myths, and dogmas. As noted, such belief structures are not confined to primitive societies but are an essential part of the belief structure of modern societies.

The changes in lifestyles and technology of the past centuries have led to a proliferation and elaboration of ideologies. Each attempts to provide positive mental models that tend to focus on the actions and valued outcomes defined as crucial to the hindering or fostering of the vision embodied in the ideology (Downs: 1957; Higgs 1987; Munger and Hinich 1992). The positive mental models in an ideology comprise action-outcome mappings that relate the utility-relevant outcomes to the possible actions among which the individual could choose. For example, consider Milton Friedman's discussion about the social responsibility of business. He argues that the best way to be socially responsible, which we assume here to be an argument in the chooser's utility, is to maximize profits. Sowell (1980) further develops this argument, showing the crucial problems of information in attempting to deal with the effects of one's actions on unknown others.

Given the action-outcome mappings of an ideology, the normative or vision parts of an ideology identify the aspects of reality that are crucial to achieving one's goals. A Marxist would see the employment relation as an exploitive one: All profits produced in the capitalist production process result from the extraction of "surplus value" from the workers by the capitalist employing them, as the workers are induced to work for wages lower than the value of their labor. In attempting to examine the extraction of any excess value, a Marxist economist would attempt to measure the surplus value seized by the capitalist employer. A study of the strategies used to increase the surplus taken might then go on in order to determine what the workers' movement should spend its energies fighting, and

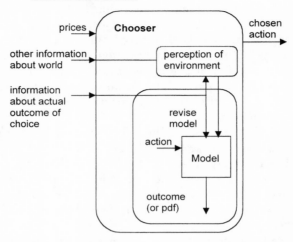

Figure 2.1. Uncertain chooser using mental models to learn directly.

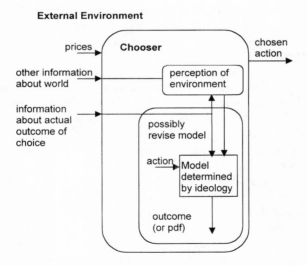

Figure 2.2. Uncertain chooser using ideology to help form mental models.

what it should ignore. Using only this view of the world, one is likely to ignore many important changes that might make 1993 different from 1848, when Marx published the *Communist Manifesto*.

Learning in the Face of Strong Uncertainty with a Shared Mental Model

Let us see how to build a model of a chooser facing strong uncertainty, who learns both directly from the world and from a shared mental model (SMM). Figure 2.1 shows the basic framework of the uncertain chooser learning directly from the external environment to improve his mental models. This process is slow and can be made more rapid by having some indirect learning in the form of artifactual models already created by others, termed shared mental models.

This learner with shared mental models is shown in Figure 2.2. Here, the SMMs are related to the idea of Bayesian priors in a Bayesian learning model. But the Bayesian approach implicitly assumes that the dimensions of the internal mental models used to represent the external world are correct, in some sense.[7] The connectionist approach and the classification models used by Holland et al. instead assume that the fundamental issue is to determine the relevant dimensions of reality for one's decision or learning purposes. For the learner, these dimensions are identified in large part by the existing shared mental models. A set of prior beliefs about action-outcome mappings is being learned as part of the shared mental model, whether traditional culture or ideology.[8]

---

[7] This is one rationale for the result of Kalai and Lehrer (1990). They argue that unless the true model of the world is already given atomic mass (strictly positive probability assigned) in the support set of the learner's prior distribution, it is impossible for the learner ever to have the true model in the support set of any posterior distribution. If the attribute space in which the distributions are defined by a learner's mental model cannot be mapped in a straightforward way into a space in which the true model can be "naturally" located, it would be impossible to learn the true model using Bayesian methods.

[8] A second tie between our approach here and a Bayesian learning model needs to be laid out. The idea of a representational redescription is just like a surprise to a Bayesian learner: Both seem to be impossible to generate from a Bayesian model. We believe, however, that this is a mistaken interpretation of the Bayesian model and not demanded by the model itself. Many of the punctuations in the learning of an individual result from the failures of a mental model to predict in situations when the individual is highly motivated, i.e., when the issue is one very important to the learner. The failure of the mental model to predict in such an important situation makes the person wish to avoid the negative reinforcement (opportunity cost that has been realized) in the future. Such motivation to learn causes the learner to mull over the problem to find its cause, and this process of reconsideration of the mental models can be viewed as giving substantial weight to the new data (the model's failure in a salient situation).

In a connectionist model, such repeated retraining on the new observation(s) can

Mental Models in a Simple Model of Communication

The SMM has another important effect. It provides those who share it, at least in the sense that they have an intellectual understanding of it, with a set of concepts and language that makes communication easier. Better communication links would lead to the evolution of linked individuals' mental models converging, rather than diverging, as they continue to learn directly from the world.

Figure 2.3 shows the idea of communication suggested by the Church-land view of knowledge representation. Agent L (for Local) has made a decision inside her mind, and wishes to explain the basis for the decision to her supervisor, agent C (for Center). The patterns in L's mind (e.g., idea A) must first be encoded in a language, such as English. This encoding would be perfect if there were a known set of dimensions in which to measure the factors that caused L to make the choice she did, and if she could state her measurements of each of these dimensions. This would constitute sufficient statistics for the decision, and communicating this data would be a perfect substitute for the neural patterns in L's mind.

But the problem is that we almost never know what factors actually influenced a decision we have made. Much of our understanding in a choice situation can be tacit knowledge, as Michael Polanyi (1983) discusses. We perceive things of which we are not even consciously aware, but which can affect a decision. Attempts to determine the factors and their weights can be made, but the basic problem is that we are always uncertain as to the dimensions of the knowledge space that must be measured. As a result, the encoding is almost certainly to be imperfect, and not all the information used by L to make the decision can be placed in the communication channel.

The communication channel itself may be noisy and imperfect, and this problem has been studied extensively. This problem is a purely technical one and is not the cause of the problems on which we wish to focus here. Instead, the decoding process at the listener, C, causes the next important communication problem. The listener must transform the

cause substantial changes in the connection weights, and thus the implicit concepts and relations embodied in the model. Although this process has not been explicitly simulated in the experiments performed by cognitive scientists, it is because their mental models have not suggested the relevance of this idea. In a Bayesian model, the idea can be interpreted as the addition of new data with substantial (nonatomic) weight attached to it. Such a new mass of data different from the priors would cause a discrete jump in the posterior distribution from the prior. Both these types of discrete changes can be interpreted as the counterpart of representational redescriptions. These changes would also generate the type of punctuated equilibrium dynamics considered in this chapter.

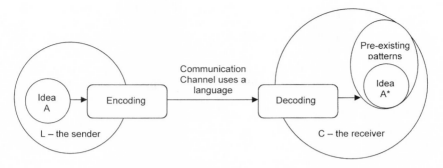

Figure 2.3. A theory of communications for two agents.

message in the communication channel into changes in the neural patterns in his mind. The decoding is affected by the preexisting patterns already in the listener's mind. The reception of a message and its interpretation by the listener, idea A*, are strongly influenced by the categories and beliefs that the listener already has about the world.

To the extent that the speaker and a listener have common features in their mental models for the concepts identified in the SMM, they are more likely to be able to encode and decode their internal ideas into a shared language, and more likely to be able to communicate effectively using single terms to stand for substantial pieces of implicit analysis embodied in the SMM. To use the example of Marxian ideas again, consider the terms *worker* and *capitalist*. To use these words in the standard classical Marxian manner is implicitly to bring in considerable pieces of analysis of the exploitation of workers in a capitalist system. The terms also may carry affective denotations, so that the listener is expected to favor the worker and disfavor the capitalist. The world seen through this set of concepts can be a world quite different from that described in a neoclassical price theory text.

If a SMM is available, the concepts embodied in the structure of mental models that several people have can be made more similar. As noted, the words used to convey the mental model ideas are used repeatedly as the espousers discuss their ideas among themselves, either orally or in written form. In consequence, the mental models of the two people should become more similar; in turn, their learning from some data observed by one of them should be relatively similar, compared to a random pair of individuals.

Mental models are shared by communication, and communication allows the creation of ideologies and institutions in a coevolutionary process. The creation of ideologies and institutions is important for eco-

39

nomic performance, as there exist gains from trade and production that require coordination. As various authors have written, a market economy is based on the existence of a set of shared values such that trust can exist. The morality of a business person is a crucial intangible asset of a market economy, and its nonexistence substantially raises transaction costs. La Croix (1989) develops a model in which this intangible asset becomes a group-specific asset for a homogeneous middleman group (such as Jewish, Indian, or Chinese traders in a society in which they are a minority). A small group that maintains itself differentiated from the rest of society can enjoy much lower transaction costs than could two randomly chosen members of the society, and can enable more transactions than would occur otherwise.

MENTAL MODELS AND INSTITUTIONS

Mental models, institutions, and ideologies all contribute to the process by which human beings interpret and order the environment. Mental models are, to some degree, unique to each individual. Ideologies and institutions are created and provide more closely shared perceptions and ordering of the environment. The connection between mental models and both ideologies and institutions crucially depends on the product and process of representational redescription. Both are, at this stage in cognitive science, quite imperfectly understood. The process of representational redescription would require an understanding of exactly how the progression in human cognition occurs. We believe that the punctuated equilibrium concept can be used to formalize this type of dynamics.[9]

The product has been more extensively analyzed than the process since there is a substantial psychology literature detailing experiments in learning. Here the agent's rate of learning varies with the difficulty of discerning expected pay-offs, and "human learning can lock in to an inferior choice, and . . . this is prone to happen where pay-offs to choices are closely clustered, random and difficult to discriminate among" (Arthur 1990: 18).

Arthur points out that this sort of finding is unfamiliar in economics "where our habit of thinking is that if there is a better alternative, it would be chosen" (18). A basic problem with this standard substantive rationality result is that the menu of choices is not really known a priori

---

[9] Hull (1988) and Campbell (1987) argue that scientific concepts evolve in a manner described by evolutionary models. Their nontechnical approach has not been formalized in explicit models; however, Higgs (1987: chap. 4) develops a model with similar dynamics of evolution in his ratchet model of governmental growth.

by the chooser. This menu is itself to be learned, and this learning can often involve exploring unknown territory. Such exploration is what Arthur is attempting to model, in a way similar to that proposed by Holland (1975) in his suggestion about a genetic algorithm for the maximization of mathematical functions that standard techniques cannot solve. Arthur speculates at the conclusion that

there is thus an 'ecology' of decision problems in the economy with earlier patterns of decisions affecting subsequent decisions. This interlinkage would tend to carry sub-optimality through from one decision setting to another.[10] The overall economy would then follow a path that is partly decided by chance, is history dependent, and is less than optimal (19).

All that is missing from Arthur's speculation is an explicit recognition of the role of ideologies in this process.

DYNAMICS OF MENTAL MODELS AND INSTITUTIONS

Arthur's speculation provides us with a tentative entering wedge to speculate further about the dynamic process of cognitive change occurring as societies and economics evolve. That society's development has been suboptimal is certainly not open to question. The path dependence of the institutional development process can be derived from the way cognition and institutions in societies evolve. Both usually evolve incrementally, but the latter, institutions, clearly are a reflection of the evolving mental models. Therefore, the form of learning that takes place is crucial.

Changes in Mental Models as Punctuated Equilibria

The usual modeling of learning in economics involves Bayesian ideas. The Bayesian learner starts out with some sort of prior distribution of beliefs over some predefined model space involving the learner's current ideas about how to think about the phenomenon that is the object of the learning. The prior beliefs are updated by some direct learning that generates observational data. This transition of prior beliefs into posterior beliefs with an unchanging model space is usually thought of as a gradual process, with the posterior beliefs some sort of compromise between the peak of the prior beliefs and the model judged most likely by the data alone (Leamer 1978). This approach misses some crucial features of

---

[10] By suboptimality here, we mean that there were technically feasible alternatives, implementable in humanly feasible institutions or organizations, that would have resulted in higher *ex ante* and *ex post* rates of economic growth, without reducing consumption levels.

learning that we believe can be captured by the approach we wish to follow. Bayesian learners are never surprised, or forced within the updating process to completely change the dimensions of the model space. Such surprises or drastically revised models can be interpreted as representational redescriptions and involve trajectories that can be described as punctuated equilibria of the sort analyzed in Denzau and Grossman (1993).[11]

Punctuated equilibrium involves long periods of slow, gradual change, punctuated by relatively short periods of dramatic changes, which we can presume to be periods of representational redescription. This reconceptualization is illustrated in two of the graphs in Hutchins and Hazlehurst. These graphs (Figures 7, 10, and 11 in the original) show the results of learning patterns directly, and with the help of cultural artifacts. The cultural learning approximately halves the time required to learn the relation between moon phases and tides. Both direct learning and the culturally mediated learning show patterns of punctuation. For an extended period, neither type of learning enables the pattern to be acquired. Then the probability of successful acquisition through mediated learning starts increasing steeply, as shown in Figure 2.4, up to about 60%, and increases slowly thereafter. The same pattern, with a less steep slope, is shown for direct learning. Figure 2.5, reproducing Figure 10 of Hutchins and Hazlehurst (1991), shows the learning results more directly. The mean squared error of the learners starts out on a plateau at 0.25 and drops precipitously in less than 10 generations to a new lower plateau at which it remains. Looking for punctuated equilibrium dynamics and the accompanying representational redescription

---

[11] This approach works at the level of the individual chooser. But many of the changes we wish to understand are social, such as changes in informal institutions or ideologies. We believe that two approaches to this aggregation problem are likely to bear fruit.

First, Kuhn (1970) argues that the choice of a new paradigm is at the individual level. In a crisis, individuals choose while facing a confusion of evidence and alternative explanations. The resolution of a scientific crisis is an intersubjective decision in the shared mental models of the members of a scientific community, come to a consensus on the new basis for their future studies. Kuhn's ideas have been important in our coming to the ideas we now espouse, and there is more to be mined in this approach. A second approach to the aggregation question involves the recent work of Bikhchandani, Hirshleifer, and Welch (1992) on informational cascades. In their model, only a small number of individuals make choices on the basis of their own mental models. The others in the society follow the choices of these decision leaders, free riding on their efforts. This approach seems to have substantial value in discussions of the shared mental models that many people acquire about religion – most people acquire their models by learning from the original texts or from the learned teachers of the doctrine. Changes in the interpretations of these teachers can be acquired as indirect learning through training or just from going along with their interpretations until one acquires the changes in one's own mental models.

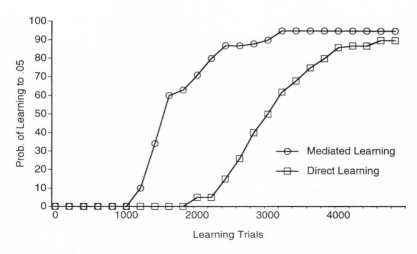

Figure 2.4. The rate of learning (to a 0.05 MSE criterion) a 2-input exclusive or with direct (experimental) learning and culturally mediated learning. *Source:* Figure 7 of Hutchins and Hazlehurst (1991: 700).

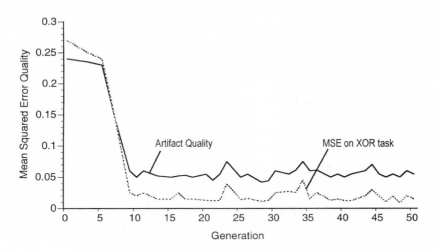

Figure 2.5. The rate of learning (measured by MSE) the moon phase–tide relation with direct (experimental) learning and culturally mediated learning. *Source:* Figure 10 of Hutchins and Hazlehurst (1991: 703).

43

requires research from the viewpoint we present here, and is yet to be performed.

The punctuated equilibrium approach to the dynamics of mental models has implications similar to those discussed by Kuhn (1970). They differ somewhat because of the crucial difference created by the attempt in science to maintain the precision of terms, as opposed to their plasticity in a popularly held and communicated mental model. In science, Kuhn argues, the relatively precise nature of concepts helps keep a paradigm or conceptual framework almost fixed for long periods. But this precision of terms must withstand the evolution of the meaning of terms, which continually occurs in popular spheres. Consider the meaning of the *Declaration of Independence* with its phrase stating that "All men are created equal." The precise meaning of this phrase in Thomas Jefferson's mind when he wrote it is vastly different from the interpretation given it by the Abolitionists 50 years later, or by most Americans today. We leave discussion of this evolution purposely tacit to allow the reader to step through the evolutionary process.

A crucial feature of this sort of evolution is the bringing of new meanings from related mental models, by analogy or metaphor. This process is a natural feature of the way our brains generalize and utilize concepts, and intellectual historians, such as Becker (1932: chap. 11), have already used the idea of an evolving "climate of opinion" to analyze the changing meaning of terminology and ideological constructs. These gradual and continual changes, in which new meanings in one field of application gradually transfer into another set of mental models, generate the ideological counterpart of Kuhn's normal science. Normal ideology with its ideological scholars and purists may attempt to resist change, but we expect that ideologies gradually change due to the changing meanings of their terms and concepts in other models, as well as changing usage in common parlance. New concepts that have become important parts of the climate of opinion, both to the intellectuals and to the population en masse, can also get brought into the set of ideas in an ideology, as the gradual accommodation of Darwinism suggests.

Let us think further about this process of accommodation and change in shared mental models. The process does not always progress smoothly or easily. Instead, ideological purists, like religious fundamentalists, try to resist any change, and their resistance may generate a crisis. Such a slowing of gradual change through attempts to maintain purity would create an increasing gap between the general climate of opinion and the "pure" ideology. An example of such a gap seems to be occurring in Castro's Cuba today, and is argued by Przeworski (1991: 1–9). When the ideology finally changes, if it does, it would generate a punctuation, i.e., a short, relatively rapid change. Gradual evolutionary change and the incorporation of new elements also can endogenously generate a crisis for a different reason. The basis for this crisis would be the discovery of a lack of logical consistency in the ideology, or the discovery of a new set of implications that are viewed as disturbing by adherents of the ideology. The communication of this sort of problem could then be used by an entrepreneur to make a punctuated change in the ideology or religion to further the entrepreneur's own goals.

The existence of discovery and surprise is related to another cognitive problem. We simply do not have the abundance of cognitive resources such that our mental models can actually be logically coherent, or that we can be certain that our ideological beliefs are logically coherent.[12] Many individuals can understand the inconsistency among three statements, e.g., God is desirous of humans living in happiness, God is omnipotent, and evil exists and makes humans unhappy. These three statements, interpreted naturally, result in a logical inconsistency that has been termed the Paradox of Evil, which some human religions attempt to resolve. But in the move to four statements, as in Arrow's Theorem, we seem to pass across a complexity boundary. Most people find the Arrow result paradoxical, even after having been presented with it. That it was only "discovered" in the 1940s suggests its complexity, even though the underlying axioms had been used for some time. The fact that Arrow himself got the proof wrong in both the 1951 and the 1962 editions of the book is suggestive of the complexity of the logical incoherence problem.

If we cannot immediately see, or even at times understand an argument about, the logical incoherence among four (or eight) statements, then it is quite likely that logical incoherence could exist in any modestly complex ideology. To demand such coherence of an ideology, as Hinich and Munger (1992: chap. 1) do, is to talk about a world in which cognitive resources are truly abundant, and not finite, a view that Cherniak

---

[12] As Cherniak (1986: 79–80) notes, this question of logical consistency is a very difficult problem as characterized by mathematical complexity theory (technically termed an NP-complete problem, not solvable in polynomial time), and the only known algorithms for implementation are exponential time ones. By a calculation of the sort used on any combinational explosion problem (like the British Museum algorithm that would allow monkey typists to write all of Shakespeare), it has been shown that it is impossible for all the possible calculation resources of the entire universe, computing for all of the time the universe has existed, to determine the logical consistency of more than 138 propositions, assuming they all are well defined. Even if 138 propositions is sufficient for stating an ideology, the cognitive limitations of a finite human agent are vastly more limited than the calculation suggests. Higgs (1987: 37) suggests that ideology is "a somewhat coherent, rather comprehensive belief system about social relations." This seems a definition that is much more defensible than requiring logical coherence initially, and at all times – a seemingly impossible task given the plasticity of language.

terms "We have God's mind." An ideological entrepreneur who learns of an incoherence or a disturbing implication of the ideology could utilize this in order to help reinterpret that ideology in ways more suitable to the entrepreneur's goals. We believe that some of the numerous religious controversies that have helped create new sects have been a consequence of both disturbing implications and incoherence problems.

CONCLUSION

We began this essay by noting that it is impossible to make sense out of the diverse performance of economies and polities if one confines one's behavioral assumptions to that of substantive rationality in which agents know what is in their self-interest and act accordingly. But once we open up the black box of "rationality," we encounter the complex and still very incomplete world of cognitive science. This essay is a preliminary exploration of some of the implications of the way by which humans attempt to order and structure their environment and communicate with each other. Does the argument have relevance for social science theory? Certainly it does. Ideas matter, and the way by which ideas evolve and are communicated is the key to developing useful theory that will expand our understanding of the performance of societies, both at a moment of time and over time.

At a moment of time, the argument implies that institutions and the belief structure are critical constraints on those making choices and are, therefore, an essential ingredient of model building. Over time, the approach has fundamental implications for understanding economic change. The performance of economics is a consequence of the incentive structures put into place, that is, the institutional framework of the polity and economy. These are, in turn, a function of the shared mental models and ideologies of the actors. Whether we pursue the framework suggested by Arthur (1992) or the notion of punctuated equilibrium for the dynamics of mental models, we get some common results. The presence of learning creates path dependence in ideas and ideologies and then in institutions. Arthur argues that a concept discovered by an individual that is useful in explaining the world is more likely to persist in his/her mental models, and this implies path dependence. The same path dependence is implied by our related evolutionary interpretation. In both approaches, systems of mental models exhibit path dependence such that history matters, and in both approaches, suboptimal performance can persist for substantial periods of time.

3

The Institutional Foundations of Political Competence: How Citizens Learn What They Need to Know

ARTHUR LUPIA AND MATHEW D. MCCUBBINS

Decades of survey research document a long list of political questions that the common citizen cannot answer.[1] Less well documented is what this lack of information implies about citizen competence. A common conclusion is that citizens who cannot answer political questions (i.e., those who score low on typical survey-based measures of political sophistication or knowledge) are not competent participants in the political process. We reject this conclusion.

We argue that for many of the most common political tasks – such as voting in a presidential election or for or against a piece of legislation – competence requires very little information. Moreover, we contend that what little information competent performance requires in these contexts can be learned from others (e.g., political parties, elite endorsements, friends, and family).

In drawing such a conclusion, we join others (e.g., Downs 1957, Popkin 1991, and Sniderman, et al. 1991), who argue that people can use heuristics or information shortcuts to make competent decisions with limited information. However, we depart from these arguments by focusing on the conditions under which these cognitive shortcuts have such beneficial effects. Specifically, we examine how political institutions help people sort through the many heuristics or shortcuts often available to them.

We find that political institutions make it easier for citizens to learn *what they need to know* by affecting citizens' beliefs about who can and cannot be trusted. We build our argument in the following way:

First, we ask the question "What do citizens need to know?" We answer this question by explaining how much information citizens need to make a *reasoned choice* – the same choices they would have made if

---

[1] This chapter extends an argument introduced in Lupia and McCubbins (1998). Consequently, our essay draws extensively from that source.

they knew more about the consequences of their actions.[2] We find that reasoned choice requires very little information for a wide range of political decisions.

Second, we ask "How do citizens learn what they need to know?" Our answer begins with the premise that people can learn from either personal experience or the testimony of others. In many political situations, however, only the second option is available, as politics often presents problems for which personal experience provides insufficient knowledge. Therefore, for many political decisions, reasoned choice requires learning from others.

We then identify conditions under which people can learn from others. We argue that learning from others is no trivial matter. At a minimum, *learning requires persuasion* – one person's successful attempt to change another's beliefs.

Persuasion in political contexts can be difficult. Differing ideologies and competition for scarce resources give political actors a reason to mistrust one another. Persuasion, however, requires a basis for trust. That is, the targets of persuasion cannot be led to change their beliefs if they believe that a speaker cannot be trusted to reveal what he or she knows. Without trust there is no persuasion; without persuasion, people cannot learn from others; and without learning from others, it is very difficult for citizens to learn what they need to know.

So, when can political actors learn what they need to know? The answer to this question is where the underappreciated role of political institutions comes in. In most extant explanations of persuasion, including Aristotle's *Rhetoric* and Hovland et al. (1953), analysts focus

---

[2] There exists a centuries-old debate about what democracy *should* do. This debate has involved many great minds, is wide ranging, and is totally unresolved. We do not believe ourselves capable of resolving this debate. However, we strongly believe that we can make the debate more constructive. We can do so by clarifying the relationship between what information people have and which types of decisions they can make. Our research agenda is firmly about determining the capabilities of people who lack political information. It is designed to resolve debates about how much information voters, jurors, and legislators need to perform certain tasks. So, while our research may help to clarify debates about what democracy should do, it will not resolve these debates.

We mention this because our relationship to the debate about what democracy should do motivates our definition of reasoned choice. Our definition of reasoned choice allows the reader to define an amount of knowledge that is required for reasoned choice. Some readers may argue that a reasoned choice requires knowledge of very technical matters, while others may argue that a reasoned choice requires less knowledge. Note that the difference between these viewpoints reduces to different views on what democracy should do. Therefore, our definition of reasoned choice is purposefully precise with respect to the relationship among information, knowledge, and choice and is purposefully vague with respect to most normative debates about what democracies should do.

on aspects of the speaker's *character* (e.g., honesty, ideology, or reputation) as a necessary condition for persuasion. If a speaker lacks the right character, then the standard conclusion is that the speaker cannot persuade.

We offer a different explanation. We use a formal theory of political communication to prove that persuasion need not be contingent upon personal character. We show that while a perception of trust *can* arise from a positive evaluation of a speaker's character, it need not do so because *external forces can substitute for character*. These external forces can generate a basis for trust, persuasion, and the possibility of learning in contexts where none of these outcomes would otherwise occur.

Political institutions are a common source of these critical external forces. Many political institutions allow citizens to observe a speaker's costly effort, to know that a speaker faces the threat of verification (i.e., cross-examination), or to know that a speaker faces penalties for lying. When institutions create these kinds of forces, they can make a speaker's incentives transparent to the audience he or she is attempting to persuade. As a result, political institutions can clarify a speaker's trustworthiness to citizens; provide effective substitutes for a speaker's character; allow people to make more effective decisions about whom to believe; allow citizens to learn what they need to know; and allow people who lack information to make reasoned choices.

We build most of our chapter's argument on the basis of work in formal theory. In the chapter's penultimate section, however, we describe our laboratory experiments on the relationship between external forces, persuasion, and reasoned choice. There, we summarize the results of more than 40 experiments in which we varied subjects' information of their political environs and the institutional context in which they were to interact. Our experiments allow us to observe circumstances under which our theory predicts that institutional interventions (i.e., such as those that allow a subject to know that a speaker faces the threat of verification) should – and should not – help subjects make reasoned choices despite a lack of information. The experimental results support our conclusions and contradict the notion that reasoned choice in common political contexts requires anything approaching full information.

We conclude that common, survey-based demonstrations of citizen ignorance provide inadequate gauges of citizen competence. Unless the questions asked are representative of what citizens *need to know,* and unless these questions account for the ways in which citizens learn what they need to know, these surveys imply little or nothing about any citizens' ability to make a reasoned choice.

Our research also clarifies the importance of integrating the institutional context of political decision making into attempts to explain human behavior. Political communication and political decision making do not occur in frictionless vacuums. Instead, they occur in contexts where external forces, such as political institutions, affect incentives and expectations. We should direct more of our attention to understanding how institutions affect who trusts whom, who persuades whom, and who learns what needs to be known. With more careful thinking about the interaction between human cognition and the incentive effects of political institutions, we stand to gain a much greater understanding of why voters, legislators, and jurors do what they do.

WHAT DO CITIZENS NEED TO KNOW?

Most citizens have scant information about politics. Indeed, four decades of survey research show that citizens cannot recall basic political facts (e.g., Delli Carpini and Keeter 1991), do not have a consistent understanding of ideological abstractions (e.g., Converse 1964), and fail to recall or recognize the names of their elected representatives (e.g., Jacobson 1992, Neuman 1986). A common conclusion to draw from such studies is that citizens who cannot answer political survey questions are unable to make reasoned political choices. That is, it is presumed that limited information prevents reasoned choice.

The problem with the conclusion is that for it to be true, the following assumption must also be true: People can make reliable predictions about the consequences of their actions *only if* they know a detailed set of facts about these actions. However, we reject the conclusion that limited information prevents reasoned choice because the special assumption is false. Citizens can and often do use limited amounts of information to make the same decisions they would have made if more informed. To see how, suppose that a particular set of facts is sufficient for a reasoned choice (e.g., suppose that knowing Bill Clinton's position on 100 political issues is sufficient). Then, if a person does not know these facts, and cannot access any other facts that allow her to make the same choice, then she cannot make a reasoned choice. In this case, knowing the initial set of facts is necessary for reasoned choice. If, however, there exists another, perhaps simpler, set of facts that leads her to make the same choice (i.e., Bill Clinton is endorsed by the Sierra Club), then knowing the initial set of facts is not a prerequisite for reasoned choice. When a few, simple pieces of information can lead citizens to make the same choices as many, complex pieces of information, citizens who want to make reasoned choices need not know very much.

This way of thinking about the relationship between information and choice provides a more sensible way to interpret survey data on citizens' information. That people cannot explain or have forgotten *why* they do what they do is a general fact of life (Churchland 1995: 22). Therefore, we should expect even people who make reasoned political decisions to be unable to answer detailed questions about their choices (see Fiorina 1981, Lodge 1995 for related arguments). It follows that a person's inability to answer detailed survey questions correctly may reveal nothing about the quality of his decisions.

But what do citizens need to know? Establishing that reasoned choice does not require complete information is not the same as showing how much citizens need to know. For the answer to that question, we direct your attention to the *calculus of attention*. After all, learning (acquiring information) requires attention. So, the answer to the question "What do citizens need to know?" is equivalent to the answer to "To what types of information should citizens direct their attention?"

The Calculus of Attention

Our calculus begins with one of the most basic lessons of modern cognitive science: *Learning is active and goal oriented*. Though people seem to learn many things without even trying, the simple fact is that humans often choose when and what to learn. This finding is consistent over time and across individuals.[3] To see why, consider three simple facts. First, learning requires effort. Second, effort is a scarce resource for everyone. Third, and a consequence of the first two facts, *people choose* what and when to learn. Thus, *learning is active*.

What we learn depends on how we direct our attention, but attention is a scarce resource. In general, when we pay attention to one stimulus, we do so at the expense of paying attention to other stimuli. For instance, at noisy gatherings we often *choose* to pay attention to one conversation at the expense of attending to another (Jackendoff 1980). When visiting Disneyland, we listen for our children's screams (of delight or otherwise) and not to others. If we want to exit a room, we attend to the location of a door instead of attending to the color of an end table. To survive, we must make good use of our limited capacity for attention.

In what follows, we assume that the purpose of directing scarce attention is to avoid the risk of future pain and increase the opportunity for future pleasure. In essence, we assume that people are goal oriented (i.e.,

---

[3] See Holland, Holyoak, Nisbett, and Thagard (1986), Kandel, Schwartz, and Jessel (1995), and Newell (1990) for reviews of this literature and elaborations of the argument that learning is goal oriented.

rational) and that the purpose of paying attention is to make reasoned choices.[4]

Knowledge. To make reasoned choices, people need to *know* something about the consequences of their actions. They need to know about relationships of the form "If A, then B." To gain this knowledge, they need not learn fundamental truths about the causal processes of our universe; they need only have beliefs that generate accurate predictions about the consequences of their actions. We define *knowledge* as the ability to make accurate predictions.[5] We say that a prediction of the form "If A, then B" is accurate if the *ex ante* belief "If A, then B" matches the *ex post* observation. If you can, in 2000, correctly predict the winner of the 1948 presidential election, then we say that you have knowledge about the topic in 2000. Similarly, the more accurate predictions you can make about the incentive effects of a new tax policy, then the more you are knowledgeable about that topic. We argue that the desired consequence of paying attention to a stimulus is to acquire knowledge sufficient for reasoned choice.

When thinking about knowledge it is important to remember that knowledge and information are different. Knowledge is the ability to make accurate predictions; information is data. Knowledge requires information because accurate predictions require data – at a minimum you need some data to verbalize the prediction you are making. By contrast, you can know a long list of facts and fail to put them together in a way that allows you to make accurate predictions. Thus, while knowledge requires information, you can have information without having knowledge.

The Calculus. So, what do citizens need to *know*? In *The Democratic Dilemma* (Lupia and McCubbins 1998), we present a more com-

---

[4] Our definition implies that rationality and concern for others are not mutually exclusive. People who do things out of concern for others act self-interestedly. This must be true because people *choose* whom to care for. Moreover, this choice is itself correlated to past experiences with pain and pleasure – concern for others must be physically embodied in the cognitive and emotional apparatus of the caring person. Thus, if past events lead a person to have a concern for others, then it is rational to be altruistic. Our definition of rationality requires only the feeling of pain and pleasure; it does not restrict the source of such feelings to material concerns for one's self.

[5] Readers from cognitive science will note that our definition of knowledge closely approximates the modern definition of intelligent performance. We use the term *knowledge* here because it is far more common in social science parlance. For an extensive discussion of what constitutes knowledge, see Chapters 2, 3, and 6 of Newell (1990).

plete *calculus of attention.* To answer the question at hand, we focus on only parts of that calculus. We begin by describing the benefits of attention.

The expected benefit from attending to a given stimulus comes from the new knowledge that the stimulus imparts. To be beneficial, a stimulus must help an individual make new and accurate predictions about the consequences of her actions. If a stimulus does not cause an individual to change her actions (i.e., take new or different actions), then the benefit derived from paying attention to the stimulus is zero. If a stimulus leads an individual to change her behavior, and this change prevents a painful mistake, then the benefit is *positive.* If, on the other hand, the stimulus leads an individual to change her behavior and this change causes the individual to make a painful mistake, then the benefit of paying attention to the stimulus *is negative.*

We define the expected benefit of paying attention to a given stimulus as $E(Benefit) = \Sigma_M((P_{Prev} - P_{Cause}) * E(Mistake))$. $E(Mistake)$ refers to the pain that a mistaken choice is expected to produce; P_{Prev} refers to the perceived probability that paying attention to the stimulus will prevent such a mistake; P_{Cause} refers to the perceived probability that paying attention to the stimulus will cause a costly mistake. The sign Σ_M denotes the summation over the set of all possible mistakes. The point of this simple equation is to show that if paying attention to a given stimulus reduces the likelihood of a costly mistake, then it increases the expected benefit of paying attention to that stimulus. Conversely, if paying attention to the stimulus increases the likelihood of a costly mistake, then it decreases the expected benefit of attention.

Thinking about the benefits of attention this way leads to the following conclusion: More information is neither necessary nor sufficient for reasoned choice. Put another way, additional information is beneficial *only if it prevents a costly mistake (or, alternatively, if it causes a reasoned choice).* If people expend effort acquiring information that does not ultimately prevent them from making a costly mistake, then, from the *ex post* perspective, they squandered a scarce resource. So, if a person knows (*ex ante*) that new information will affect no decisions, then he or she should not pay to learn it.

If we also consider another part of the calculus of attention – the fact that stimuli are costly to attend to (i.e., the often high opportunity costs of attention) and to process (i.e., the transactions costs of attention) – then we see why people have an incentive to rely on simple pieces of information that allow them to avoid many costly mistakes and to make many reasoned choices. If cognitively cheap, pain-decreasing (or pleasure-enhancing) information is sufficient for reasoned choice, then people have little incentive to obtain more detailed information.[6]

Comparing the benefits of attention to its costs reveals why people reject so many opportunities to acquire political (and many other types of) information. Even if people could acquire "complete information," the fact that information is valuable only if it prevents costly mistakes would dampen their desire to do so.

This calculus also explains voter decisions to attend to a candidate's party identification, work experience, involvement in scandals, sound bites, interest group ratings, endorsements (e.g., supported by labor), or personal appearance, instead of learning a candidate's complete legislative voting history, policy portfolio, or name. Voters have an incentive to attend to simple stimuli that promise high returns. When voter opportunity costs are high, they have an incentive to rely on the most effective, cognitively costless cue they can find. They have no incentive to believe everything they hear or to treat all cues equally. For example, attending to a candidate's partisanship promises a higher return when candidates from different parties compete against one another than it does in nonpartisan or primary elections where the cue provides less information. The opposite is true for interest group and elite endorsements when such cues correlate with the schisms that divide party members (e.g., for some Democrats, a Sierra Club endorsement is a perfect substitute for a party label).[7]

---

[6] The idea that individuals use shortcuts or cues is not new (e.g., Downs 1957, Popkin 1991, Sniderman et al. 1991). We expand on this scholarship by deriving the conditions under which shortcuts will be used and the criteria that people use when they have many different shortcuts to choose from. That is, an individual (who does not already possess complete information) relies on an information shortcut when he or she perceives it to be cognitively cheap and correlated with an increase in pleasure or a decrease in pain. In this situation, an individual has no incentive to become completely informed. If there are more information shortcuts available than a person can attend to, then he or she has an incentive to attend to the shortcut that is cheapest and most highly correlated with pleasure and pain. Our extension implies that the effectiveness of any shortcut, such as party, is not automatic or constant across situations. Instead, as we demonstrate theoretically in Chapter 3 of *The Democratic Dilemma* and experimentally in Chapters 7 through 9, a shortcut's effectiveness and usefulness vary across individuals and contexts in predictable ways.

[7] This claim is subject to the caveat that the endorsement is credible. Our research on heuristic decision making is distinct from most others in the respect that we identify the determinants of an endorsement's (or heuristic's) credibility in Chapter 3 of *The Democratic Dilemma*. So while many examinations of heuristic decision making point out the existence of heuristic usage, our research identifies conditions under which any individual heuristic will (and will not) be used. Note also that voters may believe that all the issues they care about are correlated with the candidate's position on a single issue, such as abortion. Thus, they may rationally seek information about a candidate's position on the "hot button" issue and not bother with other information.

In sum, reasoned choice requires knowledge; knowledge requires *some* information; information requires attention; and attention is scarce. Therefore, reasoned choice requires that people direct their attention in systematic ways. Cognitive science paradigms reveal that learning is active. When we combine the implications of this insight with the economist's insights about costs, benefits, and incentives, we find that people are wise to attend to cognitively cheap stimuli that are sufficient for them to make reasoned choices and avoid costly mistakes. They are wise to ignore all of the other sordid details of political life.[8]

HOW DO CITIZENS LEARN WHAT THEY NEED TO KNOW?

In addition to defining *what citizens need to know,* we must also identify *when citizens can learn what they need to know.* It is to that task that we now turn.

Reasoned choice requires knowledge; that is, people must be able to predict the consequences of their actions. To obtain this knowledge, people have two options. First, they can draw knowledge from personal experience. Second, they can draw knowledge from what other people say, write, or do.

In many political settings only the second option is available. This is true because politics generates problems that are unfamiliar to people's "own experience and uncorrected by trial and error" (Lane 1995: 117). In these settings, personal experience does not provide sufficient knowledge for reasoned choice. Therefore, in many political settings, a person who wants to make a reasoned choice must have the opportunity and the ability to learn from others.[9]

Learning from others requires *persuasion,* where persuasion is *one person's successful attempt to change the beliefs of another.* In settings where reasoned choice requires learning from others, persuasion is a necessary condition for reasoned choice. To see why, suppose that person

---

[8] Our argument here parallels rational ignorance arguments of the type offered by McKelvey and Ordeshook (1986) and Wittman (1995).

[9] Political settings vary in the number of opportunities they offer. At one extreme, voters in major elections have opportunities to learn from newspaper articles, news broadcasts, television advertisements, direct mail, speeches, rallies, interest group endorsements, voter information pamphlets, workplace conversations, and family debates. Congressmen have opportunities to learn from party leaders, the votes cast in committee, lobbyists, staff, colleagues, and experts in the executive. Jurors have opportunities to learn from eyewitnesses, expert witnesses, attorneys, and the presiding judge. At the other extreme, some political settings offer no opportunities to learn. For people in these settings, only personal experience can generate reasoned choice.

A's ability to make a reasoned choice depends on what she can learn from person B. If B can persuade A, then reasoned choice is possible. By contrast, if B cannot persuade A, then A cannot make a reasoned choice.

A common claim about persuasion is that a speaker's personal character, along with the content of his statement, determines who can persuade whom (e.g., Aristotle's *Rhetoric*, Hovland et al., 1953). That is, if the speaker lacks character, then he or she cannot persuade.

By contrast, we argue that persuasion does not require character assessments of any kind. In Chapter 3 of *The Democratic Dilemma*, we use a formal theory of strategic communication to derive a different set of necessary and sufficient conditions for persuasion. We present these conditions below. In the presentation, the principal represents a voter, juror, or legislator, and the speaker represents a person or group (e.g., a political campaign, an endorsement-making political party or interest group) from whom the principal can take advice.

The Conditions for Persuasion

The following conditions are individually necessary and collectively sufficient for persuasion:

- The principal must perceive the speaker to be trustworthy and the principal must perceive the speaker to have the knowledge she desires.
- Absent external forces, persuasion requires perceived common interests and perceived speaker knowledge [e.g., personal character of the type described as necessary in the classic theories of persuasion].
- In the presence of external forces, these requirements can be reduced. In other words, with respect to persuasion, external forces can be substitutes for common interests (and for each other).

In *The Democratic Dilemma*, we prove that *incentive-altering external forces offer an alternate basis for one person to trust what another person says.* The forces we describe are present in culture, norms, markets, and, most importantly for our argument in this chapter, political institutions. These forces affect persuasion by altering what people *choose* to say and what people *choose* to believe.

How these forces work should be familiar to any member of an advanced industrial economy. For example, every day millions of people buy goods from, and sell goods to, people about whom they know little or nothing. Each of these transactions requires some degree of trust (e.g., that the currency offered as payment is legitimate and that a good has its advertised characteristics). Since buyers and sellers do not know each other well, they must have an alternate and effective means for evaluating credibility. One such mean is the external forces that substitute for unobservable personal characteristics. Laws and customs are forces that realign strangers' incentives, giving people a basis for trust in billions of situations where it would not otherwise exist. These external forces are the substitutes that make advanced economies possible. We argue that analogous substitutes make advanced democracies possible because they allow people to learn from others.[10]

How Institutions Help People Learn

By providing substitutes for personal character assessments, external forces affect who can learn from whom. Three such forces are *penalties for lying, verification,* and *observable, costly effort.* Each force is common to politics and can be introduced by the design of political institutions.[11]

The first force is *penalties for lying.* Penalties for lying are the costs that a speaker must pay when he or she says something false. Our motivation for focusing on penalties for lying is the explicit fines levied on people who lie (e.g., in cases of perjury) and the losses in valued reputations for honesty that result from being caught making false statements.[12]

Penalties for lying facilitate persuasion when they give a principal a reason to believe that she can distinguish speakers who make truthful statements from those who do not. Penalties for lying play this role when they decrease the expected benefit of lying to the speaker. To see how this works, consider the following example:

> Suppose that the speaker knows, but the principal is uncertain about, whether x is *better* or *worse* than y for the principal. Suppose further that the principal and the speaker have conflicting

[10] This type of argument has a well-established lineage in certain subfields of political science and economics. For example, economists in the subfields of economic history (North 1990), industrial organization (e.g., Williamson 1975), and mechanism design (e.g., Baron 1989; Myerson 1983, 1989) have demonstrated an important set of relationships among external forces, individual incentives, and collective outcomes. In addition, political scientists, such as McKelvey and Ordeshook (1986), show how voters can substitute simple poll results for more complex information.

[11] Verification, penalties for lying, and observable, costly effort cover the range of effects that external forces can have on communication. Verification affects the manner in which the principal receives the speaker's statement. It is independent of any costs associated with making statements. Both penalties for lying and observable, costly effort affect the speaker's costs and are independent of the manner in which the signal is received. Penalties for lying are a simple example of statement-specific costs. Observable, costly effort is an example of communication costs that are independent of what is said.

[12] While we focus on the case where these costs are common knowledge, our results are robust to the assumption that the principal is uncertain about them. Note also that other statement-specific costs, such as rewards or penalties for telling the truth, have similar dynamics.

interests. That is, if x is *better* for the principal, then the speaker loses $20 when the principal chooses x; if x is *worse* for the principal, then the speaker earns $75 when the principal chooses x. Suppose further that if the principal chooses y, then the speaker earns nothing, and that the penalty for lying is $50. In this example, the penalty is big enough to dissuade the speaker from lying when x is *better* for the principal; that is, the speaker has to pay $50 to avoid losing $20. It is not big enough to do so when x is *worse* for the principal; that is, the speaker can pay $50 to earn $75. So if x is *better,* then the speaker will only say *better,* and if x is *worse,* then the speaker may say *better* or *worse.* Therefore, if the principal hears the statement *worse,* then the penalty for lying allows her to infer that the statement must be true.

In general, a principal who believes that the speaker faces a penalty for lying can make one of the following two inferences upon hearing a statement from the speaker: (1) the statement is true; or (2) the statement is false and the value to the speaker of lying is greater than the expected penalty. When penalties for lying have this effect, they provide a new window from the principal's perceptions to the speaker's incentives and provide a basis for trust.

The second force is *verification.* We represent verification as follows: After the speaker speaks, but before the principal chooses, the principal learns (with verification probability v) about the veracity of the speaker's statement. Verification works by posing the threat that the principal can discern true signals from false ones. This threat changes the speaker's incentives in the following way: As the probability of verification increases, the probability that he can benefit from sending a false signal decreases. Verification can affect the speaker's incentives when he and the principal have conflicting interests. By contrast, when the speaker and principal have common interests, verification is not a threat.

A third external force is *observable, costly effort.* We represent costly effort as a cost that the speaker must pay to say certain things. Intuitively, there is a cost for almost any cognitive task, and speaking is no exception. The logic underlying this effect closely follows the old adage, "actions speak louder than words."[13]

When someone takes an observable, costly action, he reveals something to others about the intensity of his preferences. For example, if a

---

[13] The logic underlying this external force is equivalent to the logic of Spence (1973), the seminal paper on costly signaling in economics. For simplicity, we describe the case where the cost of effort is known. It is trivial, however, to extend our results to the case where the principal does not know, but can form beliefs about, both the magnitude of the effort required for the speaker's speech and the shape of the speaker's utility function.

knowledgeable speaker pays $100 for the opportunity to persuade us, then we can infer that the difference in expected value to the speaker between what the speaker expects us to do after hearing his statement and what he expects us to do if we do not hear his statement is at least $100. Therefore, even if he ultimately delivers his statement in a language that we do not understand, the speaker's payment informs us that our choice is important to him. Observable costly effort can allow the principal to make a new inference about the speaker's interests. Specifically, the principal can infer something about the extent to which the speaker's preferred alternative differs from the one that she would have chosen otherwise.

The Institutional Foundations of Trust

Our explanation of how and what people learn from each other provides insight into how political institutions help people make reasoned choices. To see this insight, consider two arguments, both of which we present in outline form. The first argument is familiar:

- Reasoned political choice requires political knowledge.
- This knowledge usually requires the testimony of others; learning from others requires persuasion.
- Therefore, reasoned choice usually requires persuasion.

The second argument is as follows:

- Some institutions contain incentive-altering external forces.
- External forces can affect what speakers say and help principals evaluate a speaker's credibility.
- Affecting what speakers say and helping principals evaluate credibility can help them learn what they need to know.
- Therefore, some political institutions make reasoned choice possible in contexts where it would not otherwise occur.

Combining these two arguments produces the conclusion that *political institutions can help people who lack information make reasoned choices*. This outcome occurs when institutions provide speakers with incentives to reveal what they know and principals with the ability to perceive speaker incentives accurately. By contrast, when such institutions are not present, then people who have no other way to learn what they need to know are incapable of reasoned choice.

Perhaps the clearest example of an institutional design that generates reasoned choice is found in courtrooms. Jurors face an environment where personal experience is usually insufficient for reasoned choice (e.g., they cannot go back in time to a crime scene). The witnesses and attorneys who attempt to persuade them are people whom they have never met and will likely never encounter again. Jurors, therefore, have very limited information about the speakers' personal character. Further, jurors know that the prosecution and defense have conflicting interests. In this environment, jurors may be uncertain about which speakers share common interests with them.[14] However, jurors can rely on the fact that all testimony is subject to verification (through cross-examination and the collection of evidence) and penalties for lying (e.g., perjury). These aspects of judicial institutions provide a substitute for character judgments, clarify speakers' incentives, and allow people to make better judgments about whom to believe.

Some electoral institutions have similar therapeutic effects. Consider laws that make it easier for voters to observe costly campaign efforts. Campaign-finance disclosure laws, for example, require that campaign committees and lobbyists publicly identify all significant contributors and how much was contributed by each.[15] This enables voters to identify which groups or individuals support a given candidate or initiative and how much a change in the status quo policy is worth to them. If a person is reasonably happy with the status quo, and would thus like to see only a small change in policy, and if she observes the sponsor of a ballot initiative spending several million dollars to affect the election, then, without any further information, she can infer that the initiative proposes a very large change in the status quo and that she should oppose it.

Spending by candidates can have the same effect. In a primary election, for example, where party cannot serve as a cue, voters can observe how much each candidate spends to gauge the differences among them. If a challenger, in this case, mounts a very expensive campaign against an incumbent, voters can infer, again without any other information, that many knowledgeable contributors believe that there are substantial personal and policy differences between the challenger and the incumbent.[16] In sum, if a voter observes a knowledgeable person giving up something of value for the purpose of obtaining a particular outcome, then the voter can use that observation to learn how he or she should vote.

[14] Of course, the presiding judge may share common interests, but it is unclear that he or she is knowledgeable about the evidence. Also, the presiding judge is often more concerned with procedure than with justice.

[15] Examples of financial disclosure laws include the Federal Elections Campaign Act of 1974 and the California Political Reform Act of 1974. While *Buckley v. Valeo* struck down many of the provisions of the California Political Reform Act, including those concerning expenditure limits and source restrictions, the extensive public disclosure rules were left untouched.

[16] Because the incumbent has access to a variety of free resources, gauging the incumbent's costly effort is much more difficult (see Jacobson 1990).

EXPERIMENTAL EVIDENCE ON THE EFFECT OF EXTERNAL FORCES

It is one thing to claim theoretically that external forces affect whether and how citizens can learn what they need to know; it is another to demonstrate the power of such a claim empirically. In *The Democratic Dilemma,* we attempt such demonstrations by reporting on a series of experiments designed to clarify how external forces affect persuasion and reasoned choice. Most of our experiments took place in a formal laboratory setting. In this section, we offer a very brief review of the experimental results that are relevant to our argument in this chapter.

In the first half of 1996, we ran a series of experiments on information, persuasion, and choice. Our subjects were undergraduates at the University of California, San Diego. We recruited these subjects by posting flyers on the UCSD campus. These signs told prospective subjects how to make an appointment for an experimental session.[17]

When subjects came for their appointments, we paid them a nominal amount (usually $2) just for showing up. We then asked subjects to read and sign a standard consent form. The form told them that they would be in an experiment on "decision making." All subjects signed the form and stayed for the duration of the experiment.

We designed our experiments to be close analogies to the situations faced by the speaker and the principal in our formal theory. Therefore, our experiments had a principal and a speaker. As in our model, the principal's job was to choose one of two alternatives, while the speaker's job was to make one of two statements to the principal about his or her choice. Specifically, we asked the principal to predict the outcome of a coin toss, about which he or she was uncertain (i.e., we asked the principal to predict whether an unobserved coin toss landed on heads or tails). We asked the speaker to take an action or make a statement to the principal that could inform the principal about whether heads or tails would be a better prediction.

To make subjects' incentives analogous to the principal's and speaker's incentives in our model, we paid the principal and speaker for their actions. We paid the principal a fixed amount, usually $1, for a correct

---

[17] Our flyers gave prospective subjects a number to call for an appointment. Our research assistants fielded these calls, verified the callers' age (18 years or older) and undergraduate standing, and assigned experiment appointment times to eligible callers. Typically, we scheduled more subjects than we needed in a given experiment due to an expected 20% no-show rate. When extra subjects arrived, we admitted into the laboratory only the number needed for the experiment on a first-come, first-admitted basis. We then paid the extras $5 and invited them to sign up for another experiment. No person was a subject in our experiments more than once.

prediction. We tested some of our theory's hypotheses by varying the speaker's information and incentives. In some cases, the principal knew that the speaker also earned $1 when the principal made a correct prediction (i.e., the speaker and principal had common interests). In other cases, the principal knew that the speaker earned $1 when the principal made an *incorrect* prediction (i.e., the principal and speaker had conflicting interests). In still other cases, we made the principal uncertain about how the speaker earned money and, in particular, whether he or she and the speaker had common or conflicting interests.

Simultaneously, we varied the extent to which such external forces as penalties for lying and the opportunity to engage in observable, costly effort were present. We also varied the speaker's knowledge and the principal's beliefs about the speaker's knowledge. In sum, we tested our theory's hypotheses by varying perceived speaker attributes, actual speaker attributes, and external forces.

Figure 3.1 summarizes the results of our experiments. It shows how two dependent variables, persuasion and reasoned choice, varied over different types of experimental treatments. Our measure of persuasion in the figure is the percent of times that the principal's prediction matched the speaker's statement. When the observed percentage of matches was significantly greater than the percentage that would most likely occur by chance (which, in most cases, was 50%), then we observe evidence of persuasion. Our measure of reasoned choice in the figure is the percent of times that the subjects predicted the coin toss correctly. When the observed percentage of correct predictions was significantly greater than the percentage that would occur by chance (which, in most cases, was 50%), then we observe evidence of reasoned choice and of subjects who were able to learn what they needed to know.[18] Note that all numbers reported in Figure 3.1 refer to experimental trials in which the principal *did not* observe the coin toss that he or she was asked to predict.[19]

The patterns depicted in Figure 3.1 are representative of each of our

[18] To see why we predict reasoned choices at the rate of chance, rather than 0% persuasion and 0% reasoned choice, recall that the conditions for persuasion are not satisfied when the principal *has no reason to base her actions on the speaker's statement*. To achieve 0% in the figure, the principal would systematically have to do the opposite of what the speaker recommends. However, to take such an action implies that the principal *is conditioning her action on the speaker's statement,* which is contrary to the prediction of the model in the case described. Instead, we expect the "principal" to guess the coin toss outcomes without systematic regard to whether her prediction matches or contradicts the speaker's statement.

[19] In our book, we tested our hypotheses using strings of observations rather than a simple evaluation of sample means. The former provides a much more rigorous evaluation of causal claims than the latter.

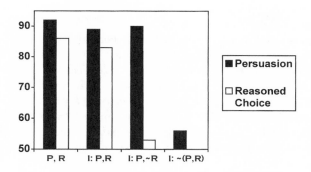

Figure 3.1. Results from laboratory experiments.

many laboratory experiments. The patterns reveal that our theory provides a powerful forecast of the observed experimental behaviors.

The leftmost set of bars in the figure depicts the trials in which it was common knowledge that the speaker had knowledge of the coin toss and common interests with the principal. These are the trials where we expected to see persuasion and reasoned choice without the presence of external forces (i.e., without an institutional intervention). And this is what we observed. In these trials, the frequency of persuasion was 92% (174/190) and the frequency of reasoned choice was 86% (164/190). This set of bars is labeled "P, R" to denote the fact that they are trials in which our formal theory leads us to predict persuasion and reasoned choice.

The next three sets of bars depict trials in which the principal either knew or had a reason to believe that he/she and the speaker had conflicting interests. The difference between the three sets of bars is the extent to which external forces sufficient to substitute for perceived speaker interest were present. In some trials, we introduced external forces into the experiment in amounts large enough that our theory leads us to predict levels of persuasion and reasoned choice matching those described in the leftmost set of bars in Figure 3.1. In other cases, we introduced no or insufficient amounts of external force. For these trials, our theory predicts only random occurrences of persuasion and reasoned choice.

The second pair of bars is labeled "I:P, R." The "I" in the notation reflects the fact that these trials contained institutional interventions. The "P, R" refers to the fact that these are trials for which our theory predicts the institutional variations to be sufficient for persuasion and reasoned choice. These are trials that contained interventions, such as a penalty for lying, sufficient to allow the principal to distinguish speakers who make truthful statements from speakers who do not.

For example, in the most extreme of our penalty for lying experiments, we set the experimental parameters in such a way that if the speaker made a *false* statement and the principal made a *correct* prediction, then the speaker reaped net earnings of *minus $1*. If the speaker made a *false* statement and the principal made an *incorrect* prediction, then the speaker earned nothing. When the speaker made a *true* statement, his or her earnings depended on only the principal's prediction – the speaker earned one dollar for an incorrect prediction and nothing for a correct prediction.

In these trials and others less extreme, the frequency of persuasion was 89% (394/444) and the frequency of reasoned choice was 83% (368/444). These percentages are similar to the frequencies observed when the speaker and principal knew that they shared common interests. As a result, the experiments support the claim that external forces substitute for common interests under the conditions specified by the theory.

The third pair of bars is labeled "I: P, ~R." Again, the "I" refers to the institutional intervention in the trials and the "P" refers to our theory's prediction that we should observe the speaker persuade the principal in these trials. The "~R", however, refers to the fact that we do not expect a high frequency of reasoned choice in these trials. Our theory leads us to believe that these are trials where the institutional intervention gives the principal a reason to trust a speaker but is not sufficient to induce the speaker to tell the truth.

These are trials where external forces are present in amounts that should lead the principal to be persuaded by the speaker *all of the time* and should lead the principal to make reasoned choices *most of the time*. The reason for the difference is that the external forces are present in amounts that help the principal reduce errors probabilistically but do not help the principal eliminate all errors. For example, suppose that the principal and speaker know that there is a very high probability that a speaker's statement will be verified. There are verification probabilities that are sufficiently high to induce the principal to believe the speaker because the threat of verification induces most (but not all) types of speaker to tell the truth. If the principal is unfortunate enough to encounter one of the few speaker types who have conflicting interests with the principal and can gain enough from deceiving her, given the very small chance that verification will not occur, then the institutional intervention will induce persuasion, but not reasoned choice. In these trials, the frequency of persuasion was 90% (104/116) and was indistinguishable from the previous two sets of bars. The frequency of reasoned choice, however, was 53% (62/116) or approximately the rate of chance.

The final pair of bars, labeled "I: ~(P,R)," summarizes behavior for cases where neither the conditions for persuasion nor the conditions for reasoned choice were satisfied. In these trials, we instituted penalties for lying or verification probabilities that, according to our theory, would be too small to induce the principal to trust the speaker.[20] In these cases, we expected that the principal's predictions should be *independent* of the speaker's statement and that the principal should make a correct prediction approximately half the time (the rate expected by chance for predicting a coin toss). Figure 3.1 shows that our expectations were again fulfilled: Persuasion (56%, 108/192) and reasoned choice (44%, 84/192) occurred at approximately the level of chance.

Overall, when we set experimental parameters to satisfy our theory's conditions for persuasion, the speaker was persuasive about 90% of the time. Otherwise, the speaker "persuaded" only at a rate equal to chance (approximately 50%). Thus, our theory provides a powerful and efficient way of understanding how people in our experiment learned what they needed to know and how political institutions can help people learn what they need to know.

CONCLUSION

In general, evolved creatures will neither store nor process information in costly ways when they can use the structure of the environment and their operations upon it as a convenient stand-in for the information processing operations concerned. That is, know only as much as you need to know to get the job done.

– Clark 1989: 64

People lack detailed information about most of the decisions they make. In this essay, we have attempted to describe some the conditions, identified explicitly in *The Democratic Dilemma,* under which limited information does not prevent reasoned choice. We have explained that reasoned choice rarely requires detailed information and that people have incentives to be very selective about what information they attend to. We have explained that politics often forces people who want to make reasoned choices to rely on the testimony of others. And we have explained how political institutions help people sort through the testimony that others offer them. In so doing, we identified the institutional

---

[20] See note 18.

foundations of political competence. We revealed that institutions matter for politics, not only because they can shape people's incentives but also because they can affect who can learn from whom.

Lastly, our explanations challenge the many critiques of democracy that are based upon underinformed critiques of the common citizen. Democracy need not be threatened by the fact that relatively few Americans have memorized trivia, such as the names of their U.S. senators, or that few can recall, without looking, the content of the U.S. constitution's seventh amendment. Unless an analyst can prove that knowledge of these facts is a necessary condition for reasoned choice, the fact that people lack such information is insufficient justification for concluding that voters cannot perform their democratic duties. Our theory and evidence suggest that it is wrong to assume that citizens who cannot recite passages from a civics book are less competent than those who can.

4

Taking Sides: A Fixed Choice Theory of Political Reasoning
PAUL M. SNIDERMAN

Does it make sense to speak of ordinary citizens as being able to reason about political choices? The most widely accepted answer, certainly since publication of Philip Converse's (1964) seminal study, "The Belief Systems of Mass Publics," is less than reassuring. Setting aside only a thin stratum of the politically engaged and aware, ordinary citizens as a rule do not pay close attention to politics, are not well informed about it, and have not thought through their ideas about it (Delli Carpini and Keeter 1996). The architecture of mass belief systems is believed more nearly to resemble, to borrow a metaphor from Rae (1981: 2), a jester's church rather than a cathedral, with their principal compartments unconnected or even butting into one another. The political convictions that citizens avow tend to have embarrassingly little to do with their actual positions on the issues of the day (e.g., Levitan and Miller 1979). Moreover, the political rights that they declare sacred in the abstract – freedom of expression, due process of law, among them – often disappear in the heat of controversy (McClosky 1958). Their political stands are, in sum, minimally grounded on political principle, minimally informed by a knowledge of political affairs, minimally stable, and, above all, minimally coherent.[1]

Minimalism, it is fair to say, is still the accepted view of public opinion. Of course in political science, to describe a particular view as the most widely accepted is only to say that it is the one most often attacked. Indeed, on my score card, the principal activity in the field of public opinion research, over the last two decades, has consisted in challenging one or another feature of the portrait of mass belief systems that Converse drew three decades ago.

One increasingly prominent line of criticism of minimalism centers on

---

[1] For a detailed review of minimalism as a research program, see Sniderman, Brody, and Tetlock 1993.

the idea that citizens can manage to reason about political choices coherently, notwithstanding their minimal levels of political information, by taking advantage of shortcuts in reasoning – or judgmental heuristics as they formally are dubbed. I propose to focus critically on the notion of heuristics, in part because it is specifically the line of argument that my colleagues and I have been advancing for the last decade. Those inside a research program often have a better opportunity, even if those outside it usually have a stronger incentive, to identify just where it has come up short.

I mean to state pretty assertively the limits of the heuristics approach as a general theory of the conditions under which citizens can make political choices coherently. My larger objective, however, is constructive, not critical. It is to lay out a broader theory of political reasoning I am in the process of developing with Philip Tetlock. It is a joint effort – if the words are mine, the thoughts are ours – and very much a work in progress. Although evidence can be brought to bear at many of the crucial points of contention, we are very far from being able to meet our burden-of-proof duty. I shall accordingly concentrate on the logic of the analytical story we propose to tell.

This analytical story, though more encompassing and, I hope, more revealing than our original account, takes as its starting point very nearly the same question that we have been grappling with from the beginning. How is it possible for citizens to make political choices coherently, if indeed they can, given how little they know about politics? Very nearly the same question, but not exactly. For the crux of the matter, as it seems to us now, is not by what means, but rather under what conditions, citizens manage to make approximately coherent political choices.

This seemingly small difference in formulation signals a fairly sizable change in conception. Initially, we asked how citizens effectively can simplify political choices so as to make them coherently. Putting the question this way led us, like virtually everyone else, to start the explanatory process by focusing on the characteristics of citizens. How much attention do they pay to politics? What do they know about it? What political ideas do they hold and how are they organized? Answer these questions, and we should be in a position to figure out how citizens make political choices. Or so it seemed then. Now, I am persuaded, we had the order of things wrong. Citizens do not operate as decision makers in isolation from political institutions. If they are in a position to overcome their informational shortfalls by taking advantage of judgmental shortcuts, it is because public choices have been organized by political institutions in ways that lend themselves to these shortcuts.

On this institutional view, to understand how citizens make the political choices they do, it is first necessary to understand the kinds of choices that they make as citizens. This shift in focus from citizens as choosers to political institutions as the organizers of political choices commits us to a trio of premises: first, that citizens can reason about political issues coherently, so far as they can, because the form of public choices they make has been fixed for them; second, that political institutions, above all the party system, fix the form of public choices; and third, that the distinctive form of public choices has much to do with how citizens actually go about making them. By way of working out this fixed choice theory of political reasoning, I want first to outline our initial research program on heuristics; then I propose to concentrate on a notion integral to the theory we are developing – the concept of a choice set.

SIMON'S PUZZLE AND THE CITIZEN AS INTUITIVE DECISION THEORIST

For all the cross-questioning of the classic model of public opinion, all sides agree on a central plank of minimalism. Moments of exceptional crisis or controversy aside, the attention that ordinary citizens pay to politics tend to be intermittent, cursory, erratic. And, paying little attention to politics, it is only to be expected that ordinary citizens will know embarrassingly little about public affairs; indeed, so little that for decades it has been a popular parlor game for public opinion researchers to elicit astonishment by citing instances of the political ignorance of the general public, my personal favorite being the finding from a 1980s survey that 4 in every 10 Americans believed Israel to be an Arab nation (Sniderman, Brody, and Tetlock 1991: 15).

It would be one thing if public inattention and ignorance was episodic, and indeed, early on it was argued that citizen disengagement from politics was only a public commentary on the banality of politics in the 1950s (see Nie, Verba, and Petrocik 1976). Subsequent studies, however, have put emphasis on the suggestion that citizens would more assiduously involve themselves in public affairs if only politics were more ideologically charged, and indeed, according to the most recent systematic study, the level of citizen knowledge, adjusted for increased educational opportunities in schooling, quite possibly has gone down (Delli Carpini and Keeter 1996). Any theory of political reasoning, it follows, must bite the bullet and concede that the public's minimal knowledge of political choices is chronic rather than episodic.

With our acceptance that citizens' disengagement from politics is chronic, it has recently been argued that the conclusion to draw in turn is that "most people really aren't sure what their opinions are on most political matters" (Zaller 1992); indeed, that most of the people, most of the time, just "make it up as they go along."[2] In this view, most citizens have about as many reasons to support as to oppose any given governmental policy, and their position on any given occasion therefore hinges on chance and accidents of question wording that tilts them, for a moment, in one direction rather than another. This conclusion, if correct, dissolves the problem of political reasoning. There is no point in developing a theory of how citizens make public choices if the crucial factors are matters of happenstance.[3]

As it happens, I do not think that anyone seriously supposes this is the rule. On political matters that are arcane or remote from their concerns, citizens often have little idea what course of action the country should pursue; and large numbers of them may, as Converse's (1964) seminal study suggested, make up a position on an issue, rather than acknowledge they have failed to form one.[4] But I do not know of any evidence that suggests, or indeed any observer who really believes, that when it comes to welfare, crime, affirmative action, the death penalty, the use of American troops overseas, or a host of other issues at the center of political controversy, most citizens choose a position by happenstance.

But how is it possible for large numbers of citizens to know where they stand on political issues, given how little they know about politics? In deference to Herbert Simon, I call this Simon's puzzle.

For the last decade my colleagues and I have worked on Simon's puzzle. Broadly, the avenue we have followed is this: The public choices that citizens are asked to make are, taken head-on, complex; the fund of information they have to work with, at any given moment, thin. If they are to make approximately rational choices (in the standard economic sense of the term), then they must simplify the choice itself, and this they can do by taking advantage of shortcuts in reasoning, or judgmental heuristics.

The argument is general. Consider a classic example of a heuristic, taken from the world of budgeting – incrementalism. Suppose the task is to draw up a university's budget. No one has the information (or the time) to fix expenditures in every category, starting from scratch.

---

[2] "Making It Up as You Go Along" is the title of Chapter 5 in Zaller's *The Nature and Origins of Mass Opinion*.

[3] Zaller, for example, though arguing in favor of nonattitudes in the first half of his book, brings attitudes back in the second half. There is an irony to an argument that contends that citizens do not have opinions but do have ideological predispositions.

[4] Converse, in fact, found only one that fitted the black-and-white model, and it was, for that matter, distinguished by being double-barreled, with respondents asked about government assurance of electricity and private housing.

Taking Sides: A Fixed Choice Theory

By taking last year's expenditures as a starting point, however, one can readily manage multiple marginal changes. Budgetary incrementalism is thus a simplifying strategy that makes an otherwise impossibly complex task manageable. Ordinary citizens similarly find themselves routinely confronting political choices that are unmanageably complex. But, we reasoned, if they can hit on a way to simplify such choices effectively, they may nonetheless be able to make them coherently. As a first step in working through this idea, Henry Brady and I focused on how citizens figure out not where they themselves stand on major issues, but rather where politically strategic groups – above all, liberals and conservatives – stand on them (Brady and Sniderman 1985). Whether ordinary citizens know what this particular pair of political grapplers stand for is of more than passing interest. The classic position has long been that, even if there are terms in which mass publics can effectively make sense of political choices – and there may well not be – the politically crucial point is that they cannot understand these choices in the terms that they are actually posed by political elites – that is to say, ideological terms (see, e.g., Campbell, Converse, Miller, and Stokes 1960).

Taking advantage of the notion of judgmental shortcuts, we argued in favor of a measure of overlap. A nontrivial fraction of the public at large could, we reasoned, figure out where liberals and conservatives stand on major issues of the day, provided they knew where they themselves stand and how they feel about the ideological alternatives. These two elements, put together in the right way, provide a judgmental shortcut, the likability heuristic, as we dubbed it, allowing ordinary citizens to figure out what liberals and conservatives stand for, even if they cannot explain what liberalism or conservatism as political philosophies are about.

As I am myself about to criticize this approach, perhaps I can get a word in first about the criticisms of others. According to Luskin (2000), "the trick behind the likability heuristic, simply put, is to infer that groups you don't like take positions you don't agree with." Unfortunately, this gets things wrong several ways over.[5] In the first place, citizens' feelings contribute to the heuristic if, but only if, they are cognitively consistent: If you like liberals, you must understand that you are supposed to dislike conservatives, and vice versa. And in the second, rather than relying simply on how people feel toward politically strategic groups, as Luskin contends, the heuristic hinges as much on people's

---

[5] By way of example, Luskin suggests a correction for guessing, no doubt helpfully meant but gratuitous, since guessing is a specific component of the model for estimating the likability heuristic.

beliefs as their feelings. The two points, taken together, are crucial. Follow Luskin's formulation, and you succumb to "false consensus" effects, supposing that others are more like you than they actually are the more you like them. Follow the likability heuristic, by contrast, and you will estimate reasonably accurately what politically strategic groups actually stand for on the issues of the day, very much including being able to recognize when groups you like take positions different from your own.

More generally, there have been objections that our research program has overstated the case for citizen reasoning.[6] On this view, we claim – wrongly – that poorly informed citizens can reason as effectively about political choices by relying on their feelings as well-informed citizens can by relying on their ideas. And had we claimed this, we certainly would have been wrong. In fact, we have repeatedly and publicly argued in behalf of a pair of interlocked propositions: that citizens can compensate for informational shortfalls by taking advantage of efficient heuristics *and* that whether they can take advantage of efficient heuristics itself depends on their level of information. Simply put, it takes smarts to take advantage of smart moves (see Brady and Sniderman 1985).

But if the criticisms of our research program seem to me wide of the mark, what do I think are its genuine weaknesses? Citizens are, it suggests, intuitive decision theorists. When they lack the information necessary to make the choice head-on, their fallback strategy is to take advantage of effective shortcuts in judgment.

How, exactly, did they come to hit upon these shortcuts? Two conditions have to be met for the likability heuristic, for example, to yield approximately correct answers. First, citizens must know their own position on the issues; not a trivial condition, since it requires that citizens already have in place one of the elements of judgment that heuristics were introduced in the first place to account for. Second, for the likability heuristic to yield accurate estimates, citizens must put together their likes and dislikes for opposing groups consistently. They must, that is, know that just so far as they like liberals, they should dislike conservatives, and vice versa. But isn't this perilously close to presupposing that they understand the very aspect of judgment that the concept of heuristics is invoked to explain?

I do not think there strictly is a problem of tautology, but I do believe that application of heuristics to politics presupposes background considerations that the concept was itself supposed to illuminate. And we

[6] For illustrations of this view, see Richard Johnston, Andre Blais, Elisabeth Gidengil, and Neil Nevitte 1996: 22 and 282, and Robert Luskin 2000.

can see a deeper problem if we consider a different judgmental shortcut – the "self-help" heuristic.[7] The intuition behind this heuristic is straightforward. In deciding who is entitled to government assistance, citizens apply a simple rule of thumb: If those for whom help is being sought have been trying to help themselves, then they will favor government helping them; if not, not.

The rule, so stated, seems consensual. It is, however, crucial to distinguish between agreement on the meaning of a rule and agreement on its application. Consider, for the sake of concreteness, how citizens go about making a choice as to whether government should help blacks more or blacks should do more to help themselves. The notion is that ordinary citizens compensate for the thinness of their political information by taking advantage of the self-help heuristic, favoring government help for blacks if they believe blacks are trying to help themselves, opposing it if they believe blacks are not. Notice that everyone taking advantage of the heuristic is following the same rule, but the point politically is that they disagree in applying it to blacks. The question at the center of the politics of race is not whether, as a general proposition, people who are trying to help themselves show themselves to deserve help from others, but instead whether blacks are trying to help themselves. What stands in need of explanation, it follows, is not why a citizen will oppose government help for others if he has concluded that they are not trying to help themselves, but why he concludes that blacks are not trying to help themselves. But if the judgment as to whether a particular group is or is not trying to help itself is built into the self-help heuristic, doesn't this presume the very judgment we are attempting to explain?

Finally and most generally, our initial emphasis on judgmental heuristics as devices for organizing political choices owed much to William James's perspective on perception. We supposed that paying as little attention to politics as they do, citizens experience a "blooming, buzzing confusion" when they come to think about political choices. If they are to make coherent choices, we reasoned, they must find a coherent way to organize this "blooming, buzzing confusion." And this, we suggested, they do by taking advantage of judgmental shortcuts, or heuristics.

In a frankly Jamesian spirit, our research program on heuristics presumed that perceivers organize the field of perception. But how reasonable is it to presuppose that citizens are in a position to organize and impose order on the political choices they are asked to make? If they are as inattentive and ignorant about politics as advertised, how do they

---

[7] Originally, this was labeled the desert heuristic, a less-than-fortunate, because a less-than-transparent, choice.

come to be so inventive in devising effective shortcuts in organizing political choices and so expert in imposing them on political choices? By way of working out an answer, I think it useful to focus not on the attributes of citizens as choosers, but on the characteristics of the choices they make as citizens.

THE CONCEPT OF A CHOICE SET

Thirty years ago, the Free Speech Movement convulsed the University of California at Berkeley. Nothing like it had occurred, and meeting after meeting was held in an effort to make sense of what was happening. One still stands out in my memory. At a particularly dramatic juncture, Norman Jacobson, a political theorist, spoke to the graduate students in political science. Without attempting to argue for a particular course of action, he argued that the key to choosing a course of action is to understand that we do not have our choice of choices; we have to choose from the alternatives on offer.

As practical advice, that seemed to me helpful then. As a theoretical intuition, it seems to me instructive now. Whatever is or might be true in "direct" democracies, in representative democracies, citizens get to choose only from among the alternatives on offer. But the role of alternatives in organizing political choice has been elided. That seems to me valid as a general proposition, and whether true across the board, true in our case. We had, so far as we had a self-conscious theoretical point of reference, a Lewinian perspective. Behavior, Kurt Lewin had declared, is a function of the person and his situation, or as he famously put it, $B = (f) \, P, S$. For nearly the whole of my career, Lewin's formula has seemed to me the right formulation. All behavior, political behavior very much included, could be accounted for in terms of the characteristics of the person, or of his situation, or of the two taken together. Personal and situational characteristics – the two exhausted the universe of causal considerations. The task in the analysis of choice, I therefore supposed, was to understand in detail the impact of both. This no longer seems to me helpful. The difficulty is not whether Lewin's formula is sufficiently capacious; with enough effort and ingenuity, any and every factor, dispositional and circumstantial, can be squeezed in. The question is whether, applied to politics, Lewin's formula cuts Nature at her joints.

In thinking of situational factors, I now think it is necessary to distinguish between the choice context and the choice set. The choice context encompasses the circumstances in which people make political choices that guide the choices they make, and roughly corresponds to what ordinarily we mean when we say that situational factors affect the choices that citizens make. Construed distally, the choice context includes

74

external factors, "attack advertising," for example; construed proximally, it includes immediate features of the interview situation, the ordering of questions, for example. The choice set, by contrast, consists in the alternatives open for choice. For political choices, the choice set consists characteristically in alternative courses of action framed in terms of government policies. The proposition I want to argue for is that how people go about making a choice hinges on how the choice set – the alternatives open for them to accept or reject – is organized.

To make this proposition do useful work, two conditions have to be met. It is necessary, first, to identify a causal mechanism by which political choices become organized and, second, to specify the distinctive features of political choice sets that bear on the process of choice itself.

A theory of public opinion, it follows, must begin with a theory of political institutions. Rather than presuming that citizens, operating on their own, organize the "blooming, buzzing confusion" of politics, it makes more sense to suppose that political choices, so far as they are organized, are organized for citizens by political institutions. But which institutions, and how, and why?

As Herbert McClosky demonstrated a generation ago,[8] at the level of political activists, the Democratic and Republican parties, so far from being Tweedledee and Tweedledum, represent communities of co-believers, the one committed to liberalism, the other to conservatism. This intersection of party and ideology provides, I want to suggest, the crucial mechanism in the institutional organization of choice sets in the American political system. To win public power, the parties must compete, and a central aspect of this competition is their effort to define the terms of political choice.

Our opening claim is thus that political parties, under the direction of overarching political orientations, fix the terms of public choice for citizens at large. Our corollary claim is twofold: first, that it is because of the particular way that political institutions fix the terms of public choice that a sizable number of citizens can make political choices approximately coherently, notwithstanding their informational shortfalls; and second, that how citizens go about making political choices is tied to how public choice sets are organized. To illustrate the reasoning behind both claims, I want to consider the nature of public choice for citizens.

THE NATURE OF PUBLIC CHOICE

What kind of choice are citizens asked to make as citizens? This question has not gotten much in the way of attention. On the contrary, it

---

[8] Herbert McClosky, Paul J. Hoffman, and Rosemary O'Hara 1960.

seems a taken-for-granted premise that political choices are not taken to be distinctive in form, but instead fall quite tidily under general decision theory and judgment. This taken-for-granted premise has contributed, I want to suggest, to mischaracterizing what making a public choice involves for citizens and, in consequence, to mistaking whether they are capable of making it coherently. Consider, by way of specific example, a problem that Quattrone and Tversky (1988: 722) pose in their exploration of the psychology of political choice:

Suppose there is a continent consisting of five nations, Alpha, Beta, Gamma, Delta, and Epsilon. The nations all have very similar systems of government and economics, are members of a continental common market, and are therefore expected to provide very similar standards of living and rates of inflation. Imagine you are a citizen of Alpha, which is about to hold its presidential election. The two presidential candidates, Brown and Green, differ from each other primarily in the policies they are known to favor and sure to implement. These policies were studied by Alpha's two leading economists, who are of equal expertise and are impartial as to the result of the election. After studying the policies advocated by Brown and Green and the policies currently being pursued by the other four nations, each economist made a forecast. The forecast consisted of three predictions about the expected standard of living index (SLI). The SLI measures the goods and services consumed (directly and indirectly) by the average citizen yearly. It is expressed in dollars per capita so that the higher the SLI the higher the level of economic prosperity.

The three projections concern

1. The average SLI to be expected among the nations Beta, Gamma, Delta, and Epsilon.
2. The SLI to be expected by following Brown's policy.
3. The SLI to be expected by following Green's policy.

The forecasts made by each economist are summarized in Table 4.1.

Quattrone and Tversky continue: "Suppose that as a citizen of Alpha, you were asked to cast your vote for Brown or Green. On the basis of the information, whom would you vote for? [Brown, 28%; Green, 72%]."

To demonstrate that attitudes toward risk are a function of whether outcomes are perceived as gains or losses, relative to a reference point, Quattrone and Tversky presented to a second group of respondents the same cover story, but different economic forecasts (Table 4.2). And, indeed, the variation in the reference made a difference, with Brown now getting 50 percent of the vote.

Take this as a specimen example of the nature of public choice from the perspective of decision theory. Contrast it with a formulation from the perspective of public opinion studies, taking as a specimen example a standard policy choice from the National Election Studies: Some people

Taking Sides: A Fixed Choice Theory

Table 4.1. *Projected SLI in dollars per capita (A)*

	Other Four Nations	Brown's Policy	Green's Policy
Economist 1	$43,000	$65,000	$51,000
Economist 2	$45,000	$43,000	$53,000

Source: Quattrone and Tversky 1998: 722.

Table 4.2. *Projected SLI in dollars per capita (B)*

	Other Four Nations	Brown's Policy	Green's Policy
Economist 1	$63,000	$65,000	$51,000
Economist 2	$65,000	$43,000	$53,000

Source: Quattrone and Tversky 1998: 722.

think that the government in Washington should increase spending for programs to help blacks. Others feel that blacks should rely only on themselves. Which makes more sense to you? Should the government help improve the position of blacks, or should they rely only on themselves?

Simplifying political choices is a key part of what we mean in saying that political institutions organize political choices. The decision-theoretic task conspicuously is complex; the public opinion choice, strikingly simplified.[9] What matters as much are the ways in which public choice is simplified. Four define public choice: tense, mood, person, and the organization of alternatives.

Tense

Consider first the matter of tense. In the Quattrone-Tversky example, citizens are asked to vote based on their prediction of the future performance of the economy, conditional on the election of alternative candidates. The tense is thus future. Idiosyncratic details of this particular example to one side, decision-theoretic judgments are standardly future

[9] For the record, I am cheerfully aware that I am taking the public opinion as a representation of the politics of issues. Beyond observing that accomplishing this actually is the raison d'être of opinion surveys, I would ask for indulgence on the grounds that I, notwithstanding my vocation as a public opinion researcher, am going to be arguing for the primacy of political institutions.

oriented, taking, among other forms, estimates: (i) of ranges of gains or losses (e.g., expected standard of living gains or increases in unemployment); (ii) of probabilistic outcomes (e.g., how likely is a given consequence and how much variance or uncertainty is there in our likelihood estimates); and (iii) of trade-offs (e.g., balancing levels of unemployment and inflation). In all these cases, judgment tends to take the form of "if, then," and requiring calculations of the comparative attractiveness of alternative future states of affairs.

The presumption that political judgments are future oriented, if true, matters because tense and competence are connected. Over a wide range of problems, Kahneman and Tversky have demonstrated the limits of competence of ordinary citizens (and even of experts) in making probabilistic choices of this sort (Kahneman, Tversky, and Slovic 1982). It is hotly debated how far the Kahneman-Tversky emphasis on judgmental biases and error applies to economic choice. But it is my impression that its application to political choice tends to be taken for granted. Partly this is because it seems obvious that ordinary citizens, lacking information about politics, are vulnerable to errors in making political choices, giving too much weight to vivid recent events (the sorts of events likely to be "cognitively available") and too little weight to abstract statistical data (the sorts of information that are difficult to weave into causally compelling or emotionally evocative narratives).

If citizens, to make the choices citizens are asked to make, have to make probabilistic calculations, it would be tough to defend the role they play in democratic politics. But precisely the point, from my point of view, is that they are not asked to be intuitive statisticians. As against a standard decision-theoretic task, what distinguishes public choice is not merely that the alternatives respondents are asked to select between are identified and narrowed to two, but as crucially that the choice between alternatives is *not* framed in terms of a probabilistic calculus. No mention is made of odds or likelihood; nor is there a requirement for the explicit balancing of chances of positive and negative outcomes. As part of the process of answering the question, citizens may make calculations about future states of affairs, if they believe it appropriate and feel themselves competent to do so. But doing so is not an explicit requirement for performing the task – indeed, not even an earmarked strategy. The tense of the choice is the present, not the future.

Mood

Mood is another distinguishing feature of political choice. Consider the standard distinction between descriptive and prescriptive judgments. In the making of political choices, citizens are asked what course of action the country *should* follow. Prescriptive judgments, to be sure, are tied to descriptive ones in practical reasoning. But the express role of the public in democratic politics is not to act narrowly as a jury, as finders of fact. They are instead empowered to serve as judges, as arbiters of what ought to be done.

Terms like "ought" and "should" signal, obviously enough, that the object in making a public choice is the designation of right and wrong courses of action. Less obvious, I think, is the distinctive sense in which right and wrong are to be understood. On a common view, agreement in politics obtains over the ends to be accomplished – who objects to peace or prosperity? – and dissensus centers on the means best suited to accomplish them. Differences over right and wrong, so conceived, represent disagreements about the optimal means to achieve consensually valued ends. This view is not without its uses, but another is more telling. Because policy is contested, ideas of right and wrong tend to blur the distinction between the instrumental and the consummatory. In selecting one course of public action as right and rejecting another as wrong, citizens wind up taking the point of view that the right course of action is of value, not just because it is a means to an end they value but because it is, in and of itself, an end they value. In politics, means become ends.

Political beliefs, because of this blurring of instrumental and consummatory considerations, have an evaluative smear. I recognize that it used to be fashionable to distinguish between belief (or cognition) on the one side and feeling (or affect) on the other, but this distinction, applied to social attitudes, turned out to be academic: Empirically, the two tend to be inseparable. As a rule, it is not possible to measure what people believe about most political issues without, also, measuring how they feel about it. It is not possible because political beliefs characteristically run together views about what is and what ought to be.

The evaluative smear that results matters because of its organizational and informational consequences. Here, however, it is the sources, not the consequences, of this evaluative smear that interest me. On the hypothesis I am suggesting that the properties of the choice set primarily shape the choice process; the characteristics of the chooser do so only derivatively. Citizens' responses to politics, on this hypothesis, are shot through with judgments as to what should and should not be done, not because they have a mysteriously endogenous propensity to think in terms of right and wrong, but because the political choices they are asked to make as citizens are posed in these terms.

Person

Person is, together with tense and mood, a constitutive feature of the public choices that citizens, in virtue of being citizens, make. From the point of view of the citizen, the choice notionally is posed in the first person singular: As between these alternatives, which do I prefer? But it only appears so because the choice task is elliptically framed. Expressed at fuller length, it is first person plural, not singular. The alternatives between which a choice is made represent general courses of action, typically that the country as a whole, occasionally a particular group again taken as a whole (e.g., blacks or women), should follow. What I as a respondent am being asked to decide is what is best, not for me distinctively, but for us collectively.

It is because political choices are posed in the first person plural that they are public choices; and it is because citizens commonly understand them to be public choices that accounts of public opinion, centered on the maximization of material – and individual – self-interest, tend to misfire. Just so far as choosers understand political choices to be public choices, the considerations that they take into account characteristically tend to be sociotropic, not egocentric. As a citizen asked what we should do, I will be inclined to base my choice on public policy on my judgment of what is best for the country as a whole, and not on what is best for myself considered as a separate individual, except incidentally so far as I take the latter to be a proxy for the former. In this respect, the person and mood of public choices mutually reinforce the understanding of public choice as calling for an assessment, in James March's terms, of the logic of obligation rather than of consequences.[10] In the making of public choices, self-interest, rational choice style, thus tends to play a minor role, its major role in making private choices notwithstanding.

Organization of Alternatives

The final, and arguably the most important, characteristic of political choice sets that I want to take up is the organization of alternatives. Notice that two questions, and not just one, have to be dealt with. First, where do the alternatives come from? Second, how are they organized? I want to say a word about both.

Parties and candidates, under the terms of electoral competition, solicit popular support by making a case in behalf of the course of action they favor government following or against the course their opponents favor it following. Their aim is to win political power,

[10] James G. March and Johan P. Olsen 1989.

but just so far as they must make a compelling case to win it, the organization of alternatives is marked by four features: They are (1) organized in advance, the act of choice consisting in the selection (rather than the formulation) of alternatives; (2) are radically limited in number, typically to two; (3) are disjunctive, one or another being open for selection, but not both;[11] and (4) are mandatory, with at least one having to be selected on pain of otherwise being excluded from the choice process itself.

The view I originally favored treats citizens as intuitive decision theorists. Citizens make the task of political judgment manageable by simplification, and they manage this by taking advantage of judgmental shortcuts. To put things this way, I am now persuaded, puts the cart before the horse. Citizens can overcome informational shortfalls about politics, not because they (mysteriously) can simplify public choices effectively, but because these choices are systematically simplified for them. Issue alternatives are organized in advance, typically binary, mutually exclusive, and characteristically exhaustive.

But how is it possible for citizens to make connections across issues? Again in keeping with our overall hypothesis, we take issue consistency conceived programmatically to be conditional primarily on the organization of choice sets by institutional factors external to the chooser, and only derivatively by factors internal to the chooser.

By way of throwing some light on the organization of alternatives across choice sets, I want to say a word about Converse's discussion of issue constraint. In his classic paper on mass belief systems, Converse considered three mechanisms for connecting preferences across issues coherently: logical, psychological, and sociological constraint. In his view, the first is obviously not up to the job. Even supposing there were genuine laws of political reasoning dictating logically necessary connections of positions across issues, it is not plausible to suppose that ordinary citizens are well acquainted with them, let alone well drilled in their application. As for psychological constraint, although disparate issues may engage common underlying personality needs, given the range and diversity of political issues, personality cannot plausibly be a general mechanism for programmatic consistency.

By default, the one plausible mechanism, in Converse's view, is social constraint. Roughly the notion is that citizens gravitate to sets of political positions congruent with their social location. Thus, blue-collar

---

[11] Logically, issue alternatives in a choice rarely are mutually exhaustive. The impression that they are arises out of the efforts of political parties that their preferred alternative dominate all others, including that of the other party. We refer to this, accordingly, as pseudo-bipolarity.

workers favor a more liberal package of policy views; the better-off, a more conservative package. I say roughly, because Converse attaches a rider. The influence of social location is conditional on political awareness, which has the politically interesting corollary of both pointing to, and accounting for, asymmetries between classes in programmatic awareness of where their political interests lie. But even in principle, social constraint can account for connections over only a narrow range of issues, chiefly economic and redistributional, and in practice, its influence even there is restricted. To account for connections across wider sets of issues, it is necessary to invoke a fourth mechanism of constraint.

Some time ago, Edward Carmines and James Stimson (1989: 136) proposed a mechanism to account for changes in issue space. Citizens' attention to politics, they observed, is episodic, peaking during presidential campaigns, falling off between. It follows, they argued, that "Presidential campaigns are a time of relatively intense political learning. Candidates are the teachers. By becoming associated with positions on salient political issues, candidates define the contents of issues. And because in the norm there are only two major candidates, voters in this period of unusual political involvement face considerable persuasive pressure to constrain their own positions, but only on salient issues, to the same unidimensional and bipolar space occupied by the candidates."

"Candidate-bundling," Carmines and Stimson's tag for this constraint mechanism, is tailor-made to account for idiosyncratic changes in "what goes with what." By contrast, to account for programmatic connections across choice sets, "party-bundling" is a more appropriate candidate. Parties, operating as agents of ideology, bundle issues at both elite and mass levels. At the elite level, it is agreed that political parties require a core of activists if they are to mount effective campaigns. Just so far as ideological commitments mobilize partisan activists, parties have an incentive to achieve a measure of coherence across issues. The argument at the elite level carries us some distance, but it stops, I think, one train stop short. To attract the support of their partisans in the electorate as a whole, they have to present themselves not as opportunistic actors but as agents acting under an obligation to devise a principled and coherent approach to public policy. They are, to be sure, interested in what is to their advantage, but the point is that it is to their advantage to present their specific issue positions not as ad hoc preferences but as expressions of a larger and principled orientation toward public affairs. The incentive of political parties to achieve a measure of programmatic consistency, if so, is rooted in their effort to achieve support in the larger public, as well as to sustain it among their inner core. Just so far as parties accomplish this, choice sets across issues are themselves connected.

Previous work, my own very much included, has taken the characteristics of citizens as the starting point. Here, I take the characteristics of political choice sets as the point of departure. Their form is fixed, if the party system has performed its task, in four respects: (i) Public choices are focused in the present, and do not expressly require, as a condition of making a choice, explicit calculation of future states of affairs; (ii) they are phrased notionally in the first person singular but are posed actually in the first person plural, defining the task as public and not merely individual; (iii) they call for an assessment in terms of the logic of obligation rather than of consequences; and (iv) the alternatives are explicitly stated, limited in number, redundant across choices, and characteristically mutually exclusive and exhaustive. Tense, mood, person, and organization of alternatives are thus the principal features of public choices.

The presentation has been schematic. A proper analysis will be conditional. The characteristics of political choice sets vary, sometimes qualitatively, often quantitatively. In a given political system, alternatives may tend to bipolarity; but they do not do so uniformly. The choice sets of some issues are more sharply contrasted than those of others, and connections across some sets of issues are clearer than across others, and ditto for both more so at some points in time than at others. Variations in the organization of alternatives across issues, eras, and regimes have much to do with the conditional dynamics of public choice. Variation of these various forms is the implicit premise in our argument, and the most obvious dimension of variation is the party system.

How, exactly, does the idea of choice sets apply to multi- rather than two-party systems? Absent research, I rely on intuition. The attractions of simplicity of structure are irresistible, and so my own guess favors a tendency to collapse nominally multipolar party systems into functionally bipolar ones. Although only a tendency, variable across systems and – within them – across individuals, the hypothesis of the institutional basis of efficient political reasoning can be cast in the form of a thought experiment. Transplant Americans to a political order where – whether because of the chaos of institutions or the enfeeblement of ideology – the structure of political choice sets is either more complex or more obscure than here, and they will have still more difficulty in grasping the order of politics.

I have focused on only one element of a theory of public choice, the characteristics of choice sets. A proper account must take cognizance of two others: the characteristics of the choice context and of the chooser. But my focus, limited as it is, has at least the virtue of highlighting the limits of my own work.

5

How People Reason about Ethics

NORMAN FROHLICH AND JOE OPPENHEIMER

Once upon a time there was an independently wealthy social activist. She worked very hard championing the causes of the poor and the oppressed. She did community organizing in poor black neighborhoods and worked at establishing day-care centers. The pay was not great and she had other talents, and so it seemed clear that she was not doing it for the money. Her actions seemed the epitome of ethically motivated behavior. One day she found herself in need of a dining room table and proceeded to the local flea market. There, at a stand presided over by an obviously poor, frail, old black man, she discovered a solid oak dining room table exactly of the sort she wanted. True, it was grimy and shabby looking, but she could see that it was of excellent quality, and with a little work could be made to look very fine indeed. And the price was only $45, well below its true market value. And so she proceeded to bargain with that little old man, brought the price down to $40, and walked away with a real deal. The bargain she struck might, in contrast to her behavior in her work, be thought of as ethically questionable.

So, in different contexts, our social activist was capable of both high-minded and petty behavior. For our purposes, the moral of the story is that ethical behavior is no simple matter. To understand it, we may have to examine a variety of contextual factors that both induce and mediate it.

Indeed, although ethics has a very long pedigree in philosophy, there is, even now, no universally agreed-upon definition of ethics. But by all accounts, ethics deals with some aspects of morality (often identified as the "applied" side of ethics). And morality always seems to involve relations between oneself and others.[1] For our purposes, we will stipulate

---

[1] Of course, morality can involve relations between one human and a nonhuman. Thus we need to keep a broad definition of "others" in mind.

that a situation involves an ethical question when the best interests of two or more parties do not coincide, or put another way, when the preferred alternatives of the two parties do not coincide.[2] In particular, a sufficient condition for a decision to have ethical content is that, in the decision, improving the payoff to one party requires bearing some cost by another.

Implicit in this definition is the notion that to "resolve" an ethically problematic decision, some balancing of one's interests with that of another's must take place. This places ethics near the antipode of self-interest. But most philosophers have long understood ethical concerns to begin with the reining in of self-interest. This is not to assert the illegitimacy of one's self-interest. Rather, it is to specify the territory under exploration. And, of course, individuals in any situation may, or may not, believe that their choices can affect the welfare of others. Further, that belief may, or may not, be accurate. If the principals lack the relevant information, there may be no ethical component to the behavior even if, with better information, the situation would call for it. Thus, the evaluation of an act as ethical or not must take into account an inherently subjective component. We seek to discover whether there are

- cognitive conditions that lead one to place limits on self-interest in decision making; and
- patterns to the limits one places on self-interested decision making, that is, varieties of ethical orientations.

The evaluation of a choice as being ethical or not requires knowledge of whether an individual is actually limiting self-interest or simply acting instrumentally (even if it is in a way that appears to limit those interests) for some other gain. Hence, data for a research program on ethical behavior must be able to reveal whether observed behavior is, or is not, self-interested.[3] It would be most convenient if we could observe humanity's everyday encounters and use these data as the basis for our conclusions. But for reasons that will become clear, we need to go well beyond observing everyday behavior to test for the existence of other-regarding behavior.

For any of our findings to be correctable, we will have to identify, and even measure, empirical other-regarding behavior as a moral or ethical

---

[2] All distributional or zero-sum issues would, therefore, have an ethical component. This definition obviously doesn't get us to bedrock; after all, what are "best interests"? On the other hand, we must stop somewhere, and there probably is some agreement as to what constitutes the important interests of a person.

[3] It goes without saying that this can be tricky. For a (somewhat overly) detailed research design, consider Batson 1987.

response to situations (see Frohlich and Oppenheimer 1997). The small building blocks of observations in the experimental literature can be used to build a case regarding the way we, as human beings, reason about ethical matters. We will try to show that the apparently other-regarding responses found in the literature (which we presumably also find as an everyday component of human behavior) are what they appear to be and are generalizable to a range of ethical situations and contexts. But, we will argue, the extension to other contexts is likely to be far from a simple matter.

A research program based on observing and understanding decisions faces some preliminary difficulties. As noted above, decisions are a function of the subjective understanding of the individuals. Given our interest in decisions with ethical content, we note that some contextual conditions will highlight some ethical aspects of the situation for the decision maker. They might even engender a particular ethical orientation toward that situation. Exactly what conditions are contextually important in ethical theorizing, and how do these conditions affect individuals' responses? Are some conditions more likely to trigger the behavioral responses that ethical theory prescribes? Of course, there is the further question of what people actually notice in their decision situations and the comparison of this with what ethical theory would say they *ought* to notice. Are the observed behaviors universal responses, or are they mere cultural artifacts, learned differentially in different societies?[4]

REASONING ABOUT ETHICS

One can't travel very far in the study of ethics and behavior before one meets the skeptic. The skeptic questions the very existence of ethical behavior. In starkest terms, the skeptic believes all behavior to be self-interested. Thus the skeptic raises the fundamental existential, and even ontological, question regarding other-regarding behavior (and hence self-interest). After all, concern for others, as expressed by such terms as altruism, is probably the foundational concern of moral or ethical theory. The skeptic's question is particularly problematic in the context of rationality theory. It has often been claimed that we can reduce virtually all other-regarding behavior to self-interest. And, truth be told, at some level this must be possible: Neurologically, the behavioral impulses (or values) are all generated in the brain of the same person. So reductionism appears plausible and possible; but is it useful?

---

[4] This is a key point in the arguments regarding cultural relativism in ethics. We do not pretend to be initiating this discussion de novo. There is a long and rich tradition of such inquiries. Consider, for example, the work of Axelrod (1984), who tries to identify conditions that would develop patterns of cooperation.

In part, the issue here is definitional. If the values of one individual reflect the welfare of both self and others, certain difficulties must be overcome prior to the commencement of serious theorizing. First, we must analytically separate self-interest and other-regardedness. After all, to state that the individual must get something out of the other-oriented behavior would appear tautological. At the very least, the individual is acting in terms of his or her values. For our purposes, and for the sake of clarity, we propose a stipulative solution by defining other-regarded preferences as those that include the placing of a value on others' consumption bundles or welfares.[5] Second, there is the question as to how to avoid infinite feedback loops if one actor's welfare is a function of another's and conversely.[6] This problem was worked out some time ago (see Frohlich 1974 and Valavanis 1958). Such loops can be precluded by insisting that we differentiate between direct (first-stage) payoffs and secondary payoffs. Thus, if (x_{is}, y_{it}) is a vector of i's consumption bundle of s private goods, x_{is}, and t public goods, y_{it}, then i may be said to be other-regarding or if i's welfare $U_i = U_i(x_{is}, y_{it}, x_{js}, y_{jt})$, where the last two terms enter into the function nontrivially. Or, alternatively, $U_i = U_i[x_{is}, y_{it}, U_j(x_{js}, y_{jt})]$. The traditional self-interest assumption posits that the last two terms of the first expression and the last of the latter are null.

To understand how individuals can and do relate to ethical situations, we can look at the attributes of such situations and see how these attributes might (and should) affect the individual's choices.

The attributes of a situation include but are not restricted to

1. The number of other individuals involved in the situation. For example, the number of individuals affected by a collective project helps determine the total effects on others of any action.
2. The structural characteristics of the situation (i.e., how all relevant individuals would be affected by the different choices available). That is, the specific relations between the choices of each of the individuals and the payoffs that they themselves and the others each receive.
3. The perception of the situation by (or information available to) the individuals making choices.

Since any individual must choose relative to his or her subjective conception of the situation, there can be divergence between the objective

---

[5] We can stipulate this as something like i's preferences, R_i, are a function of j's consumption of goods x_j or j's welfare, U_j. In other words: $R_i = f(U_j, x_j)$ or $R_i = f(U_j, U_j)$.

[6] These loops come about as follows: Say i values j's welfare, and the relationship is reciprocal. Then, were i to give j, say, \$1, j's welfare would increase. Since i would be happier, and j values i's welfare, j would have a secondary gain.

state and the subjective understanding of it. This divergence may be in both the number and identity of other affected individuals, as well as in the impact of any choices on all individuals. The reality may or may not be objectively specifiable, and it may or may not correspond to how any person perceives the situation.[7]

Clearly, variation in any one of these elements of an ethical situation may engender different responses from individuals. The empirical questions we propose to address can then be ordered as follows:

- First, can we differentiate between selfish and other-regarding values and behavior; and can we demonstrate that the other-regarding values exist?
- What might trigger other-regarding behavior?
- Can we discover any patterns that might help us understand how people reason about ethics and behave in ethical situations?

We end by putting forth conjectures of universal behavioral characteristics with regard to other-regarding decisions.

Reasoning about Other-Regarding Behavior: Existence and Varieties

Many behavioral scientists have traditionally assumed self-interest to be the template individuals use to evaluate options. Moreover, many have held that if properly and carefully searched for, other-regarding behavior either would prove to be nonexistent or relatively rare and unimportant. This has been especially true of economists, who have built much of their theoretical structure on the self-interest assumption.[8]

An Early Experiment. A number of years ago, we conducted a series of experiments designed to identify whether, and how, subjects, under laboratory conditions, would exhibit behavior that took into account the welfare of others. We also wondered whether such dispositions would

[7] Many factors may account for divergences between subjective understanding and the objective conditions. We would highlight, at this time, an individual's history of interactions in similar situations with the same or similar individuals. Also important are the aspects of the objective situation highlighted in any presentation. Both can be influential in determining how an individual perceives a given situation, and hence reacts.

[8] Not all aspects of economics are constructed on such assumptions. So, for example, the social choice literature and game theory have eschewed self-interest. Indeed, Kenneth Arrow has argued that for a way around his impossibility theorem to exist, individuals *must* have a broader basis for preferences than simple self-interest (Arrow 1973: 122–123).

be related to other identifiable aspects of the individuals (Frohlich et al. 1984).

The experiments were structured to focus on the question of self-interest. Students in classes at the Universities of Manitoba and Maryland were recruited into an experiment. All subjects were told that they were paired with another person (anonymously) in another class. In class, a research assistant gave subjects a sheet of paper containing a set of choice situations. The choices were nonstrategic. Each choice would unequivocally establish a payoff for the chooser and an (unknown) other. Subjects were told to record their choices and that one of the choice situations would be selected at random to determine a payoff to the chooser and the other student. To insure reliability, the choices were administered seven times over the course of a semester. A few weeks after the last administration, subjects collected their payoffs individually from a departmental secretary by showing up, at their convenience, and identifying themselves.

In Figure 5.1, eleven choice situations are represented. In each, the subject is to choose one row. The first number in each row represents the payoff to the chooser, the second, that to the recipient. The choice situations were designed to distinguish among four different types of preference functions. Choice 11 demonstrates what they are. An individual who chose Row A would maximize her own payoff, and the choice would correspond to simple self-interested maximizing behavior. Contra Row A, every other alternative yields a lower return to the chooser, and presumably would be chosen only if the different payoff to the other party were of importance to the chooser.[9] The choice of Row B would involve a decreased payoff for the chooser, but an increase for the paired other, and hence connotes Altruistic preferences. A chooser of C takes a decrease in payoff, but gains an increased difference between his own payoff and the payoff of the paired other, a motive we characterize as Difference Maximizing. D connotes Egalitarianism since a chooser would be giving up some payoff in order that both receive the same payoffs. Thus, the experimental design reflects our attempt to identify the existence, prevalence, and characteristics of self-interested and three types of other-regarding behavior: Altruism, Egalitarianism, and Difference Maximizing.

The results of that experiment showed that the self-interested behavior was modal (42.7%). More choices were consistent with a preference

[9] Of course, misunderstandings, errors, and other extraneous factors can also lead to deviations from the hypothesized, individually maximizing payoff choices. These factors were minimized by the research design: Subjects repeated the experiment numerous times on separate days.

Situations to reveal Altruistic Deviance from Self-Maximizing Preferences:

1.

A. 8,7

B. 7,14

2.

A. 8,7

B. 5,14

3.

A. 8,7

B. 3,14

Situations to reveal Egalitarian Deviance from Self-Maximizing Preferences:

4.

A. 8,7

B. 6,6

5.

A. 8,7

B. 3,3

6.

A. 8,7

B. 0,0

Situations to reveal Difference Maximizing Deviance from Self-Maximizing Preferences:

7.

A. 8,7

B. 7,2

8.

A. 8,7

B. 6,1

9.

A. 8,7

B. 5,0

Situations to reveal a choice from among the set of Preference Types:

10.

A. 7,7	Egalitarianism
B. 7,6	Difference Maximizing
C. 7,8	Altruism

11.

A. 8,7	Self-Maximizing
B. 7,8	Altruism
C. 7,5	Difference Maximizing
D. 7,7	Egalitarianism

Figure 5.1. Experimental situations for revealing other-regarding behavior. *Note:* The first number represents the subject's payoff; the second number represents the payoff to the person paired with the subject. In situation 1, a choice of B yields the subject 7 units and the other person 14 units.

function that was strictly self-interested than with any other type. But other-regarding behavior was far from negligible. Averaging across the test dates, 57.3% of all subjects made some other-regarding choices. Instances of Altruism (19.6%), Egalitarianism (22%), and Difference Maximizing (19.4%) were all observed. A skeptic might argue that the apparent other-regarding behavior was simply error, but a number of factors put the lie to that interpretation. Other-regarding behavior, for example, exhibited consistency and specialization. Almost no one (7 out of 151 subjects) made a choice that was consistent with more than one type of other-regarding behavior. In addition, the choices were designed to test for price sensitivity of the other-regarding preferences. The three types of other-regarding choices scaled at between .83 and .89 with regard to price sensitivity. The preferences for the states of others seemed to behave like preferences for traditional goods.

To check for other indications that the choices reflected true underlying preferences, social/demographic correlates of the choices were examined. Differences were found between the distribution of other-regarding behavior in Canada and the United States (the experiment was run in both Manitoba and Maryland), with altruism being more pronounced in the United States and Difference Maximizing in Canada.[10] No male/female differences were found in the choices per se. However, an examination of the relationship between the type of choice and self-identification with a political party revealed significant relationships between type of other-regarding choices and partisan preferences, especially in Canada.[11]

In sum, these early experiments demonstrated the consistent existence of other-regarding behavior in a significant subset of the experimental population in a replicable, controlled experimental environment. Moreover, it showed these inclinations to be reliable, price sensitive, and correlated with other plausible preferences. These experiments can be criticized: Although subjects did not know with whom they were paired (and could not find out), they had to pick up their payoffs at the end of the entire experiment from a departmental representative. This contact meant that the subjects were not assured of anonymity. Thus, the choices of the subjects could be affected by the subjects' attempts to please the experi-

---

[10] Although this result may be confounded by the fact that students in Canada were recruited from a business school while those in the United States were arts and sciences students, the fact remains that differences were found.

[11] In both countries, gender played a mediating role between choices and partisan preferences. In Canada, male Conservatives were more prone to difference maximizing and disinclined toward altruism; male Liberals leaned toward egalitarianism, and male New Democrats (social democrats) inclined toward altruism and away from difference maximizing. Females followed no discernable pattern. In the United States, the relationships showed significantly only in females. Female Democrats were inclined toward egalitarianism and against difference maximizing, whereas female Republicans favored difference maximizing. But some of this lack of significance may be due to small samples in the United States (28 males and 27 females).

menters. But they certainly established findings at variance with the traditional self-interest assumptions in economics, yet consistent with notions of rational choice.

Dictator Experiments.   With the growth of game theory as a field of study in economics, a few years later some economists (mainly working in game theoretic and experimental areas) began to treat the assumption of self-interest less as an axiom and more as a bold, testable conjecture. Other social scientists have joined in the effort. This has led to a number of experimental tests of the conjecture. Most direct tests have had a similar basic structure, one which resembles, but simplifies and refines, the experiments for revealing other-regarded behavior. They are known as dictator experiments.

Dictator experiments were explicitly designed to insure the two-way anonymity of the subject: protecting the chooser's identity from both the experimenter and the paired other. This is done by having subjects in one room (called Room A) each receive an envelope with money in it. In a privacy booth, they then each take what they want and leave the rest for an anonymously paired other in the second room (called Room B) by dropping the resealed envelope in a box.[12] This anonymity deprives the choosing individual of any motive to choose in order to get a reputational, or other, secondary gain from either the experimenter or the paired other.[13]

Very roughly, one could describe the results of these traditional dictator experiments as follows: About one-half to two-thirds of the subjects take all the money; half of the others (i.e., between one-sixth and one-quarter) leave half of the money for the other person; virtually all the rest leave less than half, but there are some few who leave a lion's share for the other person.[14]

[12] More details of the experiment are relevant in that they help ensure the double anonymity of the choosing subject: See Roth 1995a for a discussion of the designs. It should be noted that the current design deviates from that reported in our early experiments. For example, the game played here is purely distributional, or zero sum. Our early experiments were variable-sum games.

[13] Contra the need for anonymity, it should be noted that despite the imperfect anonymity, in the Frohlich et al. 1984 experiments, 19% of the subjects showed no compunction in exhibiting (nasty) difference-maximizing behavior, and 47% were unshamefacedly self-interested. This result is quite similar to the results in current dictator experiments (see the discussion in note 14).

[14] It is perhaps instructive to compare the results of these dictator experiments with the results of our early experiments as described. The results reinforce each other nicely. The dictator experiments are not designed to discriminate between self-interested behavior and difference-maximizing behavior: Both types of preferences would lead a subject to keep all the money. Hence, the 64% of subjects in Hoffman et al. 1996 who took all the money roughly correspond with the 65% who were either self-interested or difference maximizing in the Frohlich and Oppenheimer

Dictator experiments improve the research design by increasing the anonymity of subjects making the choices and by focusing solely on simple division problem. Hoffman et al. (1996) interpret the results of a series of experimental variants of the dictatorship protocols. In these, the psychic distance between the subjects and the experimenter is varied. At one extreme there is a so-called double-blind condition. Subjects are called upon to divide a provisional payoff of $10 in cash with an unknown, unseen other in another room. No one can know the subject's identity because the subject makes the division of dollars behind a screen, when the experimenter is out of the room, replaced by a randomly selected student monitor running the experiment. No record is available to link the subject's choice with the subject. The subject's decision cannot be known to the experimenter. Hence, no experimenter can reward or punish the subject on the basis of her choice. At the other extreme, the subject must reveal a tentative division to the experimenter before actually receiving any payoff, thus violating the subject's anonymity with the experimenter.

Results from these experiments show the existence of an experimenter effect, as posited. In the most anonymous condition, 64% of the subjects keep all $10 bills. In the least anonymous condition, roughly 18% take it all. Intermediate levels of anonymity engender intermediate levels of division. Increased anonymity between subject, experimenter, and the recipient of largesse seems to increase self-interested behavior. But it does not extinguish other-regarding behavior. If, in the most anonymous condition, 64% leave nothing, that still leaves 36% who leave something.

Increasing the anonymity of the dictator and/or the social distance between dictator and potential recipient was designed to reveal the true nature of other-regarding behavior. But the separation of dictator from both recipient and experimenter may have introduced another confounding factor. Roberta Frohlich, a perennial critic of context-thin experiments, upon hearing about the results of some anonymous experiments, posited the following explanation: "Dictators don't believe that anyone is there." Indeed, in the anonymous double-blind experiment there is an absence of definitive evidence that there really are others in another room who will receive whatever money left by the dictator. Although some dictators may have believed the experiments are as

(1984) experiments. In both experiments, the rest of the subjects may be assumed to exhibit some form of beneficent other-regarding behavior (altruism, egalitarianism, or perhaps some other form). Among those who do leave money, about half leave exactly half of the money and most of the rest leave less. This also roughly corresponds to the division between altruists and egalitarians found in our earlier experiments.

depicted, others could well question the real impact of leaving money in the envelope.

To test for this possibility, we designed a set of double-blind dictator experiments in which subjects anonymously answered questions about their beliefs in the existence of others and the fate of the money to be left in the envelope purportedly for the paired other (Frohlich and Oppenheimer 1996b). Subjects took with them out of the experiment a chit with a number on it and were, without warning, intercepted in the hall and asked to fill out a questionnaire, anonymously, putting their number, unknown to the experimenter, in a sealed envelope with the questionnaire. Out of a total of 41 dictators, 23 left an amount greater than zero for the other person. The quotations that follow are from responses in these experiments. The anonymity can be seen to function for some, albeit imperfectly (Frohlich and Oppenheimer 1996b):[15]

(Amount left: 0; Place: Maryland) "I took all of the money and all of the pieces of paper. I believed that there were 'Room B' people because I met other people along the way who were going to a different room. I assumed that that was Room B. I took everything because I thought they would never know if I didn't give them any money, and therefore, I wouldn't feel guilty. The amount of money made no difference."

But the research design raised questions in the minds of some other regarding the true nature of the experiment:

(Amount left: 0; Place: Canada) "I am a student and I needed the money. I doubted the existence of Room B. I took the opportunity (and the money), as I do not care about the person with whom I am paired. You snooze you lose."

Note that the latter dictator reports doubt regarding the existence of others, but the doubt doesn't seem to have played a major role since raw self-interest is the reported motivation. Some others who, it ought to be noted, tended to give more, had other interpretations of the experimental frame, including doubts that the anonymity would actually be maintained:

(Amount left: 5; Place: Canada) "I made the decision that I did because if we are saying out loud what we left in the envelope I didn't want people to think I was greedy."

So even carefully designed experiments must be subjectively interpreted by the subjects, and there is no certain isomorphism between the *objectively* constructed and *subjectively* understood realities.

But the bottom line was that subjects' beliefs regarding the true nature

---

[15] For brevity, we present only a single representative comment to illustrate each point we wish to emphasize. We also report the amount left in the envelope for the other person, and the place in which the experiment was run, Maryland, United States, or Manitoba, Canada.

of the experiment affected their behavior. About 25% of the variance of the money left is reflective of beliefs regarding the existence of others who are to receive the money, and the less likely they believed the money would go to the others, the less they left. And on the basis of the comments written on the questionnaire, a number of individuals (at least 6 of the 18 who left nothing) seemed to be choosing as if the outcomes were gambles, and a form of probabilistic discounting was affecting much of the behavior. Consider the following comments:

(Amount left: 0; Place: Canada) "I really didn't believe that someone was paired with me. When making my decision I thought about whether or not if I was indeed paired with someone – should I leave half for them and take half for me. Since however I concluded there probably wasn't anyone in the other room, I took all of the money myself."

(Amount left: 1; Place: Maryland) "I wasn't sure whether or not there are people in the other room."

In the most anonymous conditions in dictator experiments, significant amounts of money are left and variations in context affect the amount left. These data support the previous evidence cited (Frohlich and Oppenheimer 1984) for the existence of other-regarding behavior. But additional experiments have demonstrated that other factors of the decision context can affect behavior, giving further credence to the existence of other-regarding behavior.

Roth (1995) presents an excellent review of the dictator and closely related literature and notes (282): that a laboratory experiment framed in a market context generates choices that are more self-interested than does a laboratory "dictator" environment. He also notes that two different procedures for paying subjects have been used. In some experiments, subjects were paid a show-up fee for attending the experiment; in other experiments, not. The amounts left were different under the two conditions, being higher when subjects were not paid a show-up fee. In that case, the modal behavior was to leave half of the money for the other person. More than 40% of the subjects left one-half of the money when subjects were not paid a show-up fee! This behavior is consistent with an assumption either that benevolent other-regarding preferences exhibit diminishing marginal returns (re others' payoffs) or that they are sensitive to other distributional characteristics of the payoffs between the self and others (perhaps to a minimum payment others are entitled to for showing up).[16]

Grossman and Eckel (1996) have argued that the lack of context in the double-blind dictator experiment threatens the external validity of

---

[16] See Frohlich and Oppenheimer 1992 for a discussion of the ethical importance of floor or minimum incomes in income-distribution problems.

any results found. Put simply, it is hard to find real-world situations devoid of contextual details. Such "thin" contexts, as they appear in the laboratory, may make it more difficult to interpret what is at the base of other-regarding behavior. Their point is that when some attributes of the other person are invoked, they can change what a chooser leaves in the envelope. By always sterilizing the context, we can't come to understand what triggers other-regarding choices: Elements of the context may be what leads people to behave altruistically.

They (1996) have run a number of experiments in which they varied the characteristics of the recipient of the monies: changing the nature of the other's need or entitlement. In one variant, they introduced information on the potential recipient's behavior in previously played modified dictator games. In another, they made the recipient a charity. They altered the gender of subjects. And they even altered the benefit associated with leaving money for the other – matching funds left to increase the value to the recipient of any money left by the subject. Not surprisingly, they found contexts to be important. Each of the varied factors changed behavior significantly.[17]

Some Conclusions about Context and Other-Regarding Behavior

Designers of the dictator experiments hoped that they would confirm the empirical simplicity of self-interest as the universal template, but it hasn't quite worked out that way. And, in retrospect, achieving a definitive answer to such a simple research question is problematic. After all, what evidence could falsify the self-interest hypothesis? Technically, it might be thought that if there is a statistically significant (say, with a $p < .05$, or $p < .01$), and persistently observable, gap between the observed amount left in the envelopes and 0, we have falsified the hypothesis. But this does take into account other experimental findings, such as those of Saijo et al. 1992. Their findings showed that even in pure cooperation games, one often gets levels of cooperation of only around 80%. The 20% shortfall seems to reflect errors of judgment by the subjects. Falsification would require more than 20% variance from zero. And the data tend toward falsification. In the majority of experimental tests of self-interested behavior, the amount left, as well as the number of subjects leaving money for the second person, are unlikely to be explicable as simply an error of understanding as they are in the Saijo experiments. The residuals are much higher in the dictator experiments.

Current efforts at establishing a purely self-interested explanation for choice seem to have foundered, or at least stalled. The results from the

---

[17] Similar findings were reported in experiments by Cain (forthcoming).

various experiments described in this chapter indicate that the degree to which self-interest accounts for observed behavior in laboratory experiments seems to be a function of a number of variables. The degree of anonymity/social distance seems to matter, but even when controlling for it, other variables enter and affect other-regarding behavior. Hence, the problem of more complex individual motivations and the role of context must continue to haunt theorists of "nonmarket" decision making and economics, and give comfort to those who posit the possibility of ethical behavior.

And so we begin to exorcise the skeptic. The empirical program of ethical inquiry is a meaningful enterprise that may help us understand the nature of human ethics. Having established that main point, we must now consider how investigating other decision contexts may enable us to build on our findings.

REASONING ABOUT FAIRNESS AND DISTRIBUTIVE ISSUES

In this essay we have been concerned with establishing the existence of other-regarding behavior interpreted as interacting utility. But other forms of ethical concern and other bases of ethical behavior exist. Individuals may hold that certain types of actions are simply "right" and may base their choices on following the appropriate ethical rules.

In the Frohlich and Oppenheimer dictator experiments (1996b) already described, a number of individuals who left money admitted to doing so because it was the right thing to do. Indeed, even a subset of dictators who admitted doubts about the existence of people in a second room reported that they didn't use probabilistic discounts in making their decisions. The comments of 11 individuals (out of the 24 who left some monies)[18] indicate that they chose on the basis of moral rules. Here a range of comments is provided to illustrate the variety of different rules that may have governed subjects' decisions:

(Amount left: 1; Place: Maryland) "I thought if there were people in the other room they deserved to make at least $6/hr. so I left $1 to add to Oppenheimer's $5."

(Amount left: 3; Place: Canada) "I decided to do what I did because it is human nature to be selfish, but on the other hand most of us do have a small, little conscience."

(Amount left: 5; Place: Canada) "I chose to leave the amount that I did because I felt that it was a fair amount, in terms of equality. I know I would have felt cheated if I got less than half so what I did is left $5

---

[18] One Canadian individual who gave nothing cited such rules as dictating that he take all the money he received and give it to his church for charity.

98

and 5 slips of paper so that whoever got my envelope (if they did exist) would feel that they had not been cheated. But I was also thinking of taking all $10 and splitting it with the monitor since he didn't get any extra money and since it was only a small amount of money, he deserved something. I <u>know</u> he exists."

(Amount left: 5; Place: Maryland) "The world isn't fair but that doesn't mean that we should not try to make it fair (i.e., I split it 50/50)."

(Amount left: 5; Place: Maryland) "I wanted to be fair to whoever was paired with me so I decided we would split the money. I was fairly confident there were actually people there. Even if there weren't others, I feel I have been fair."

(Amount left: 5; Place: Maryland) "I was not at all convinced that there really were people in Room B, but since there could have been, my conscience wouldn't let me take more than half. My Christian value system strongly affected my decision."

(Amount left: 10; Place: Canada) "I have left all 10 bills for the simple reason that the money does not belong to me and as promised the professor has paid $5. I don't want money which is not mine. Thank you."

The relatively large number of individuals who say they made their decisions on the basis of a deontological decision structure is evidence for another factor influencing the way people reason about ethics. See Olson 1967 and Prior 1967 for a quick summary of some of the bases for deontology in ethical reasoning. Implicit in some of the rules seems to be a concern for distributive justice.

CONCERNS FOR DISTRIBUTIVE JUSTICE

For the most part, the experiments we have discussed involved one-shot or transient, two-person relationships. In these situations, the main factors that would appear to explain other-regarding behavior have been interdependent preferences and choices based on ethical decision rules. But other contexts involve more people and many other ways in which the welfare of others are affected by an individual's choice. And this can lead the individual to marshal more complicated ethical judgments. For example, rather than being directly and solely concerned about the welfare of others, an individual may be concerned about the fairness of a pattern of the distribution of payoffs among individuals.[19] The concern for fairness may be the primary motivator, rather than the direct concern for the other. There are many empirical contexts in which fairness is likely to be a salient factor: Families, teams, working groups, and coali-

---

[19] These differences in motivation may be characterized as a difference between altruism and notions of fairness, such as egalitarianism.

tions are just a few that come quickly to mind. In examining how people reason about ethics, it may be important to go beyond simple binary determinate choices to differentiate among underlying motives.

One of the earliest such experiments (Miller and Oppenheimer 1982) looked at the role of fairness in the choice of coalitional partners and outcomes in voting contexts. As with the other experiments described in this chapter, the test was based on whether individuals would choose to take lower monetary payoffs for themselves in order to ensure a fairer distribution of payoffs across players. But in this case, the context was a coalition game involving more than two players. They found that individuals, in the absence of anonymity, allowed concern for fairness to affect their choices. Individuals accepted substantially lower payoffs than they need have.[20]

Later experiments (Roth 1995) have been concerned about precisely which environments seem to support and squelch such motivations. They found that some contexts extinguish all but simple self-interested behavior. In other words, concerns for fairness seem vulnerable to the institutional structure of the choice. But since a concern for fairness does exhibit itself in a number of well-defined and replicable choice situations, it is potentially important to consider the factors that might affect its emergence.

Hoffman and Spitzer (1985) were among the first to examine the role that entitlements play in defining (at least subjectively) what might constitute a fair division of money in an experiment. They found that when the right to divide money between oneself and another is determined by means of a mechanism based on skill or knowledge, the divider (the prototype of the dictator) was more inclined to take a larger proportion of the money than when the assignment of the division right was done at random. In a series of scenarios sketched to subjects via phone calls, Konow (1994) demonstrated that willingness to surrender resources to another party was a function both of entitlements and the needs of the other. And Kahneman, Knetsch and Thaler (1986) have demonstrated that, even in market contexts, the definition of what constitutes a fair pricing policy is dependent on the context of the exchange.

Perhaps the most celebrated modern attempt to address the question of fairness in distribution is John Rawls's *A Theory of Justice* (1971). Rawls addressed, from a philosophical point of view, that which might constitute fairness in the organization of society in general, and in the

---

[20] A number of other experiments have been run to expand these findings. See, for example, Eavey 1986 and Eavey and Miller 1984.

distribution of what he called "primary goods" in particular. In one of his most widely commented upon arguments, he presents a sort of thought experiment in which he proposes how one might consider an ideal way of reasoning about distributive justice. A key component in his argument is the hypothetical device of a set of representative individuals reasoning from behind a veil of ignorance in what he called an "original position." This arrangement is presumed to invoke impartial reasoning among the individuals – reasoning which takes the interests of all into account in an evenhanded fashion. A crucial link in Rawls's argument is the notion – shared in many philosophical circles – that impartial reasoning applied to an ethically problematic situation yields a solution with a claim to ethical validity. The bite in Rawls's argument is that the individuals in question are not allowed to know what role they are to play in society. Not knowing which position they are to occupy, they must weigh everyone's interests fairly in their choices of the principles that will determine the payoff structure in society. In this way, ignorance induces impartial reasoning. By explicitly using the assumptions of rationality and self-interest, Rawls attempts to identify their normative implications when they are applied in a context of impartial reasoning.

In a series of experiments (Frohlich and Oppenheimer 1992), we have shown that many of the conditions identified in Rawls's argument can be approximated in the laboratory and that experimental methods can be used to identify what constitute fair outcomes regarding income distribution. In experiments conducted in Canada, the United States, Poland, Australia (Jackson and Hill 1995), and Japan (Saijo et al. 1996), under a number of experimentally varied conditions, the vast majority of experimental groups (about 75% in each country) were able to reach consensus on the same principle as the fairest for the distribution of income in society. That principle guaranteed a minimum income for all in society, with the proviso that after those needs were funded, no constraints should impede individuals' earnings. Groups were committed to the notion that a guaranteed floor income was required, but they rejected the imposition on a ceiling for incomes.

Groups' deliberations were taped, and an analysis of their conversations revealed that the preferred principle was favored because it constituted a compromise among three competing ethical imperatives that lie at the heart of the distribution problem: need, entitlement, and efficiency. These are also the dimensions identified by Konow (1994, 1995). There was general consensus that 1) there would always be some deserving poor who, for reasons beyond their control, could not support themselves and merited support at some level above survival; 2) individuals who exert efforts to earn income should be entitled to a reasonable proportion of their earnings and so the support that they give to the deserving poor should not be overly confiscatory; and 3) the level of support granted the deserving poor should not be so high as to encourage individuals to shirk work responsibilities and rely on a guaranteed income. This is to ensure that all who could work have an incentive to do so. The level of support for the deserving poor (the floor income without a ceiling on the high producers) constituted the compromise between these competing imperatives. In their discussions, subjects often explicitly referred to the trade-offs among these ethical principles. And in that sense, the ethical principles were treated similarly to economic goods, much as the subjects in the simple division problems treated others' well-being.

Those experiments indicate that in some ethical situations, subjects from diverse cultures can reach agreement on what is fair. Further, they show that reasoning about fairness resembles, in still other ways, individual reasoning about purely self-regarding matters. For example, we saw (Frohlich and Oppenheimer 1992) that compromises regarding ethical values seem to take place analogously to compromises on other values (see their Chapter 6 on how the groups went about setting an income floor).

Ethical Behavior in Collective Action Situations

Many substantively important ethical situations outside the laboratory involve the strategic interdependence of individuals' choices. To study how individuals reason about ethics, therefore, it is also important to examine laboratory situations in which the payoffs to the individuals involved are strategically interdependent.

The problem of the social distribution of income carries within it, implicitly, a collective-action problem. The total product of a society can be viewed as a divisible public good toward which each member of society can contribute by exerting productive energy.[21] And the problem of collective action (Olson 1965) to achieve a group benefit is perhaps the area that has attracted the greatest scholarly interest among students of social problems. Often modeled as an *n*-person prisoner's dilemma game, hereafter referred to as an N-PD (Hardin, 1971, 1982), the models juxtapose the self-interested choice of withholding valuable resources from a group effort with the socially beneficial choice of contributing those resources. In the prisoner's dilemma, the only theoretically justifi-

---

[21] Indeed, this widely understood fact may be the major barrier against the libertarian notion of a minimalist state (cf Nozick 1974).

able outcome is said to be that of noncooperation, or the Nash outcome (see Binmore 1993).[22]

However, evidence of socially oriented behavior has been reported in prisoner dilemma–type situations since the first description of the game by Flood (1952, 1958) and others. This behavior has been reported both in laboratory experiments and in reports of "field" data (Baumol and Oates 1979). Other-regarded motivations furnish one possible explanation for the observed cooperation. But it is often difficult to know precisely what is generating the behavior.[23] In a review of the experimental literature in this area, Ledyard (1995) found a wide variety of circumstances under which individual behavior diverged from the self-interested economic prescription. But he noted (1995: 170) that in well-designed experiments, "about 20–25% of the aggregate contributions (are) unexplained."

Other-regarding or fairness-oriented behavior furnishes a possible explanation for these widely reported divergences from the prescriptions of the self-interest assumptions. But, in these situation as well, it is important to note that contextual details dramatically affect behavior and, presumably, some aspects of the weighting of ethical considerations in the reasoning that leads to individual choices. Certainly these details affect individuals' propensity to cooperate at some cost to themselves. Some contexts – again, markets are a good example[24] – seem to squelch most other-regarding behavior. Other factors – for example, simple forms of communication – can ensure virtually complete cooperation.

---

[22] Other sorts of games have been used to describe collective action (see Frohlich et al. 1975; Hardin, 1982; and Schelling 1973). In cases where an individual can make a difference under some circumstances, but not all, even altruists may not find they are sufficiently efficacious to warrant contributing to a collective effort. Hence, it can be very difficult to tell whether behavior that is not supportive of the socially optimum outcome is motivated by selfishness. It often could be just as easily explained by rather simple consequentialist behavior.

[23] For example, when there is a consistent but small level of disconfirming data, one is always attracted to the idea that the disconfirming data reflect noise in an experimental design. One serious study that lends credence to such a view is by Saijo and Yamaguchi 1992. They found that cooperation rates in N-PD games or games involving voluntary contribution mechanisms to public goods with no provision points and without communications typically settle down to about 20%. But, of course, that result can also be interpreted as the "altruists" and or "egalitarians" identified in previous experiments. Changing the payoffs so that the game has a dominant cooperative strategy, they observed just about 20% noncooperative behavior. One interpretation they put forward is that we can expect about 20% error in choices. But again, that 20% may just be our old enemy, the "difference maximizer."

[24] Perhaps the most astounding results showing the importance of context are those reported by Plott (1983). He shows that in the case of externalities in an unregulated market (112) the public good can go virtually ignored. He then goes on to show that nonincentive compatible systems of regulation do little to correct the situation (115).

Recently, we constructed a two-phased experiment that parallels the structure of a repeated (5-person) N-PD. All groups of subjects played a repeated N-PD without communication in Phase 2. But in Phase 1 there was a variety of experimental conditions. In some groups, subjects made decisions that were not tied to their *own* payoffs during Phase 1. Rather, the choices led to payoff outcomes that then were reassigned randomly to members of the decision group.[25] This was done to invoke impartial reasoning within an N-PD context. This "impartial transformation" of the prisoner's dilemma has a dominant strategy of complete cooperation and may be viewed as a device for aligning individual and group interests. By aligning individual and group incentives, this arrangement was expected to lead to more cooperative behavior and to invoke ethical motivation in individuals (Frohlich and Oppenheimer 1995 and 1996a). As mentioned, different communication conditions were also introduced in different treatments within groups in Phase 1. It was anticipated that in Phase 2, which was constituted as a set of subsequent rounds of the simple 5-person N-PD, with no communication, the subjects who had experienced impartial reasoning would exhibit more cooperative (ethical) behavior.

These experiments showed that impartial reasoning can move groups a long way toward optimal provision of benefits. But the use of the impartiality device had two unanticipated consequences. First, subjects playing the N-PD from an impartial point of view, although they were more successful in achieving cooperative outcomes in Phase 1, evidenced no relationship between their reported ethical concerns and their behavior. By contrast, individuals in a control group playing a regular N-PD showed a strong and significant relationship between their ethical concerns and behavior. In the second phase of the experiments – when both experimental and control groups played repeated, regular N-PD's[26] – higher levels of cooperation persisted in the group that played the *regular* N-PD. In other words, the effect of greater cooperation due to impartial reasoning was not only transient – in that it disappeared after Phase 1 – it seemed to undermine subsequent cooperation and leave the group worse off than those in the control group who had played a regular N-PD.

One possible interpretation of these findings is that the device of impartial reasoning – by virtue of the very fact that it aligns individual

[25] Some groups, as a control, played a regular N-PD without such payoff randomization during this phase.
[26] Another variation in the experiment allowed for forms of communication in Phase 1. We found that communication, especially when subjects were in a regular N-PD, led to an improved level of cooperation after communication was ended (i.e., in Phase 2).

and group interests – may blind participants to the ethical dilemmas inherent in the situation. As Professor Steve Turnbull commented at a presentation of the results: "It prevents subjects from flexing their ethical muscles." By removing the opportunity to wrestle with the dilemma, the device may be cuing individuals simply to follow their individual interests, and may cause self-interested behavior to be reinforced and carried over into subsequent decisions.[27]

Our results suggest that when sequential decisions are made, and the earlier decisions are ones that do not involve ethical tension but invite individuals to exercise simple self-interest, those early decisions may blind individuals to the ethical dilemma they face in subsequent decisions and may undermine ethical reasoning. Their subsequent behavior, therefore, may yield worse outcomes than would have been obtainable had they had practice in wrestling with ethical dilemmas.[28] The decision context and experience matter.

CONCLUSIONS

There are powerful disputes concerning how individuals reason about ethics. The findings we have cited and discussed are still preliminary. But it appears that there is an irreducible core of behavior that looks like, smells like, and is best thought to be: moral behavior. The data indicate that its existence is not preposterous. It puts the burden on the skeptic. The simplest assumption that can account for the facts appears to be a moral concern. In general, the value one places on one's own consumption is only one of many values. To figure out how people reason about decisions with numerous values, we must identify some of those other values and how people deal with conflicts among those values.

At this point, we cannot develop an overall theory of the general subject. But we can identify a number of properties about how people reason about choices when the welfare of others is at stake. We can say a few things about the existence of other-regarding as well as other forms of ethical behavior, and we can identify factors that affect both the invocation and form of this behavior.

The following italicized statements are the minimal lessons we can carry away from the experiments designed to confront the self-interest conjecture and moral behavior:

[27] Note that this would be consistent with conjectures that markets would squelch other-regarding behavior.
[28] Of course, this tendency must be contrasted with the contrary tendency for subjects in repeated rounds of prisoners' dilemmas to reduce their contributions as they experience free riding by others.

- First, recall that even when deciding in context-free situations, about half the observations violate the simplest version of the self-interest assumptions. *A substantial subset of individuals consider the welfare of others, as a value, in itself, when making a decision.*
- But for a substantial number of individuals, ethical choices may be determined on the basis of rules, which are simply believed to be right (Frohlich and Oppenheimer 1996b). *Some individuals use deontological rules, which are at variance with purely self-interested behavior.*

Given the existence of ethical behavior, we can conclude that the form it takes is sensitive to the characteristics of the chooser and the object of the behavior. Thus a number of characteristics can affect behavior:

- The relative moral status of the other party in an experiment matters (see Cain forthcoming, as well as Eckel and Grossman 1996). *Individual choices to help others are mediated by judgments of moral worthiness.*

But we can also make some general statements about the form of ethical behavior. Many instances of ethical behavior resemble traditional economic behavior in their characteristics. They are subject to the same calculi as are evident in other economic decisions. This is important in that it opens the possibility of analyzing a number of forms of ethical behavior with traditional economic tools:[29]

- The relative cost-benefit context matters (Cain 1998; Eckel and Grossman 1996; Frohlich et al. 1984; Frohlich and Oppenheimer 1992; and Roth 1995). *Individual choices to help others usually reflect costs and benefits leading to marginal calculations.*
- The perceived likelihood of others actually being helped by the behavior affects other-regarding behavior (Frohlich and Oppenheimer 1996b). *Individual choices to help others are subject to probabilistic discounting.*[30]
- Moreover, the context of the decision matters, and this includes the institutional structure within which the decision is made (Roth 1995; Frohlich and Oppenheimer 1996a). *Some social contexts, such as markets, turn off, while others turn on, other-regarding behavioral patterns.*

---

[29] This may be less true of deontologically motivated behavior.

[30] The impact of this on behavior in collective-action situations with high stakes and substantial ethical content could be severe. For example, in discussing the "good German" syndrome, Oppenheimer (1985) shows that if such discounting takes place, we can expect that where no one individual is very likely to make a difference, substantial failure of ethical behavior can be counted upon to enable political evil to remain unchallenged.

- A decision context's anonymity matters (see Hoffman et al. 1996), although the extent of the effect may be affected by uncertainty invoked by experimental design factors (Frohlich and Oppenheimer 1996b). *Individual choices to accept a lower monetary payoff may really be designed to capture broadly construed reputational payoffs (including anticipated reciprocity).*

In general, it is clear that the way in which an individual acts in a situation, either in the laboratory or in the rest of the real world, is subject to the model he or she uses to interpret the situation.[31] And the model used depends on a variety of cues imbedded in the decision context. Much variability in behavior may be attributable to the contextual factors facing decision makers and the way in which these factors evoke different models.

What then can we conclude? Starting with the skeptic from Missouri who demanded, "Show me!" we have seen that the landscape of ethical behavior is far from barren and leaves much room for exploration. The skeptic appears to have been answered: Humans are often capable of moral behavior. And luckily, perhaps, the moral behavior of humans can be understood in ways that are similar to other sets of behavior, with many of the same basic patterns. Less obviously, it would appear that moral behavior may be triggered by and affected by just a few parameters of a situation. And, further, empirical methods can be used to dig more deeply into the origins of the trust and other factors needed to support moral behavior in a community.

If experimental studies continue to yield insight into the bases and nature of moral behavior, in the long run, the accrued knowledge will have an impact throughout the behavioral sciences. Understanding the relationship between a decision structure and the individual's decoding of the situation by its cues is sure to be useful in the design of public policy (and other institutions) (Frohlich and Oppenheimer 1995). Finally, the philosophical study of ethics will also be affected. This does not mean, of course, that the empirical world will dictate the nature of the "oughts" of concern to philosophy. But the accumulated understanding about how humans form moral judgements, and the increased understanding of the shapes that such judgments take, is sure to influence how we argue about and understand ethical matters.

---

[31] Of course, the most influential scholarly example of this is Tversky and Kahneman 1981.

6

Who Says What? Source Credibility as a Mediator of Campaign Advertising

SHANTO IYENGAR AND NICHOLAS A. VALENTINO

As every election day approaches, voters all across the country are forced to endure "saturation bombing" in the form of political advertisements from every manner of candidate and cause. During the 1996 campaign, for instance, the major presidential candidates aired 5,700 advertisements in the Los Angeles media market. Campaign advertising is now such a strong force that political analysts habitually attribute electoral outcomes directly to some facet of the candidates' advertising tactics. In 1996, leading newspapers diagnosed the "winning" strategy of the Clinton campaign's ad team the day after the election.

It is hardly surprising, of course, that the very political consultants who design the advertisements claim that these messages influence electoral outcomes.[1] But more objective sources, including a substantial body of social science research, also support this conclusion. Whether one learns about it in the *New York Times* or the *Public Opinion Quarterly*, campaign advertising seems to matter.

Although there is an emerging consensus about the efficacy of advertising (see Goldstein 1997; Shaw 1997), little is known about the psychological mechanisms relating campaign advertisements to support for the sponsoring candidate. Most prior research has been preoccupied with refuting the "minimalist" conception of political campaigns (see Iyengar 1996). Higher-order questions concerning the specific attributes of persuasive advertisements or the reasoning process employed by voters remain unanswered. This essay takes a first step toward understanding

We acknowledge the generous support of the National Science Foundation, the John and Mary R. Markle Foundation, and the University of California.
[1] In 1996, for instance, Bill Knapp of the Democratic consulting firm of Squier, Knapp, and Ochs assessed his firm's contribution as follows: ". . . it was an unprecedented effort by the party to resuscitate the party. This was a party that was dead. It was flat. There were road marks on our backs." (*New York Times*, November 7, 1996, B1.)

the mechanism of persuasion by specifying and testing one particular psychological account of the "winning" message.

Given its wealth of evidence on attitude change in a variety of contexts, the literature of social psychology is the natural springboard for political advertising research. This literature differentiates between message-based and cue-based accounts of persuasion. According to the former, the audience is prompted to consider the arguments contained in the message, retrieve relevant supportive or antithetical information from memory, and adjust the "target" attitude appropriately. In cue-based models, the audience attends to more easily assimilated "signals" or associations that operate as decision-making shortcuts. For example, cues can be derived from the gender or race of the sponsoring candidate; the spokesperson making the "pitch" for the candidate; attitudes concerning the sponsoring candidate's political targets; and vivid images, emotion-evoking music, humor, negativity, and other nonsubstantive elements of a message.

The evidence from attitude change research indicates that in everyday situations involving efforts to persuade, cue-based processing predominates. Thus, in most situations, the recipient accepts or rejects persuasive messages based on an evaluation of the source's credibility (the research bearing on credibility is reviewed by McGuire 1985; for an extension to political attitudes, see Lupia 2000). Presumably, reliance on cues is more efficient for the recipient of the message than assembling and processing arguments; reliable sources provide a relevant and simple shortcut for deciphering the information value of the message. However, when recipients are highly involved in the persuasion situation (as, for instance, when the decision at hand represents a major financial commitment or when the recipient possesses high "expertise" on the subject), they typically focus more on the content or substance of the message than on associational cues. When the recipient is either motivated or expert, attitude change research finds that the logical or textual content of the message is more likely to influence attitude change than evaluations of the message's source (for reviews of this research, see McGuire 1985; Petty and Cacioppo 1984).

Given what we know about the typical voter's level of political engagement and familiarity with political appeals, the cue-based model of persuasion would seem especially applicable to the case of campaign advertising. Most voters lack the motivation and/or resources to acquire even the most elementary level of factual knowledge about the candidates and campaign issues (Buchanan 1991; Popkin 1991). They encounter information about the campaign not because they actively seek it out, but rather because it is sometimes difficult to avoid. In such low-involvement environments, voters' reactions to visible cues – including a candidate's party affiliation, gender, or physical appearance – take on special importance as mediators of campaign advertising (see McDermott 1997). In terms of the classic shorthand of message-learning theory – "who says what to whom" – "who" (source-related variables) can be expected to surpass "what" (message-related variables) as facilitators of political persuasion. The impact of political advertisements is more likely to be conditioned by what voters know, or are willing to infer, about the sponsor of the ads than by the particular statements, claims, or promises made in the ads.

Unlike the social psychological literature, which typically treats source and message characteristics as unrelated, we argue that credible political advertising depends jointly upon who makes a statement and what is said. A credible advertisement is one that "resonates" with voters – that is, is congruent with their preexisting beliefs about the competing candidates' strengths or weaknesses. Thus, in our view, campaign communication is most persuasive when it plays upon – or interacts with – voters' prevailing expectations or predispositions.

The most important political predisposition in the context of American campaigns is partisanship. Most Americans acquire a sense of party identification at an early age, and this psychological anchor remains with them over the entire life cycle (Jennings and Niemi 1981; Sears 1983). Not only are voters socialized to consider themselves Democrats or Republicans, but they also learn to attribute differing policy positions to Democratic and Republican candidates. For instance, candidates are considered especially responsive to the interests of the groups or movements that comprise the party coalitions. Democrats are thought to represent the interests of blue-collar workers, racial minorities, women, and environmentalists. Republicans are considered sensitive to the claims of businesspeople, the wealthy, "born-again" Christians, and white males. Based upon these beliefs about responsiveness to group interests, voters also impute differences in the willingness and capability of the parties to resolve policy problems. Republicans are expected to exhibit a strong sense of fiscal responsibility, opposition to "big government," and a tough posture on crime and national defense. Conversely, Democrats are expected to reduce unemployment, maintain government social welfare programs, and help minorities and women overcome discrimination and inequality (Ansolabehere and Iyengar 1994; Baumer and Gold 1995; Petrocik 1996; for an extension to European parties, see Budge and Fairlie 1983; Kleinnijenhuis and de Ridder 1997).

Such ingrained expectations about the commitment and performance records of candidates serve as important filters for interpreting and understanding campaign communication. In general, this argument suggests that political campaigns should be fitted to the party's reputation:

A Democrat should be better off using advertisements that emphasize her intent to reduce unemployment, whereas a Republican should promote his support for a more punitive criminal justice system. Campaigns in which defense and military issues are central will work to the advantage of the Republican, whereas emphasis on social security and child care will benefit the Democrat. In short, campaign communication that conforms to voters' expectations is most likely to be credible and compelling.

This essay assesses the role of credibility in political advertising by examining the "fit" between the issue content of particular advertisements and the sponsoring candidate's party affiliation. Our evidence stems from a series of field experiments carried out in southern California during the 1992 senatorial elections, the 1994 gubernatorial campaign, and the 1996 presidential campaign. The results consistently demonstrate that when candidates focus on issues that match their party affiliation, they enjoy significant electoral advantages.

In Study 1, we examined the electoral success of U.S. senatorial candidates when they broadcast a campaign advertisement that dealt with crime, unemployment, or "women's issues." We found that campaign advertising on gender-related issues or unemployment was optimal for Democratic candidates Barbara Boxer and Dianne Feinstein, and that they gained least by advertising on crime. Our second study moved beyond the examination of a single candidate's advertising to focus on the campaign "dialogue" between the advertisements of gubernatorial candidates Kathleen Brown (the Democratic challenger) and Pete Wilson (the Republican incumbent). Here, the results indicated that Ms. Brown fared best when both candidates converged on the issues of education or unemployment, and, conversely, that Wilson's prospects were brightest when the candidates advertised on crime or immigration. Finally, our third study examined the ability of presidential candidates Bill Clinton and Bob Dole to sway voters with advertisements that addressed the scope of government social welfare programs, taxes, or illegal drugs and immigration. In this case, the results showed that President Clinton's support peaked when the campaign agenda concerned government funding of social security and other benefit programs, whereas Senator Dole was most effective when the candidates addressed issues of illegal drugs and immigration.

METHODOLOGY

We rely on experimental methods. The advantages and disadvantages of experimentation are well known. Unlike surveys, experiments yield precise causal inferences about the effects of campaign advertising. The

111

experimenter carefully selects the campaign messages that will be tested. Participants are assigned at random to conditions where they are exposed (or not exposed) to these specific campaign messages. This random assignment assures that the groups are equivalent in all respects but for exposure to particular campaign ads. These simple techniques provide researchers with the all-important ability to attribute any observed difference between the experimental and control groups to the effects of the experimental stimulus.

Of course, experiments have their own liabilities. Most are administered upon "captive" populations – college students who must serve as guinea pigs in order to gain course credit. As the eminent experimental psychologist Carl Hovland warned many years ago (Hovland 1959), college sophomores are not equivalent to "real people." A further weakness of the typical experiment is the somewhat sterile, laboratory-like environment in which it is administered. This research environment bears little resemblance to the cacophony and confusion of election campaigns.

We enhanced the realism and generalizability of our campaign experiments in several ways. Each of our experiments took place during an actual campaign and featured real candidates – Democrats and Republicans, liberals and conservatives, males and females, incumbents and challengers – as the advertising sponsors. Moreover, the advertisements that made up our experimental stimuli were highly realistic. They were selected either from actual advertisements used by the candidates during the campaigns (in 1994 and 1996), or they were produced by us to emulate typical campaign advertisements (in 1992). In the case of our own productions, we spliced together footage from actual advertisements or news reports using studio-quality editing technology, making it difficult for all but the most sophisticated viewers to detect any differences between the experimental manipulations and the "real thing."[2]

An especially important step toward boosting the generalizability of our results was the use of a subject pool that was reasonably representative of the southern California voting-age population. Unlike the usual social science experiment, which relies heavily on conscripted college sophomores as subjects, our participants were people from many walks of life and included adults of all ages, employed and unemployed, whites, African-Americans, and Hispanics, men and women, city dwellers and suburbanites, and so forth.

The sites for each experiment were furnished to resemble, as closely as possible, the normal conditions in which a person views political

---

[2] Out of a total of more than 2,000 subjects, 3 indicated at the debriefing stage that they harbored suspicions over the authenticity of the political advertisements they had seen.

advertisements. Comfortable couches and chairs were arranged in front of a television set, with houseplants and wall hangings placed around the room. Respondents were offered coffee, cookies, and soft drinks to enjoy during the viewing sessions. In most cases, family members or friends took part in the experiment at the same time, so that respondents did not find themselves sitting next to a stranger while viewing the political advertisements.[3] Participants were recruited by the use of flyers and announcements in newsletters, as well as by personal contact in shopping malls, all offering payment of $15 for participation in "media research."

The sites selected for each experiment were virtually identical in layout and decor. Each site consisted of a two-room office suite located in or near a retail shopping area. One of the rooms was used as a viewing room and the other was used for filling out questionnaires.

In 1992, we administered the experiment in two locations. The first was located near Westwood, a predominantly Democratic neighborhood located just south of the UCLA campus. The other was located in Costa Mesa, a small city in conservative Orange County. In 1994, our site adjoining several major office complexes was located in downtown Los Angeles. In 1996, we expanded the facilities to include three sites. One was located again in Westwood, in a popular shopping mall. The second was based in a small shopping area in Moorpark, a conservative northern suburb of Los Angeles. The third site was located in Manhattan Beach, a coastal city southwest of Los Angeles. This variety of locations helped to ensure a large and diverse subject pool.[4]

The Designs

We relied on two different experimental designs. The first (administered during the 1992 and 1994 campaigns) embedded the experimental advertisements into a 15-minute recording of a recent local newscast. Candidates advertise heavily during local news programs (because the audience for news includes a large proportion of likely voters), and the appearance of the experimental campaign advertisement in the local newscast was thus inconspicuous. Other news stories and product advertisements were selected carefully so that they were not relevant to the experimental stimulus, and these same filler stories and ads were used in combination with each political advertisement.

[3] While participants were free to converse with each other during the viewing sessions, they completed their responses to the questionnaires individually, often in separate rooms.

[4] Information concerning relevant socioeconomic and political attributes of the experimental participants is provided in the Appendix.

The "newscast" design was administered in two different versions containing either one or two campaign advertisements. In the one-advertisement design (employed in 1992), we limited the experimental manipulation to a single 30-second commercial. In these studies we produced the experimental advertisement ourselves, the ad addressed either a "Democratic" or "Republican" issue, and we manipulated the resonance of the ad by airing it on behalf of both the candidates. One set of participants, for example, saw an advertisement aired by Democrat Dianne Feinstein that discussed rising unemployment and her support for job-training programs and economic development tax incentives. Another set of participants saw the identical advertisement, this time on behalf of Feinstein's Republican opponent, John Seymour. In other conditions, participants watched a Seymour (and Feinstein) advertisement that called for tough new anticrime measures. In this way, we varied the degree to which one or the other of the candidates' ads was especially credible.

The two-ad design (which was used in our study of the 1994 gubernatorial campaign) expanded the scope of the manipulation to include two advertisements, one from each of the candidates. Within this "paired" arrangement, we varied the issue agenda of the campaign, so that participants were exposed to spots dealing either with the Democratic issues of unemployment and education or the Republican issues of crime and illegal immigration.

In 1996, we introduced a different one-ad design in which participants simply watched a videotaped collection of nine television advertisements, one of which was an advertisement from the 1996 presidential campaign. The ads corresponded to those being aired in southern California by Bill Clinton and Bob Dole.[5] The presidential ads we examined addressed illegal immigration, drug abuse, federal spending on social programs, and cutting taxes.[6]

---

[5] In general, we synchronized our participants' exposure to the 1996 ads with the candidates' ad buys.

[6] Protecting and preserving federal social programs was a thematic mainstay of the Clinton reelection campaign. Attempting to capitalize on the Republicans' "Contract with America" and their subsequent efforts to curb the rate of growth in entitlement expenditures, numerous Clinton ads depicted Senator Dole and Speaker Newt Gingrich as advocates of "cuts" in social security, Medicare, student loans, child care, and other benefit programs. Clinton's positive ads focused on the president's steadfastness in resisting congressional Republicans' efforts to slash government programs and agencies. Dole's ads on social welfare programs tended to focus on "wasteful" spending (e.g., "midnight basketball") and on labeling President Clinton as a "big spender." Senator Dole's ads on the subject of taxes contrasted his 15 percent tax-cut plan with the tax increases supported by President Clinton. Clinton's ads in the taxes category either attacked Dole's tax-cut plan ("risky" and a threat to the health of the

Indicators

Our basic indicator of candidate preference was the respondent's intended vote choice following exposure to a campaign advertisement. This variable was coded as a trichotomy, with intended votes for Democratic candidates set equal to +1, votes for Republican opponents set equal to −1, and respondents who expressed no preference or who remained unsure of their vote being scored as zero. In effect, this indicator measures the Democratic candidate's lead over the Republican.

Since there were two concurrent Senate races in 1992, we pooled across both elections.[7] That is, depending on the sponsor of the advertisement they were exposed to, respondents chose between Barbara Boxer and Bruce Herschensohn or between Dianne Feinstein and John Seymour. For respondents assigned to the control condition (in which there was no campaign advertisement), the vote choice indicator was defined as the average margin by which the Democratic candidates were favored in the two Senate races. As a result, the effect of the experimental manipulation in the 1992 studies is the difference between the lead of either Democrat in each advertising condition and the average lead of both Democrats in the control condition.

Democratic versus Republican Messages

We categorized advertisements as Democratic or Republican according to the reputations of the parties with regard to specific issues. As described, we paired advertisements sponsored by each candidate in each election that concerned a specific issue. Our sample of Democratic issues included unemployment (1992 and 1994), education (1994), women's rights (1992), and government funding for social welfare programs

economy) or depicted Dole and Gingrich as supporters of tax increases themselves ("taxmen for the welfare state").

In the case of illegal immigration, Dole used a series of attack ads concerning the administration's failure to curb the flow of illegal immigrants. Clinton used a "rebuttal" ad in which he claimed credit for strengthening border patrols and protecting American workers from illegal immigrants.

In the general category of crime, Dole's ad campaign concentrated on teenage drug abuse. We included a pair of Dole ads that featured footage from the famous 1992 MTV interview in which Clinton admitted to having used marijuana while a college student. The Clinton crime ad focused on the passage of the Brady Bill and police chiefs' support for the legislation.

[7] Prior to pooling across the races, we tested and rejected the hypothesis of election-specific effects. That is, we found no significant interactions among the Democratic candidate's level of support, the issue agenda of the advertising campaign, and the Senate election (Boxer versus Herschensohn or Feinstein versus Seymour).

(1996). Unemployment was particularly salient in 1992 when the severe recession forced all four senatorial candidates to address the issue in their advertising. We created an ad in which the sponsoring candidate indicated his/her support for job-training programs. A similar theme was prominent in the 1994 gubernatorial campaign, as Brown attacked Wilson for the state's loss of jobs and Wilson claimed credit for having implemented various job-stimulus programs.

The year 1992 was hailed as the "year of the woman" in American politics. With two prominent women Democrats running for Senate seats in California, it was to be expected that gender-related issues would heat up as the campaign progressed. We produced an ad on behalf of both Democrats (but not on behalf of their Republican opponents) in which they stated their support for abortion rights and pledged to support legislation against sexual harassment in the workplace.

In 1994, we tested another traditionally Democratic appeal – the quality of public education. Kathleen Brown aired ads criticizing the poor quality of California's public school system and promising to modernize teaching. Pete Wilson countered with ads pledging to protect state funding of public schools.

The final Democratic issue – which featured prominently during the 1996 campaign – focused on government spending for social welfare programs (most notably Social Security and Medicare). President Clinton repeatedly reminded voters of Republicans' efforts to weaken these popular benefits, while Dole attempted to portray Clinton as a liberal Democrat who favored handouts and programs that created "big government."

Our sample of issues owned by Republicans included crime (1992, 1994, and 1996) and immigration (1994 and 1996). Of course, crime is a perennial issue in political campaigns, and it was especially prominent during the 1992 senatorial campaigns in the aftermath of the Los Angeles riots. We created ads in 1992 that described the sponsor as a forceful advocate of "law and order." In 1994, Pete Wilson contrasted his support for "one strike" legislation for major crimes with his opponent's opposition to the death penalty. Kathleen Brown attempted to engage Wilson on the crime issue by airing an ad in which she blamed Wilson for increases in youth crime and described her proposal to build "boot camps" for juvenile offenders. A variation on the theme of crime took center stage in 1996 when Dole invested heavily in ads attacking the Clinton administration's record on teen drug usage.

The issue of illegal immigration was used extensively during the 1994 gubernatorial campaign. Capitalizing on the publicity generated by

Proposition 187, Wilson aired several advertisements citing his tough stance on the issue. Brown countered by attacking Wilson's proposal to deny access to health care and education to the children of illegal aliens. Senator Dole revived the immigration issue in 1996 by airing ads (specifically targeted for California voters) that documented the significant increase in the number of illegal immigrants and the adverse consequences (including higher crime and overcrowding in the schools) of immigration for Californians.

In 1996, we also tested a number of ads from both candidates concerning taxation. Dole attempted to position himself as a tax cutter, while Clinton attacked Dole's tax-cut proposal. The issue of taxes provides an interesting variant on the notion of resonance concerning temporary shifts in party ownership, especially with regard to economic issues. Traditionally, Republicans might be expected to own the tax issue. During the Reagan years, Republican candidates at every level of government successfully depicted themselves as "tax busters," while simultaneously painting their Democratic opponents as "tax-and-spend liberals." However, several contextual factors may have worked to erode the traditional Republican advantage on taxes. In 1992, Clinton successfully challenged Bush on the basis of a poorly performing economy, effectively positioned himself as a "centrist" following the Republican gains in 1994, and then presided over a rapidly recovering economy. On the basis of his recent economic accomplishments, we might predict that in 1996 Clinton could temporarily "lease" the issue of taxes from the Republicans (see Petrocik 1996).

In summary, we expect that Democratic candidates will benefit when the subject of the ad campaign is unemployment, women's rights, education, or government funding of social welfare programs. Conversely, we anticipate that Republicans will enjoy greater credibility when the campaign issue agenda consists of crime or illegal immigration. Given the recent history of the issue, we make no prediction on the issue of taxes.

RESULTS

Our first test of credibility as a mediator of campaign advertising analyzes the electoral support for the candidates in relation to the issue agenda established by the advertising campaign. As shown in Figure 6.1, the candidates' electoral prospects were enhanced when the issue agenda of campaign advertisements matched their party affiliation.

The first panel in Figure 6.1 displays the results for the 1992 California Senate campaigns. In these elections, support for the Democratic

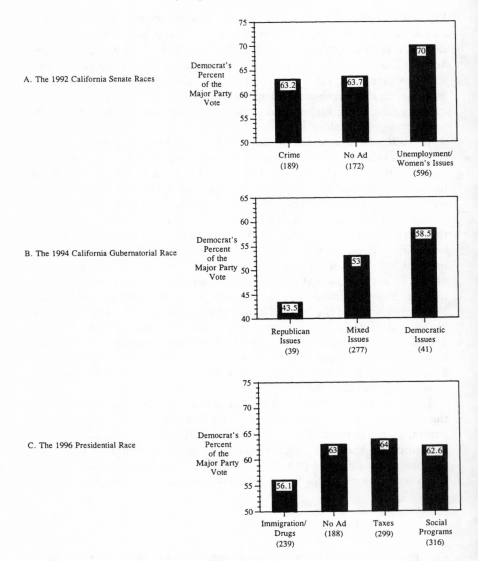

A. The 1992 California Senate Races

Democrat's Percent of the Major Party Vote

Crime (189) No Ad (172) Unemployment/ Women's Issues (596)

B. The 1994 California Gubernatorial Race

Democrat's Percent of the Major Party Vote

Republican Issues (39) Mixed Issues (277) Democratic Issues (41)

C. The 1996 Presidential Race

Democrat's Percent of the Major Party Vote

Immigration/ Drugs (239) No Ad (188) Taxes (299) Social Programs (316)

Figure 6.1. The effects of the campaign issue agenda on vote choice.

candidates increased by nearly 7% when the agenda switched from Republican (crime) to Democratic (employment or gender-related) issues. When respondents were exposed to ads about crime, support for the Democratic candidates was 63.2%, no different from the level among

118

those who saw no political ad at all. This finding suggests that the Republican candidates in these particular races were unlikely to win under any circumstances, but their prospects significantly worsened when respondents saw ads involving women's rights or unemployment.

A similar pattern emerged in the 1994 gubernatorial campaign. As displayed in Panel B of Figure 6.1, when both candidates addressed education and jobs, Democrat Kathleen Brown won handily (with 58.5% of the two-party vote). When the issue agenda was mixed and each candidate advertised on his or her strengths, the race was a standoff (Brown received 53% of the vote). Finally, when both campaigns advertised on crime or immigration, Wilson was the decisive victor (receiving 56% of the vote). Clearly, the candidates' choice of issues was crucial to the outcome of the race. Had economic issues predominated, Brown might have been elected; however, the Wilson campaign was able to tap into the public's fear of crime and illegal immigration and thereby succeeded in pushing economic issues to the background.

The results from the 1996 presidential race further reinforce the notion that a candidate benefits when the central issues of the ad campaign are "owned" by his or her party. As illustrated in the third panel of Figure 6.1, among participants exposed to ads about the future of Social Security, Medicare, college loans, and job training, Clinton enjoyed widespread support (62.6%). On the other hand, Clinton's vote share was weakest (at 56.1%) when respondents were exposed to advertisements about the traditional Republican issues of illegal immigration or drug-related crime. Surprisingly, participants exposed to ads about taxation were just as likely to vote for Clinton as those who watched ads dealing with social welfare. These results suggest either that "cutting taxes" is no longer an inherently Republican appeal or that there is a centrist trend in public opinion that resists large shifts in the economic status quo (as represented by the Dole tax-cut proposal). The relatively strong performance of the economy, coupled with the radical nature of the Dole tax plan, may have combined to grant Clinton special credibility on the tax issue in 1996.[8]

To test these differences further, we controlled for party identification, gender, education, and respondents' previous presidential vote. Tables 6.1 and 6.2 present these multivariate tests.[9]

The dependent variable in these analyses, as mentioned, is the

---

[8] Continuing the trend of recent years, President Clinton supported and signed into law the Taxpayer Relief Act of 1997 that dramatically reduced the tax rate on capital gains for individual taxpayers.

[9] We are required to present these tests separately because the 1994 study utilized a two-ad design making it impossible to isolate exposure to a particular message from one of the candidates.

Table 6.1. *The effects of the campaign issue agenda on vote choice*

	1992	1996
	California Senate Races	Presidential Race
Issue Agenda	.06**	.05**
Party Identification	.26***	.40***
Gender	.08**	−.04
Education	.08***	.01
Previous Presidential Vote	.16***	.41***
R²	.24	.57
N	953	1034

Note: The dependent variable is the Democratic candidate's percentage point lead in the major party vote. Entries are unstandardized OLS regression coefficients. Issue agenda is coded −1 for participants exposed to ads on Republican issues (crime in 1992 and immigration/drugs in 1996), 0 for participants exposed to no ads in 1992 and no ads or ads on taxes in 1996, and +1 for participants exposed to ads on Democratic issues (unemployment and women's issues in 1992 and social welfare programs in 1996). Party identification is coded Democrat = 1, Independent = 0, and Republican = −1. Gender is a dummy variable with Female = 1. Education is scored from 1 = "some high school" through 5 = "post-college." Previous presidential vote is coded Bush = −1, Other = 0, Clinton = 1, $* = p \le .10$, $** = p \le .05$, $*** = p \le .01$.

percentage point lead for the Democrat. A trichotomous variable was created to measure the issue agenda in each campaign. Messages focusing on Republican issues were coded −1, while those focusing on Democratic issues were coded +1.[10] Exposure to messages involving taxation, or exposure to no political advertisements at all, was coded equal to 0. Thus a positive coefficient on the issue agenda variable corresponds to the average increase in the lead for the Democratic candidate associated

[10] This specification was chosen to conserve degrees of freedom. Another specification of advertising type was also tested, where each issue was given a dummy variable in the regression analysis with null ads representing the baseline. The mean shifts associated with these dummies were nearly identical to these results.

Table 6.2. *The effects of owned versus mixed campaign issue agendas on vote choice in 1994*

		1994 Gubernatorial Race
Campaign Issue Agenda		.11*
Party Identification		.34***
Gender		.10
Vote on Prop. 187		.34***
Previous Presidential Vote		.26***
Constant		-.12
	R^2	.40
	N	356

Note: Table reprinted with permission from Iyengar, Valentino, Ansolabehere, and Simon, 1996, "Running as a Woman: Gender Stereotyping in Political Campaigns," in P. Norris, ed., *Women, Media, and Politics* (New York: Oxford University Press). The dependent variable is the Democratic candidate's lead in the major party vote. Entries are unstandardized OLS regression coefficients. Campaign issue agenda is a trichotomous variable where respondents exposed to consistently Republican messages (on crime or immigration) were coded −1, the null/mixed dialogue group received a score of 0, and respondents exposed to consistently Democratic messages (on education or unemployment) were scored as +1. Party identification is coded Democrat = 1, Republican = −1, Independent = 0. Gender is a dummy with Female = 1. Education is a dummy variable where college graduate is coded 1 and all others are coded 0. Previous presidential vote is also a dummy variable: A vote for Clinton is coded 1 and all others are coded 0. Proposition 187 was a ballot initiative designed to deny state-funded, nonemergency health and education services to illegal immigrants. Respondents who approved of the initiative were coded −1, those who disapproved were coded +1, and all others were coded 0. * = $p \leq .10$; ** = $p \leq .05$; *** = $p \leq .01$.

with moving from Republican to neutral issues, or from neutral to Democratic issues. In the first row of Table 6.1, we see that the Democratic lead increased by an average of 6% for each level of the trichotomous variable corresponding to the issue agenda of the advertising campaign, even after controlling for various alternative influences on vote choice. Thus, moving from Republican issues to Democratic issues led to a 12% increase in support for the Democrat.[11]

The effect of the issue agenda was quite similar in 1996 and was also statistically significant. The coefficient of .05 indicates that moving from Republican issues (immigration or drugs) to Democratic issues (spending on social programs) boosted the Democrat's support by 10%.[12]

Table 6.2 presents the results from the 1994 California gubernatorial race. Even with the introduction of several control variables, Kathleen Brown's lead surged significantly when campaign advertising focused on Democratic issues. Each level of the campaign agenda variable was associated with an increase of 11 percentage points in support for Brown. Thus, when both candidates focused on education or unemployment, rather than on crime or illegal immigration, the Democrat improved her electoral support by an impressive 22%. Overall, these results confirm the pattern revealed in Figure 6.1; shifting the issue agenda of the campaign significantly affects the fortunes of the candidates.

To this point, we have been concerned with the issue agenda of campaign advertising, without regard to the specific source of the advertisements. But in order to test precisely hypotheses about source credibility as a mediator of campaign advertising, we must look separately at voter reactions to issue appeals by candidates from each party. Our second test, therefore, considers the credibility of campaign advertising as a function of both message content and source. We examined differences in voter choice when particular candidates aired advertisements dealing with particular issues. Does a Democratic advertisement on unemployment sway more voters than a Democratic advertisement on crime? Conversely, are Republicans more effective with advertisements on crime than on unemployment?

This test requires a one-ad design in order to isolate the effects of individual candidates and individual issue appeals. Therefore, we can present evidence only from the 1992 and 1996 campaigns. Figure 6.2 displays the mean level of support for Democratic candidates for each level of the issue agenda established by each of the sponsoring candidates.

In 1992, both Democratic senatorial candidates improved their prospects by 9 percentage points when they advertised on job creation and women's rights, and actually worsened their chances (by two points) when they advertised on crime. The Republicans were generally ineffective no matter what issue they used, as indicated by the almost identical

[11] When we specify advertising type as a dichotomous variable with Republican issues = 0 and Democratic issues = 1, the mean difference in Democratic support is 11%.

[12] Again, when specified as a dummy variable with Republican messages = 0 and Democratic messages = 1, the effect on Democratic support is +10%.

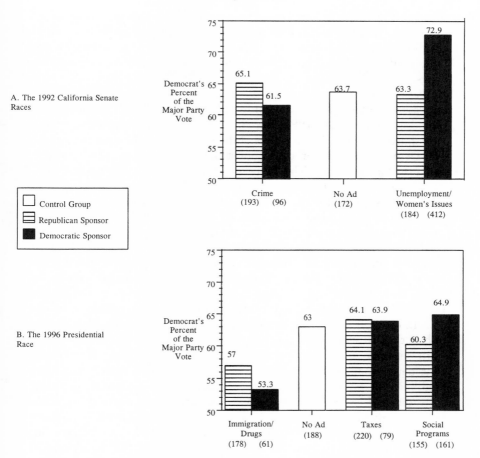

A. The 1992 California Senate Races

Control Group
Republican Sponsor
Democratic Sponsor

B. The 1996 Presidential Race

Figure 6.2. Advertising effects broken down by issue agenda and sponsor.

levels of support for the Democrat across the advertising categories in Panel A of Figure 6.2.

Turning to the 1996 campaign, Clinton maximized his vote share (64.9%) when he advertised on social welfare programs and minimized his vote share (53.3%) when he addressed the Republican issues of illegal immigration and drugs. Conversely, Dole's most successful messages involved immigration and drugs. The issue of taxes appeared to favor Clinton in that he maintained his commanding lead over Dole when advertising on this issue, while Dole's tax-related ads worsened his position considerably. Overall, the evidence in Panel B of Figure 6.2 indicates that Clinton was invulnerable so long as he did not stray into Republican territory. For Dole, attacks on Clinton as a tax-and-spend liberal and appeals on the basis of his tax plan only played into Clinton's hands. Dole could only be competitive when his advertisements centered on drugs or immigration.

We again tested the statistical significance of these differences in a regression analysis that included multiple controls. These results are presented in Table 6.3. In 1992, Republicans were unable to improve their vote share significantly, regardless of their choice of advertising messages. The Democrats, however, could boost their lead substantially by advertising on "their" issues. The 11-point shift associated with each level of the trichotomous campaign agenda variable translates into a 22% increase in support for the Democrats when they chose to advertise on employment or women's issues instead of crime.

In 1996, the Democrat's choice of ads again significantly influenced his lead. Shifting from immigration and drugs to spending on social programs produced a 12 percentage point ($.06 \times 2$) increase in Clinton's support. Conversely, Dole's optimal result was when he advertised on crime and immigration, though the effect was not significant. When Dole's ads concerned social welfare issues, his level of support fell by 6%. In effect, any Dole ad not dealing with drug abuse or immigration only served to worsen his position vis-à-vis Clinton.

In summary, we have demonstrated that issue content is a significant determinant of the persuasiveness of campaign advertising. The credibility of political advertising is enhanced when candidates resort to traditional issue appeals – appeals on which their party has a long-standing advantage in the minds of voters. We can test this hypothesis even more precisely in 1996 because in that study, we included items that directly tap viewers' beliefs about the credibility of televised political advertising. In particular, we asked respondents to indicate how well the terms "informative" and "misleading" applied to "commercials for political candidates or organizations." Responses to these items were used to construct an index of credibility, which runs from −1 (uninformative and misleading) to +1 (informative and not misleading).[13] Because we insisted that respondents evaluate the believability of political advertising in general and not the specific ads they had just seen, this is an

---

[13] The exact wording of the questions was as follows: "Now we're interested in how you react to commercials for political candidates or organizations. Please indicate in general how well political advertising can be described by the terms listed below. Remember to consider political ads in general, not ads from any particular candidate or organization." The response options provided ranged from "very well" to "not well at all."

Table 6.3. *The effects of the campaign issue agenda on vote choice by sponsoring candidate*

	1992		1996	
	Republican	Democrat	Republican	Democrat
Issue Agenda	-.02	.11***	.03	.06*
Party Identification	.23***	.29***	.39***	.36***
Gender	.10*	.09	-.04	-.06
Education	.10***	.07***	-.01	.00
Previous Presidential Vote	.15	.15***	.41***	.45***
Constant	-.18*	-.05	.14*	.12
R²	.19	.29	.57	.58
N	447	677	733	485

Note: The dependent variable is the Democratic candidate's percentage point lead in the major party vote. Entries are unstandardized OLS regression coefficients. Issue agenda is coded −1 for exposure to ads on Republican issues (crime in 1992 and immigration/drugs in 1996), 0 for exposure to ads dealing with issues on which neither party could claim outright ownership (taxes in 1996), and +1 for exposure to ads on Democratic issues (unemployment and women's rights in 1992, social welfare programs in 1996). Party identification is coded Democrat = 1, Republican = −1, Independent = 0. Gender is a dummy with Female = 1. Education is coded from 1 = "some high school" through 5 = "post-college." Previous presidential vote is coded Bush = −1, Clinton = 1, Other = 0. $* = p \le .10$, $** = p \le .05$, $*** = p \le .01$.

especially strict test of the credibility hypothesis. Figure 6.3 presents these results.

Panels A and B of Figure 6.3 present the mean credibility scores for each sponsoring candidate and the issue content of their messages. There are three levels of issue content corresponding to "owned issues" (issues on which the sponsoring candidate's party is favored), "opponent's issues" (issues on which the opposing candidate's party has the edge), and "ambiguous issues" (on which neither party may have a clear advantage). For Dole, ads dealing with crime and immigration fall into the owned-issue category, ads on taxes are classified as ambiguous with respect to ownership, and advertising on the budget is considered tres-

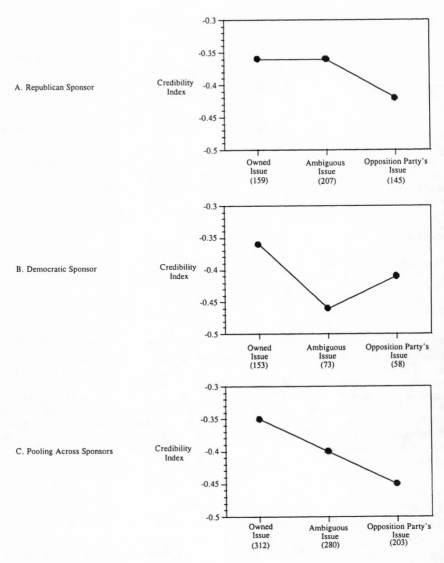

A. Republican Sponsor

B. Democratic Sponsor

C. Pooling Across Sponsors

Figure 6.3. Source and content differences in credibility of campaign advertising in 1996. *Note:* Entries are mean credibility ratings for each type of ad aired by each sponsor, drawn from a regression model controlling for respondents' partisanship, education, ethnicity, gender, and interest in politics. Owned issues include social programs for Clinton, and crime and immigration for Dole. "Taxes" were considered an ambiguous issue with regard to ownership. Clinton on crime or immigration, or Dole on social programs were considered opposition-owned issues. Cell sizes are in parentheses. Credibility is measured with an additive scale consisting of two items in which respondents are asked how well they feel "informative" and "misleading" describe political ads in general. The scale runs from −1 ("not informative at all" or "very misleading") to +1 ("very" informative or "not misleading at all").

passing into Democratic territory. Of course, the reverse logic would apply to advertising by Clinton.

Before addressing the effects of issue content and partisanship of the sponsoring candidate on the credibility index, it is noteworthy that campaign advertising was rated much more negatively than product advertising. The sample mean for campaign advertising was −.39, indicating that a large plurality of participants rated political ads as lacking in credibility. For product advertising, the sample mean was −.03, indicating that roughly equal numbers of participants rated product ads as informative and truthful as uninformative and misleading. From the perspective of the audience, campaign advertising is clearly tainted.

The results in Figure 6.3 accord well with our previous findings. In Panels A and B, credibility was highest when Dole advertised on traditional Republican issues and when Clinton's appeal was consistent with his party affiliation. Although none of the observed differences were statistically significant, they at least suggest that political advertising is more likely to be considered credible when the message and messenger match.

Since the theoretical notion of credibility can be generalized across individual candidates (and because the pattern of differences we noted was so similar for both Dole and Clinton), we pooled across candidates and subjected the credibility index to a multivariate analysis that controlled for individual differences in attitudes toward campaign advertising. Panel C of Figure 6.3 presents the adjusted credibility means within each level of issue content.[14] As anticipated, the effects of issue content were significant – moving from the "owned issue" to the "opposition party's issue" category yielded a .10 downward shift ($p < .05$) in the average level of credibility. This finding strongly supports our original hypothesis: Respondents rate advertisements as significantly less credible when the sponsor's party and the issue focus of the ad are incongruent.

In summary, our evidence reveals that campaign advertising is most effective when the sponsoring candidates pitch their message to the traditional strengths of their parties. Voters tend to place their credence in advertisements that correspond to the sponsor's partisan reputation. This pattern holds for senatorial, gubernatorial, and presidential campaigns. *Ceteris paribus*, the candidate whose issue agenda fits better with voters'

---

[14] The adjusted means were computed by regressing the credibility index against the issue content trichotomy, in addition to participants' ethnicity (whites granted political ads higher credibility), gender (women were more favorable), education (credibility ratings were higher among the less educated), and political interest (the higher the level of interest, the higher the credibility rating).

stereotypes about the capabilities of the political parties will carry the day.

CONCLUSION

Our evidence suggests that candidates have a strong incentive to focus on issues that resonate with their party affiliation. A candidate's party affiliation conveys information about his or her ability to deal with particular issues. Our results suggest quite strongly that candidates should seek to exploit such reputational advantages. A Democrat who calls for educational reform or for more stringent enforcement of gender discrimination laws will be taken more seriously than a Democrat who favors the death penalty or more aggressive monitoring of terrorist groups.

An important implication of these findings is that in competitive races, where both candidates tend to be well financed, the total amount of advertising purchased by a candidate may be secondary to the selection of the appropriate message. In both the senatorial and presidential studies, the sponsoring candidate who chose to advertise on the "wrong" issue was better off showing no advertisement at all. This pattern suggests that it is the issue agenda of the campaign, rather than the volume of each candidate's campaign communication, that influences voters.

Another important implication is that campaigns are unlikely to provide meaningful dialogue about the important issues of the day. Our results suggest that candidates have a strong incentive to focus on issues that resonate with their party affiliation, no matter what the opposition chooses to discuss. Though candidate dialogue (both candidates addressing the same issues) is undoubtedly the best way for voters to make enlightened choices, candidates cannot be expected to sacrifice their own electoral chances by engaging the opposition on issues that place them at a disadvantage. In the long run, this strategy contributes to the confusion and tumult of campaign communication, and to the dissatisfaction voters feel with the candidates (for a general model of campaigns that predicts the absence of dialogue, see Simon 1997).

The results provided by our experiments are probably conservative estimates of the importance of source credibility in campaign advertising inasmuch as all the elections under consideration were relatively "high stimulus" races characterized by well-known and well-financed candidates whose campaigns generated considerable news coverage and publicity, in addition to paid advertising. When voters encounter advertising from less-visible candidates, the importance of the candidates' party affiliation is likely to be amplified. In general, we might expect that source-related cues increase in importance as voters' store of information about particular candidates declines.

The use of the sponsoring candidate's attributes as a basis for inferring his or her positions on political issues extends well beyond the candidate's party affiliation. Gender and race are especially visible attributes, and the popular culture provides several associations between these traits and political ideology (see McDermott 1997). Thus, in the case of gender, messages involving stereotypically "masculine" issues, such as crime or national defense, should be especially persuasive when the sponsor is a male war hero. On the other hand, child care and nutrition will fit well with voters' beliefs about the credentials of a candidate who happens to be a mother. Ansolabehere and Iyengar (1994) and Iyengar et al. (1996) have assessed the relative credibility of male and female candidates on the issue of sexual harassment. Their results showed that advertising on this issue yielded significant gains for both women running for the U.S. Senate in 1992, but virtually no return for presidential candidate Clinton.

In conclusion, our evidence suggests once again that in low-involvement persuasion situations, it is the interplay between "old" and "new" information that governs the effects of mass communication. Political campaigns are classic low-involvement situations: Most viewers are less than fully captivated by political campaigns and pay only casual attention to campaign advertisements. Given the fleeting nature of most voters' exposure to campaign advertising, it is the advertiser's ability to evoke what voters already "know" about the candidates that makes the difference between effective and ineffective advertising campaigns.

Appendix. *Socioeconomic and political attributes of experimental participants*

Participant Profile	1992	1994	1996
Median Age	33	32	37
Percent With College Degree	53	54	50
Party Identification			
Republican	24	31	33
Independent	31	32	26
Democrat	45	38	39
Race			
Asian	7	15	4
Black	20	22	8
Hispanic	8	12	8
White	62	51	75
N	954	661	1042

7

Affect as Information: The Role of Public Mood in Political Reasoning
WENDY M. RAHN

Levels of political information are notoriously low in the American mass public. How is it that people arrive at political judgments in the absence of detailed information? In recent years, students of American public opinion have latched onto the notion of "heuristics," or simplifying rules of thumb, to explain how it is that people get by (Sniderman, Brody, and Tetlock 1991). These forms of "low-information rationality" (Popkin 1991) are thought to cut information-processing costs and lead some people to make the same sorts of judgments that they would have made had they been better informed. Lupia's (1994) study of voting on California ballot issues, for example, shows how less-well-informed voters can emulate the behavior of well-informed voters by relying on the cues provided by interest groups and political leadership.

In this chapter, I will argue that affective (i.e., emotional) experiences affect political reasoning and facilitate low-information rationality. In everyday discourse, "being emotional" is seen as dysfunctional, often resulting in decisions or actions that are later regretted. However, I wish to make the case that certain kinds of affective experiences can be useful, rather than dangerous, because they help inform the individual about the state of his or her world. This affective information can substitute for more cognitively expensive forms of information and can aid people in their attempts to form political opinions.[1]

I wish to thank Lynn Smith-Lovin for her work on the 1996 General Social Survey emotions module, Daniel Stevens for his research assistance, and the editors for their comments.

[1] While not the focus of this chapter, it is worth noting that affective experiences may have implications for a wide range of cognitive and behavioral processes (Martin, Ward, Achee, and Wyer 1993). For example, when a feeling "signals" that the individual should pay heed, affect can motivate increased attention to important stimuli. In such cases, people may forgo simplified strategies of information processing, with the result that decisions are actually "better" than if they had not been affectively infused (see, e.g., Marcus and MacKuen 1993; Schwarz, Bless, and Bohner

Affect as Information

It is not a new idea to political science that affective reactions may indeed be functional (see Marcus and MacKuen 1993; Sniderman, Brody, and Tetlock 1991). This chapter builds on earlier work by conceptualizing and measuring a specific form of affective experience, one that I call public mood. Public mood is the affective state that captures how individuals feel about the society in which they live. With two surveys and one experiment, I reveal a link between public mood and the ways in which people seek and process political information. That is, I show that variations in how people feel about their society correspond to systematic variations in how they form judgments about other matters, such as NAFTA. My efforts support the contention that affective states, such as public mood, affect how people think about politics and facilitate low-information rationality. My efforts also reinforce the growing realization (e.g., Damasio 1994; Lodge and Taber 2000) that basic cognitive processes, such as those that underlie political reasoning, cannot and do not operate independently of affective experiences.

WHAT IS PUBLIC MOOD?

Definition

As we have conceptualized it in various studies, public mood is a "diffuse affective state, having distinct positive and negative components, that citizens experience because of their membership in a particular political community" (Rahn, Kroeger, and Kite 1996: 31). The nation-state is the political community that has been the focus of our research to date.[2] Membership in a nation-state provides individuals with a national iden-

---

1991). Affect can also create long-run efficiencies in information processing. Positive affect, for example, may lead people to rely on well-developed prior knowledge structures (Bodenhausen, Kramer, and Süsser 1994). Because these knowledge structures (e.g., schemas, prototypes, and stereotypes) make information processing more parsimonious, cognitive capacity is freed up, allowing the information processing system to engage in other important tasks (Bless, Clore, Schwarz, Golian, Rabe, and Wölk 1996). Emotions, therefore, help to regulate attention (Derryberry and Tucker 1994). At high levels of arousal, positive and negative affect states, of course, may become dysfunctional, such as in manic-depressive illness or panic attacks. But at ordinary levels, affective states are now widely perceived in many areas of psychology to be functional for human rationality.

[2] In principle, there is nothing in the definition of public mood that restricts its reference point to the nation-state. For example, one can imagine experiencing public mood in a city or a state whose team wins a World Series or Super Bowl. In practice, however, our investigations of the properties of public mood have focused on the nation-state. Our focus is predicated on the idea that despite the ostensible weakening of the nation-state as a form of political organization, nation-states continue to be "the largest collectivities with which individuals have forged strong identifications" (Wrong 1994: 230).

tity, a type of social identity that functions as a "means of locating and defining individual selves in the world" (Smith 1991: 17). National identity is usually reinforced through explicit instruction and continually re-created through subtle means, such as product advertising, weather maps, and sports reporting (Billing 1995).[3]

Self-categorization as a member of the American political community has important affective consequences. Because American national identity "extends the self" beyond the level of the individual, events that are group relevant, but not necessarily self-relevant, can instigate emotional responses.[4] Thus, public mood is a type of "social emotion," a concept developed by the psychologist Eliot Smith (1993) to distinguish feelings that arise because of group attachment, rather than more individually based experiences. To cite recent examples, the threat of military action in the Persian Gulf might make national identity salient, evoking feelings of anxiety and distress. And many Americans cheered when the U.S. gymnast, Kerri Strug, landed a gold-medal–winning vault during the 1996 Summer Olympic Games. When national identity is made especially salient, as in these kinds of situations, public mood can become an integral part of a person's private mood (Rahn and Hirshorn 1997).

As a type of affective experience, public mood belongs to that category of affective reactions that involve awareness of the target of one's feelings (in this case, the national political community), but potential unawareness of the source for these sentiments. These forms of "dedicated affect" include many types of experience. The anxiety that a claustrophobic feels in an elevator, for example, has a well-defined target, and the individual may even recognize that the fear is unreasonable. But the origins of these feelings may not reside in any explicit event in a person's life. Less extreme than phobias are widely shared feelings about certain classes of objects, such as the delight evoked by the sight of a baby or the recoil in response to certain animals. Plutchik (1994), for example, reports a study conducted by the ethologist Desmond Morris (1967) in which he asked children watching a zoo program to tell him which

---

[3] The kinds of events, people, and activities that are relevant to public mood processes depend on "collective representations," to use Durkheim's phrase, about the nature of national identity. These representations help citizens in a given national political community "imagine" the nation and its inhabitants (Anderson 1983). This imagining process is carried out by political leaders and citizens, and is formalized and perpetuated in such institutions as the mass media, the arts, citizenship and commemorative ceremonies, explicit instruction in school, and election campaigns (Anderson 1983; Bennett 1992; Billing 1995; Merelman 1986; Rahn, Brehm, and Carlson 1997; Spillman 1997).

[4] Smith and Henry (1996) provide experimental evidence that evoking a social identity results in a cognitive merger of the in-group with the self.

animals they liked or disliked the most. Leading the list of disliked animals were snakes, followed by spiders. Crocodiles and lions tied for third place. According to Plutchik, "The animals the children disliked most shared one important feature: they are dangerous to humans" (1994: 344). When the children were asked why they disliked these creatures, however, their responses mostly centered on physical attributes, such as "slimy" or "hairy." Fear reactions to certain animals make perfect sense from an evolutionary point of view, and provide people with a basis for "reasoning backwards" from their emotional response to the belief that such creatures should be avoided.[5] But the "real" sources for these feelings may lie in our evolutionary past, and therefore cannot be accessed consciously.[6]

Public mood shares with other forms of dedicated affect an "address."[7] That is, the feelings are about something that can be explicitly named. But the sources for these feelings may lie outside conscious awareness; they have been forgotten perhaps, or the sources are so diffuse and multiple that adumbrating all of them would prove impossible.

In addition, public mood is an attribute of *individuals,* not "the public." In principle and in reality, public mood varies across individuals and over time for the same individual. A morning news item about U.S. children's test scores, for example, may make some individuals discouraged. But later, a record stock market close may lift some of these spirits, even if one does not have any investments. Public events are the source of public mood, and my interest here is in determining how

---

[5] Batson, Turk, Shaw, and Klein (1995) use the phrase "reasoning backwards" to refer to the process by which one uses one's feelings about a target to infer back to the values or beliefs that must have been responsible for them.

[6] Attitudes are also a form of dedicated affect (Jerry Clore, personal communication). With attitudes, one lacks awareness of the source for one's feelings, either because the critical event that led to the attitude formation was not salient at the time or because so many events or bits of information with affective implications have gone into the attitude that they are forgotten, as in on-line processing (Lodge, McGraw, and Stroh 1989). The "likability heuristic" that helps people decide what opposing groups want in politics is described by Sniderman, Brody, and Tetlock in precisely these terms: "Suffice it to observe that affect [toward groups] itself may be the residue of long biographies of cognitive transactions" (Sniderman, Brody, and Tetlock 1991: 115). And affect toward groups may also provide a basis for "reasoning backwards" to beliefs about them (Sniderman, Brody, and Tetlock 1991).

[7] Public mood and other forms of dedicated affect are distinguished from affective states that lack an "address." Undedicated affect is characterized by unawareness of source (which it shares with dedicated affect) and by the lack of a specific target object that is the focus of one's feelings. Free-floating anxiety, for example, is characterized by the fact that a source for these feelings cannot be located, nor can a specific target for anxiousness be specified.

individual-level shifts in public mood affect individual capacities for political information processing.[8]

Effect

How might we expect public mood to affect the way that people seek and process information about politics? Ongoing research in psychology and cognitive science provides some clues. Consider, for example, the idea that some dedicated affective states provide a means for individuals to make choices without spending a great deal of effort thinking about them. This type of effect has been brought to light most explicitly in studies conducted by the Damasios and their colleagues (Bechara, H. Damasio, Tranel, and A. Damasio 1997; see more generally, A. Damasio 1994). For example, in one study they had normal participants and "emotion-impaired" patients play a card game in which decks of cards were associated with rewards and penalties.[9] People in the study did not know when a penalty card would be turned over, nor did they know how long the game would last. Certain decks had cards yielding high rewards but also large penalties; other decks carried less reward and less risk. Participants were asked to make choices among the decks about which cards to turn over. The decks were structured in such a way that the expected utility of drawing from the low-reward–low-penalty decks was much higher than the expected utility of drawing from the other decks.

Participants without brain damage quickly began eliciting anticipatory autonomic responses before turning over a card from the high-risk decks, and they ultimately learned to avoid choosing from them. The patients, however, never developed this anticipatory response, although some did come to learn that choosing from certain decks carried higher penalties. Normal participants who developed the anticipatory responses often did so after turning over only 10 cards; yet they were unable to articulate the strategy responsible for these feelings until some 70 turns later. And even though three of the normal participants never reached the "conscious" reasoning stage, they were still able to make advantageous choices. Even more astonishing, the three brain-damaged partici-

---

[8] Of course, certain events, such as the Olympic example I mentioned, or the *Challenger* disaster, may move nearly everyone up or down at the same time because exposure to information about the event is virtually universal and the feelings evoked by the incident are consistently in the same direction across individuals. As a result, we could witness substantial aggregate volatility in the average level of public mood. In this chapter, however, I limit myself to examining individual-level effects of public mood.

[9] The impairment of these subjects was due to brain damage to the prefrontal cortex, an area of the brain implicated in emotional responding.

pants who were able to generate the insight that some decks were better than others were still not able to choose well. Apparently, the "hunches" normal participants developed in advance of acquiring explicit knowledge of the rule allowed them to proceed as if they had knowledge of the rule. This anticipatory feeling, which the researchers label a "covert bias," assists "the efficient processing of knowledge and logic necessary for conscious decisions" (Bechara et al. 1997: 1294). Based on these results, it appears that affect is often prior to more explicit cognitive strategies. Moreover, knowledge of the correct cognitive strategy, if unaccompanied by a "covert bias," does not by itself lead to utility-maximizing choices.

DOES PUBLIC MOOD AFFECT INFORMATION PROCESSING?

In this chapter, I base my claim that public mood affects the processing of political information and facilitates low-information rationality on my analysis of three distinct studies. My first two analyses are conducted on data from the 1996 General Social Survey (GSS), a national survey conducted by the National Opinion Research Center (see Kite and Rahn 1997, for evidence from local samples). I was able to administer six public-mood questions to a randomly selected subsample of approximately 700 GSS respondents. The mood markers I used in this particular study were worried, angry, upset, frustrated, enthusiastic, and hopeful. Respondents were given five options for indicating how frequently they felt these emotions when thinking about the United States: "always," "most of the time," "some of the time," "rarely," or "never."[10]

Analysis 1: Public Mood and NAFTA Preferences

I first examine the correspondence between public mood and opinions about the desirability of NAFTA. In response to a question asking whether the United States benefits or does not benefit from NAFTA membership, fully 9% of the GSS sample admitted to never having heard of

[10] The public mood measures ask respondents for "generalized" mood ratings over a retrospective, but indefinite, time frame. Research by Parkinson and colleagues (Parkinson, Briner, Reynolds, and Totterdell 1995) on the accuracy of retrospective ratings of personal mood finds that retrospective reports of generalized mood are somewhat affected by current mood state, but in general, memory for affective experiences is, in fact, strongly determined by averaging across actual momentary mood states; that is to say, memory for mood is largely accurate. There is no reason to suspect that retrospective ratings of public mood are any less accurate than ratings of personal mood.

NAFTA, and another 47% said they "didn't know" whether the United States benefits. NAFTA, in other words, despite being the focus of many public debates, had low salience to the mass public. But almost half of the sample did offer an opinion one way or the other, and so the question is, on what basis did they decide that NAFTA was a good or bad thing?

To determine the basis of opinions on NAFTA, and to provide a compelling set of control variables against which I can evaluate the role of public mood, I begin my analysis by considering the many factors that previous scholars have used to explain opinion formation (see generally, Boniger, Krosnick, and Berent 1995; Kinder 1983; Zaller 1992): personality and predispositions, such as authoritarianism (Feldman and Stenner 1997; Geddes and Zaller 1989); general "postures" (Hurwitz and Peffley 1987); ideology (Converse 1964); partisanship (Campbell et al. 1960; Jacoby 1988); group cues (Converse 1964; Lupia 1994); social identities (Conover 1984); values (Feldman 1988); self-interest (Green and Gerken 1989); and information and knowledge (Bartels 1996; Delli Carpini and Keeter 1996; Dimock and Popkin 1995).

Many analogs of these factors for the NAFTA case study are available in the 1996 GSS in some form. For example, general posture toward free trade is assessed with a Likert question about whether limits on imports should be imposed in order to protect the U.S. economy. Partisanship and ideology are measured in the usual ways. The impact of reference groups is measured with a dummy variable for union membership. Domain-specific information is measured by responses to questions that asked respondents how much they had heard about NAFTA. And general knowledge is (rather poorly) measured by years of educational attainment. Self-interest is not easily defined on the NAFTA issue, but I include a measure of retrospective personal-financial assessments in order to pick up the role of personal-economic considerations.[11]

With these controls in hand, I now wish to pose the question, how does public mood affect opinion formation? To answer this question, I regressed NAFTA opinion (coded 1 for benefits, 0 if the United States doesn't benefit)[12] on the factors named above, the usual complement of demographic controls, and a measure of public mood valence, computed by subtracting the average frequency of negative feelings from the average frequency of positive feelings. All variables, except age and edu-

[11] My equation initially included a measure of authoritarianism. Its coefficient was virtually 0 and far from significant. In order to preserve cases, this variable was not included in the final equation.

[12] People who responded "don't know" to the NAFTA opinion question are excluded from the analysis.

Table 7.1

NAFTA Opinion Direction (1=U.S. Benefits, 0=Does Not Benefit)	
	Unstandardized Coefficient (Standard Error)
Public Mood Valence	.68*** (.16)
Union Membership (1=Member)	-.16# (.09)
Age	-.004* (.002)
Education	.010 (.011)
Race (1=Black, 0=Else)	.12 (.11)
Personal Financial Retrospections (1=Better than year ago)	-.05 (.07)
Sex (1=Female, 0=Male)	-.02 (.06)
How much heard or read (1=Lots)	-.21# (.11)
Party Identification (1=Strong Republican)	-.27*** (.10)
Ideology (1=Extremely Conservative)	-.06 (.14)
General Trade Orientation (1=Strongly disagree imports be limited)	.45*** (.11)
Constant	.47* (.24)
Adj. R^2	.15
N	288

***$p \leq .001$ ** $p \leq .01$ * $p \leq .05$ # $p \leq .10$, two-tailed

cation, which are coded in years, are scored to lie between 0 and 1, facilitating direct comparisons of the unstandardized coefficients.

The results, displayed in Table 7.1, are striking. The impact of public mood, quite simply, is enormous when compared to these other consid-

137

erations. Of course, other considerations are also operative, namely party identification and union membership. Members of unions, not surprisingly, were less positive in their evaluations of NAFTA's effects. And Republicans, despite their endorsement of free trade in the abstract, were less likely than Democrats to believe that a Clinton-supported policy is beneficial to the United States. Specific information about NAFTA is also important. Those people who have heard a lot about the issue tend to be more dubious about NAFTA's benefits, all else equal.

In Table 7.2, I show that the effect of public mood on opinion varies with the amount of information one holds about the issue. There, I divided the sample into three groups: those who had heard "a lot" about NAFTA; those who had heard "quite a bit"; and those who heard "not much" or "nothing at all." When I ran the equation separately within these three groups, some interesting patterns emerged, albeit the small number of cases makes comparison hazardous. The magnitude of the public mood coefficient is much smaller for those people who had heard a lot about NAFTA: They were much more able to link their general free-trade postures and their party identifications to their opinions; the coefficients are of considerable magnitude (.835 and −.60, respectively) compared to the low information group (.06 and −.39 respectively). The middle group was able to make use of a general posture toward free trade in evaluating the benefits of NAFTA, without, however, abandoning public mood. As Zaller (1992) argues, some considerations, apparently, depend on having some information in the first place so that appropriate linkages can be made to underlying predispositions (such as general postures on free trade or partisanship) or group interests (such as belonging to a union). Indeed, in the high-information group, there appears to be the partisan polarization that characterizes intense, two-sided information environments (see Zaller 1992).[13] Public mood, on the other hand, seems to have a greater impact on policy preferences at the lower end of the information range. For those less knowledgeable, this general-purpose consideration may be the only one operative. For those more informed, affective information is just one source of many, and it only starts to lose its utility at the very highest range of information, when partisan and other predispositions come to dominate.

Analysis 2: Generalized Trust in Others

In the domain of opinion formation, public mood exists alongside other potential determinants, notably partisanship and other ideologically

---

[13] Average NAFTA opinion among highly informed, strong Republicans was .41; for strong Democrats in this group, .71. In contrast, among the less informed, the averages were .48 and .60, respectively.

Table 7.2

NAFTA Opinion Direction by Information Levels			
	Low Specific Information	Medium Specific Information	High Specific Information
Public Mood Valence	.67** (.28)	.80** (.25)	.39 (.40)
Union Membership	-.006 (.17)	-.21# (.12)	-.28 (.28)
Age	-.005 (.004)	-.004# (.002)	-.007 (.005)
Education	.02 (.02)	.001 (.02)	.001 (.02)
Race	-.05 (.19)	.18 (.22)	.008 (.23)
Sex	-.11 (.11)	.03 (.08)	-.006 (.13)
Personal Financial Retrospections	-.007 (.13)	-.09 (.11)	.07 (.20)
Party Identification	-.39* (.18)	-.19 (.14)	-.60* (.25)
Ideology	-.06 (.28)	.003 (.21)	-.30 (.25)
General Free Trade Orientation	.06 (.23)	.50 (.17)	.84*** (.23)
Constant	.57	.16	.98
Adj. R^2	.06	.13	.27
N	90	141	57

***p ≤ .001   ** p ≤ .01   * p ≤ .05   # p ≤ .10, two-tailed

tinted predispositions. Depending on the information environment and the framing of the policy choice, public mood may or may not be useful to individuals in reaching some sort of political judgment on these policy issues. But how do people form judgments in areas that are less subject to the to and fro of partisan and interest-group conflict? Here, possessing general or specific knowledge would seem to provide one with no obvious *political* linkages since these connections have not been made by political elites. This may be one reason that Zaller's (1992) opinion-formation model appears to perform best in attitude areas that are driven by partisan cleavages, such as electoral choice and policy disagreements. But for other types of attitudes, such as trust in government, the model does not appear to apply as well: "The reception-acceptance model is designed to capture the diffusion of particular ideas and messages, not the spread of amorphous moods and humors" (Zaller 1992: 300). Because it is specifically conceptualized to measure at the individual level these "amorphous moods and humors," public mood may have some utility as an explanation for attitudes precisely in those areas in which ideological, partisan, and other political predispositions don't apply.

I examine this proposition in the context of generalized trust in others, the origins of which have become the object of intense scholarly interest because of the connection between general, or social, trust and "social capital" (Putnam 1993). In societies marked by high levels of trust, desirable collective outcomes – such as well-functioning governments, economic growth, and low crime rates – are more likely because trust lowers transaction costs, facilitates cooperation for mutual benefit, and inhibits shirking (Fukuyama 1995; Putnam 1993). How social trust gets produced, then, is an important question to people in many different fields of inquiry.

Arriving at an assessment about whether "most people" are trustworthy would seem a most difficult task, for any one person is likely to have direct experience with only a very small fraction of the category, "most people." And unlike the evaluation of NAFTA opinions, partisan predispositions would seem to be of little use, as no politician or interest-group representative is against trust. So how does one decide to tell a survey interviewer that "most people can be trusted" or "you can't be too careful in dealing with people"? Does public mood play a role?

One could decide, for example, that most of the time, others can be trusted because it is in their self-interest to behave in a trustworthy way. Your judgment of the trustworthiness of most people "encapsulates" your knowledge of the incentives facing them. An important source of these incentives includes abstract systems of social, political, and economic organization that govern transactions among people (Seligman 1997). Confidence in these systems, particularly confidence in the state (Gambetta 1988; Levi 1996) may allow you to trust others, even those whom you do not know. By this account, trust is instrumental and is based on being aware of the incentives others face.

Another account places the origin of trust in social learning. Information gleaned from previous encounters with other people may provide for the individual a basis for generalizing to new interactions. Learned trust allows one to make judgments about others without the knowledge of their incentives (Hardin 1993). In this "intuitive Bayesian" (Hardin 1993) account, a person with a high capacity to trust is a person who has been blessed with many fruitful experiences with others. The "leap of faith" that trust requires comes from optimism that others provide benefit rather than harm (Uslaner 1996). The civic engagement Putnam (1993) found in northern Italy may help create this optimism by providing people with settings in which they have positive dealings with others. And people without the capacity to trust are those who have had interactions with others that have taught them that trust is not justified.

A shortcut to this kind of learned-trust calculation may involve the use of the "cognitive miser's heuristic" (Orbell and Dawes 1991), or the projection of one's own level of trustworthiness onto others. The logic is as follows: Since I plan to behave in a trustworthy (or untrustworthy) way and others are similar to me, then they will do what I plan to do. Perceived similarity can be imputed on the basis of shared characteristics. The basis for similarity may be "imagined" rather than based on direct familiarity, such as in the case of shared group identity (Kramer, Brewer, and Hanna 1995; Seligman 1997).

There are thus numerous reasons that might lead our beleaguered survey respondent to offer a generalization about the likely trustworthiness of that amorphous category of folks, "most people." And many of these have been tested already in a model of social trust developed by Brehm and Rahn (1997). And all of them have some support, with personal optimism, confidence in government, and civic engagement doing most of the heavy lifting, though direct personal experience plays a small supporting role.

What I would like to consider here is that the decision to trust most people may be even simpler than these theories imply, a gut reaction rather than a considered evaluation of all these possibilities. In deciding whether most people are deserving of trust, individuals could avail themselves of the "affect-as-information" heuristic, implicitly asking themselves the question, "how do I feel about the society in which I live?" If the response is enthusiasm, an individual may "reason backwards" to the belief that it is because most people are pretty decent. If one feels worried, angry, upset, or afraid, on the other hand, the inference may be that these feelings arise because people cannot be counted on.

Testing this requires pitting public mood against some of the other bases for trust judgments. A thoroughgoing test is made difficult by the construction of the GSS sample. Some of the crucial items were administered to only half or two-thirds of the full sample, and because the public-mood questions were asked of only one-quarter of the GSS sample, we are left with the situation that the number of usable cases is small. In addition, the GSS did not ask about group involvement in the 1996 survey. However, they did ask all respondents whether they voted in the 1992 presidential election, and so I can use reported turnout as one indicator of civic involvement.[14]

I use a measure of fear of crime in one's neighborhood and a measure of the alteration in one's financial status in the last year to reflect recent personal experiences that might contribute to judgments of others' trust-worthiness. I also include a measure of authoritarian predispositions, measured by the importance adults place on obedience in child rearing (Feldman and Stenner 1997). Civic engagement is captured with the turnout variable, as already mentioned. Race, to some degree, reflects one's environment, and educational attainment, the investment that has been made on one's behalf by one's parents (Hardin 1993). And age is used to capture cohort effects on trust that are still not well understood, though they may be based, in part, on the rapid rise in materialistic value orientations that occurred in children who were part of the late baby boom or postboom generations (Rahn and Transue 1997).

As in our earlier analysis, confidence in government is measured by a scale that includes confidence ratings of Congress, the Executive Branch, and the Supreme Court ($\alpha = .67$). Responses to these questions were averaged, and the resulting scale was recoded to lie between 0 and 1. Personal optimism is measured by a question asking how many days in the past week the respondent felt happy, and it ranges from 0 to 7 days. Public mood is measured as before. The dependent variable is a scale based on the degree to which respondents felt that most people were trustworthy, fair, and helpful ($\alpha = .66$). With the exceptions of age and education, which are measured in years, and personal optimism, which is measured in days, variables are scaled to lie between 0 and 1.

Table 7.3 displays the results of this analysis. As with NAFTA opinions, there is a significant correspondence between respondents' public mood and their assessments of others' trustworthiness. Personal optimism, authoritarianism, and civic engagement (as measured by turnout) are also of some importance. The effects of confidence in government, fear of crime, and age – variables that we found in our earlier analysis to be of some importance – appear to be completely mediated through the other variables in the model. I interpret these results as evidence that one's public mood summarizes confidences in governing authorities, perceived security in one's neighborhood, and distinctive cohort experiences, plus myriad other factors that are impossible to catalog in full. Public

[14] The GSS is administered in the spring. Respondents who were not eligible to vote in 1992 are excluded from the analysis.

Table 7.3

The Origins of Social Trust (1=Trusting)	
Public Mood Valence	.60*** (.16)
Age	.0016 (.002)
Education	.02* (.01)
Race	-.14# (.07)
Sex	.003 (.05)
Personal Financial Retrospections	.06 (.07)
Personal Happiness	.03** (.01)
Fear of Walking Alone at Night? (1=Yes)	-.008 (.05)
Turnout in 1992 (1=Yes)	.173** (.06)
Importance of Obedience in Child rearing (1=Most Important)	-.19** (.07)
Confidence in National Government (1=A Great Deal)	-.03 (.11)
Constant	-.44*
Adj. R^2	.28
N	169

***$p \le .001$ **$p \le .01$ *$p \le .05$ #$p \le .10$, two-tailed

mood corresponds with strong patterns in respondents' trust assessments and acts in a way that is consistent with the notion that it summarizes a lot of detailed information about the political community. Put another way, Table 7.3 provides evidence that public mood affects political reasoning and facilitates low-information rationality.

I performed the same analysis within different educational strata – those with more than a high school education versus those with less edu-

Table 7.4

The Origins of Social Trust by Level of Education		
	12 years or less	13 years or more
Public Mood Valence	.72*** (.21)	.52* (.23)
Age	.003 (.002)	.001 (.003)
Education	.07*** (.02)	.006 (.02)
Race	-.18# (.09)	-.05 (.11)
Sex	.06 (.07)	.02 (.07)
Personal Financial Retrospections	.193* (.097)	-.003 (.09)
Personal Happiness	-.002 (.016)	.07*** (.02)
Fear of Walking Alone at Night?	-.12# (.07)	.05 (.07)
Turnout in 1992	.14* (.07)	.20* (.09)
Importance of Obedience in Child rearing	-.13 (.09)	-.30* (.11)
Confidence in National Government	-.12 (.15)	-.06 (.15)
Constant	-1.1***	-.28
Adj. R^2	.39	.26
N	75	94

***p ≤ .001   ** p ≤ .01   * p ≤ .05   # p ≤ .10, two-tailed

cation – in order to see whether, as before, the effect of public mood varies with knowledge. As seen in Table 7.4, the coefficient on public mood is large for both groups. Its size, however, is somewhat diminished for the well educated, suggesting that its influence may be somewhat muted for those with more cognitive resources, although the small number of cases makes this difference statistically unreliable. The main difference between the two groups seems to lie in the use of recent personal experiences or predispositions in making tı ments. Authoritarianism and personal optimism, both personalı, dispositions the origins of which are a combination of biology aı experience, are much more important for the better-educated group. For the less-well-educated group, however, the coefficients for retrospective assessments of personal-financial well-being and fear of walking at night in one's neighborhood are sizable in comparison to their counterparts in the well-educated group. Notice, too, that both race and years of education are important for those in the less-well-educated group. To the extent that these are demographic stand-ins for the quality of one's personal experiences, they conform to the pattern as well.

The foregoing analyses of NAFTA and social trust suggest that public mood may supply an important source of information for making many different politically relevant judgments. The main variation observed in these analyses is that the better informed appear to be less reliant on public mood and more reliant on various kinds of predispositions. In the NAFTA case, these predispositions are political; for social trust, the predispositions are based in personality. Therefore, a tentative generalization that emerges from these tests is that the better informed have less need for public mood, and so the extent to which public mood affects political reasoning and facilitates low-information rationality is greater for those with less information.

Analysis 3: A Misattribution Experiment

So far, the argument for the informational role of public mood has been based on examining its impact in a cross-sectional survey setting. Such analyses are always vulnerable to objections about the nature of causality. Does public mood cause the judgments being examined or does it work the other way around?[15] To answer this question, Jerry Clore and I conducted an experiment within a survey in which we made use of the so-called misattribution paradigm. Schwarz and Clore (1983) were the first to establish firmly the informational role of moods by using this type of experimental design, and our study replicated its logic.

---

[15] I believe that the reverse causality argument is implausible with respect to opinions on NAFTA, because so few people had opinions about it. In contrast, virtually everyone answered the public mood questions. For social trust, the argument is potentially more compelling. However, when I estimated, via two-stage least squares, a reciprocal model of trust and public mood, this analysis completely supports the recursive results reported in Table 7.3. The coefficient for the social trust to public mood link has the wrong sign and is statistically insignificant ($\beta = -.01$, $p < .84$).

The basic element of a misattribution experiment involves providing some subjects with an explanation for something, and then comparing their responses to others who were supplied with an alternative explanation. Schwarz and Clore (1983) used a variation of the misattribution paradigm to study the impact of current mood state on judgments. In their studies, the experimental treatment involved providing some subjects with an explanation for their feelings that would discredit them as a basis for evaluation. For the experimental control group, no such attribution was provided. The informational role of affect could then be established by comparing these two groups of subjects. For subjects not provided an explanation, Schwartz and Clore expected to find a correspondence between mood and judgment; that is, subjects in good moods would evaluate the target object (in this case, their own lives) more positively than subjects in negative moods. For misattribution subjects, however, mood was expected to be viewed as less reliable and, therefore, its information value discounted, resulting in reduced mood-congruency effects.

In one version of this basic design, the researchers called people up under the guise of conducting a public opinion survey. In some cases, these phone calls were made on warm, sunny days; in others, on rainy days. As expected, people called on sunny days reported higher levels of momentary happiness, or mood, than people called on rainy days. In all cases, people were asked to rate the quality of their lives "overall." However, some people were led either directly or indirectly to connect the weather to their current moods. In the direct condition, the interviewer explicitly stated that the purpose of the survey was to see how the weather influences a person's mood. In the indirect condition, the interviewer in an aside more innocuously asked, "By the way, how's the weather down there?" For subjects called on rainy days, self-reported overall life satisfaction depended on whether they were supplied, either directly or indirectly, the link between the weather and their current mood state. Rainy-day subjects not supplied with the weather attribution reported much lower levels of general life satisfaction than rainy-day subjects cued to the fact that the weather just might have something to do with their mood. Moreover, rainy-day subjects supplied with the weather attribution were just as satisfied with their lives as sunny-day subjects.

In our version of the misattribution paradigm, we purchased a few minutes of interviewing time in early 1994 on a national continuous telephone survey conducted daily by the University of Wisconsin's Survey Center, and 646 respondents were randomly assigned to one of two conditions, misattribution or control. In the control condition ($n = 336$), respondents were first asked the public mood questions, followed by a series of Likert-type political-attitude statements. In the misattribution condition ($n = 310$), a manipulation designed to get respondents to doubt the relevance of their public moods was inserted in between the measurement of public mood and the political judgments. The interviewer asked the respondent: "Please answer true or false: These feelings I've had about the country are due mostly to the way the United States is portrayed in television advertising and on TV programs." After recording the respondent's answer, the interviewer moved on to the political-attitude items.

Our choice of television as the attribution target was based on two things. First, we needed to suggest a source for public mood feelings that people would see as plausible. But second, this source had to be seen as dubious enough to get respondents to second-guess their own feelings as reliable. Television seemed to meet this criterion as well. For example, in 1974, less than 18% of respondents in the GSS said that they had hardly any confidence in television. By 1994, which was the year we did our experiment, the percentage of no-confidence responses had nearly doubled.

Our attribution manipulation, however, was not as successful as we had hoped. Less than half of the respondents ($n = 120$) assigned to the misattribution condition actually responded "true" to the interviewer's question about TV, and so we were forced to differentiate the misattribution condition into two, nonexperimental groups, "true responders" and "false responders."[16] The predictions for the design are as follows: Subjects in the control condition should show public mood effects on at least some judgments because their feelings about the country act as a source of information, and this information has not been called into question. Subjects in the "false" group should also show public mood effects on judgment, but for a different reason: By rejecting the misattribution suggestion of television, respondents implicitly affirm the validity of their feelings. In other words, the control and the "false" groups should resemble each other in terms of the average levels of the political judgments. For respondents in the "true" condition, however, we expect to see the discounting of public mood on political judgments because by attributing their feelings to television, subjects implicitly cast doubt on their reliability as information sources.

To examine these predictions, we treated each respondent's political judgment as a deviation from his or her overall judgment mean, in order to control for within-subject variability that might arise from the ques-

---

[16] The "true" group did not differ significantly from the "false" group with respect to age, race, personal mood, party identification, economic assessments, or job performance ratings of President Clinton and Congress. However, the "true" group was less educated.

tion format (e.g., acquiescence bias) or perspective effects (Green 1988; Wilcox, Sigelman, and Cook 1989). Because we use deviations rather than raw scores, a positive value indicates that the judgment was more positive than an individual's average judgment; negative scores mean the reverse. The seven judgments listed below were then submitted to an analysis of covariance in which group (control, true, false) was a between-subjects variable and education was a covariate:

- *Trust in government:* You can generally trust the government to do what is right.
- *External efficacy:* People like me don't have any say in what government does.
- *Responsiveness:* If public officials are not interested in hearing what the people think, there is really no way to make them listen.
- *Group conflict:* In America, we don't have to worry about group conflicts tearing up the country like they did in Yugoslavia.
- *Problem-solving efficacy:* It seems like as Americans, we can no longer find ways to solve our problems.
- *Global efficacy:* The United States can accomplish quite a lot in the world, provided that our leaders and the people really want to do it.
- *Security threat:* It won't be long until another strong country will start being a troublemaker for the United States now that the Soviet Union is gone.

Of these seven judgments, three showed significant differences ($p \leq$ .04) by attribution group: trust in government, external efficacy, and group conflict. Consistent with expectations, the means in the control and false groups do not differ. But in the true group, two of the judgments (group conflict and trust in government) are significantly more positive, and the efficacy item is significantly more negative, in comparison to the control and false groups.

The pattern in the data in Figure 7.1 suggests that the attribution to television caused the "true responders" to engage in correction of their judgments for the now-discredited influence of public mood feelings. Judgments that were more negative than a respondent's average judgment were "corrected" in a more positive direction; the more positive efficacy judgment was corrected in a negative direction. These results suggest that people may possess "naive theories" about the biasing impact of emotions that are used as a basis for readjusting judgments if it is believed that the initial value of the judgment was unduly influenced by some factor deemed to be inappropriate (Wegener and Petty 1995). Respondents in the false condition, however, did not need to correct their judgments, because they had affirmed their feelings by rejecting television as their source. Therefore, their judgments resemble those made by

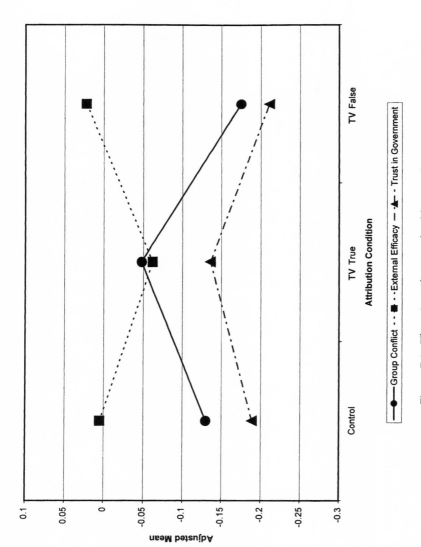

Figure 7.1. The misattribution of public mood.

respondents in the control condition, those individuals who were not made aware of the emotional aspects of their opinions.

CONCLUSION

There are many forms of low-information rationality available to citizens. I have endeavored to show in this chapter that public mood may be extremely important in informing some kinds of judgments. It is not that public mood causes individuals to ignore other information; rather, it appears to be most serviceable precisely in those situations when other information may be lacking or when the judgment is inherently a difficult and complex one. To the extent that public mood serves as a "barometer of the nation" in the same way that personal affective states serve as a "barometer of the ego" (Mayer and Hanson 1995), it may efficiently integrate the affective implications stemming from many aspects of American life, from the economy to popular culture.

PART II

Internal Elements of Reason

8

Reconsidering the Rational Public: Cognition, Heuristics, and Mass Opinion

JAMES H. KUKLINSKI AND PAUL J. QUIRK

There has been a marked change in the way political scientists think about the American citizenry. Beginning with the advent of survey research in the 1940s, students of public opinion took a dim view of citizens' political capabilities. Consistently finding a public profoundly lacking in political knowledge and sophistication, they became skeptical of the individual citizen's ability to make intelligent political decisions or to participate effectively in the political process (see Kinder 1983 and Sniderman 1993 for comprehensive reviews).

Over the past decade, leading scholars have offered grounds for a much more positive view of citizen competence. They do not dispute the finding of widespread political ignorance or claim that the citizen's command of politics has recently improved. Rather, they offer two arguments to suggest that even an uninformed citizenry can participate in politics competently. One is that individuals use heuristics – mental short-cuts that require hardly any information – to make fairly reliable political judgments. By this means, Sniderman, Brody, and Tetlock (1991: 19) write, "people can be knowledgeable in their reasoning about political choices without necessarily possessing a large body of knowledge about politics." The other argument is that public opinion is rational in the aggregate, even if individual opinion is prone to error (Page and Shapiro 1992; see also Converse 1990). Individual errors cancel out in the process of aggregation, and thus collective opinion conveys real and true information about the citizenry's preferences.

The two proposals struck a chord among political scientists. Sniderman, Brody, and Tetlock's *Reasoning and Choice* (1991) and Popkin's *The Reasoning Voter* (1991) stimulated widespread attention to political heuristics.[1] Subsequent studies also found that individuals achieve a

---

[1] Even earlier, several contributors to Ferejohn and Kuklinski (1990) had stressed the utility of political heuristics. See Carmines and Kuklinski (1990), Ferejohn (1990), and McKelvey and Ordeshook (1990).

kind of rationality generally adequate to the tasks of citizens (see, for example, Lupia 1994, Lupia and McCubbins 1998, and Mondak 1993). Page and Shapiro's *The Rational Public* (1992), along with work by Stimson and colleagues (Stimson 1991 and Stimson, MacKuen, and Erikson 1995), resurrected research on the properties and movement of collective opinion, concerns that students of American politics had over-looked for years.

The enthusiasm for the political-heuristics and collective-opinion approaches is understandable. Each defines an agenda of significant research. Both offer plausible mechanisms for competent citizen perfor-mance, and both have produced significant supporting evidence. Not least, the notion of a competent citizenry is normatively attractive. It but-tresses efforts to expand citizen participation and credits the citizenry for some of American democracy's success.

Nevertheless, we propose an alternative perspective that is more skep-tical about the citizen's competence – especially in choosing policy pref-erences, responding to policy rhetoric, and influencing policy making. In the pages that follow, we first review the work on political heuristics and collective opinion. Although both bodies of work make major contribu-tions, we argue that the research does not warrant broad claims of citizen competence. Indeed, it leaves open the possibility of significant distor-tions in public opinion. We next note that research in the basic sciences of human cognition – neural science, cognitive psychology, and evolu-tionary psychology – has converged on several findings that are relevant for models of mass politics. Contrary to the political-heuristics and collective-opinion perspectives, these findings suggest that human cogni-tion is not well adapted to the tasks of citizens. We then review a variety of evidence focusing on distortions specifically in political judgment. Most of it comes from our own experimental survey work, some of it from so-called deliberative polls and recent developments in public policy. Taken together, this evidence portrays the public as prone to send misguided signals to policy makers. In closing, we summarize briefly and comment on some implications of recent trends in American politics.

POLITICAL HEURISTICS, COLLECTIVE OPINION, AND THE "RATIONAL PUBLIC"

To what extent has a compelling case been made for a politically com-petent, rational public? In this section, we first take up the work on polit-ical heuristics, which raises the most fundamental considerations, and discuss it at length. We then consider more briefly the literature on col-lective opinion.

154

Political Heuristics

Advocates have identified many kinds of political heuristics. In elections, the classic voting cue is, of course, the political party (Campbell, Converse, Miller, and Stokes 1960). By merely attending to party labels, voters can compensate for a lack of reliable information on the candidates' policy positions. Popkin (1991) identifies a multitude of other voting strategies on which people can draw. These include attributing issue positions on the basis of a candidate's demographics or those of his supporters; using evidence about personal character to make inferences about political character; assuming that the president controls the economy; and using returns in early presidential primaries as evidence of the candidate's merit.

In judging either candidates or policies, people can use public statements by elected officials, interest-group leaders, or others as cues. Citizens who know very little about a pending bill, for example, can look to the statements of particular officeholders they have come to trust (Carmines and Kuklinski 1990; Mondak 1993). Alternatively, they can consider the positions of interest groups whose policy preferences they are generally inclined to support or oppose (Lupia 1994). Such cues arguably eliminate the need for substantive information about an issue.

Among the most provocative heuristics political scientists have proffered is Brady and Sniderman's likability heuristic. Brady and Sniderman (1985) argue that people can use the likability of certain political groups – blacks and whites, liberals and conservatives – to make reasonable judgments of where they stand on policy. To use the heuristic, a person must have relevant policy preferences and also have affective responses toward a pair of groups. She can then attribute a position close to her own to the liked group and a more distant position to the disliked group – in effect, using her feelings toward the groups as information about their positions.

That citizens apparently can draw on such a variety of heuristics is fortunate. For one thing, the rules of thumb that scholars have identified cover the two primary tasks that citizens perform: voting and evaluating public policy. For another, most citizens face conditions of limited information most of the time. By any serious standard, even the *relatively* well informed fall short of being *well* informed. So, political heuristics would seem indispensable to any citizen who is trying to make a well-grounded judgment.

But have researchers convincingly made the case that citizens achieve, in Popkin's words (1991), "low information" or "gut" rationality? For students of heuristics to make their case, they need to show, first, that most citizens routinely use particular heuristics in particular situations and, second, that the use of those heuristics leads to good or at least reasonable decisions. We discuss each issue in turn.

The Use of Heuristics. We accept that people sometimes use the kinds of decision-making heuristics discussed. A harder question is whether most people appropriately use them most of the time. The case for the benefits of a heuristic falters if only a few people use it in the relevant circumstances.

Empirical work in the heuristics tradition has not addressed the frequency with which citizens use heuristics in the real world. It is easy to understand why: The data are hard to come by. Such data would describe people's mental processes under real-world circumstances when, for example, they express a policy preference, evaluate a campaign appeal, or decide for whom to vote. And the data would need to be collected over a large number of decision-making situations. To expect such data would be unreasonable.

We therefore pursue a different strategy. It is simply to ask this question: Are there reasons to believe that people fail routinely to use the kinds of political heuristics that scholars have posited? We think there are.

First, as we will argue below, a cognitive-sciences perspective suggests that people indeed do use heuristics, but hardly as rational strategies specifically tailored for each kind of decision.[2] Rather, people take their heuristics off the shelf, use them unknowingly and automatically, and rarely worry about their accuracy. An inherent part of human nature, these broader, less discriminating sorts of heuristic generally trump strategic decision making.

Second, as Delli Carpini and Keeter (1996: 51–53) observe, people often lack the contextual knowledge needed to use heuristics intelligently, or in fact to use them at all. For a voter in a primary election to learn significantly from an earlier primary in another state, for example, he would need to know whether that state is generally liberal or conservative. Most citizens undoubtedly lack the necessary command of political geography.

Finally, the information necessary to use heuristics might often be missing from the citizen's environment. Consider cue taking. When researchers provide people with statements attributable to prominent groups or political leaders, they readily take the cues (Carmines and Kuklinski 1990; Lupia and McCubbins 1998; McKelvey and Ordeshook 1990). In the political world, however, usable cues are not regularly

---

[2] For an imposing theoretical and empirical treatment of heuristics as such rational strategies, see Lupia and McCubbins (1998).

available. Statements by leading officials endorsing or opposing proposals in Congress appear infrequently on network news programs (Althaus 1996). If cues do not appear, citizens cannot use them.

These arguments are admittedly only speculative. Nevertheless, they identify potential barriers to the effective use of political heuristics. They suggest that citizens might actually employ some of the heuristics proposed in the literature less often than scholars have implied.

Heuristics and Good Political Decisions. Putting the question of actual use aside, we now examine the central claim of the heuristics literature: that by drawing on certain heuristics, citizens reach sound judgments. In labeling judgments as "good," "sound," or "competent," the difficulty is to find criteria independent of the decision-making process. Scholars cannot deem a judgment good simply because people reach it by using a heuristic, or because they feel satisfied with it.[3] Unfortunately, as in any other public-opinion research, standards of quality turn on values, debatable facts, or both. In general, we can discriminate between better and worse political opinions only by positing normative criteria, which are in all cases open to criticism (Price and Neijens 1997).

To their credit, students of political heuristics have not punted on the question of competence, which is a safe move but one that makes public-opinion research irrelevant to any assessment of democratic politics. In establishing criteria, these researchers have employed the same general strategies that any scholar would draw on. In some instances, they have relied on their own political knowledge, or that of other experts, to designate a decision as good or not so good, or to judge the worth of a given kind of information. In others, they have identified a criterion group – assumed to be well informed and yet otherwise representative of the appropriate population – and then tried to ascertain how closely people's judgments resemble those of the criterion group.

To repeat, we have no quarrel with these general strategies for assessing competence, as such. However, we question some of the applications of the criteria and the conclusions that advocates have reached about the effectiveness of certain heuristics. To show why, we briefly discuss four examples.

1. In his study of voting on the California automobile insurance referendum, Lupia (1994) shows that relatively uninformed voters who had access to a relevant cue were able to mimic voters who had somewhat more information. Specifically, voters who knew only the insurance

---

[3] At times, the political-heuristics advocates have seemed content to make a very limited claim – that heuristics help people make judgments with which they are satisfied (Popkin 1991; Sniderman, Tetlock, and Brody 1991). We do not dispute this effect. Taken by itself, however, such a claim merely evades the issue of competence.

industry's position on the competing propositions voted similarly to a criterion group that scored in the top third on a multiple-choice test on the key provisions. Both groups voted differently than did people who had neither kind of knowledge. In short, knowing the industry position apparently worked as well as knowing the specific provisions.

As Lupia himself stresses, however, this finding demonstrates competent performance by the industry cue takers only if we assume that those who knew the provisions relatively well were indeed adequately informed. In fact, there is no evidence that they knew much at all about the merits of the debate. As we stated, being *relatively* well informed falls far short of being well informed. In fact, the relatively well informed voted as one would expect the uninformed to vote. They massively supported a proposition – the winner in the referendum – that mandated a 20 percent rollback of automobile insurance rates. The appeal of a price rollback to voters is no mystery. But such a measure is rarely warranted in a competitive industry. Moreover, economists and insurance experts overwhelmingly oppose rate controls for automobile insurance (Lascher and Powers 1997). And in any event, the California measure was not successfully implemented. A similar measure adopted in Ontario, Canada, was quickly reversed. In our view, the evidence from the California referendum suggests that even relatively well informed citizens responded heavily to extraneous factors – dislike of insurance companies and wishful thinking about their rates, for example – rather than making an informed assessment of the merits.

2. Another rule of thumb is to evaluate the incumbent president on the basis of the economy's current performance (Popkin 1991; also see Fiorina 1981 and Key 1966). In using this heuristic, Popkin suggests, voters make a "simplifying assumption" that the president controls the economy. That assumption is not just a simplification, however. It is mostly false. A commonplace of informed commentary is that the president's ability to influence short-term economic performance is exceedingly modest (Hibbs 1987: 255–279; Woolley 1998). Thus, the economic-conditions heuristic captures little information about a president's skill or priorities. For the most part, it merely rewards good economic luck and punishes bad. To the extent that it creates incentives for presidential management, those incentives are notoriously perverse – favoring the sacrifice of long-term growth and monetary stability for a small boost in current activity, especially in an election year (Nordhaus 1975; Tufte 1978).

3. In a cleverly designed study, Mondak (1993) shows that when Reagan's endorsement was mentioned in poll questions about policy issues, people used it as a cue to form preferences. Moreover, the effect varied with Reagan's approval rating: The more popular he was, the

greater the effect of his endorsement. In one sense, this looks like discriminating cue taking. But consider this: Reagan's policies did not vary
with his popularity. Nor, therefore, did the policy significance of his
endorsement. Thus, the evidence on the effects of Reagan's approval does
not indicate rational cue taking aimed at achieving desired policies.
Rather, it points to the effect of a source's prominence or attractiveness
on persuasion.

4. As we noted, Brady and Sniderman offer the likability heuristic
(1985) as a method for people to identify the preferences of certain
groups. Oddly, however, this heuristic entails people's doing just the
opposite of what Lupia's California referendum voters apparently did.
In the California study, voters used a group cue – the insurance industry's position on the referendum – to form their preferences. In the likability study, people already have preferences, and they combine them
with feelings toward groups to estimate the groups' positions. Taken
together, the two studies suggest a circular argument that preference formation depends upon group cues, and yet attribution of group positions
depends upon prior preferences. In order for the argument that likability leads to competent decisions to be compelling, its advocates will have
to break out of this circular argument and show that people's existing
preferences are in some sense "right."

In the end, we are not saying that political heuristics are never helpful
or even that these authors' claims for the advantages of various heuristics are clearly wrong (see Mondak 1994 for a generally positive review).
We do not doubt, for example, that using party labels to evaluate candidates leads individual voters to the right candidate choice, in view of
their policy preferences, most of the time (Lau and Redlawsk 1997).
Rather, our point is simply that the benefits of the heuristics described
in some of the leading studies are in fact debatable. Accordingly, any
broad conclusion that people achieve competence via heuristics is also
debatable.

Collective Opinion

Ironically, the collective-opinion perspective proceeds from the very same
finding whose dismal implications it has sought to overcome. Thirty
years earlier, Converse (1964) had found massive instability over time in
individuals' attitudes about politics. In his view, this instability indicated
that most citizens did not even have true attitudes about political issues
and thus answered survey questions, in effect, randomly. In a remarkable turnabout, collective-opinion scholars have found a basis for optimism in this very randomness.

Individual-level randomness, they contend, implies that aggregated opinion can readily be quite rational and well behaved. The individual-level errors, because random, will cancel out; and collective opinion will move, as it should, mainly in response to real-world events. A popular saying warns, facetiously, "bad information drives out good information." The collective-opinion school claims almost the opposite: Bad information drives itself out; good information survives.

In our view, there are grounds for skepticism about the benefits of aggregation. First, it is far from clear that the errors in individual citizens' political judgments are largely random. Modern research in cognitive psychology has shown that bias and distortion are systematic properties of human cognition (Kahneman, Slovic, and Tversky 1982; Nisbett and Ross 1980). People process information in similar, imperfect ways; so in dealing with the same information, they tend to make the same mistakes. Moreover, in some Monte Carlo simulations, Althaus (1996: chap. 3) has shown that collective opinion can be quite sensitive to such error. He shows that unless the proportion of informed individuals is very high, or systematic error is indeed minimal, the error in collective opinion is often sizable. In short, there is no safety in mere numbers.

Second, advocates of collective rationality assume that citizens will receive reliable information from the media, interest groups, or public officials. In fact, the information these sources provide – presumably the citizens' main connection with the real political world – can easily be severely unbalanced and not particularly helpful. Put aside concerted efforts by politicians to deceive the public.[4] Even in their normal policy-making activities, elected officials make no effort to provide objective information. They use whatever rhetorical devices are likely to work. There is no presumption that the balance of effective rhetorical opportunities in a political debate happily reflects the balance of real information with respect to it. Indeed, the public itself will sometimes induce pronounced biases in the information that it receives. If the public has strong predispositions about an issue, politicians will avoid taking positions or providing information that challenges those predispositions. For example, if people reflexively oppose raising taxes, or if they have an irrational fear of chemical wastes, elected officials likely will not offer opposing views.

Let's turn now to the empirical evidence that scholars have presented to support claims of collective rationality. It indeed demonstrates some

---

[4] In fact, Page and Shapiro themselves are concerned about certain forms of elite deception and manipulation; they fear that elites mislead the public to benefit powerful economic groups, to bolster aggressive foreign policies, and so on. Without disputing those concerns, we would suggest that the principal elite bias is probably to reinforce those biases that are already prevalent in mass opinion.

reassuring properties of collective opinion. Overall, though, the evidence falls short of supporting broad claims of a rational public; in fact, the findings do not rule out significant collective bias.

The principal study is Page and Shapiro's (1992) monumental analysis of the movements of aggregate opinion recorded in 50 years of opinion polls. This study clearly establishes two findings. First, collective opinion is normally stable, with dramatic change very unusual. The public is rarely seized by the "momentary passions" so deeply feared by the Founding Fathers. Second, collective opinion responds to changing conditions and information in intelligible ways. The movements of opinion are not arbitrary. Support for defense spending has increased with international tensions, support for antipoverty and employment programs with unemployment, and so on.

These findings are also quite consistent, however, with an error-ridden collective opinion. One reason is that Page and Shapiro do not specify, a priori and in any discriminating fashion, what patterns of change should count as rational. In some cases, the favorable interpretation is debatable. Should support for defense spending really vary with international tensions? Considering that a strong defense is needed for deterrence even in times of apparent harmony, perhaps not. That world conflicts influence citizen support for defense is understandable, not necessarily rational.

More important, such patterns of change do not speak to biases that might exist more or less constantly over a long period of time. Suppose that during the cold war, the public consistently supported a defense budget that was twice as large as an informed assessment would have recommended. Off the mark by 100 percent, this support could appear rational by Page and Shapiro's criterion, so long as it varied with the level of international tension. Similarly, collective opinion could favor unrealistically low taxes and yet still respond to the budget deficit; it could favor excessively harsh criminal sentences and still respond to crime rates; and so on. The movement of collective opinion cannot speak to constant biases in that opinion.

The research on collective opinion should relieve some of the worst fears about mass politics. The public does not become agitated for slight cause or demand policies completely lacking elite support. The research fails fully to demonstrate, however, that public opinion is consistently a constructive force, expressing the public's true preferences fairly accurately. As with the empirical work on political heuristics, the findings do not rule out even major distortions in public opinion.

In the next section, we set out some basic propositions of a different approach to studying mass opinion – one that draws on recent developments in basic research on human cognition (also see Lupia and McCubbins 1998).

A COGNITIVE-SCIENCES PERSPECTIVE: HARD
WIRING, EVOLUTION, AND THE TASKS OF
CITIZENSHIP

Theories of mass political behavior, in our view, should build upon and comport with basic findings about human mental processes in the cognitive sciences – including cognitive psychology, evolutionary psychology, and even neural science. Some of the convergent findings in these fields have considerable bearing on the debate about citizen competence.

Basic Findings on Human Cognition

In particular, six broad findings of recent cognitive-sciences research are highly relevant for developing well-grounded theories of mass behavior.[5]

1. Much of human cognitive capability is "hard-wired," built into neural circuitry that is part of our genetic inheritance. Children learn to speak, infants recognize some laws of physics, and people become intuitive psychologists – in each case, sooner and with less effort than would be needed for a tabula rasa. Such hard-wired capabilities substantially reduce each individual's need for learning. They also, however, reduce flexibility. People's mental processes are only partly shaped by the experiences and requirements of their own lives.

2. Natural selection designed these hard-wired mental processes to meet the demands of survival and reproduction that faced our human ancestors, primarily in the Stone Age. These humans lived by foraging in small nomadic bands on the African savanna. The crucial tasks were self-defense, finding food and shelter, mating and childrearing, and achieving social cooperation for these purposes. We still have the mental equipment that evolved in this environment. The entire period of agricultural and industrial civilization, about one percent of human history, has been too short to produce further biological adaptation.

Our minds thus are not designed to deal with the demands of contemporary technological societies. As Pinker writes (1997: 42): "They are not wired to cope with anonymous crowds, schooling, written language, government, police, courts, armies, modern medicine, formal social institutions, and other newcomers to the human experience." He

---

[5] We draw on a large number of works in this section. The most important include Barkow, Cosmides, and Tooby 1992; Bogdan 1997; Churchland 1995; Churchland and Sejnowski 1992; Damasio 1994; Hauser 1996; LeDoux 1996; Pinker 1997; and Plotkin 1998. Most of these books place a heavy emphasis on evolution. In following this lead, we recognize that evolutionary theory's currently high status could wane quickly. We also acknowledge the inherent problems of testing evolutionary theory.

could have added all the apparatus of democratic politics: the media, elections, referenda, political rhetoric, and opinion polls. Of course, all of these institutions are designed to function with humans; they cannot be completely alien. Nevertheless, human capabilities and dispositions are often problematic for their functioning. Parents and teachers invest enormous effort, for example, inducing children to study in school. If nomadic foragers had needed book learning to survive, it would come more easily now.

3. The mind is not a single, general-purpose calculator that applies universal principles to deal with all kinds of problems. Human mental capacities are "modular," that is, domain specific and independent: one module for mothering, another for attending to danger, another for judging character, and so on. These modules contain very specific built-in assumptions about how the world works and which responses are useful. They are deployed automatically, without conscious thought, and have limited flexibility. Metaphorically, we look quickly for an appropriate mental tool; if we pick up a hammer, whatever we are dealing with gets pounded.

Although the general capability for critical reasoning can intervene and correct faulty assumptions in some of these processes, it plays a minor role in many decisions. Indeed, competence in reasoning depends heavily on learning in context. Experiments have shown that people do poorly at applying abstract logic in the absence of detailed contextual knowledge (Cosmides 1989; Wason 1966). We can figure out what follows from "all cows eat grass" mainly because we know a lot about cows.

4. Under many circumstances, people make judgments in notably unreliable ways without realizing that they are doing so. Psychologists distinguish between "central" and "peripheral" processing (Fiske and Taylor 1991: 475–480). In central processing, used when attention and motivation are high, people employ more mental resources, think more systematically, and allow data to shape inferences. In peripheral processing, used when attention and motivation are low, they employ fewer resources, rely on simple heuristics, and use top-down, stereotypic inferences (Fiske and Taylor 1991: 475–480).

Peripheral processing is not simply an abbreviated or economical version of central processing – as in the abandoned notion of the "cognitive miser" or the current notion of "low-information rationality." It uses quite different strategies. And importantly, people do not take account of the shortcomings of peripheral processing by making tentative judgments, or discounting conclusions for their uncertainty. Rather, they use problematic methods without recognizing their character and take the results for granted.

5. Human emotion systems interact with cognitive processes in complex and subtle ways. On the one hand, emotions are indispensable for decision making (LeDoux 1996). Inarticulate "gut feelings" often reflect real information that is not available for conscious processing (Schwarz and Clore 1988). Rationality often breaks down in brain-damaged patients who cannot experience emotions (Damasio 1994). On the other, because emotions rely on learning and memory systems that work very differently from those involved in cognitive processing, they also adversely affect thinking and rationality. From the standpoint of making sound judgments, emotion systems are too easily conditioned, overgeneralizing from isolated episodes. They make crude inferences, recognizing few distinctions. And they resist revision, recording emotional memories essentially permanently. Moreover, most of the effect of the emotions is unconscious, not subject to rational scrutiny. And in the constant interaction between emotion and cognition, emotion generally dominates.[6]

Some of the consequences are widely recognized. As LeDoux notes (1996: 228–230), we have too many fears. Many people suffer debilitating mental illnesses, which are mainly of emotional origin. More relevant for politics, emotions distort judgment even among the mentally healthy. We need not assume that these properties of the emotion systems are adaptive in every context or even in general. LeDoux speculates that the brain is still evolving toward a more balanced relation between emotion and cognition.

6. Finally, cognitive processes generate systematically false beliefs to promote certain kinds of behavior (Barkow, Cosmides, and Tooby 1992; Hauser 1996; Pinker 1997). Perhaps best known, people hold high opinions of groups to which they belong and low opinions of those to which they do not. Thus, for example, soldiers see their fellow troops as braver, smarter, and stronger than the enemy. However inaccurate such perceptions might be, they help to sustain cooperative ventures. People also fool themselves about their own dispositions and capabilities. One function of such self-deception is to make our promises and threats appear more convincing to others (Hauser 1996). There are other cognitive distortions – such as overconfidence, the confirmation bias, and biases of causal attribution – that also nudge behavior in various ways.

The behavioral effects of these built-in distortions were presumably advantageous in the evolutionary past. In all likelihood, many are still useful. But the skewed perceptions will sometimes do harm. In particu-

---

[6] More specifically, most of the activity of the emotion systems does not produce conscious feelings. And the neural pathways that carry messages from the emotion systems to the cognitive systems are far more extensive than those running in the opposite direction.

lar, they will undermine performance in those tasks that mainly require accurate judgment.

Implications for Mass Politics

What do these findings imply for the study of politics? They do not directly predict specific patterns of political behavior. We believe, however, that they have three general implications for mass politics.

The Presumption of Adaptability. First, researchers should not presume that any particular feature of human cognition is well adapted to the tasks of citizens. In view of natural selection and the capacity for learning, we expect cognitive processes to be highly adaptive in some global sense; nothing about how people think will be simply pointless or unfortunate. Even so, we can account for departures from "low-information rationality" in politics in several distinct ways.[7]

People might rely on decision-making processes that perform satisfactorily in other areas of life but that are less suitable for politics. For example, people may have learned to employ certain criteria for choosing friends, work partners, and so on. If they use these same routines to choose political leaders, they might overlook criteria that are uniquely important to evaluating leadership.

Moreover, people may use cognitive processes that produce dysfunctional responses generally – not only in politics or other special contexts – because they promoted survival and reproduction in the ancestral environment and have been incorporated in the genetic code. Considering the transformation that has occurred in the conditions of human life since the Stone Age, there seems to be hardly any limit to the potential for such malfunctions. What worked for nomadic hunter-gatherers could easily fail badly for citizens of a postindustrial democracy. Although we can only speculate here about the role of evolved responses in mass politics, we suspect that the conditions of the ancestral environment help to account for some important aspects of political behavior. Judging from anthropological research, ancestral humans fought frequent wars and faced a high likelihood of death by homicide (Barkow, Cosmides, and Tooby 1992; Pinker 1997) The hazardous conditions presumably rewarded stereotyping, ethnocentrism, and quick-trigger responses to fear and anger, major traits that frequently create conflict in modern politics. Our Stone Age ancestors also lived a precarious existence eco-

---

[7] It is possible to define low-information rationality, trivially, as the use of any information whatsoever, no matter how unreliable. ("I like his tie. I guess, then, I'd like his policies.") The concept is significant only if it implies the use of relatively efficient methods of judgment.

nomically. They were in danger of starvation; and yet, lacking money and refrigeration, they had little ability to store surpluses. On the one hand, therefore, any substantial loss of resources might be fatal; but an equivalent gain might largely go to waste. Such conditions may underlie people's well-documented tendency to discount gains in relation to losses (Kahneman and Tversky 1984; Tversky and Kahneman 1981).

Finally, ancestral humans also lived in an information environment radically different from ours – with no writing or formal arithmetic, few concerns about remote consequences, and little or no specialized knowledge. This environment may account for the relative ineffectiveness of abstract and systematic information in persuasion (Cacioppo and Petty 1979; Cacioppo and Petty 1985): To the extent that we possess evolved processes for responding to persuasion, they are not adapted for this newfangled information. And it is understandable that the source of a message, how strongly it is expressed, and how it fits people's existing beliefs will often shape their responses more than any rational assessment of its content will (Hauser 1996; McGuire 1969, 1985).

For all of these reasons, then, we cannot assume that the cognitive processes people use in making a particular political judgment are well adapted to that use. To the contrary, if close observers see such processes as irrational or generally misleading, they probably are.

The Nature of Heuristics. A second broad implication of the cognitive-sciences perspective, implicit in the first, is that we should expect systematic bias in heuristic judgments. Ironically, political scientists have borrowed the concept of heuristics from psychology while overlooking its main significance in that literature. Viewing heuristics as rational strategies for dealing with ignorance, political scientists have stressed how they enhance competence. They have not looked for problems with them.

For the most part, cognitive psychologists look at heuristics differently. They see the use of heuristics as automatic, unconscious, and frequently dysfunctional (see, for example, Kahneman, Slovic, and Tversky 1982; Nisbett and Ross 1980). Research has shown that people use arbitrary starting points to anchor estimates, use accessibility in memory to estimate frequency; use a source's attractiveness to judge her credibility; and draw inferences from predetermined scripts and stereotypes. In cases that do not fit their implicit assumptions, heuristic judgments produce serious departures from rationality. For the most part, as Piattelli-Palmarini (1994: 6–7) writes, the resulting errors are "inaccessible to correction." We use unreliable rules of thumb with no awareness of doing so.

That the political scientists' concept of heuristics differs from the psychologists' does not make it incorrect. To a large extent, the difference reflects distinct starting points and standards of comparison. The psychologist starts with the layperson's commonsense perception that people are generally rational. (We feel at least that we ourselves are rational.) Heuristic judgments disappoint such expectations, often profoundly. In describing their effects, therefore, psychologists highlight the error. Political scientists, on the other hand, start with the research showing that people are politically ignorant. They find evidence that political heuristics can save people from being strictly clueless. So unlike psychologists, they are inclined to stress the positive side.

Such differences in perspective and emphasis are largely understandable. What is not warranted, in our view, is political scientists' virtual abandonment of the psychologists' notion of heuristics and its expectation of serious distortion. It is the psychologists' version that comports generally with cognitive-science findings and is supported by extensive laboratory research (Wittman 1995 criticizes the heavy reliance on experiments). Heuristics as discriminating strategies, well adapted for particular uses, is at best part of the story.

Expectations for Citizen Competence.   The third and main implication of the cognitive-science findings is that, on the whole, we should not expect a great deal of ordinary citizens' political judgments. In general, people will use available information effectively and make good decisions only under favorable conditions. These occur primarily when a task is intrinsically simple, when helpful capabilities or dispositions are hard-wired, or when institutions or other environmental conditions promote competence.

Consider some cases. People usually know what they're doing in mating, mothering, and making friends. The reason is that these tasks have not changed fundamentally since the Stone Age. People also usually know what they're doing in managing a large investment portfolio, if they have that job. This task is complex and of recent origin. However, portfolio managers are likely to have M.B.A. degrees, they receive rapid and informative feedback, and they have strong incentives for good performance. They even have training and professional literature to help them avoid cognitive biases (Hammond, Keeney, and Raiffa 1998). Unfortunately, the tasks of citizens in a democracy are less conducive to avoiding dysfunction. There are four difficulties in particular.

1. The political process calls upon ordinary citizens to answer very hard questions. According to some views of this matter, the citizens' task is quite easy (Sniderman 2000; Wittman 1995). The structure of political conflict pares down and clarifies citizens' choices so that they require

only a few simple operations: choosing a broad preference about the role of government, such as a liberal or conservative ideology, and matching it up with the appropriate party or candidate (Sniderman 2000). We agree that such a task is manageable for many people. Indeed, we agree that a political process that elicited primarily that form of participation could generally count on satisfactory citizen performance.

But, in fact, citizens are invited and sometimes compelled to do much more. In primary elections, the voters select the parties' nominees for various offices, including the presidency. The candidates are not pre-screened for their character, policy views, or governing skills. And party labels are unavailable. Voters have to assess the relevant attributes themselves or live with the results of not doing so.

Moreover, rather than merely choosing a broad direction for government, citizens help to select and even design specific policies. In many states, of course, voters choose policies directly through initiatives and referenda. They can also have a large influence, though less directly, by responding to polls about issues. Most important, in our view, voters respond to campaign appeals about issues. Such appeals, often framed negatively, are the bread-and-butter rhetoric of contemporary campaigns (Ansolabehere and Iyengar 1995). Voters' responses may virtually dictate policy choices.

In exerting such influence, people do not abstract out the ideological location of a policy, signal a preference on that basis, and ignore all of the policy's specific features. They support or oppose entire policies: Clinton's health-care reform plan, the Republicans' welfare reform, and so on. Ultimately, they send signals about whatever features actually elicit their response – not just getting tough on crime, for example, but three-strikes-and-you're-out; not just reducing welfare but a two-year limit; and not just responsive government but term limitations. Getting one's preferences right on such specific matters is no easy task.

2. The conduct of political debate makes pertinent, reliable information for these hard, political choices difficult to find. Politicians are not in the business of educating the public. Instead, they use rhetoric to trigger the psychological mechanisms that distort judgment. They present isolated, unrepresentative facts; they frame issues tendentiously; and they seek to evoke an emotional response, rather than encourage rational deliberation. The media rarely attempt to sort out a debate in an orderly way. Observers of politics are too accustomed to all this to find it remarkable. But from the standpoint of understanding citizen competence, it is important to know that the information people receive is typically sketchy, misleading, or manipulative.

3. The structures of modern democracy give ordinary citizens almost no incentive to think carefully about politics. Because informed deliber-

ation is a collective good, individuals lack not only the incentive to be well informed, but even the incentive to use their limited information in thoughtful ways. People make political judgments half-consciously, as an incidental part of another activity – such as watching television for entertainment. They employ the error-prone methods of peripheral processing (Cacioppo and Petty 1985). They make little use of their critical faculties, and rarely wonder if their judgments are accurate.

4. Perhaps most important, politics rarely provides usable feedback on the methods people use for political judgment. For comparison, consider the nonpolitical case of a technologically challenged faculty member, Jim, buying a computer for his office. To avoid several days of tedious research, he simply imitates the purchase made by his apparently more expert colleague, Wendy; in brief, he uses a copy-Wendy heuristic. He soon knows if the machine suits him. And he can use that information to decide whether to use copy-Wendy in selecting a printer. His learning about the value of the heuristic depends on his experiencing the consequences of the first decision, obtaining the new computer and finding out whether it works.

Using heuristics in the political domain is entirely different. If a voter uses an irrelevant or misleading cue to pick a candidate, no one tells him his choice was wrong. The candidate might not be elected. If elected, in our fragmented political system, she may not control policy outcomes. And if her policies are adopted, discovering their effects will generally be very difficult. By the time the candidate's merit becomes clear, if that ever happens, the voter will not remember why he decided to vote for her. Even in the unlikely event that he is interested in improving his political heuristics, therefore, he'll have a hard time doing so.

In short, then, a cognitive-sciences perspective on mass politics suggests that citizens often will make problematic judgments. In the following section, we summarize more direct evidence on the specific causes of dysfunction.

BIAS IN POLITICAL JUDGMENT: EVIDENCE FROM EXPERIMENTAL SURVEY RESEARCH

Our question here is simple: In using political information and making political judgments, do people perform more or less rationally? Or do they exhibit suboptimal behavior of the sort that a cognitive-science perspective predicts?

To answer this question, we present evidence from experimental survey research. Such research can reveal how people respond to specific kinds of information, identify distortions in those responses, and suggest explanations based on well-documented properties of human judgment.

For reasons we will discuss, considerable caution is required in extrapolating these findings to real-world political behavior. We will address that problem with some additional evidence in the "Conclusion and Implications" section.

The evidence comes mainly from studies that one or both of us have conducted with various collaborators (Michael Cobb, Norman Hurley, Robert Rich, and David Schwieder). For one recently completed analysis, we present data. For the most part, we merely summarize studies that have been reported elsewhere.

Policy Stereotypes

To form sound policy preferences, people should receive and use policy-relevant information in a reasonably balanced way. For example, they cannot systematically screen out information that demonstrates the benefits of a program, or that reveals its adverse consequences. We know that people misperceive the policy-relevant world in various ways – for example, grossly overestimating the proportion of the federal budget that goes to foreign aid. We also know that they have stereotypes of racial and other groups that sometimes affect policy judgments (Gilens 1996; Judd and Downing 1995). We were interested in knowing whether people form stereotypes, or equivalent schemas, that directly concern programs or policies.

To investigate such policy stereotypes, we (Kuklinski, Quirk, Schwieder, and Rich 1997) asked a sample of Illinois residents to make estimates on a series of items about welfare: the percent of all families that are on welfare, the proportion of the federal budget that welfare absorbs, the average annual benefit amount for a family of three, the percentage of welfare mothers who are on welfare for more than eight years, and the percent of welfare mothers who have less than a high school education.[8] We found that most people made errors in a consistent direction. They had either pro-welfare or anti-welfare stereotypes. As one might expect, the more common stereotype was anti-welfare – with people overestimating the percent of all families on welfare, the proportion of the budget that goes to welfare, the average annual benefit, and so on.

In accounting for these findings, we suggested that people use their welfare-policy stereotypes to fill in missing information about the program, its consequences, and related matters. For a person with a neg-

---

[8] The items, selected with the help of experts in welfare policy, represent some of the main facts relevant to arguments for or against welfare programs; some of them tend to support welfare and some to oppose it.

ative stereotype, for example, activating the concept of "welfare" might activate "welfare mothers" and "wasteful spending on inessential items." These thoughts would permit inferences, such as that "welfare benefits are too generous," that "government spends a lot on welfare," and so on. The person would then use these inferences to make specific estimates, such as the percentage of the budget that goes to welfare.

We do not yet fully know the dynamics of this process – for example, whether perceptions shape attitudes or vice versa. Most likely it is both. Nor do we suppose that such stereotypes have similar effects in all policy areas. In certain long-standing policy debates, however, systematically biased policy stereotypes should exacerbate the polarization of conflict, exaggerate the intensity of feelings, and produce greater support for radical measures.

Overconfidence

The highest form of knowledge, Socrates famously observed, is knowledge of one's own ignorance. A rational citizen would recognize his or her areas of ignorance about politics, and use this awareness in deciding on which matters to withhold judgment, defer to leaders, or look for more information. It appears, however, that people generally lack that ability.

In the same study of welfare attitudes and perceptions we just described (Kuklinski, Quirk, Schwieder, and Rich 1997), we also measured people's degree of confidence in their factual beliefs. In general, people's accuracy on the welfare items was little better than random guessing. Yet on any given item, a large majority of the respondents said they were very confident or fairly confident that their perceptions were right. Even among respondents in the lower two-thirds of an index of accuracy, 20% reported feeling very confident on all six factual items. Another 40% reported feeling between very and fairly confident on the average item.[9] To be sure, some of this high reporting of confidence stems from the survey interview process itself; nonetheless, the figures are markedly higher than is justified.

From the standpoint of the psychology literature, it is not surprising that people are overconfident in their political beliefs. As research has

---

[9] To ensure that respondents did not merely make casual guesses and then feel compelled to express confidence in them, we examined the relationship between a directional (pro- versus anti-welfare) index of factual beliefs and two questions about welfare policy. The regression equations also included measures of two political orientations (political ideology and partisan identification) and three values (humanitarianism, egalitarianism, and anti-governmentalism), all known to be strongly related to welfare preferences. Even after controlling for these factors, factual beliefs influenced policy preferences in the expected direction. At a minimum, therefore, these beliefs were well integrated into people's attitudes.

171

demonstrated, people express unjustified confidence in their judgments on a wide range of subjects (Allwood and Montgomery 1987; Griffith and Tversky 1992; Mayseless and Kruglanski 1987). Nor is such expression a mere social convention. In one classic study (Fischhoff, Slovic, and Lichtenstein 1977), many respondents were willing to bet their own money on their inaccurate judgments.

Widespread and pronounced overconfidence in political opinions may have mixed consequences for the political process. On the one hand, it may encourage more vigorous participation. On the other hand, however, it may also obstruct deliberation and learning. In some circumstances, it may undermine appropriate trust in elected representatives.

Resistance to Correction

If correct information becomes accessible, rational citizens would be expected to update their beliefs and adjust their policy preferences accordingly. Lack of information should be a matter of costs, not of principle. However, we find evidence that people are inclined to resist or ignore new factual information.

In the welfare study, we gave a randomly selected group of respondents the correct information on the same factual questions about welfare that we described. To focus respondents' attention on the information, we presented each fact separately (in the guise of asking respondents whether they had heard it), and required a response (yes or no). The group thus had the opportunity to update their preferences in light of new and correct information. We then compared their policy preferences to those of respondents who had not received the correct information – whose beliefs, as we have noted, tended to err in an anti-welfare direction. The preferences of the two groups did not differ. The respondents who received correct information apparently either dismissed it or did not incorporate it in their policy preferences.

To probe the limits of such resistance, we undertook a smaller, second study to find out whether people will use factual information when its relevance to their policy preferences is made obtrusively obvious. We divided student respondents into two randomly assigned groups to receive different versions of a questionnaire. For Group 1, we first asked the respondents to estimate the percentage of the budget that goes to welfare. Next we asked them to indicate what percentage *should* go to welfare. We assumed that these items would induce the respondents to contrast their estimated and preferred levels of spending. A respondent might think, for example, "About 20 percent of the budget goes to welfare, but only about 5 percent should go to it." Finally, we

172

asked these respondents to indicate their degree of support for welfare spending.

For Group 2, we also asked the two questions about their estimated and preferred levels of spending. Instead of proceeding immediately to ask about their support for welfare, however, we then told them the correct figure for actual spending. For most respondents, the correct figure was substantially lower than what they had estimated, and even lower than what they had said they preferred. Such respondents were placed in a situation where the relevance of the correct information was hard to miss. Its salience had been drastically (and artificially) inflated, and it implied that actual spending was already below an acceptable level. In contrast with the lack of response to correct information indicated in the survey findings, Group 2 respondents expressed more support for welfare spending than those in Group 1. In this extreme condition, in other words, factual information made a difference.

There are great difficulties in testing for the effects of correct information in survey research – among them, the uncertain appropriateness of any selection of information, and the inability to match real-world conditions for learning and reflection. With that caveat, we believe these findings are suggestive: People appear to have factual premises that are significant to their thinking about policy issues. In some cases, these beliefs are likely to be stereotyped and highly skewed. If people are given correct information, they likely will ignore it – unless it is presented in ways that virtually compel attention and reflection. But such presentations rarely occur in a large-scale democracy.

The Influence of Easy Arguments

When considering a policy proposal, public officials and others make arguments for or against it, which the media then report. Citizens read or hear some of these arguments, and some use them in varying degrees to make up their minds about the issue. Rational citizens will respond mainly to the substantive persuasiveness of the arguments, and not merely their rhetorical features. In fact, however, people respond disproportionately to certain forms of argument – what we call "easy arguments" – even when those arguments lack substance almost entirely.

In a recent study, Cobb and Kuklinski (1997) categorized arguments along two dimensions: pro versus con, and hard versus easy. Pro arguments favor a proposal; con arguments oppose it. More relevant here, hard arguments differ from easy ones in their structure, complexity, and ease of absorption. Hard arguments use reasoning or evidence to support claims about the consequences of a proposal. They take some mental work to understand and likely evoke little emotional response. Easy arguments, in contrast, are simple and symbolic, making strong assertions without providing support. They are designed to have emotional impact: "If NAFTA passes, you'll lose your job." Hard arguments convey more genuine information than easy ones, which hardly convey any at all.

To ascertain how argument types affect persuasion about policy proposals, Cobb and Kuklinski (1997) conducted an across-time experiment in which subjects received one argument at each of three points in time. They gave different groups different types of arguments (hard-con, hard-pro, easy-con, or easy-pro) and measured subjects' policy preferences on NAFTA and national health care at the outset of the experiment and after each exposure to an argument. Although the results differed across the two policy domains, easy arguments (especially easy-con arguments) generally had greater influence than hard ones. Pure assertion, which can evoke emotion and is easily represented in memory, is what most readily changes opinion.

The preference for easy arguments will often affect collective opinion. It will cause distortion whenever one side in a debate can appeal to easy arguments, even if largely misleading, while the other side has more to explain. This occurred, for example, in the brief, one-sided debate over President Clinton's nomination of Lani Guinier to head the Civil Rights Division of the Justice Department. Seizing on her advocacy of cumulative voting systems, opponents labeled Guinier a "Quota Queen" and her ideas "undemocratic." Supporters tried to explain that cumulative voting merely ensures more nearly proportional representation. But that exceedingly hard argument did little to help Guinier's cause. We expect that cases of one-sided advantage in easy arguments are fairly common in political conflict.

Biased Interpretation of Messages

When politicians speak, citizens need to listen. They must do this not only to evaluate leaders and sort them out as allies or opponents, but also to use the politicians' statements as cues to inform their political judgments. Elite messages, however, do not simply pass unchanged through the auditory canals and into the minds of listening citizens. People must interpret them. In doing so, according to some evidence, people often overlook the content of the message and focus on unreliable peripheral cues.

In the spring of 1992, Kuklinski and Hurley (1994, 1996) conducted a survey that asked African-Americans in the Chicago metropolitan area to answer the following item:

174

We would like to get your reaction to a statement that_____recently made. He was quoted in the *New York Times* as saying that "African-Americans must stop making excuses and rely much more on themselves to get ahead in society." Please indicate how much you agree or disagree with_____'s statement.

For each respondent, the ostensible source of the assertion was one of four politicians: George Bush, Clarence Thomas, Ted Kennedy, or Jesse Jackson – respectively, a white conservative, a black conservative, a white liberal, and a black liberal. Respondents were randomly assigned to one of the four sources, and a fifth group received the statement without attribution. All respondents indicated whether they agreed or disagreed with the statement. At a later point, they were asked to recall the statement. Some interpreted the statement, indicating what it meant to them.

Ignoring the source's ideology almost entirely, the respondents agreed with the statement when attributed to either of the black sources and disagreed with it when attributed to either of the white sources. Two different processes explain this pattern. Some of these African-Americans heard the messenger but not the message. As measured by recall, they paid scant attention to the message itself. They based their judgments simply on their trust and affection for the two black political figures. Others heard the message and recalled it, but they interpreted it on the basis of the source's race. When either Bush or Kennedy was the attributed source, blacks construed the statement as "white people are writing us off." When it was Jackson or Thomas, they interpreted it as "we black people can do it on our own." Ironically, it was Jackson and Kennedy who had helped to spearhead the civil rights movement, whereas Bush and Thomas had largely opposed it.

In using race as their primary cue, then, African-Americans ignored the most relevant information available to them, namely, the source's political ideology and record on civil rights. However valuable as a cue a leader's race might be at other times, in this instance it blotted out any awareness of the basic structure of national politics.

Overresponse to Policy Positions

Rational citizens will make some effort to take information for what it's worth. Whenever possible, they will prefer to avoid making decisions on the basis of obviously unreliable inferences. Here too, however, we find that people fall short.

Using other data from the Illinois survey, we considered how people use sketchy information about a candidate's position on a single issue to make voting decisions. Do they discount their judgments on a particular issue when they have hardly any information about it? Or do they treat these judgments as gospel truth?

Our examination of this matter uses two sets of survey questions. One set, incorporating an experimental design, was designed to determine how different pieces of information about a candidate would affect voters' support for him. Respondents were divided randomly into five groups of about 250 to receive different versions of a single question. In all versions, respondents received four items of information about a hypothetical member of Congress who was running for reelection, and then were asked how likely they would be to vote for him. The first three items of information were the same for all groups. Respondents were told that the member was serving his first term; that he had visited the district frequently; and that he had made a speech "that you liked." These common items were intended to establish a moderately favorable presumption in favor of the incumbent.

The experimental manipulation concerned the fourth item, which was different in each group. Group 1 was given the innocuous datum that the incumbent was 47 years old. It provides a baseline, representing the support that would occur with no negative information. Group 2 was told that the incumbent was frequently absent from Congress and had missed a number of important votes. It gauges the loss of support from evidence of a general failure to perform: the electoral penalty for substantial nonfeasance. Group 1 and 2 responses set the upper and lower bounds of support, respectively.

Each of the remaining groups was told of a different hypothetical vote the incumbent had cast – each of which we expected many respondents to disapprove. The statements were that the incumbent "had voted against a major bill to reduce the budget deficit" (Group 3); that he had "voted to cut medical care for the elderly" (Group 4); or that he had "voted to cut medical care for the poor" (Group 5). We did not identify these items as criticisms. But the items did describe the votes with the blunt expression of negative campaign advertising. As in such advertising, we provided no information about the provisions of the bill the member had supported or opposed, the rationale for the member's vote, the alternatives, or the likely consequences.

To state the findings simply, people tend to make an electoral mountain out of a policy molehill. In the baseline group (Group 1), only 12% of respondents said they were unlikely to vote for the candidate (see Table 8.1). Given some mildly positive information about an incumbent and no negative information, few wanted to throw him out. Confronted with the habitual no-show, by contrast, 64% of Group 2 respondents withdrew support. As we expected, people deemed frequent absence from important votes a serious failure.

Table 8.1. *Support for hypothetical member of Congress, given*
various types of information

	Likelihood of vote for the incumbent	
Information	Very or fairly likely	Not very or not at all likely
47 years old	78%	12%
often absent and missed votes on important bills	30	64
voted against a major bill to cut the budget deficit	68	25
voted to cut medical care for the elderly		
all respondents	45	52
respondents opposing Medicare cuts (74%)	34	64
voted to cut medical care for the poor		
all respondents	45	50
respondents opposing Medicaid cuts (66%)	35	65

Most important, responses in the issue-item conditions resemble those in the no-show case. The vote against a major deficit-reduction bill had the weakest effect, with a rejection rate of 25% (Group 3). Votes to cut health care for the elderly or for the poor were more powerful, eliciting rejection from 52% and 50% of respondents, respectively (Groups 4 and 5) – nearly the effect of nonattendance. Moreover, respondents who said later in the interview that they opposed cuts in the relevant program expressed an even greater disposition – equivalent to that for the no-show – to punish the incumbent for these votes. Judging from this evidence, then, people do not discount casual and uninformed judgments about policy positions. To the contrary, respondents were as willing to penalize a member of Congress for a single vote, on a complex issue described in a single phrase, as they were to penalize a member who often didn't vote at all.

The second set of questions was designed to determine whether such decisions to punish on a single issue even reflected people's policy preferences on that issue accurately. We measured support not only for cutting the Medicare and Medicaid programs generally but also for several specific approaches to doing so – options for reducing the programs' costs that had been actively considered around the time of the survey.[10] In fact, many of the respondents who would have punished an incumbent for cutting these programs themselves supported or had "no feeling" about some of these measures. On Medicaid, a 56%–29% majority of such respondents favored transferring responsibility to the states. On Medicare, 79% favored reducing benefits for high-income recipients. In a word, a great deal of the electoral punishment was, from the standpoint of the respondents' own policy preferences, undeserved.

To be sure, we have presented evidence from a highly simplified survey experiment. Nonetheless, two well-documented cognitive biases – overconfidence and the fundamental attribution error – predict such an overresponse to minimal information about candidates' policy positions (Allwood and Montgomery 1987; Fiske and Taylor 1991: 67–72; Griffith and Tversky 1992; Heider 1958; Ross 1977; Mayseless and Kruglanski 1987). People overconfident in their judgments don't ponder alternative positions; and people who attribute an incumbent's vote entirely to his personal dispositions don't stop to consider that he might have voted in response to compelling circumstances. If people are quick to conclude, even with minimal evidence, that a vote was objectionable and that an incumbent cast it from bad motives, we should not wonder that negative, highly misleading political advertising is effective (Ansolabehere and Iyengar 1995).

Of course, the large effects of these survey items do not imply comparable impacts on voting in an actual election. Even assuming a far smaller actual impact, however, an excessive and erroneous response to a major campaign issue might swing the result in a competitive race. And even more likely, it might send powerful and misleading signals about issues to policy makers. Finally, the overresponse to sketchy and tendentious issue appeals explains why there are "third rails" in politics,

---

[10] Respondents were divided randomly into two groups, for questions about either Medicare or Medicaid, and were given four options to support or oppose: reducing the health-care services that beneficiaries received; requiring that services be obtained through prepaid plans like HMOs; requiring beneficiaries to pay more money out of pocket for health care; and (for Medicare) reducing benefits for high-income recipients, or (for Medicaid) transferring authority to the states.

issues that responsible policy makers want to address but dare not touch.

Judging from all this research, then, various and sometimes severe distortions can occur in people's political judgments. They hold inaccurate and stereotyped factual beliefs, hold their beliefs overconfidently, resist correct information, prefer easy arguments, interpret elite statements according to racial or other biases, and rely heavily on scanty information about a candidate's policy positions.

A skeptic could still argue that such distortions are only of marginal importance in politics. Our findings almost certainly overstate their real impact. One reason is simply that people may behave differently in answering a survey than they do in other aspects of political life. (Of course, answering surveys is itself part of political life.) A second reason is that each of our studies deals narrowly with certain elements of political judgment – factual beliefs, responses to issue positions, influences of different sorts of argument, and so on. In real-world politics, political judgments could have so many elements and be affected by so many stimuli that none of the cognitive errors people make would have much impact. Cognitive errors could cancel out, not only in collective opinion but even at the individual level. In the next section, therefore, we introduce some evidence that more directly addresses real-world political consequences.

COLLECTIVE BIAS: FURTHER EVIDENCE

Two kinds of observation bear more directly on the role of cognitive distortion in real-world mass politics. One concerns changes in opinion that occur in so-called deliberative polls; the other, the events of policy making in certain areas of high salience. Neither sort of evidence, it should be emphasized, is without significant ambiguity. Taken together, however, they provide some additional support for our line of argument.

The well-known deliberative polls that James Fishkin and Robert Luskin have conducted permit comparisons between a representative group of citizens and an obviously pertinent better-informed group – namely, the same individuals after they have been brought together for a weekend of intensive learning and deliberation (Fishkin 1997). Assuming that the deliberations improve information and reduce error, we can use the difference in opinion before and after deliberation as a crude indicator of the error.

Consider, in this light, some of the results. In a 1996 Austin, Texas, gathering, support for a flat tax decreased from 44% before deliberation to 30% afterward; support for a tax reduction for savings increased from 66% to 83%; support for maintaining current levels of foreign aid increased from 26% to 41%. There were even larger shifts in a series of regional deliberative polls on energy issues. In one, for example, support for increased reliance on renewable energy fell from 67% before the deliberation to 16% afterward; support for investment in conservation increased from 11% to 46%. It turns out, then, that on a variety of issues, people's initial preferences deviated substantially from their more informed and deliberative ones (Fishkin 1997: 214–220).

This evidence has certain limitations. Most important from our standpoint, one might interpret the findings alternatively – namely, that the briefings or discussions were themselves biased, and that the changes in aggregate opinion merely reflect that bias. Yet that account of the changes does not appear very likely. Fishkin and his associates work diligently to ensure balance in the briefings and deliberations. Participants themselves consider them fair.[11] We find it more plausible, therefore, to regard the findings as evidence of error, in relation to well-informed opinion, in pre-deliberative public opinion.

Although even more subject to interpretation, the ultimate real-world test of the importance of collective bias lies with its influence, if any, on public policy making. If collective opinion is indeed often biased, and if the bias does indeed affect policy making – both assertions we have not proved – then a variety of important policies should exhibit the expected effects. In fact, although alternative accounts are readily available, there is no shortage of plausible cases. In the rest of the section, we will merely sketch a few such cases and comment briefly on the general issues of interpretation.

The most widely criticized feature of national policy in recent decades was the running of massive federal-budget deficits from the early 1980s to the mid-1990s (Kettl 1992). Such deficits originated with President Reagan's use of unorthodox, highly optimistic fiscal projections in appealing to voters in the 1980 presidential campaign (Campagna 1994; Stein 1984). After the election, Reagan used popular support to push his supply-side tax cut through a skeptical Congress (Kernell 1993). Efforts to reduce the deficit in subsequent years often foundered on public resistance to tax increases and spending cuts and on political rhetoric designed to exploit that resistance.

After the collapse of the Soviet Union, the United States responded only very modestly to Russian requests for large-scale economic assistance to help ensure a successful transition to liberal democracy (Mroz 1993; Snyder 1996). In view of the United States's huge stake in the

---

[11] In the January 1996 poll, about 81% of the participants agreed that the briefing materials were "mostly balanced," and 94% felt that the group leaders had not sought to influence opinions (Fishkin 1997: 224).

Russian reforms, such aid had strong support in the foreign-policy community. But a major economic-aid program for Russia ran up against the public's general aversion to foreign aid and its specific hostility toward former communists. American policy makers largely deferred to the public's reluctance. Indeed, former President Richard Nixon publicly chastised President Bush for his failure to lead on the issue.

A great deal of economic analysis suggests that federal environmental regulations have often been unduly severe – with costs of compliance vastly exceeding estimated benefits (Crandall 1997; Landy et al. 1990). Indeed, according to estimates by the nonpartisan Government Accounting Office, the costs of the ozone standards adopted by the Environmental Protection Agency in 1997 will exceed their benefits by approximately a factor of 10 (Crandall 1997). The severity of such regulations appears to reflect the public's virtually automatic support for strong pollution controls and general unawareness of the resulting costs (Landy et al. 1990: 280–282). There are similar accounts of policy making on energy pricing, nuclear power, welfare reform, criminal sentencing, and Social Security, among other areas.

As we have suggested, the interpretation of such cases is not straightforward. In particular, ordinary citizens may just disagree with the presumed experts, who in any case are never unanimous. The public may reject most experts' view of the world on some rational grounds. After the collapse of the Soviet Union, for example, people may have believed for cogent reasons that economic aid would not help the Russian democracy. Alternatively, the public may value different objectives than those that the more informed take for granted. People may have wanted to deny aid to former communists more than they wanted stability in Russia. On such accounts, a more informed public would still reach the same conclusions.

In some of these cases, however, policy making may indeed reflect bias and error in mass judgment. Often, these errors arise because one group of elites tries strategically to evoke them for purposes of gathering public support. Returning to our example, we find the following account at least plausible: Most people knew very little about the situation in Russia. They thus were highly susceptible to the influence of symbolism, emotional memories, and other sources of error. Some politicians exploited the resistance and helped intensify it; others played it safe and did not vigorously advocate aid. The result was a stingy aid program that put the nation's vital interest in a democratic Russia at risk.

CONCLUSION AND IMPLICATIONS

We have cautioned against overly optimistic accounts of a politically competent, rational public. Not only are citizens minimally informed, as nearly all scholars agree, but they are also prone to bias and error in using the limited information they receive. As a result, they will sometimes send distorted signals to policy makers, which in turn can exert perverse influences on public policy.

We have not sought to specify the conditions under which cognitive error in mass opinion causes serious difficulties for democratic politics. In closing, we will offer a general speculation with broad implications for the condition of American political institutions.

The risk of distortion in mass opinion, we believe, will depend on where people focus their attention and on what kinds of judgment they attempt to make. In general, people should do better when they make inferences from the broader and longer-standing features of politics: political parties, social groups, ideologies, and established leaders. Heuristics based on these features should work, when people actually use them. People should have more difficulty when they make inferences from or directly assess narrower or shorter-term features: singular events, aspiring leaders, changing social or economic conditions, and, in particular, specific policies. Thus, for example, using party labels to evaluate candidates will work fairly well for most citizens in most races. But using campaign appeals about issues to evaluate candidates or parties will work much less well – and will often create perverse incentives for policy makers.

If this distinction is generally correct, there is cause for concern about developments in American politics. The citizenry has increasingly focused attention on the elements of politics where it is likely to make unreliable judgments. Citizens' attachments to and concern about political parties have declined in recent decades. With the rise of primary elections, the voters are now directly responsible for assessing the aspiring leaders in nomination contests. And with the rise of public opinion polls, decision making by referendum, and issue-oriented political campaigns, they are increasingly called upon to choose specific policies. In short, American politics probably has become more susceptible to distortions in mass opinion in recent years.

9

Three Steps toward a Theory of Motivated Political Reasoning

MILTON LODGE AND CHARLES TABER

The human understanding, when it has once adopted an opinion . . . draws all things else to support and agree with it. Though there may be (more) instances to be found on the other side, yet these it either neglects or despises, or else by some distinction sets aside and rejects.

– Francis Bacon, *New Organon* (1621)

In this essay we propose a theory of motivated reasoning that can account for why both ordinary citizens and political sophisticates are prone to follow Bacon's dictum. Three subtheories – hot cognition, on-line processing, and a "how-do-I-feel?" heuristic – working together, provide a three-step mechanism for how we believe citizens think and reason about political leaders, groups, and issues.

This tripartite theory of motivated reasoning starts with the notion that all social concepts are affect laden; all social information is affectively charged (Bargh 1994, 1997; Fazio, Sanbonmatsu, Powell, and Kardes 1986; Fazio and Williams 1986; Lodge and Stroh 1993; Taber, Lodge, and Glathar 2000). This is the *hot cognition hypothesis* (Abelson 1963). Specific to politics, all political leaders, groups, issues, and ideas you have thought about and evaluated in the past are now affectively charged – positively or negatively, strongly or weakly – and this affective tag is stored directly with the concept in long-term memory.

On-line processing (Anderson and Hubert 1963; Lodge, Steenbergen, and Brau 1995; Park and Pennington 1986) is a mechanism for updating the value of affective tags attached to concepts in memory. The OL

Research funded by NSF Grant SES-931351. With special thanks to Aron Galonsky, Jeff Jones, and Jason Lucas for helping to program, run, and analyze the hot cognition experiment, and to the numerous scholars who saved us from even more grievous errors, among them: Bob Boynton, Joe Cappella, Nehemia Geva, Jim Gibson, Brian Jones, "Skip" Lupia, Mat McCubbins, Kristen Monroe, and Sam Popkin.

183

theory holds that when people see their task as forming or revising an overall impression of a person, place, event, or idea, they automatically extract the affective value of the message and then spontaneously, when the information is before their eyes so to speak, revise their summary evaluation of the object (Lodge, McGraw, and Stroh 1989; Sanbonmatsu and Fazio 1990). This OL Tally – representing a running score of all prior evaluations (minus a decay function) – is then rejoined to the concept and restored to LTM where it is available for subsequent evaluations of that person, group, event, or issue.

And finally, when one is asked explicitly or implicitly for an evaluation of a political object, a *"how-do-I-feel?" heuristic* (Clore and Isbell 1996) captures the affective tally attached to the concept and "moves" it into working memory, thereby signaling the affective coloration of the object, "telling" the individual at the moment of recognition how much she or he likes or dislikes him (her, it). At the instant you comprehend an object, say at the very moment you realize that the letters C-L-I-N-T-O-N in a news headline signify the concept Clinton, your affect toward Clinton comes to mind. The crucial hypotheses, of course, are where, when, and how this affective tag colors the subsequent processing information on Clinton.

Working in tandem, the tripartite model unitizes affect and cognition. Feelings become information. The three subtheories – for better or worse – couple together affect and cognition in long-term memory and bring them simultaneously to mind in the judgment process. Hot cognition says that all political objects are affectively charged; the on-line model provides a mechanism for updating these affective tallies; and the "how-do-I-feel?" heuristic automatically brings this affect to bear on the judgment process. Should this theory of motivated reasoning prove to be a reasonable approximation of how people routinely think about government and politics, it would have important substantive and normative implications. The clear expectation is that most, if not all, citizens will be *biased reasoners*, finding it nearly impossible to evaluate any new information in an evenhanded way. The tendency is to evaluate incoming information to support preconception and to devalue contrary evidence. These processes may be conscious, as when a lawyer makes a case, but the tripartite model suggests a more insidious bias toward preconception in the very mental mechanisms on which citizens rely for all information processing.

The three mechanisms, which we see as typically acting in consort, simplify the processing of information by freeing one from having to compute an evaluation piecemeal from an object's attributes. Bias – the failure to treat evidence fairly – will most likely creep into reasoning processes when

- one's attitudes are challenged (Kunda 1990; Stevens and Fiske 1995);
- an affective judgment is called for (Fazio 1995);
- one's attitude is strong (Abelson 1987; Krosnick and Petty 1995);
- the consequences of being wrong are weak (Tetlock 1985);
- the judgmental task is complex (Eagly and Chaiken 1993);
- "objective" information is not readily available or the evidence is ambiguous (Tversky and Kahneman 1974);
- disconfirming evidence is not highlighted (Klayman and Ha 1987);
- counterarguments come easily to mind (Lord, Ross, and Lepper 1979);
- one is distracted or under time pressure (Petty and Cacioppo 1986b).

To our way of thinking, each of these contextual factors is characteristic of how most citizens routinely confront the political system. From this perspective, then, emotion and reasoning are inseparable, unitized in memory, and therefore next to impossible to disentangle in the everyday course of information processing. This being the case, we think it likely that most citizens most of the time will be decidedly "partisan" in what and how they think about and reason about political leaders, groups, events, and issues.

In this chapter, we lay out the arguments for how and why the simple mechanisms of hot cognition, on-line processing, and the "how-do-I-feel?" heuristic work together automatically to promote motivated political reasoning, and then in the discussion, make the argument that this reliance on one's affective on-line tally is not necessarily bad or "irrational." In fact, we argue that the summoning up of one's OL Tally by the "how-do-I-feel?" heuristic is both a virtue and a vice (Clore and Isbell 1996): On the plus side, the reliance on the affective tally allows one to avoid the more cognitively taxing task of constructing a judgment from whatever evidence is available in memory. Empirically, the OL Tally proves to be a better summing up of one's past evaluative experiences than are preferences based on the recollection of pros and cons that come to mind on the spur of the moment (Sanbonmatsu and Fazio 1990), or worse yet, evaluations based on the reasons people give when they are asked explicitly why they like or dislike some person, place, or thing (Nisbett and Wilson 1977; Wilson and Hodges 1992). Moreover, recent evidence from neurology (Damasio 1994) suggests that the mechanisms of motivated reasoning provide vital direction for the reasoning process. Without them, people may be unable to establish and pursue goals, perhaps the most basic requirement of rational information processing (Elster 1989; Lupia and McCubbins 1998; Morrow 1994). But – this is the rub – the very same mechanisms that promote and bring the on-line tally to mind are very likely to bias the processing of new information, since decision makers "know" how much they like or dislike the political object *as they are evaluating the new evidence,* and they also know whether or not a new piece of tally-relevant information is pro or con.

A THEORY OF MOTIVATED REASONING

There is a good deal of evidence in both psychology (Anderson and Hubert 1963; Hastie and Park 1986; Hastie and Pennington 1989) and political science (Lodge, McGraw, and Stroh 1989; Lodge, Steenbergen, and Brau 1995) that evaluations are drawn on-line, in real time, with summary impressions updated on the fly at the moment of recognition after but one or two exposures (Park 1989). In much of this research, the focus has been on how information is integrated into a summary evaluation of people, places, ideas, and things, with results typically showing that the summary impression reflects one's evaluation of the object better than does the individual's recollection of the factors that originally contributed to the evaluation. Much of this research, ours included, treats the individual decision maker as a passive responder to whatever messages happen to impinge on consciousness, the simple updating rule being to increment one's OL Tally if the message is positive, decrement if negative (Boynton and Lodge 1994). This is surely a bizarre portrait of human reasoning, too lifeless even for homo-not-so-sapiens, for we know that oftentimes people do not simply accept information at face value but sometimes mull it over, denigrating and counterarguing evidence that doesn't match their expectations or fit their predilections. In this chapter, we extend the analysis of OL processing to the study of political reasoning and suggest mechanisms for how and why this affective tally – once formed for a candidate, party, or issue – will likely influence *subsequent information processing,* typically promoting biased decision making. We seek an account of when and how citizens collect, assess, reassess, and integrate political information in a biased way.

Our starting premise (following Kunda 1987, 1990) is that *all reasoning is motivated.* Keeping it simple and focusing on reasoning about things political, citizens are goal oriented. Their motives fall into two broad categories: accuracy goals, which motivate them to reach a correct or otherwise optimal conclusion (Baumeister and Newman 1994; Fiske and Taylor 1991), and directional goals, which motivate them to justify a specific, preselected conclusion (Kruglanski and Webster 1996). Crossing these two goal dimensions yields a four-category typology, depicted in Figure 9.1. Neither of these goal dimensions is ever entirely absent, apart from the ideal worlds of philosophy and fiction, and so the two dimensions in Figure 9.1 range from weak to strong goals of each type.

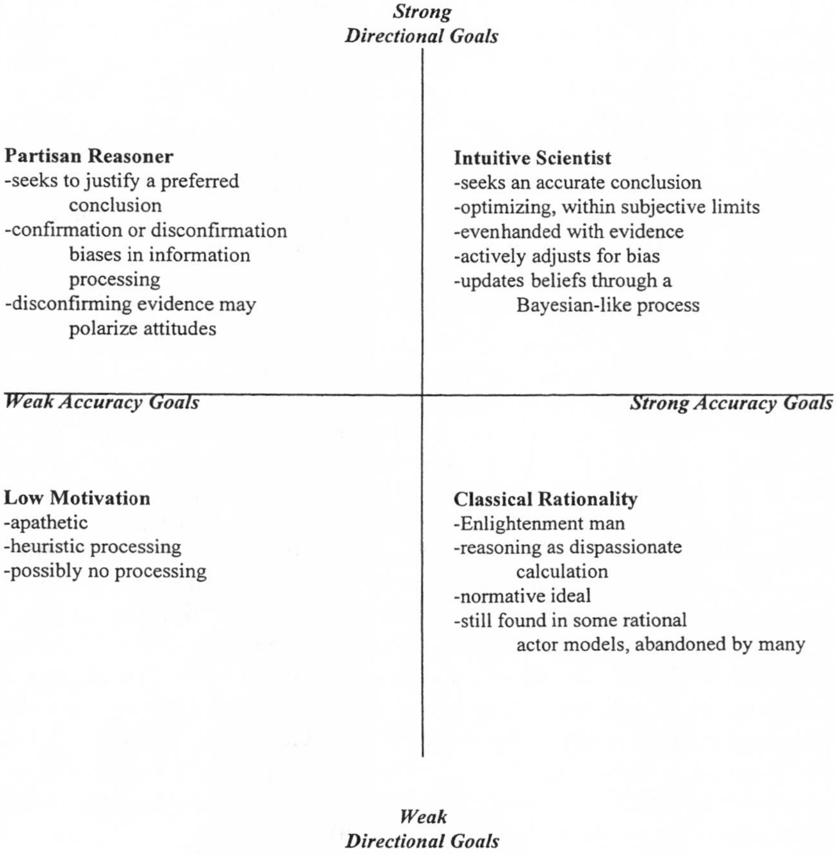

Strong
Directional Goals

Partisan Reasoner
-seeks to justify a preferred
    conclusion
-confirmation or disconfirmation
    biases in information
    processing
-disconfirming evidence may
    polarize attitudes

Intuitive Scientist
-seeks an accurate conclusion
-optimizing, within subjective limits
-evenhanded with evidence
-actively adjusts for bias
-updates beliefs through a
    Bayesian-like process

Weak Accuracy Goals   *Strong Accuracy Goals*

Low Motivation
-apathetic
-heuristic processing
-possibly no processing

Classical Rationality
-Enlightenment man
-reasoning as dispassionate
    calculation
-normative ideal
-still found in some rational
    actor models, abandoned by many

Weak
Directional Goals

Figure 9.1. A typology of motivated reasoning.

Citizens are always motivated, in some measure, to be accurate, but they are unable completely to ignore their preconceptions and prior affect. The constant tension between the drives for optimal accuracy and belief perseverance underlies all political reasoning.

Figure 9.1 distinguishes four types of motivated reasoning as a function of the relative mix of accuracy and directional motivation. First, in situations that excite little motivation, depicted in the lower left quadrant, citizens will be relatively apathetic. They will be unwilling to expend much effort in processing information and will most likely rely on simple heuristics for any decisions they make. Second, the lower right quadrant represents situations with strong accuracy but weak directional goals. This is the normative ideal of classical rationality that has been the target of a wide variety of philosophical and empirical criticisms. Here, citizens will be largely motivated by a concern for "optimal accuracy"; they should process information dispassionately and completely. Many rational-choice and game theorists today consider this view a straw man, arguing for a narrower and more subjective (dare we say psychological!) view of rationality (e.g., Elster 1989; Lupia and McCubbins this volume; Morrow 1994), which may be found in the third quadrant of Figure 9.1. This "rational decision maker" carefully weighs pros and cons in order to maximize the likelihood of achieving preferences. When so motivated to be *intuitive scientists,* people are most likely to work toward their goal by attempting a thorough search and evenhanded evaluation of the evidence. Aware that they are also subject to directional goals, these intuitive scientists actively adjust – sometimes even overadjust – for biases in information processing. Despite their best efforts, however, we suspect that few "rationalists" will truly escape their prejudices, preconceptions, and prior passions. The most rigorous scientists have their preferred theories and so will intuitive scientists. Finally, the upper left quadrant depicts the *partisan reasoner,* who seeks to support a preferred goal or evaluation. Biases in information processing will be more pronounced as partisans actively counterargue contrary information while too readily accepting supporting information. There are limits, however, to the lengths to which partisans will go to preserve preconceptions. They still feel some pressure, albeit weak, for at least the "illusion of objectivity" (Pyszczynski and Greenberg 1987). Indeed, the persuasion literature clearly shows that even those committed to their positions can be persuaded by strong and credible counterevidence (Festinger 1957; Petty and Cacioppo 1986).

Though differences may exist in individual styles of reasoning (e.g., "need for cognition"), we believe that the more interesting differences in modes of reasoning stem from contextual variation. The same citizen may exhibit low motivation in one context, be evenhanded in another context, and partisan in a third. Our theory is aimed at explaining the impact of these contextual variations on information processing, rather than developing another personality typology. In other words, political reasoning is driven by the interaction of individual motivation and situational context. To place this theory of motivated reasoning in perspective, we start with a simple depiction in Figure 9.2 of the processing steps people may go through when reasoning about a persuasive message. We will describe the steps briefly in terms of the rationalist decision maker and then return to a discussion of partisan reasoners after laying out a more detailed process model.

Three Steps toward a Theory

DECISION STEPS	
1	**Problem Definition/Goal Activation**
2	**Gathering Evidence**
3	**Assessing Implications**
4	**Reassessment**
5	**Integration**

Figure 9.2. Stepwise decision model.

Step 1. Defining the Problem/Establishing Goals. Something in the environment attracts attention, raising a question or problem that confronts or sets up a goal. Problems are typically interpreted by reference to how things worked out in the past, to prior cases, examples, or analogies, which may now be activated because of their perceived similarity to the current situation (Holyoak and Thagard 1995; Khong 1992; Taber forthcoming). If the problem is salient, goals are established and the judgment process begins. Accuracy goals, which are strengthened when one expects the judgment to have real personal consequences, lead to the consideration of multiple possible cases or analogies. That is, alternative interpretations of the problem may be considered by an intuitive scientist in an effort to be impartial and open to varying perspectives on the problem.

Step 2. Gathering Evidence. Sometimes one is a passive, exposure-driven witness to information, as is often the case when watching the evening news with one eye open (Iyengar and Kinder 1987), which typically triggers one or another heuristic that will skim the surface of the message (Mondak 1993; Pratkanis 1989; Sniderman, Brody, and Tetlock 1994). At other times, the very same individual may take a more active role, perhaps by searching long-term memory for similarities between one or another characteristic of the issue and some analogous representation in memory (Zaller 1994), or by looking through the newspaper for details about a particular story (Lau and Redlawsk forthcoming), or by asking a friend's opinion about some political leader or issue (Huckfeldt and Sprague 1995; Mutz 1992). More active processing will occur when motivation is strong. Accuracy goals spark deeper, broader, and a more evenhanded search for evidence, as the intuitive scientist seeks the truth.

Step 3. Assessing Implications. One becomes immediately aware of the implications of each piece of information in the message brought to mind

189

in Step 2. This is an *automatic process* of spreading activation, as associations (Neely 1963) and the implications of messages spontaneously
"pop" to mind without conscious effort or design (Uleman and Bargh
1989).

Step 4. Reassessment of Implications. Here, one consciously reassesses
the automatic implications drawn in Step 3, perhaps by rethinking their
credibility or importance. Although the step from evidence to implication is automatic – meaning that the implications cannot be prevented
from becoming conscious – an individual could, given the cognitive
wherewithal and sufficient motivation, choose to reassess, modify, or
reject the implications of associations activated by the message (Devine
1989). The intuitive scientist may actively try to ferret out and correct
for biases that may have emerged in the automatic retrieval of implications from memory.

Step 5. The Integrating of Information. The evidence and implications
must at some point be drawn together into a summary assessment of the
person, problem or object. When motivated to be accurate, people will
try to weigh all the evidence impartially before reaching a conclusion.
If the evidence or implications are in conflict or are ambiguous – an
all-too-common outcome awaiting those who scrupulously seek out all
relevant evidence – the integration of evidence into a summary judgment may not be easy. Many different models have been suggested
for integrating considerations into a summary judgment (Taber and
Steenbergen 1995). Though virtually all models put this step last,
people oftentimes reach preliminary conclusions at earlier points in the
overall judgment process (Berelson, Lazarsfeld, and McPhee 1954;
Campbell, Converse, Stokes, and Miller 1960) or rethink a choice when
some event reframes the issue (Jones 1994). Figure 9.2 indicates an
"ideal" rather than a necessary or even typical ordering of steps.

Our goal is to pull these processes into a model of motivated political reasoning that can account for why it is that biases can so easily over-
whelm the objective quality of arguments and why it is that many a
seemingly good rationalist turns into a partisan reasoner in the course
of evaluating political candidates and issues. What we have to date are
three pieces to the puzzle: the theories of "hot cognition" and OL processing, and the "how-do-I-feel" heuristic.

THE ARCHITECTURE OF MOTIVATED REASONING

Because the devil lives in the details, in this chapter we need to look
closely at the cognitive architecture underlying these information-

processing mechanisms (Lodge and Stroh 1993). A cornerstone of any model of political reasoning is the citizen's preexisting knowledge and predilections. These long-term factors – functionally speaking – require firstly a *long-term memory* (LTM) for retaining one's beliefs and predispositions, and secondly a *mechanism* for "moving" one's knowledge about leaders, parties, and issues from long-term memory into *working memory* (WM) where it can be processed (Rummelhart and Norman 1977; Sanford 1986). Think of working memory as that small part of LTM that you are consciously attending to at the moment. Attention is very limited, perhaps to the magic number 7 ± 2 bits or chunks of information, hence the need for heuristics and other simplifying mechanisms for thinking and reasoning.

LTM is organized associatively, much of it structured conceptually. We can represent knowledge structures in LTM as a configuration of *nodes* linked to one another in a network of associations and a spreading activation mechanism for "moving" information from LTM to WM and back again. Semantic node-link networks can represent all kinds of concepts. Figure 9.3a depicts a fragment of one citizen's concept of Bill Clinton.

Were we able to tap a citizen's complete political knowledge structure, there would be tens of thousands of nodes with many connections to and from Clinton, including perhaps his demographics (Clinton is president), looks (tall), stand on issues (pro death penalty), perceived traits (intelligent; wishy-washy), and maybe an abstraction or two (that he is "sort of" liberal).

As depicted in Figure 9.3b, nodes are connected by *links,* representing the association among nodes. Each link between nodes depicts the nature of the node-to-node relation. Links represent a belief or what Judd and Krosnick (1989) call an "implicational relation." These associations can be positive (represented here by a plus sign) or negative (a minus sign). Here, our good citizen believes CLINTON is a DEMOCRAT and believes Clinton favors gun control, but that Clinton is not likely to cut taxes.

The next key element of semantic network models (depicted in Figure 9.3c) is the notion of *belief strength*. The strength of association between nodes is represented here by the size of the plus and minus signs: The more strongly an individual believes one concept is related to another, the greater the probability that the activation of that node will energize its linked nodes in the network. This respondent is confident that CLINTON is a Democrat, less sure that he is "pro gun control," and only somewhat confident he will not cut taxes.

To get a network model to work, we also need the notion of *node strength*, depicted in Figure 9.3d by the thickness of the circles depict-

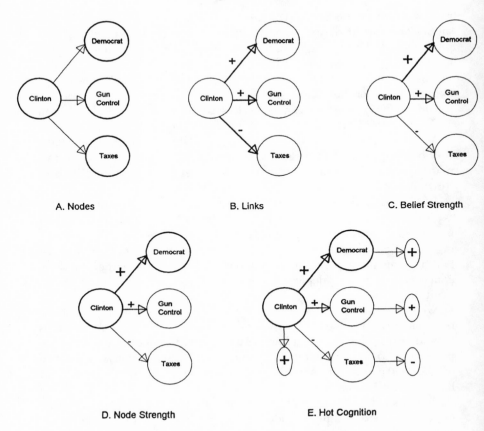

Figure 9.3. Node-link architecture of political beliefs and attitudes.

ing nodes. Node strength represents the accessibility of a node in LTM – the ease by which a stored attribute that is laying dormant in long-term memory can be retrieved from LTM – that is, its probability of being energized and "popped" into working memory. Here, both CLINTON and DEMOCRAT have great node strength, making them readily (perhaps even chronically) accessible considerations in the judgmental process, whereas the gun control and taxes issues have less node strength (Lau 1989). Which nodes come to mind, that is, get into WM – *a node's accessibility* – is a function of the frequency, consistency, and recency of activation, and contextual triggers of the message.

All well and good, that is the *classic, cognitive model* of information processing. The problem with this model and virtually all such cognitive models is that they are silent about the role of affect in the judgmental

192

process. This is a major shortcoming inasmuch as the sociopolitical world is characterized by affect-laden beliefs (what we, following Bob Abelson [1963, 1973] call "hot cognition"), and consequently such purely cognitive models fail to provide a realistic account of how evaluations of candidates, parties, and issues are formed, maintained, and revised.

Knowledge structures that integrate cognition with affect can be represented in a node-link structure, as in Figure 9.3e. We posit that affect is attached *directly* to its conceptual node. The plus and minus signs with each node depict this citizen's positive feelings toward Clinton and toward gun control, but to taxes, negative. This model, taking its lead from Fazio and his colleagues (1986a, 1986b, 1995), brings affect center stage (Fiske 1981, 1982; Sears, Huddy, and Schaffer 1986), in positing that every node in memory that had been evaluated in the past is now affectively charged, "hot," that is, stored in LTM with an OL Tally attached, some objects positively charged, others negatively. To wit: All objects in LTM representing sociopolitical concepts are *affect laden,* have "tag strength," which varies from weak to strong, as indicated in Figure 9.3e by the size of the plus or minus sign.

That is our architectural depiction of a knowledge system. Well and good, but how does information get from LTM to WM? The mechanism is called *spreading activation.* Activation represents the "firing" or energizing of a node as a result of seeing, hearing, or thinking about that concept. In this process, the node in LTM switches from being dormant to a state of readiness with the potential to be moved into WM. (Were you just thinking of George Washington's wooden teeth? Are you now?)

The top panel of Figure 9.4 (adapted from Barsalou 1992: 46) depicts the *activation process,* the process whereby information is popped into WM from its dormant state in LTM. On the Y axis is level of activation; on the X axis is time (measured in thousands of a second). The rise time from dormant-state baseline to its recognition threshold is almost instantaneous, on the order of 20 to 100 milliseconds. Given sufficient "node strength," activation moves concepts from LTM to WM where they can be processed. Not depicted here but of great consequence is the rapid decay rate of activation. Unless reactivated or somehow kept in conscious memory, activation potential decays quickly, on the order of a couple of hundred milliseconds.

To follow the activation process, imagine that the person reads the word "Clinton" in a newspaper headline. As the concept CLINTON becomes active – it pops into consciousness. As the concept CLINTON is energized, activation spreads along its associated links to related concepts, thereby *priming* in our good citizen such strong semantic associ-

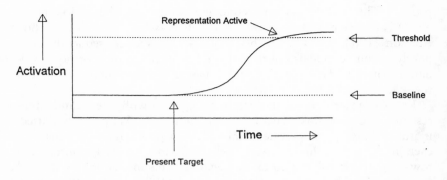

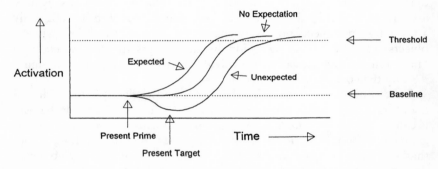

Figure 9.4. Activation of a concept in LTM.

ations of CLINTON as he is a DEMOCRAT. Priming means that as activation reaches these associated connections, their activation also begins to rise above baseline.

Think of priming through spreading activation as producing expectations. The bottom panel of Figure 9.4 shows the activation of associations under different expectations. First, consider how the activation of one node primes the detection of its *expected categories*. Start with "Clinton" in a newspaper headline. When a category is expected – say, for example, the word CLINTON priming DEMOCRAT – the activation level for DEMOCRAT rises above baseline, thereby requiring less activation to pass threshold, and thereby increasing the probability of this association popping into working memory. So, priming *facilitates the linking up of associations in LTM*. Seeing, hearing, or thinking about Clinton facilitates the speedy recognition and categorization of his strongest associations, thereby contributing to the coherence of thought inasmuch as associated concepts (e.g., DEMOCRAT) have a better chance of getting into WM, being processed faster and "framing" the interpretation of subsequent information.

Now consider how spreading activation can *inhibit* the processing of *un*expected categories. If an instance occurs unexpectedly, more bottom-up processing is necessary for the concept to pass threshold and enter into WM. So, for example, if the word "Flowers" were categorized initially, this would inhibit the recognition of unrelated concepts, such as "CLINTON" or "DEMOCRAT," and would consequently require more time and effort to categorize them. So, *inhibition decreases* the speed of categorization and the probability that unrelated concepts will come to mind. The middle course in Figure 9.4 is a control condition. So, for example, if the prime were BBB ("triple B") – conveying no semantic expectations – it would give no information about what would likely follow and neither facilitate nor inhibit the recognition and categorization of concepts.

THE MECHANISMS FOR MOTIVATED REASONING

Simple though it may be – essentially an affect-enabled ACT* model (Anderson 1983, 1993) – this simple node-link model with affective tags can account for many of the characteristics of human information processing (Boynton and Lodge 1996). Moving in step with contemporary thinking about attitudes (Fazio 1995; Petty and Krosnick 1995), we view attitude as an association in memory between an object and a summary evaluation of the object, with the term "object" being defined very broadly to include people, places, ideas, things, and events. In the simplest version, the summary evaluation is unidimensional, representing a single distillation of judgments made on-line as stimulus information is processed. The associative strength between an object (e.g., politician) and its evaluation (bad) is conceived as varying along a continuum from nil, an object with little or no affective association (from this perspective a "nonattitude," Converse 1970; Fazio 1986) to objects with strong associative strength. Whereas nonattitudes require effortful retrieval, the stronger the association between an object in memory and its affective evaluation, the less effort needed to bring the attitude to mind, with objects carrying strong tag strength being activated almost effortlessly, perhaps automatically on their mere exposure (see Bargh, Chaiken, Govender, and Pratto 1992). What makes the notion of automaticity important is the finding that many (possibly most) attitudes are *chronically accessible on their mere exposure*; that is, the object and its affective tag pop into consciousness spontaneously, without conscious processing, on the objects' mere exposure.[1]

The key point here – representing a paradigmatic shift in our thinking about political information processing – is that the very same mechanism that brings thoughts into consideration also carries the affective coloration of these thoughts to mind. If – as postulated in Figure 9.3e – affect is attached directly to a corresponding cognitive node and "travels" with the cognitive node from LTM to WM on activation of the "how-do-I-feel?" heuristic, it follows that simply thinking about someone or something will bring affect to mind, where it may affect the evaluation of new evidence and subsequent decision making. If, indeed, affect travels with the cognitive node from LTM to WM, then affect need not be constructed or recomputed afresh when citizens are exposed to political information. Affect-free, evenhanded reasoning may well nigh be impossible. This combination of a cognitive structure for hot cognition and the automatic activation of hot cognition through the "how-do-I-feel" heuristic provides the theoretical basis for our motivated reasoner model: The hot cognition and OL Tally postulates set the conditions for biased reasoning on activation of the "how-do-I-feel?" heuristic by *depositing one's prior beliefs and feelings in WM at the exact same time new information is being evaluated*. Should this be the case, decision makers would know which way they would like the new evidence to point at the very moment they are evaluating it, thus making it difficult to be a "motivated skeptic" (Ditto and Lopez 1992).

A PILOT TEST OF THE HOT COGNITION POSTULATE

To turn the notion of hot cognition from conjecture to hypothesis, let us set forth an experimental paradigm for empirically testing the premise that affect is directly tagged to its conceptual node and "travels" with it into WM, where both are directly accessible when one interprets and evaluates subsequent evidence. We begin with a classic sentence-verification paradigm, which is used extensively in cognitive psychology to determine the content of knowledge structures and illustrate how spreading activation "moves" associations into WM.

As depicted in Figure 9.5, an experimental subject (S) sees a "prime" word flashed on a computer screen, say the word BIRD, for 200 mil-

---

[1] For the interested reader, there is no better introduction to the literature on automaticity than James Neely's (1977) extraordinarily clever experiments testing the Posner and Snyder (1975) dual-process theory of human information processing, which demonstrate that the meaning of well-learned concepts is activated instantaneously and effortlessly, without conscious attention, on their mere presentation and can only be overridden (thought about differently) by concerted, conscious effort.

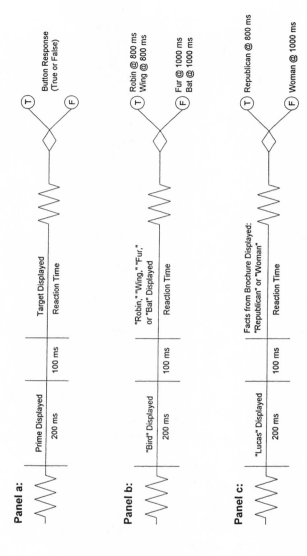

Figure 9.5. Cognitive priming paradigm (sentence verification).

liseconds, and then 100 milliseconds later – when its activation is at peak – a second word, a "target" stimulus, is presented. The S's task is to press a button labeled "True," if the prime-target statement is believed to be true, or the "False" button if the statement is judged false. Sometimes the target is an exemplar of the prime, such as "sparrow," at other times a true but less prototypical example of a bird, such as "ostrich," and on other trials, an invalid instance, such as "bat." The dependent variables are accuracy and response time – the time interval from the onset of the prime word to the button response. This paradigm can also be used to study the content of concepts by targeting the characteristics of concepts, as for example, "wings," "beak," "eats worms."

Representative reaction times (RT) are noted for the button responses. For a strongly associated concept – for example, BIRD . . . sparrow – we expect a facilitation effect, that is, relatively fast reaction times to verify the belief because of the close semantic association of the two concepts in LTM. Where the prime and targets are more distant, for example, "an ostrich is_a BIRD," we would predict a relatively slow reaction-time response, and for a BIRD . . . bat pairing, an inhibition effect. These and other cognitive priming paradigms produce robust effects (Collins and Loftus 1975; Collins and Quillian 1972). What is more, these effects are automatic – they cannot be easily suppressed (Neely 1975) – the reason being that the concepts were associated many times in the past and now come to mind spontaneously.

But what about affect? Is one's affect also primed when the concept it is attached to is primed? That is the hot cognition question. The cognitive priming paradigm has been adapted for affective priming by Fazio and his colleagues (1986), a variant of which we are now piloting in our lab to test the hot cognition hypothesis (Bargh, Chaiken, Govender, and Pratto 1992).

In the top panel of Figure 9.6 we again expose Ss to a prime and then present a target word, but in this variant of the paradigm, the S's task is to press a button labeled "plus" or "minus" to indicate whether the target word has a *positive or negative connotation*. Here again, on each trial, the name of an attitude object (e.g., politician) was presented for 200 milliseconds (ms) on a computer screen, followed by a 100 ms blank-screen interval. Then a target word – in this paradigm, an adjective – is presented in the same location. The subject's task is to indicate by a button press whether the target word is "good" or "bad" in meaning. The latency time from onset of prime word to plus or minus response is recorded:

The logic of the design was that to the extent that presentation of the attitude object name activated the evaluation associated with the attitude object, this evaluation (good or bad) would then influence how quickly subjects could correctly

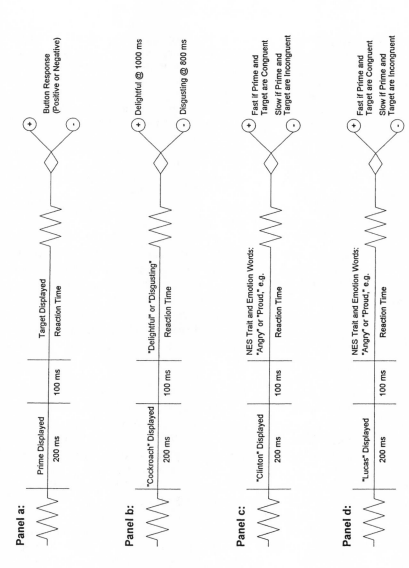

Figure 9.6. Attitude priming paradigm (Is the target positive or negative?).

classify the target adjective as positive or negative in meaning. If the adjective was of the same valence as the attitude object prime, responses should have been faster (i.e., facilitated) relative to a baseline response (e.g., the nonword letter string "BBB"). Conversely, if the adjective and prime were of opposite valence, responses should be slower. The time from the onset of the prime word to the onset of the target word (300 ms) is a critical feature of this priming paradigm as it is too brief an interval for Ss to develop an active expectancy or response strategy regarding the target adjective that follows; such conscious and flexible expectancies require at least 500 ms to develop, and to influence responses in priming tasks (Neely 1977; Posner and Snyder 1975). Given an SOA (interval from prime to target) of 300 ms, then, if presentation of an attitude object prime influences response time to a target adjective, it can only be attributed to an automatic, unintended activation of the corresponding attitude. (Bargh, Chaiken, Govender, and Pratto 1992: 894)

By way of example, in Panel b of Figure 9.6, the word COCKROACH is the prime. If the target word were "Disgusting," we would expect facilitation – a fast RT (here, on the order of 800 milliseconds) to say "Disgusting" is a negative word – a relatively fast response time because the prime and target are *affectively congruent*. Conversely, for all but entomologists, if the target word were "Delightful," we would expect inhibition – slower RTs (on average maybe 1000 ms) to say "Delightful" is a positive word – because the association is *affectively incongruent*.

Note that this is a nonreactive measure: The subject's task is to say whether the target word is positive or negative, *not* whether the word is or is not associated with the prime. This is a strong test for seeing if affect is automatically activated along with the concept itself. Our extension of the experimental paradigm to the political domain is depicted in Figure 9.6, Panels c and d. In this pretest study, we use political leaders and parties as primes (HITLER, LINCOLN, CLINTON, DOLE, POLITICIANS, REPUBLICANS, and DEMOCRATS), each prime having been rated earlier in the lab session on a 7-point like dislike scale. The target words are the trait and emotion words used in the National Election Studies (Kinder 1986), six of which are positive targets ("proud," "hopeful," "intelligent," "inspiring," "moral," and "compassionate"), while the other six adjectives carry a negative connotation ("angry," "afraid," "not qualified," "weak," "dishonest," and "prejudiced"). The prediction – what is called *the automaticity effect* – is that attitudinally congruent prime-target associations will be identified more quickly and more accurately than will incongruent prime-target pairings.

For illustrative purposes only, again reminding the reader of the pretest nature of this experimental test,[2] let us look at the primes "POLITICIAN," "REPUBLICAN," and "DOLE" as these primes generated enough between-subject variability to allow comparisons between supporters and opponents.

In Figure 9.7 the Y axis is RT – from facilitation (fast) to inhibition (slow response times), with all response latencies measured in milliseconds. On the X axis are the different types of prime by target pairings. Comparing Ss who prior to this task had rated the primes on a 7-point like versus dislike scale, we would expect those Ss who dislike POLITICIANS on seeing a negatively toned target word (or those who are favorably disposed toward politicians seeing a positively connotated target adjective) to show a general pattern of facilitation – a faster than average response time – this in contrast to the affectively incongruent associations where we anticipate inhibition – slower than average response times. We do indeed find a strong contrast effect: On average the Ss who said they disliked POLITICIANS responded more quickly when deciding whether such adjectival targets as "repulsive" and "awful" are negative than when the target words were "appealing" or "delightful," and the reverse happens for those Ss who liked (or were neutral toward) politicians.

For the concept "REPUBLICAN" (in Figure 9.8), we again find

---

[2] Perhaps because of the small *n* (60 Ss), the normally high variance in reaction-time measures, and the fact that only a few of the political primes had an adequate number of Ss at the like vs. dislike ends of the scale, we do not find statistically significant facilitation or inhibition effects across all political primes combined. We think the reasons for this are twofold: First, we suspect that many if not all of the political primes (and perhaps most if not all real-world political figures, events, and ideas) are to greater or lesser extent *affectively ambivalent;* that is, one's feelings are befuddled by contradictions. Even strong supporters of Clinton are aware of his foibles, just as pro-choice advocates feel uneasy about late-term abortions. Affective ambiguity may override the automaticity effect (Bargh, Chaiken, Govender, and Pratto 1992), as can cognitive considerations, as Zaller and Feldman (1992) show. Another possible design flaw in this pilot study that makes it difficult to make strong claims was our instruction to Ss that they say aloud the prime word *after* their button press indicating whether the target word had positive or negative connotation. We suspect that having to say the prime after responding to the target (this to insure that Ss attended to the prime) had the unintended consequence of befuddling the associative task, and this weakens the notion that the automaticity effect is triggered on mere exposure of the concept and does not require conscious effort to process. A full-fledged study will develop a measure of ambiguity toward the political primes and change the procedure so that a voice-activated switch will display the target word on the computer screen immediately on the subject saying the prime word. Given the pilot nature of the present study, we ask the reader to treat the response data as illustrative, pending a full-fledged study, although as Figure 9.7 shows, the hot cognition hypothesis appears to override the problems with the pilot study.

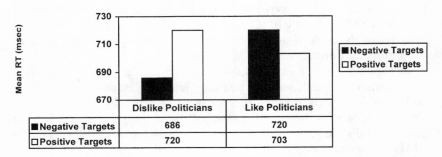

Figure 9.7. Reaction time to "Politician" facilitation and inhibition effects. *Note:* Positive targets: appealing, delightful; negative targets: repulsive, awful.

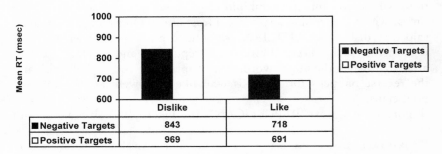

Figure 9.8. Latency to "Republicans" facilitation and inhibition effects. *Note:* Positive target traits: proud, hopeful, intelligent, inspiring, moral, compassion; negative target traits: angry, afraid, not qualified, weak, dishonest, prejudice.

facilitation-inhibition effects, albeit weaker (perhaps because we did not use the prime "Republican Party").

For "DOLE" (in Figure 9.9), we observe strong facilitation effects for those Ss who *liked* Bob Dole, but weak effects from his opponents.

A stronger test of the hot cognition hypothesis was carried out in the final stages of the experiment when Ss read a one-page, two-column campaign brochure about a hypothetical candidate, William Lucas. Along with his picture was a short biography, a brief account of his legislative experience, two endorsements, and, in one condition, an extended statement expressing his support for gun control, in the other condition, his opposition to gun control. After reading the campaign brochure, Ss were engaged in the same affective priming trials; here the prime was LUCAS, and the targets were the same twelve NES trait and emotion words (as depicted in the bottom panel of Figure 9.6). Again, the S's task

202

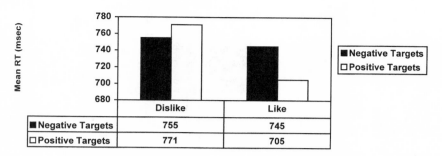

Figure 9.9. Reaction time to "Dole" facilitation and inhibition effects. *Note:* Positive target traits: proud, hopeful, intelligent, inspiring, moral, compassion; negative target traits: angry, afraid, not qualified, weak, dishonest, prejudice.

was to indicate whether the target word carried a positive or negative connotation.

In the last task, Ss were again given LUCAS as the prime but were now asked to press a button labeled "True" or "False" to indicate whether each of 12 factual statements about Lucas was true or false. This is a classic sentence-verification task (as depicted in Figure 9.5). Of the 12 factual statements, 6 were true; that is, facts presented in the candidate brochure, for example, (LUCAS (is_a) Republican) and 6 were false, for example, (LUCAS (is_a) woman).

In Figure 9.10, we trace the mean reaction times to the four one-word factual targets (since there is a word length by RT effect), as well as the mean RT to the 12 affective trait and emotion word targets. The mean RT for the affect responses was quite fast, 693 milliseconds, about the same response time observed for the earlier set of political primes, implying that an affective tally is formed quickly (Ss taking less than five minutes to read the campaign brochure) and without explicit instructions to form an impression (Ss asked to read the brochure and decide if they would likely vote for or against Congressman Lucas). But, look at the RTs for the factual verifications: much slower. On average, the time to retrieve and verify a factual attribute is two to three times slower than was the time to make a candidate-primed affective judgment, a difference we interpret as evidence that the affective tally is *directly tagged to the concept* (as depicted in Figure 9.3e), whereas – as we see it – the attributes of a person, here his party label, political position, gender, and marital status – all information highlighted in the campaign brochure – are not stored directly with the candidate node but must be summoned up as linked attributes (as depicted in Figures 9.3b–9.3d), thereby taking additional time to retrieve.

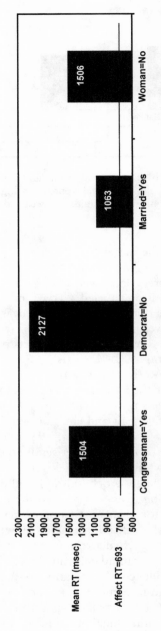

Figure 9.10. Comparison of mean reaction times: Knowledge versus affective response for candidate William Lucas. *Note:* Prime: William Lucas; targets: NES trait and emotion words.

The implication we draw from this comparison is that the OL Tally, once formed, is readily accessible to the "how-do-I-feel?" heuristic, cuing you immediately – on the mere exposure of the "object" – as to how much you like or dislike him (her, it). This is what is meant when saying the object is "hot." The affective tag "travels" with the "object" from LTM to WM where it is immediately accessible whenever one is called on to form or update an impression. Assuming that our tripartite model is a fair representation of how affect and cognition are unitized in memory and brought to mind on the mere exposure to a person, event, issue, or idea, we would expect to see one's current OL Tally impact on every step in the judgment process.

THE EXPECTATION OF BIAS IN THE DECISION-MAKING PROCESS

Some decisions are simple and straightforward, requiring little thought or cognitive effort to reach a conclusion, and some decisions are not important enough to warrant the extra cognitive effort required to gather more information or sift through the available evidence, but when decisions are multifaceted and personal involvement is high enough, people can call upon a variety of decision strategies to regulate their decision-making processes (Baumeister and Newman 1994).

In Table 9.1, we elaborate on the decision process introduced in Figure 9.2 where, you may recall, we posited a five-step sequence of cognitive processes.

This model sees the decision process as purposeful goal-directed behavior. The starting premise – common to rational as well as psychological models of judgment (Elster 1989) – is that *all decision making is motivated*. Recalling Figure 9.1, sometimes people are motivated primarily by the desire to reach an accurate, correct or otherwise optimal decision, while at other times, their primary goal is to reach a particular, preferred conclusion. So it is that both intuitive scientists and partisans, both motivated reasoners, strive to come up with strong arguments.

When motivated to maximize accuracy, one is obliged to guide and carefully monitor the decision-making process so as to consider relevant evidence and guard against biases. So motivated, the decision maker must be deliberate and explicit about procedures, ideally setting the decision rules before evaluating the evidence. This depiction of the "rational model" – largely created by philosophers – is an idealized image of scientific decision making. On the other hand, when one is operating in partisan mode, the decision maker is seen as trying to build the best possible case for a preferred conclusion. The conclusion, not the process,

Table 9.1. *The stepwise model elaborated*

DECISION STEPS	THE INTUITIVE SCI-ENTIST/RATIONALIST	INTUITIVE LAWYER/ THE PARTISAN
Activation of Goal	Need to be Accurate, Correct; Reach Optimal Conclusion	Need to Reach Specific Conclusion; Bolster and Defend Prior Attitude
Gathering Evidence	Thorough, Evenhanded Search; Considering the Opposite	Confirmation & Disconfirmation Bias; Selective Attention
Assessing Implications	AUTOMATIC PROCESS	AUTOMATIC PROCESS
Reassessment	Search for Possible Bias Adjustment. Recomputation	Override of Unacceptable Conclusions. Selective Criticism of Unwelcomed Evidence
Integration/Closure	Rules & Criteria Set in Advance. Resolve Inconsistencies; Assign Relative Weights. Bayesian Weighting of Evidence	Rules, Criteria Set to Emphasize Favorable Evidence. Non-Bayesian Integration Effect

guides the decision-making steps. To work effectively, the partisan must monitor the process by repeatedly checking the implications of the incoming evidence against the preferred outcome, for the goal is to marshal the best-available evidence in support of the preference or against an unwanted conclusion. Whereas the scientific mode relies heavily on the self-conscious monitoring of procedures, the partisan mode is typically governed by unconscious processes, for were one aware of deliberately trying to reach a preordained conclusion, it would make a mockery of the decision process (Kunda 1990).

When governed by an accuracy goal, information processing is characterized by three desiderata:

- an effort to gather relevant information, regardless of the directional push of the evidence;
- the evenhanded evaluation of the evidence; and
- the postponement of the decision until the evidence is deemed to be "good enough," such that the additional effort that would be required to increase one's confidence in the judgment would not likely change the choice.

What is important here to note – assuming the tripartite model is true – is that citizens (in particular those with strong prior attitudes), whether acting as scientist or partisan, are aware throughout the decision process of how much they like or dislike a candidate or issue (the OL Tally "tells them so"), *and* they can immediately sense the affective coloration of a new piece of information (the hot cognition postulate), which is brought instantaneously to mind by the "how-do-I-feel?" heuristic. Knowing at the very moment that the evidence being evaluated is attitudinally congruent or incongruent with one's overall evaluation makes it difficult (if not impossible) to interpret and evaluate the evidence in an impartial way. Feelings become information. This being the case, we suspect that the ideal "intuitive scientist" mode of processing is more likely to be found in undergraduate texts on the scientific method than in real-world decision making. The more common modus operandi, we think, is a decision process characterized by individuals' interpreting and evaluating information in subtle ways that lead them to reach or defend a particular, predetermined conclusion (Baumeister and Newman 1994).

In the polar model depicted in Table 9.1, the partisan mode of processing is characterized at each step in the sequence by the largely unconscious biasing of the decision-making process in ways that systematically bolster the strength and credibility of supporting evidence, while discrediting evidence contrary to one's prior preferences. Let us walk through the steps for the partisan reasoner, keeping well in mind that even the most dedicated of partisans need to come up with rational justifications for their beliefs, attitudes, and behavior (Pysczcynski and Greenberg 1987), a potent contributor, we suspect, to the oft-found positive correlation between statements of likes and dislikes and evaluation.

Step 1. The Activation of Goals. On seeing an important belief or attitude challenged by new information, decision makers are sometimes motivated to seek out one or another analogy, metaphor, example, or line of reasoning that will bolster their position (Khong 1992; Taber forthcoming). In 1991, just days before the U.S. attack on Iraq, the linguist George Lakoff sent a message out on the Internet entitled "Metaphors of War." In an extensive analysis of the metaphors used by the press, spin doctors, and the Bush administration to justify Desert Storm, Lakoff noted that supporters adopted a string of metaphors that served to frame their preferences emotionally, starting with "the rape of Kuwait" and concluding with the dangers of a Munich-like appeasement of Saddam (Hitler), while opponents countered with a cost-benefit analysis in which "blood was being traded for oil" and couched their opposition in terms of the prospect of being bogged down in a Vietnam-like quagmire (Spellman and Holyoak 1992). Metaphors, like schemas and frames, or even the simple priming words used in our hot cognition study, entrain one's thoughts and feelings in a systematic way (Leake 1991; Ram and Leake 1995).

Step 2. The Gathering of Evidence. In this step, partisans, like "intuitive scientists," can exert some control over the amount, type, and valence of information entering into the decision process. Partisans, sensing a need to support a specific, preferred conclusion, are prone to search selectively for evidence that will be favorable to their prior attitude (Volvo owners read Volvo ads), or be selectively inattentive to the prospect of contrary evidence. As an example of "defensive inattention," Sweeney and Gruber (1984) found that Nixon supporters tended to ignore the extensive news coverage of the Watergate affair, whereas Nixon haters followed the proceedings raptly. By simply controlling the TV remote, people can sometimes selectively avoid challenging information or improve the odds of seeing attitudinally congruent information.

Step 3. The Assessing of Implications. On mere exposure to a message, conscious memory is flooded with both cognitive and affective associations and implications of the message (Figures 9.3a–9.3e). Associations made in the past are most likely to come to mind now. This process of spreading activation – a core axiom of the information-processing approach (and of course its extension to "hot cognition") – is thought to be spontaneous and automatic for both those committed to accuracy and those attempting to defend their prior beliefs and attitudes. Although the step from evidence to implication is automatic, and the reception of whatever implications that pop into mind is effortless, controlled processes may be sparked, should the decision maker choose not to accept the implications at face value.

Step 4. The Reassessment of Evidence. This is the most crucial phase in the decision process, and because it is effortful, its outcome is most directly affected by motivation. In partisan mode, decision makers will be carefully critical of the disagreeable implications of associations brought to mind in Step 3, while failing to subject supportive evidence to equally critical scrutiny. Partisans can, and in hundreds of lab studies do, modify their initial assessment of evidence – its appropriateness, credibility, strength, and so forth – so as to bring the evidence in line with their priors. This they can do easily because – as suggested in the pilot test of the "hot cognition" hypothesis – people can quickly and effortlessly tell whether a piece of evidence is congruent or incongruent with their prior attitude (the facilitation versus inhibition effects in Figures

9.7–9.9). Conversely, reassessing the evidence in an evenhanded way – a hallmark of the "intuitive scientist" – is especially difficult because much of the information in the world is ambiguous, and virtually all evidence is marred by some flaws and weaknesses; hence, the counterarguing of contrary evidence seems a reasonable response to what is perceived to be "defective information."

The classic finding on the selective reassessment of evidence comes from the Lord, Ross, and Lepper (1977) study of how proponents and opponents of the death penalty evaluated pro and con arguments about the deterrent value of capital punishment. Proponents rated the pro arguments as stronger and more credible than did opponents evaluating the very same arguments, and in a thought-listing task, both groups cited many more criticisms of the attitudinally contrary evidence. The result was "attitude polarization" – Ss came away more strongly convinced of their position than when they started, despite having read an equal number of strong and weak arguments on both sides of the issue. Apparently, partisans assimilate the supporting evidence but counterargue and otherwise discredit contrary evidence, leading them to have more attitudinally congruent information in mind than before the "debate" (Edwards and Smith 1996). On the other hand, even strong partisans will bow to overwhelming evidence. So it is that patients given a negative medical report take longer to accept it than do those given a positive report, they generate more challenges to the test, and they tend to rate test accuracy lower, but after a series of efforts to undermine the validity of the bad news, many do eventually accept it (Ditto and Lopez 1992). Ever hear of a patient asking for a second opinion to a favorable test result?

Step 5. The Combining and Integration of Information. In this final step, the decision maker resolves ambiguities and conflicts, mulls over the implications of a position, and integrates the different bits of information into a new or revised belief or evaluation. To the extent that the integration of evidence into a summary judgment or choice requires conscious thought, it requires motivation. Although we treat this as the last step in the process, the theory of on-line processing sees decision making as a continuous ticktock process of incrementing and decrementing the OL Tally in real time. Tentative conclusions are being generated throughout the entire process. We think it is difficult (compliments of the "how-do-I-feel?" heuristic) to assess impartially the worth of new evidence when all the while knowing how you would like the conclusion to turn out. Given that decision makers are always aware of how much they like or dislike the person or issue, both the "intuitive scientist" and the "partisan" will call it quits when the decision is "good enough," a slippery decision point under the best of conditions, with partisans likely to end the process when their directional goal is satisfied, rather than actively seeking out disconfirming evidence. This inherent bias does not ensure, but does make it more likely, that their preconvictions will stand. Should the partisan be dissatisfied with the results – perhaps the evidence is not judged to be strong enough to convince an impartial judge sitting on one's shoulder – s/he may go back to Step 1 to reframe the problem, or skip through the sequence in search of more "compelling" evidence or a "fairer" weighting scheme (much like scientists recoding and reanalyzing data when a favored hypothesis is disconfirmed?).

Working together, "hot cognition" and on-line processing, along with the "how-do-I-feel?" mechanism for summoning up the OL Tally, are all that is needed to turn the evenhanded treatment of new information into partisan reasoning, for the OL Tally will likely conspire to bias the collection and (re)assessment of evidence. The clear expectation is that while it may be possible for people – if strongly enough motivated and under favorable conditions (as we will see) – to search carefully and treat new information that comes to mind in an impartial way, we think it is exceedingly difficult to seek out information and reappraise its implications evenhandedly when all the while knowing which way they want the conclusion to come out. This is made all the more difficult because the decision to appraise or reconsider the evidence takes time, is effortful, and is based on the assumption that one is somehow aware of having a biased set of considerations in mind and believes the need to be accurate is worth the effort that will be required to rethink the issue.

Supposing, as does our tripartite model, that people are immediately aware of the affective value of information on its mere recognition and find it automatically summoned into WM by the "how-do-I-feel?" heuristic whenever they are explicitly *or* implicitly asked for an evaluation (recall that our attitudinal priming procedure is a nonreactive task). The rationalist mode of reasoning requires the citizen to stop the process midstream, step back, and consciously challenge the considerations that immediately come to mind. Harder done than said, we think, for one's sense of the evidence is that it fits with expectations: The evidence available has a subjective plausibility to it because the cognitive associations that pop into working memory represent the most frequent and/or recent connections made in the past, and the affective coloration of these considerations is most likely to be attitudinally congruent. What reason, then, to doubt that the evidence coming so easily to mind does not reflect the fair appraisal of a representative sampling of available information? Further, we suspect that the motivation to challenge the evidence in mind is typically weak for most citizens most of the time, since neither their political opinions nor their conventional electoral behavior is likely to be seen as having direct, serious, personal consequences for their life, limbs, or self-respect.

ON THE RATIONALITY OF MOTIVATED REASONING

Assuming that our tripartite model works as advertised, a number of key "when, who, where" research questions come to the fore, chief among them: (1) Under what conditions will the citizen treat political information evenhandedly as a naive scientist should, and when will the same citizen act as a partisan reasoner? and (2) What are the consequences of relying on the "how-do-I-feel?" mechanism as a heuristic for guiding the interpretation and evaluation of new information?

To the first question, we think it *least likely* that citizens will throughly examine and evenhandedly evaluate new information

- when their motivation to be accurate is low, in particular, when the consequences of one's attitude or action are weak or when the prospect of being held responsible for one's opinions or actions is unlikely;
- when attitude strength – one's OL Tally – is strong and connections to other attitudes important;
- when information can be automatically stereotyped, as when, for example, information about a leader or issue is seen as characteristic of a party or group;
- when the issue is complex, thereby taxing resources and commitment;
- when citizens are under time pressure;
- when their train of thought is disrupted;
- when the message is one-sided (as are commercials), rather than two-sided (as in a debate), because in the former case citizens must think up the counterarguments themselves.

And this, the most controversial expectation, biased processing is most likely among those

- whose general political knowledge and domain-specific political knowledge is rich, for it is sophisticates who typically hold the strongest attitudes, with the most confidence, and who have the most facts at hand, thereby making them more able to assimilate supporting evidence and better equipped to discredit arguments that challenge their established beliefs or attitudes.

At this juncture, then, we see the prospects for the affect-free processing of information to be unlikely.

The second question – the consequences of relying on the "how-do-I-feel?" heuristic when thinking about and evaluating new information

211

– brings the issue of irrationality center stage. Trusting in the OL Tally as a mechanism for summing up one's prior evaluations of leaders, groups, and issues appears to be a good heuristic, surely better than relying solely or even primarily on the recollection of things past. But what if, as our tripartite model predicts, having one's OL Tally in mind biases the processing of new information in ways suggested by the attitude-priming experiments? Is the reliance on one's affective tally as a heuristic coloring when interpreting and evaluating political messages rational?

Traditionally, of course, the mixing of emotion with decision making – which is the springboard of motivated reasoning – runs counter to a fundamental desideratum of Western thought (Plato and Kant come first to mind) and is anathema (from Saint Augustine to Bacon to Hume to the present day) in normative descriptions of the scientific method, which contend that emotion and rationality can and should be kept apart. This dream for pure reasoning, best expressed by Descartes's "I think therefore I am," is a core belief of early economic models of political behavior (Downs 1957; Ferejohn and Fiorina 1974; Riker and Ordeshook 1968) and holds sway today in those models of rational behavior that treat the evaluation process as a purely cognitive assessment of attributes and alternatives (the lower right quadrant of Figure 9.1).

That said, there are compelling reasons *not* to disengage thinking from feeling, not to think of cognition as virtue and affect as vice. The OL Tally, on being brought to mind by the "how-do-I-feel?" heuristic, turns affect into readily available information, signaling us immediately, sometimes consciously, at other times not, whether the consequences of some bit of information are likely to be pleasant or threatening (Schwartz and Clore 1983). This assessment of how things turned out in the past need not be computed from a mental list of successes and failures – one need not spend attentional resources to tease out, mull over, and sum up problems and prospects – for one's appraisal is captured in the OL Tally. Of course, when things are not as they were or not as they should be, new information needs to be collected and old information reevaluated. Nevertheless – this an article of faith – assuming a healthy brain in a sane society (*sic*), one's affective tally, reflecting how things turned out in the past, will often provide a good guide to behavior.

What is more (Clore and Isbell 1996), the OL Tally plays an important, positive role in decision making by directing how attentional resources are allocated, priorities enforced, and subgoals created (Neidenthal and Sutterlund 1994; Simon 1967). Plato, Kant, and Descartes notwithstanding, even were it possible to be an emotion-free information processor, decision making would not necessarily be more rational. More likely, thinking and reasoning would be undirected and disordered. The best evidence available today on the prospects of pure reasoning, coming from neurological studies of people who suffer brain injuries or disease that dissociate emotions from reasoning (Damasio 1994), shows that while such patients may be able to carry out many of the cognitive tasks we think of as intelligent, such as balancing a checkbook, without the direct connection between thought and feeling, they are unable to set realistic goals, keep on task, or come to closure. For those of us lucky enough to have these connections in order, many judgments and choices can be made simply by asking ourselves "How do I feel about him (her, it)?" and letting it go at that, rather than by tallying up a list of pros and cons.

For better or for worse, affect and cognition are inseparable and perhaps inescapable. Where, when, and for whom this inexorable linking of feeling and thinking will facilitate good decision making, and when it will lead to systematic departures from a rational course of action, are important questions currently unanswered.

10

Knowledge, Trust, and International Reasoning
SAMUEL L. POPKIN AND MICHAEL A. DIMOCK

This essay challenges the argument that most citizens are susceptible to elite and media manipulation because they are too uninformed to reason about public policy. We challenge the view that citizens rarely engage in reasoning about public policy, and thus are moved mainly by media and elite influences (Bennett 1988; Converse 1964; Price and Zaller 1993; Zaller 1992). Such an argument views citizens as having nothing resembling "true" opinions on issues of public policy. When faced with opinion questions on a survey, respondents merely answer mechanically from the "top of their head" without thinking, reasoning, or deliberating (Zaller 1992: 45; Zaller and Feldman 1992).

A citizen's defense against elite and media influence and manipulation is what Converse (1964) called "constraint": People reject elite and media arguments that are inconsistent with their ideological or partisan predispositions. Unfortunately, however, only a small minority are viewed as sufficiently attentive and informed to recognize whether the messages are consistent or inconsistent with their partisan and ideological (liberal-conservative) leanings. Such cues fly over the head of most other people, and as Zaller (1992: 311) states:

Many citizens . . . pay too little attention to public affairs to be able to respond critically to the political communications they encounter; rather, they are blown about by whatever current of information manages to develop the greatest intensity. The minority of citizens who are highly attentive to public affairs are scarcely more critical: They respond to new issues mainly on the basis of the partisanship and ideology of the elite sources of the messages.

We agree that not all citizens have fully formed opinions on most issues of public policy. Without question, one very important source of information is that which is available because it has been retained in memory from recent exposure (Wyer and Srull 1989; Zaller 1992), and we accept that the framing of a question matters (Iyengar and Kinder

1987; Tversky and Kahneman 1981). But we do not accept the inference that people who have partially formed opinions, who make heavy use of available information, and who sometimes change answers when questions are reframed are incapable of political reasoning.

Even the least-well-informed citizens are able to connect a wide variety of personal attitudes and orientations with their policy evaluations, and therefore they need not simply parrot elites' opinions. There are a wide array of personal predispositions that citizens can and do bring to bear when they reason about public policy. As a result, they may have more defenses against elite and media influence and manipulation than commonly thought.

Citizens draw on a wide array of predispositions when reasoning about politics (Brady and Sniderman 1985; Ottati and Wyer 1990; Sniderman, Glaser, and Griffin 1990). Recognition of these predispositions is essential if we are to understand how citizens arrive at political judgments and how they evaluate elite and media messages (Krosnick 1988, 1989; Popkin 1994). Citizens have premises, and they use those premises to make inferences from their observations of the world around them, including what they see and hear in the media.

In this essay, we identify some of these premises. Both *knowledge* and *trust* in particular structure the kinds of inferences people make about international issues. Knowledge of American political institutions determines the context in which foreign affairs issues are perceived, and trust in one's government and trust in the people one encounters in daily life shape one's approach to the unfamiliar. Using data from the 1992 National Election Study and the 1994 "New Political Landscape" survey from The Times Mirror Center for The People & The Press, we test these hypotheses on attitudes about immigration, trade, and international involvement, attitudes which we show are strongly shaped by knowledge about and orientation toward American government and society. In short, people who neither understand nor trust their own government and who distrust their fellow citizens are also suspicious of foreigners, apprehensive about international trade, and isolationist. Our analysis suggests that these considerations are even more important determinants of international attitudes than ideology or economic perceptions.

Citizens do more than either accept or reject explicit media messages without connecting these messages to their own orientations and attitudes. The main implication of our findings is that whether citizens are processing media messages or considering the economic "bottom line" when they form their opinions, they are reasoning.

Public opinion scholars present only a slightly less narrow view of the reasoning process because they have generally paid attention to only two predispositions, partisanship and ideology. Partisanship and ideology are but two of the many predispositions that can affect our reasoning (Campbell et al 1960; Delli Carpini and Keeter 1996; Zaller 1992); and focusing on these inherently political cues has led these researchers to the conclusion that predispositions *in general* matter more as political knowledge increases (Zaller 1992: 44–45). But the notion that a high level of political knowledge is necessary to connect policy and predispositions ignores two important factors. First, it overlooks the importance of other, nonideological predispositions that might come into play, such as individuals' contextual knowledge about politics. Second, people lacking familiarity with institutions and policy processes may simply draw upon *different* sources when assembling their beliefs. For example, in U.S. congressional elections, partisanship and ideology heavily influence the choices of politically knowledgeable voters, whereas candidate familiarity and incumbency shape the choices of their less knowledgeable counterparts (Dimock 1997). In short, political knowledge does not determine our *ability* to "fill in the gaps" based upon our predispositions and background scripts, though it does shape the *manner* in which we do so.

The assumption that information is necessary to connect policy and predispositions also ignores the importance of imagination. Bettelheim (1989) has argued that under some conditions, the *less* we know, the *more* our predispositions can matter. The lack of details in fairy tales, he found, make them seem more imaginable and more credible to children who have no trouble supplying the details from their own imagination. A similar justification is given for using ink-blot tests, such that the less we actually know, the more we can project our own feelings and thoughts into a situation.[1] As Liebling (1961: 316) once put it, "when information becomes unavailable, the expert comes into his own."

Michael Delli Carpini and Scott Keeter (1991), along with a host of others, have shown that Americans are chronically bereft of civics-book knowledge about the American political system, a deficiency that increasing levels of education over the past 50 years have failed to counter. If Americans know little about their own country, how much can they know about the rest of the world? In fact, Americans' knowledge about the world was the lowest among seven advanced democracies, and strikingly so once variation in education levels is taken into account (Dimock and Popkin 1997). The world around us, as Harold Isaacs (1958) noted, is often little more than *Scratches on Our Mind*. With so little knowledge, no wonder scholars ask what possible basis Americans can have

---

[1] The playwright and author David Mamet relates this Bettelheim insight about fairy tales to theater in an interview with John Lahr, "Fortress Mamet," by John Lahr in *The New Yorker*, Nov. 17, 1997, p. 79.

for opinions about the world and what possible meaning such opinions could have (Bartels 1995).

Lacking the data to develop "informed" attitudes, where do people get their attitudes about foreign affairs? One approach to studying individual decision making, that of rational-choice scholars, emphasizes the role of personal experience and the ways that people evaluate a policy based on how it affects them directly. Thus, a person's economic experiences or perception of economic vulnerability may lie at the core of their attitudes about foreign policy. This assumption is, in fact, common among political commentators, who interpret distrust of Japan, fear of immigration, or protectionist stances as reflexive reactions to the economic changes that Levy and Murnane (1992) call the "hollowing out" of the economy.

We focus on foreign policy attitudes in this chapter precisely because most Americans have limited information about this domain. Under such conditions, the disparity between a reflexive, reactive public and a reasoning public should be most clear. If foreign policy attitudes simply reflected ideological ties or economic evaluations, then our hypothesis would not be supported. But our analysis shows that public attitudes about foreign policy reflect a reasoning process that draws upon the individual's knowledge and upon considerations much closer to home.

KNOWLEDGE, TRUST, AND INTERNATIONAL ATTITUDES

How do citizens reason about a complicated world? First, we hypothesize that the kinds of predispositions people draw upon and the kinds of shortcuts they use when evaluating international affairs are all affected by how well they understand national political institutions. We suggest that people with institutional knowledge process news, evaluate policies, and answer questions differently from those without this knowledge.[2] A tourist familiar with the geography of New York can place reports of violent crimes in perspective – knowing, for example, that the South Bronx is far from midtown Manhattan. In a similar fashion, a person with knowledge of political institutions might be better able to place reports of violence around the world in perspective, knowing the difference between a moral and humanitarian crisis like Rwanda and a civil war in a nuclear state like North Korea or China.

---

[2] We identify this characteristic by measuring knowledge about political institutions and excluding measures of familiarity with partisan and ideological dimensions that are used in broader measures of "engagement" (e.g., Zaller 1992).

We hypothesize that a tendency to experience the unfamiliar as uncertain and threatening makes persons with low knowledge of political institutions more afraid of the wider world and more concerned about immigration, trade, foreign involvement, and war. People who know about politics well enough to understand political institutions, on the other hand, can incorporate these actors and institutions into their thinking about the world.

The extent to which people trust their government and the people around them also shapes their predispositions about foreign affairs. The importance of government trust follows logically from the argument we present. Independent of the amount one knows about government, if one trusts political institutions to act effectively, one may feel less concern over foreign threats. In examining the microfoundations of Robert Putnam's (1994) analysis of declining social capital in the United States, Brehm and Rahn (1997) argue persuasively that perceptions of human nature are strongly related to confidence in government. Similarly, Brewer and Steenbergen (1997) and Dimock (1998) have shown that interpersonal trust plays an important role in shaping public support for government programs. Though familiarity with the governing institutions provides people with a context in which to interpret how policies and events will affect them, if this context is negative, political knowledge may do little to assuage their fears.

Overall, both trust in government and trust in the people around us should shape our reasoning about foreign events and policies. Independent of the specific information about these events we gain from the media, and independent of the background knowledge available to us, these measures of trust identify general predispositions that we bring to the reasoning process, predispositions that can become the foundation on which our attitudes are built. In the following analysis, we show that knowledge and trust can have at least as much influence on foreign policy attitudes as ideological predispositions or economic evaluations.

DATA AND MEASUREMENT

Our analysis consists of a series of multivariate models predicting foreign policy attitudes as the result of individual characteristics and predispositions. The data we utilize come from the 1992 National Election Study, which included a broad battery of international questions, along with a strong measure of political knowledge, and the 1994 Times Mirror "New Political Landscape" survey, which contained a question about U.S. involvement in free-trade agreements like NAFTA and GATT, along with questions about immigration policy.[3] To test our hypothesis that citizens reason about these issues, we must show that such characteristics as familiarity and trust in government, and trust in other people, play at least as great a role in shaping international attitudes as do economic evaluations and ideological predispositions.

To measure an individual's familiarity with domestic political institutions, we use a cumulative scale based on a respondent's ability to identify the offices held by important political actors (Al Gore, William Rehnquist, and Tom Foley), an individual's understanding of specific institutional rules (who nominates judges and who decides whether a law was constitutional), and that individual's familiarity with the current institutional setting (which party has a majority in the House, and in the Senate). We emphasize this measure over broader measures of political sophistication because our theory predicts that contextual knowledge about government will allow people to evaluate foreign events differently, and we in fact control for broader sophistication effects through the use of a control for education.[4] The scale for the Times Mirror study includes three comparable items about political actors and institutions (Appendix 2).

To measure trust in government, we use the standard political-alienation questions from the National Election Study. The scale consists of four questions asking respondents: if they felt they could trust government; if government wastes a lot of money, if government is run for the benefit of all; and if there are many crooks in government (see Appendix 1). The scale used in the Times Mirror study includes two comparable items (Appendix 2). Our scale measuring interpersonal trust consists of two questions: one asking if "most people can be trusted" and the other asking if people will generally try to be helpful or if they are "mostly just looking out for themselves." The Times Mirror study, unfortunately, does not include a measure of interpersonal trust, and so our analysis of trust is limited to the NES data. In both of these scales, more trusting answers have been coded positively, meaning that higher scores represent higher levels of confidence and faith.

Our models also include measures that are necessary for testing the alternative hypothesis. Since many foreign policy issues, such as free trade and immigration policy, are not inherently associated with core liberal and conservative beliefs on social and economic dimensions, we treat the extent to which ideology shapes foreign policy attitudes as a

[3] Unfortunately, more recent National Election Studies have asked far fewer questions about foreign policy issues, and have weaker measures of institutional knowledge.
[4] For discussion of the relation between political knowledge and general sophistication, see Dimock 1997; Sniderman, Glaser, and Griffin 1990; and Luskin 1987.

proxy for the relevance of elite signals (Zaller 1992). We also test both "pocketbook" and "sociotropic" models of how citizens react to economic conditions. A "pocketbook" model of public behavior asserts that individuals respond to their own economic conditions, for example, evaluating the job performance of the president by evaluating the state of one's own personal well-being. Negative reactions to immigration, trade, and international involvement correlate with negative personal economic experiences – those who feel the most economically threatened may feel the most hostility.

We use three distinct measures of personal economics to test the "pocketbook" hypothesis. The first measures job stress, combining the respondent's current working status (unemployed or laid off) with the respondent's concern about losing (or being able to get) a job in the near future. The second measures the respondent's subjective assessment of his economic situation, combining the question of whether he thinks his economic situation declined over the last year with the question asking if he felt his income was keeping pace with the cost of living. The third measure assesses personal economic experiences, such as whether medical treatment was put off, rent or mortgage was paid late, and whether he had to dip into savings to make ends meet (see Appendix 1).[5] This last measure, unfortunately, could not be replicated from the Times Mirror Survey (see Appendix 2).

A "sociotropic" model of public behavior, on the other hand, asserts that individuals evaluate incumbents, candidates, and policies based on their perceptions of national economic conditions (Kiewiet 1983; Kinder and Kiewiet 1981). In this case, opposition to foreign involvement may reflect pessimistic perceptions of the national economy. We test the "sociotropic" model with two general measures of the national economy. One is a measure of the national economy that uses a standard scale of assessments of inflation, unemployment, and the general economy, with negative perceptions coded high. The other measures pessimism about the future, combining assessments of whether their personal economy and the nation's economy will get better or worse over the next year, and whether the standard of living 20 years from now (for the next generation) will be worse than it is today.[6] Again, the Times Mirror survey is

---

[5] Consistent with Kinder, Adams, and Gronke (1989), factor analysis shows these questions to measure three distinct (though correlated) dimensions of personal economics. To be sure that the covariance between these scales was not artificially suppressing significance, we ran all of the regression and logit models with a unified scale of all questions measuring personal economic experiences and assessments, and with each scale individually. The substantive results were virtually identical in all cases, unless otherwise noted.

[6] Derived from the same factor analysis discussed in note 5, alternative coding procedures were also tested, resulting in no significant difference in results.

slightly more limited, including only a single measure of expectations for the national economy in the next year.

Finally, in every analysis we include education, age, race, gender, and income as demographic controls. We include education to be certain that we are estimating the effect of political knowledge, not the increased comprehension or cognitive ability generally associated with education. We include age because increased political knowledge is associated with life-cycle learning, and income often has an independent effect on policy attitudes, and is correlated with knowledge. We also include a dummy variable for gender in our models, which is known to be significant for attitudes about war, and a dummy variable for race, which may play a role, particularly with respect to immigration.

RESULTS

The dependent variables in our study include a range of questions measuring attitudes about international issues and U.S. foreign policy. In our analysis of the 1992 National Election Study, numerous questions were available within the issue areas of immigration, foreign involvement, and support for the Gulf War. The abundance of specific questions allowed us to develop cumulative scales to provide a more reliable estimate of an individual's attitudes in each issue area.[7] The 1994 Times Mirror "New Political Landscape" survey also contained relevant questions on related issues, such as U.S. involvement in free trade agreements like NAFTA and GATT, and two questions on immigration. All question wording and coding procedures for the two surveys are outlined in Appendixes 1 and 2, respectively. For ease of comparison, all independent variables have been coded to the 0–1 interval, as have the dependent variables.

IMMIGRATION

On the 1992 NES, the number of respondents who wanted to see immigration levels decreased outnumbered the number who wanted to see immigration increased by more than 6 to 1, with another 40% satisfied with the status quo. When asked whether the number of immigrants permitted to come to the United States should be increased, decreased, or left the same, 47% expressed an interest in decreasing immigration, and another 42% felt comfortable with current levels. When asked how likely

---

[7] The correlations between individual variables within each area were so high, and the results of logit models for each question in our analyses were so similar, that we opted for the increased reliability of scaled dependent variables for our reports here. The results of the separate logit analyses for each question are available from the authors.

the growing number of Hispanics were to take jobs away from people already here, nearly 50% felt they were "Extremely" or "Very" likely to do so. Overall, public views of immigration are cautious at best, fearful at worst. But what sorts of considerations drive these views?

A common suggestion is that economic concerns underlie public concern about immigration. We might expect individuals who feel personal economic stresses or who fear losing their own jobs to show the greatest anxiety about immigration levels. Or, it might be that a general concern about the nation's economy might drive anti-immigrant sentiment. Though both of these hypotheses seem plausible, neither allows for the possibility of voter reasoning based upon prior predispositions and knowledge. In other words, these hypotheses predict that citizen reaction to immigration represents a reflexive response to threats against the individual's own self-interest, and does not account for the broader context in which she views the issue of immigration. We hypothesize, on the other hand, that context should be highly salient – that survey responses are far more likely to reflect the citizen's own predispositions about government and others, and her own familiarity with political processes.

Column 1 of Table 10.1 shows the results of an OLS (ordinary least squares) regression using a summative scale of citizen attitudes about immigration as the dependent variable. With regard to the issue of knowledge, people whose view of the world incorporates knowledge about institutions are less threatened by immigration. The ability to place a potentially threatening issue like immigration in the context of government institutions alleviates overall concerns, irrespective of an individual's income, education, or personal economics.

With respect to the issue of trust, both trust of government and interpersonal trust are strongly related to anti-immigration sentiments as well. Our prediction that trust in government would parallel the effect of political knowledge is supported. Those who distrust government show far greater concern over immigration, to the point where they support interference from the very government they distrust, and those who feel that the people around them are not helpful or cannot be trusted show skepticism about outgroups as well. Thus, opposition to immigration arises not from people seeing "us" as the good guys and "them" as the bad guys but from general pessimism and distrust about the neighbors people already have.

There is no relation at all between anti-immigration sentiment and any of the three personal economic measures. Neither job stress and personal economic stress nor assessments of personal economics are related in any fashion to sentiments about immigration. This is particularly noteworthy since our measure of anti-immigrant sentiment is largely eco-

Table 10.1. *Reasoning about immigration*

Source:	1992 NES	1994 Times Mirror	
INDEPENDENT VARIABLES	Anti-Immigration Scale	Believes that "Immigrants are a Burden"	"Make Services Unavailable for Illegal Immigrants"
Institutional Knowledge	-0.677***	-0.702***	0.320**
Government Trust	-0.480***	-0.573***	-0.754***
Interpersonal Trust	-0.419***		
Personal Econ Experiences	0.007	0.006	0.002
Personal Econ Assessments	-0.164	-0.040	-0.043
Unemployed/Job Stress	0.043		
National Econ Assessments	-0.336*		
Future Econ Assessments	0.083	-0.019	-0.010
Ideology (Liberal High)	-0.057***	-0.095	-0.224***
Age	-0.001	-0.001	-0.010***
Income	0.019***	-0.025	0.092***
Sex (Female)	0.003	-0.002	-0.086
Race (White)	0.040	0.217	0.764***
Education	-0.605***	-0.249***	0.134***
Constant	1.413***	1.553***	-0.887***
N	1,524		
Adj. R-squared	0.132		
Log-Likelihood		268.40	281.12
Percent Correctly Predicted		66.3%	71.0%
Null		63.5%	69.8%

Note: Boldface and asterisks *** denote coefficients significant at the .01 level or better. Two asterisks denote a coefficient significant at the .05 level. One asterisk denotes a coefficient significant at the .10 level.

nomically focused, asking about whether new immigrants will "take jobs away from people already here." It is worth stressing that these insignificant coefficients are not the result of colinearity among the measures. The model can be replicated by using a single scale combining all three personal factors, or with each measure entered individually, and the results remain insignificant. Anti-immigrant sentiment is not based upon a reflexive reaction to personal economic stresses. Rather, it reflects deeper personal predispositions, and a person's ability to place this threat in the context of government institutions and ability.

Consistent with the sociotropic hypothesis of Kinder and Kiewiet (1981), the economic variable that is strongly related to anti-immigration sentiment is the assessment of how the national economy has performed. The more negative a person's assessments of the nation's economy, the stronger the anti-immigrant sentiment. With respect to immigration, confidence about the country's "bottom line" matters; however, our analysis shows that our understanding of and beliefs about government and others matter more. The significant effects of ideology (conservatives hold stronger anti-immigrant attitudes) and national economic assessments on attitudes about immigrants are consistent with more traditional models of public attitudes in which citizens follow elite signals or respond to "bottom-line" fundamentals. However, the significance of our measures of knowledge and trust suggests that citizens also draw on other considerations when assessing the impact of immigration.

The 1994 Times Mirror survey also contained questions measuring attitudes about immigration, questions which we hoped would verify our findings from the 1992 NES. Our results are mixed, however. Consistent with our NES results, whether people believe that immigrants strengthen the country or are a burden is strongly related to political knowledge and trust in government (Table 10.1, Column 2). Once again, none of the personal economic variables is related to anti-immigrant sentiment. (Recall that this survey did not contain questions about personal trust, job stress, or the national economy.)

Results differ greatly, however, when respondents are asked whether they support or oppose "changing policy so illegal immigrants are not eligible for welfare, Medicaid, and other government benefits" (Table 10.1, Column 3). In this case, we find that higher institutional knowledge is related to more anti-immigrant sentiment (making illegal immigrants ineligible for benefits), not less. Those who distrust government are again more anti-immigrant, as are whites and conservatives. But we have only surmises about why this one item shows a different relationship to political knowledge. In some way we cannot easily relate to our other results, changing policy to take immigrants off welfare or Medicaid appears to be very different from other anti-immigrant opinions. One possibility is that there is a framing effect conveyed by the phrase "changing policy." Another is that less knowledgeable people believe throwing immigrants out of welfare and Medicaid creates a bigger problem. Overall, the less knowledgeable appear to feel more threatened by immigration, and are more supportive of interdiction at the borders, but are less likely to support domestic anti-immigrant social policies.

Isolationism and Protectionism

One in four Americans agrees with the straightforward blanket isolationist sentiment that "This country would be better off if we just stayed home and did not concern ourselves with problems in other parts of the world." Likewise, over 40% of respondents wanted to see the United

States decrease aid to countries of the former Soviet Union. The roots of such political isolationism are often thought to reflect ideological ties – conservative citizens who oppose spending in general, and might pick up on the anti-involvement sentiments of conservative political elites. Similarly, it could be that isolationism reflects citizens' perceptions of economic conditions – concerns about economic problems at home might make individuals averse to the notion of foreign involvement.

We hypothesize that foreign attitudes reflect more than the reception of ideological cues or reflexive responses to economic self-interest. When evaluating uncertain international situations, individuals are likely to construct attitudes based upon domains with which they are familiar. Support for international coordination requires that one have an understanding of, or at least a faith in, one's own domestic institutions. Similarly, beliefs about the helpfulness of people around us translates into beliefs about the likelihood of international cooperation.

Our multivariate analysis lends strong support to this model of a reasoning citizen. Column 1 of Table 10.2 shows that familiarity with domestic institutions significantly decreases concerns over foreign involvement, suggesting that a person's ability to view international affairs within the context of the role of domestic institutions leads him or her to feel less isolationist. Similarly, trust in those same institutions has a parallel and independent effect. And, as with immigration, there is evidence that citizens who lack trust in the people around them tend to project that distrust when evaluating situations that are less familiar.

This hypothesis is reinforced with data from the 1994 Times Mirror survey, which asked specifically about "free trade agreements such as NAFTA or GATT." Contrary to media wisdom, opposition to these policies reflected people's knowledge about and trust in governing institutions (Table 10.2, Column 2). Isolationism is not propelled by personal finances, economic stress, or ideological cue taking. The Times Mirror survey shows us that opposition to free trade declined from 45% in the lowest information category to 23% in the highest, whereas economic evaluations and ideological predispositions had virtually no effect.

With both immigration and free trade, the same sort of logical contradiction in relations between distrust of government and policy choices emerges. People who do not trust government might be expected to want less government involvement in trade, and persons who do not trust government might be expected to want less government involvement in immigration. But people who distrust their government, in fact, want more controls on immigration and oppose free trade. We find these results particularly interesting since they imply that distrust leads people

Table 10.2. *Reasoning about international involvement*

Source:	1992 NES	1994 Times Mirror
INDEPENDENT VARIABLES	Isolationism Scale	Opposes Free Trade Agreements
Institutional Knowledge	**-0.348***	**-0.624***
Government Trust	**-0.223***	**0.694***
Interpersonal Trust	**-0.141**	
Personal Econ Experiences	-0.036	0.057
Personal Econ Assessments	-0.088	0.006
Unemployed/Job Stress	-0.076	
National Econ Assessments	**-0.281**	
Future Econ Assessments	-0.014	**-0.191***
Ideology (Liberal High)	0.001	0.056
Age	-0.002	-0.005
Income	0.001	-0.015
Sex (Female)	0.029	0.097
Race (White)	**-0.163**	
Education	**-0.114***	**-0.194***
Constant	**0.468***	0.107
N	1,554	
Adj. R-squared	0.086	
Log-Likelihood		180.87
Percent Correctly Predicted		70.0%
Null		68.9%

Note: Boldface and asterisks *** denote coefficients significant at the .01 level or better. Two asterisks denote a coefficient significant at the .05 level. One asterisk denotes a coefficient significant at the .10 level.

to be more anxious in general, and sometimes more supportive of involvement by the very same government in which they have so little faith.

Gulf War

The tendency for citizens who are unfamiliar with government to be more apprehensive about foreign affairs is a strong and consistent pattern. For example, when asked how worried they are about our country getting into a nuclear war, citizens less familiar with government are two times more likely to express concern than their more knowledgeable counterparts (data not shown). Clearly, an understanding and familiarity with domestic institutions provide a context in which global events can be understood differently. But what about when the country does get involved in international conflict, as in the Gulf War?

Table 10.3. *Reasoning about the Gulf War*

Source:	1992 NES
INDEPENDENT VARIABLES	Support for Gulf War Scale
Institutional Knowledge	**0.267****
Government Trust	**0.135***
Interpersonal Trust	0.052
Personal Econ Experiences	-0.110
Personal Econ Assessments	0.121
Unemployed/Job Stress	0.006
National Econ Assessments	**0.261****
Future Econ Assessments	**0.181***
Ideology (Liberal High)	**-0.083*****
Age	**-0.003***
Income	**0.010****
Sex (Female)	**-0.173*****
Race (White)	**0.358*****
Education	**-0.248****
Constant	**1.004*****
N	1,554
Adj. R-squared	0.167

Note: Boldface and asterisks *** denote coefficients significant at the .01 level or better. Two asterisks denote a coefficient significant at the .05 level. One asterisk denotes a coefficient significant at the .10 level.

Though support for the Gulf War was widespread, our multivariate model shows that levels of support varied systematically across a range of individual characteristics (Table 10.3). Many demographic characteristics, such as gender and race, which have had minimal effects in other models, prove to have important relationships with attitudes about U.S. involvement in this military exercise. Consistent with more traditional models of public attitudes, ideology and the economic "bottom line" had important effects on support for the war, though again, it seems that national and not personal economic evaluations are clearly the more important.

Citizens' evaluations of the Gulf War were also shaped by other considerations, however. In particular, familiarity with and trust in government once again proved to have an important effect on an individual's perspective on this issue. In retrospective evaluations of the Gulf War, respondents with low levels of knowledge about political institutions were less willing to go along with prevailing sentiments that the United States did the right thing in the Gulf War or that the Gulf War was worth the costs. Less politically knowledgeable Americans, in other words, are neither patriotic flag-wavers instinctively proud that the United States won the war, nor bandwagoneers following the lead of political or media elites. Since the retrospective questions were asked in 1992, it is possible that the survival of Saddam Hussein made the war look less successful to low-information respondents. It is more likely, given the pattern of responses, that the low-information respondents never did see any connections between the war and their own future or the country's future. Distrust of government exhibits a smaller, but statistically significant, effect as well.

CONCLUSION

Ordinary Americans do not know many of the details of foreign policy and typically give limited attention to political debate on foreign issues, but their natural gut reasoning is not devoid of substance. We have shown that ordinary Americans can call on many predispositions and past experiences. As famed baseball manager Tony La Russa put it, discussing baseball strategy, "When you trust your gut you are trusting a lot of stuff that is there from the past."

Why should knowing who William Rehnquist or Tom Foley is, or which party controls Congress, affect attitudes about immigration, foreign investment, free trade, and isolationism? We have suggested that the answer lies in the ways that institutional knowledge affects how information is processed. First, citizens less knowledgeable about the political world interpret events and assess situations based upon different predispositions. People who do not know as much about the structure of political institutions do not think like the more knowledgeable, only slower or a bit fuzzier. The less knowledgeable view the world and politics differently. Second, whereas knowledgeable voters can put international events in political context, less knowledgeable voters react to events from a less secure vantage point.

Although political knowledge is not necessary to bring many predispositions to bear, it does provide context and affect how persons process information. Persons who possess little knowledge about political institutions tend to see free trade, immigration, and international involvement as more threatening than do those who have some knowledge about the political institutions that maintain sovereignty and regulate these exchanges. It is not the persons who know about institutions and find them wanting who are the most isolationist, anti-immigrant, or anti–free trade. It is the persons who, knowing little about them, imagine even worse than that the knowledgeable critics may find.

These results parallel Rahn, Aldrich, and Borgida's (1994) experimental findings in the area of candidate assessment. Hypothesizing that persons less familiar with the political process will also have a harder time following political hearings, fights, and debates, these researchers randomly assigned subjects to groups that would receive the same information but in different formats. Their results show how knowledgeability affects citizen ability to learn about politics and politicians from debates. Less knowledgeable persons could not learn as much information from a 30-minute debate in which the statements of two politicians were interspersed as they could from two separate 15-minute speeches. In other words, when there is a long series of charges and countercharges, most unknowledgeable people lose track of the issues or principles behind the skirmishes. What might have started as good guys versus bad guys soon becomes nothing more than a free-for-all. To persons who understand the institutions of politics, a long set of exchanges between, say, Bill Clinton and Robert Dole can be as clear as a sustained volley in tennis; to persons without any knowledge of institutions, their exchange is hard to follow and becomes indistinguishable from a food fight or mud slinging. Whereas in domestic politics this confusion might lead only to boredom or disgust, in international politics, we believe it leads to perceptions of a more dangerous and out-of-control world.

The effects of low information are compounded by political distrust. Although distrust in government has not been related to turnout, it is clearly related to the premises with which people begin their policy assessments. The evidence we present here shows that high levels of concern about immigration and foreign involvement are not knee-jerk reactions to personal economic stresses or other "bottom-line" issues, but represent deeper reactions to American citizens' lack of trust and information about government. The defeat of fast-track legislation in 1997, when unemployment was at its lowest point in 25 years and distrust in government was near its highest, emphasizes this point.

The consistent influence of both governmental and interpersonal trust is of central importance to our hypothesis about citizen reasoning. When evaluating distant or unfamiliar situations, people are likely to draw upon predispositions with which they are more familiar, and about which they have more certainty. The fact that the very people who distrust government want our government to retain its power to restrict trade instead of supporting free trade, and want government to increase its control over immigration, exemplify this point. Distrust in government does not always lead to opposition to government programs. Instead, the general misgivings people have about domestic institutions translates into a broader uncertainty about these international situations, causing people to support action by the very government they distrust. Likewise, suspicion of foreigners does not reflect a nationalistic or patriotic pride.

Rather, it is the very people who distrust their neighbors who are also likely to distrust people from other countries, whom they have never met.

Overall, simply because citizens lack extensive information about foreign policy does not imply that they defenseless against media or elite manipulation. Nor do their attitudes simply reflect the economic "bottom line" as they see it. Rather, citizens adapt to limited information by drawing upon a variety of heuristics in order to evaluate foreign policies and foreign events. We therefore challenge the past research that has emphasized the role that party and ideology can play in this process, yet has found that remarkably few citizens were politically "engaged" or "sophisticated" enough to draw upon these particular predispositions (Campbell et al. 1960; Delli Carpini and Keeter 1996; Zaller 1992). This emphasis on political reference points understates the citizen's ability to reason from other predispositions, such as trust in others. There is no reason to expect that knowledge and trust are the only heuristics citizens apply to their reasoning about foreign affairs; however, by showing how knowledge and trust serve to shape foreign policy attitudes, we are taking one step toward establishing that such a reasoning process exists.

Appendix 1. *Scale construction and question wording: 1992 American National Election Study*

Anti-Immigration Scale: (alpha = .675)

V6238   How likely is it for the growing number of Hispanics to take jobs away from people already here -- extremely likely, very likely, somewhat likely, or not at all likely?

	[1] Extremely Or Very	49.02%
	[0] Somewhat Or Not At All	50.98%

V6241   How likely is it for the growing number of Asians to take jobs away from people already here -- extremely likely, very likely, somewhat likely, or not at all likely?

	[1] Extremely Or Very	49.29%
	[0] Somewhat Or Not At All	50.71%

V6235   Do you think the number of immigrants from foreign countries who are permitted to come to the Unites States to live should be increased a little, increased a lot, decreased a little, decreased a lot, or left the same as it is now?

	[1] Decreased a Little or Decreased a Lot	47.50%
	[0] Increased, Left the Same, DK/NA	52.50%

230

Concern about War Scale: (alpha = .646)

V3606 How worried are you about our country getting into a nuclear war at this time?
Are you very worried, somewhat worried, or not worried at all?

[1] Very Or Somewhat Worried	45.12%
[0] Not Worried, DK/NA	54.88%

V3607 How worried are you about our country getting into a conventional war at this
time, one in which nuclear weapons are not used? Are you very worried, somewhat
worried, or not worried at all?

[1] Very Or Somewhat Worried	55.44%
[0] Not Worried, DK/NA	44.56%

Support for Gulf War Scale: (alpha = .677)

V3608 Now we want to ask you about the Persian Gulf war that took place in early 1991.
Do you think we did the right thing in sending U.S. military forces to the Persian Gulf or
should we have stayed out?

[1] Did the Right Thing	74.29%
[0] Stayed Out/Depends/Other/DK/NA	25.71%

V3629 All things considered, do you think the war was worth the cost or not?

[1] Worth It	52.23%
[0] Not Worth It , DK/NA	47.77%

Isolationism Scale: (alpha = .326)

V3604 I am going to read you a statement about U.S. foreign policy and I would like
you to tell me whether you agree or disagree.   This country would be better off if we just
stayed home and did not concern ourselves with problems in other parts of the world.

[1] Agree	25.79%
[0] Disagree, DK/NA	74.21%

V3726 (Should federal spending be increased, decreased, or kept about the same on . . .)
Aid to countries of the former Soviet Union?

[1] Decreased	40.72%
[0] Increased, Kept the Same, DK	59.28%

<u>Political Knowledge Scale (alpha = .770)</u>

• Whose responsibility is it to nominate judges to the Federal Courts... the president, the Congress, the Supreme Court, or don't you know? (the president)	Correct Incorrect DK/NA	57.9 22.9 19.2
• Who has the final responsibility to decide if a law is constitutional or not... is it the president, the Congress, the Supreme Court, or don't you know? (Supreme Court)	Correct Incorrect DK/NA	57.6 28.2 14.1
• Do you happen to know which party had the most members in the House of Representatives in Washington before the election last month? (Democrats)	Correct Incorrect DK/NA	59.2 13.0 27.8
• Do you happen to know which party had the most members in the U.S. Senate before the election last month? (Democrats)	Correct Incorrect DK/NA	51.0 11.0 38.0

Now we have a set of questions concerning various public figures. We want to see how much information about them gets out to the public from television, newspapers, and the like. The first name is Dan Quayle. What job or political office does he now hold?

• Dan Quayle	Correct Incorrect DK/NA	87.6 1.3 11.1
• Tom Foley	Correct Incorrect DK/NA	25.7 11.7 62.6
• William Rehnquist	Correct Incorrect DK/NA	8.4 16.9 74.7

232

Trust in Government Scale: (alpha = .605)

V6120 How much of the time do you think you can trust the government in Washington to do what is right?

      [1] Most of the Time/Always   69.67%
      [0] Only Some of the Time/Never (volunteered)/DK 30.33%

V6121 Do you think that people in government waste a lot of the money we pay in taxes, waste some of it, or don't waste very much of it?

      [1] Some/Not Very Much   67.18%
      [0] A Lot/DK   32.82%

V6122 Would you say the government is pretty much run by a few big interests looking out for themselves or that it is run for the benefit of all the people?

      [1] Benefit of All   74.46%
      [0] Big Interests/DK   25.54%

V6123 Do you think that quite a few of the people running the government are crooked, not very many are, or do you think hardly any of them are crooked?

      [1] Not Many/Hardly Any   45.32%
      [0] Quite a Few/DK   54.68%

Distrust in People Scale (alpha = .635)

V6139 Generally speaking, would you say that most people can be trusted, or that you can't be too careful in dealing with people?

      [1] Most Can Be Trusted   54.19%
      [0] Can't Be Too Careful/DK/NA 45.81%

V6140 Would you say that most of the time people try to be helpful, or that they are mostly just looking out for themselves?

      [1] Try to Be Helpful   38.76%
      [0] Just Look Out for Themselves/DK/NA 61.24%

National Economic Assessments Scale: (alpha = .612)

	Better [-1]	Same/DK [0]	Worse [1]
V3527 Level of Unemployment over the past year	2.61%	17.83%	79.56%
V3529 Level of Inflation over the past year	6.24%	39.92%	53.84%
V3531 National Economy over the past year	4.55%	24.02%	71.43%

Personal Economic Assessments Scale: (alpha = .654)

	Better [-1]	Same/DK [0]	Worse [1]
V3425 Personal Economy since year ago	30.14%	35.37%	34.49%
V3429 Income in Relation to Cost of Living	11.03%	41.45%	47.53%

Future Economic Assessments Scale: (alpha = .450)

	Better [-1]	Same/DK [0]	Worse [1]
V3427 Personal Economy a year from now	32.64%	57.67%	9.70%
V3533 National Economy over the next year	29.98%	52.19%	17.83%
V3540 Standard of Living for Children	31.83%	24.31%	43.86%

Unemployed/Job Stress Scale: (alpha = .456)

V3960 How worried are you about losing your job/not being able to find a job in the near future: a lot, somewhat, or not much at all?

[1] A Lot or Somewhat	25.49%
[0] Not Much, DK/NA	74.51%

V3915 Summary of Respondent working status: respondent is Unemployed or Temporarily Laid Off.

[1] Unemployed or Laid Off	7.04%
[0] Employed, Student, etc.	92.96%

Personal Economic Experiences Scale: (alpha = .686)

V3433	During the past year have you/your family been able to buy most of the things you needed or have you had to put off buying these things?	[1] "Put Off" [0] "Able to Buy" or DK	53.26% 46.74%
V3434	In the past year did you/anyone in your family put off medical or dental treatment because you didn't have the money?	[1] Yes [0] No/DK	30.83% 69.17%
V3435	In order to make ends meet this past year did (any of) you borrow money from a bank, a lending institution, or from relatives or friends?	[1] Yes [0] No/DK	34.80% 65.20%
V3436	In order to make ends meet, this past year did (any of) you dip into your savings?	[1] Yes [0] No/DK	46.52% 53.48%
V3437	In order to make ends meet this past year did (any of) you look for a job, look for a second job, or try to work more hours at your present job?	[1] Yes [0] No/DK	41.55% 58.45%
V3439	This past year have you/your family fallen behind in rent or house payments?	[1] Yes [0] No/DK	11.46% 88.54%

Ideology

V3509, V3511, V3512 recoded into the following scale:

-3	-2	-1	0	1	2	3
Conserv or Extremely Conserv	Slightly Conserv	If had to choose, Conserv	Moderate or Haven't Thought	If had to choose, Liberal	Slightly Liberal	Liberal or Extremely Liberal

Popkin and Dimock

Appendix 2. *1994 Times Mirror Center for the People and the Press "New Political Landscape" survey questions*

Immigrants Are a Burden

Question 21 Lead In:
"I'm going to read you some pairs of statements that will help us understand how you feel about a number of things. As I read each pair, tell me whether the FIRST statement or the SECOND statement comes closer to your own views -- even if neither is exactly right.

Q21g. STATEMENT ONE: [0] Immigrants today strengthen our country because of their hard work and talents 30.9%
[0] Neither, Both, Unsure 5.9%
STATEMENT TWO: [1] Immigrants today are a burden on our country because they take our jobs, housing, and health 63.2%

Oppose Free Trade Agreements

Question 25 Lead In:
"I'd like your opinion of some programs and proposals being discussed in this country today. Please tell me if you strongly favor, favor, oppose, or strongly oppose each one."

Q25j. Free trade agreements between the United States and other countries, such as NAFTA or GATT
[1] Strongly Favor 17.7%
[1] Favor 44.1%
[0] DK/NA 10.5%
[0] Oppose 17.7%
[0] Strongly Oppose 10.1%

Make Services Unavailable for Illegal Immigrants

Q25n. Changing policy so illegal immigrants are not eligible for welfare, Medicaid, and other government benefits
[1] Strongly Favor 41.1%
[1] Favor 27.9%
[0] DK/NA 2.6%
[0] Oppose 18.1%
[0] Strongly Oppose 10.3%

236

Knowledge, Trust, and Reasoning

Political Knowledge Scale (alpha = .547)

Q17. Can you tell me the name of the current vice president of the United States?

[1] Al Gore	64.8%
[0] Other, DK/NA	35.2%

Q18. Do you happen to know which political party has a majority in the U.S. House of Representatives?

[1] Democratic party	59.5%
[0] Republicans, DK/NA	40.5%

Q19. Can you tell me the name of the president of Russia?

[1] Boris Yeltsin	45.5%
[0] Other, DK/NA	55.5%

Distrust in Government Scale (alpha = .404)

(Which statement comes closer to your own views -- even if neither is exactly right.)

Q21a. STATEMENT ONE: Government is almost always wasteful and inefficient.
STATEMENT TWO: Government often does a better job than people give it credit for.

[2] Statement One Strongly	54.1%
[1] Statement One Not Strongly	12.2%
[0] Neither/Both (volunteered) DK/NA	3.0%
[-1] Statement Two Not Strongly	13.5%
[-2] Statement Two Strongly	17.2%

Q21o. STATEMENT ONE: Elected officials in Washington lose touch with the people pretty quickly.
STATEMENT TWO: Elected officials in Washington try hard to stay in touch with voters back home.

[2] Statement One Strongly	58.1%
[1] Statement One Not Strongly	13.2%
[0] Neither/Both (volunteered) DK/NA	3.4%
[-1] Statement Two Not Strongly	11.2%
[-2] Statement Two Strongly	14.1%

<u>Economic Variables</u>

Future Personal Economics
Q26.   Over the course of the next year, do you think the financial situation of you and your family will:

[2] Improve a lot	8.6%
[1] Improve some	54.4%
[0] Same (volunteered), DK/NA	13.6%
[-1] Get a little worse	18.0%
[-2] Get a lot worse	5.4%

Personal Economic Assessments
Q38y   STATEMENT ONE: I'm generally satisfied with the way things are going for me financially
        STATEMENT TWO: I'm not very satisfied with my financial situation

[2] Statement One Strongly	36.1%
[1] Statement One Not Strongly	20.3%
[0] Neither/Both (volunteered) DK/NA	1.0%
[-1] Statement Two Not Strongly	9.8%
[-2] Statement Two Strongly	32.8%

Personal Economic Experiences
Q38z.   STATEMENT ONE: I often don't have enough money to make ends meet
         STATEMENT TWO: Paying the bills is generally not a problem for me

[2] Statement One Strongly	27.4%
[1] Statement One Not Strongly	8.4%
[0] Neither/Both (volunteered) DK/NA	1.4%
[-1] Statement Two Not Strongly	19.9%
[-2] Statement Two Strongly	42.9%

11

Coping with Trade-Offs: Psychological Constraints and Political Implications
PHILIP E. TETLOCK

A thoughtful reader of the psychological literature on judgment and choice might easily walk away with the impression that people are flat-out incapable of reasoning their way through value trade-offs (Kahneman, Slovic, and Tversky 1982). Trade-offs are just too cognitively complex, emotionally stressful, and socially awkward for people to manage them effectively, to avoid entanglement in Tverskian paradoxes, such as intransitivities within choice tasks and preference reversals across choice tasks. But what looks impossible from certain psychological points of view looks utterly unproblematic from a microeconomic perspective. Of course, people can engage in trade-off reasoning. They do it all the time – every time they stroll down the aisle of the supermarket or cast a vote or opt in or out of a marriage (Becker 1981). We expect competent, self-supporting citizens of free market societies to know that they can't always get what they want and to make appropriate adjustments. Trade-off reasoning should be so pervasive and so well rehearsed as to be virtually automatic for the vast majority of the non-institutionalized population.

We could just leave it there in a post-positivist spirit of live-and-let-live pluralism. The disciplinary divergence provides just another illustration of how competing theoretical discourses construct reality in their own image. This "resolution" is, however, less than helpful to political scientists who borrow from cognitive psychology or microeconomics in crafting theories of political reasoning. The theoretical choice reduces to a matter of taste, in effect, an unconditional surrender to solipsism.

I appreciate the editors' helpful comments on an earlier version of this essay, as well as the editorial and research assistance of Heather Kinney. The research reported in this chapter was supported by a grant from the National Science Foundation (BNS 732396) and assisted by three institutions: The Center for Advanced Study in the Behavioral Sciences, The Institute of Personality and Social Research of the University of California, Berkeley, and The Mershon Center of Ohio State University.

At the risk, therefore, of appearing to be an epistemological primitive (a pre-post-positivist), I'll pose the Stone Age question "Who is right?" And, if we can not identify a clear winner, what exactly does it mean to assert that the "truth" lies somewhere between the rationalist and cognitivist positions? What boundary conditions can we identify? When does trade-off reasoning approximate the microeconomic ideal? And when do cognitive, emotional, and cultural constraints make themselves felt? Finally, what are the political implications? Are politicians who acknowledge trade-offs candidly at a serious public-relations disadvantage (as some psychological formulations would suggest)? Can we determine when acknowledging trade-offs can be politically lethal and when it might even be beneficial?

The first section of the chapter lays out the grounds for supposing the worst about the human capacity for coping with trade-offs. The case for pessimism draws on the work of behavioral decision theorists on choice heuristics and loss aversion (Kahneman, Slovic, and Tversky 1982; Kahneman and Tversky 1979); of cognitive consistency and psychodynamic theorists on "bolstering" (Festinger 1964; Janis and Mann 1977); and of anthropologists and social psychologists on "taboo trade-offs" (Fiske and Tetlock 1997; Tetlock, Peterson, and Lerner 1996). Taken together, these arguments suggest that people are reluctant decision makers who do their damnedest to minimize cognitive effort, emotional dissonance, and moral angst by denying that important values conflict. If we assume a pluralistic polity that regularly thrusts important values into sharp conflict (Berlin 1969, 1990), this portrait of the decision maker warns us to expect chronic mismanagement of trade-offs. People, certainly the mass public but probably also elites, will be slow to recognize that core values clash; they will rely on mental shortcuts that eliminate direct comparisons between clashing values; they will engage in the dissonance-reduction strategy of bolstering to reduce the stress of those value conflicts they are forced to acknowledge; and they will resort to decision-evasion tactics, such as buck-passing, procrastination, and obfuscation, to escape responsibility for making choices that inevitably leave some constituency feeling it has gotten the short end of the trade-off stick.

The second section of the chapter qualifies this grim assessment of our capacity to cope with trade-offs. People are best thought of not as cognitive misers but rather as cognitive managers who deploy mental resources strategically as a function of the perceived importance and tractability of the problem. The value pluralism model of political reasoning is in this cognitive-managerial spirit – it specifies when people are likely to invest effort in overtly compensatory trade-off reasoning, as opposed to relying on simple, easy-to-execute heuristics. The model makes predictions concerning the main effects and interactive effects of political ideology, issue domain, institutional role, and electoral accountability on the complexity of trade-off reasoning. I survey the evidence bearing on these predictions – evidence that includes laboratory experiments on undergraduates, content analyses of both confidential interviews and public statements of elites, and representative-sample surveys of mass publics.

Finally, this chapter presents two exploratory lines of empirical work – one of which suggests that the value pluralism model may exaggerate the flexibility of trade-off reasoning (at least when such reasoning touches on taboo topics), and the other of which suggests that the value pluralism model is correct in crediting people with a metacognitive capacity to shift strategically from simple to complex to simple modes of thinking. Work on *taboo* trade-offs harkens us back to a pessimistic assessment of human rationality – a view of people as not just cognitive misers but as cognitive primitives who recoil from normatively suspect trade-offs in fear and horror. A key research question becomes: How literally should we take the designation taboo? Are taboo trade-offs "taboo" in the primal Polynesian senses of the term: (a) rooted in unreasoned aversion; (b) extraordinarily resistant to change; and (c) capable of contaminating anyone or anything associated with violations of the taboo? One set of studies investigated whether taboos are pure affect or are rooted in cause-effect beliefs about utilitarian consequences. They did so by assessing whether we could deactivate the moral outrage triggered by taboo trade-offs and present counterarguments designed to deflect common objections that people (who are not too consumed by outrage) offer to such trade-offs. A second set of studies examined the issue of contamination by assessing whether we could transform previously popular politicians into objects of scorn by revealing that their decision process violated the taboo proscription on affixing dollar values to human life. Both sets of studies suggest that taboo is an apt characterization of how half or more of college-educated samples in late-twentieth-century America deal with trade-offs that require attaching monetary values to objects, actions, rights, and responsibilities that our secular society deems sacred.

The other line of work contains more upbeat implications for defenders of mass rationality: It examines popular reactions to political rhetoric that either denies trade-offs (by claiming to possess a dominant option that is superior on all dimensions of comparison) or affirms trade-offs (by depicting choice as a complex balancing act in which different values must be given different weights in different situations). When do people see the embracing of trade-offs by politicians as evidence of moral weakness (lack of principles) and of mental confusion (trapped in the throes of Hamlet-like paralysis)? And when do they see the same style of rea-

241

soning as evidence of a mature temperament that recognizes the contradictory demands of life? And how do people react to politicians who deny trade-offs? When do they find such political figures inspiring, energizing, and charismatic, or when do they suspect demagoguery? Although trade-off reasoning is often a net political liability, there are noteworthy exceptions. Much depends on the political temper of the times: If people have been primed by recent experiences to place a negative "value spin" on trade-off denial (the shrill demagogue) and a positive spin on trade-off acceptance (the thoughtful statesman), politicians who acknowledge trade-offs can even prevail in the competition for public favor.

So, where will this leave us? The empirical battle over rationality is but three or four decades old. The opening volley – the cognitive critique of homo economicus – scored palpable hits. But the severely bounded rationality of homo psychologicus – the cognitive miser who is prisoner of his or her simplification strategies – has proven too constraining and has already been superseded by a wave of cognitive-manager models that depict decision makers who decide how to decide and who can occasionally even approximate the ideal type of economic rationality. There are reasons for suspecting that this synthetic position – the cognitive manager – strikes a compelling compromise between the economic and psychological world views. But it is hardly likely to be the last word in this dialectical process. Cognitive managers work within complex constraints, including computational capacity, emotional arousal, and cultural norms. There is plenty of room for reasonable disagreement over how tightly constraining these constraints are in specific choice tasks. This chapter traces the yin/yang progression of this debate within my own research program.

OBSTACLES TO TRADE-OFF REASONING

Psychological theorists have identified at least four mutually reinforcing reasons for supposing that people are incapable of doing what microeconomic theory postulates people do routinely.

The first obstacle to trade-off reasoning is arguably the most fundamental: the incommensurability problem created by the absence of a common metric for translating competing values into each other. By definition, trade-offs require interdimensional comparisons – balancing proverbial apples and oranges – that people do not have the cognitive equipment to perform in reliable ways. Most of us do not have carefully calibrated subjective scales to generate judgments of the form: What loss of liberty would I accept to achieve this increment in public safety? How many young American lives is it worth sacrificing to stop genocide in eastern Europe or central Africa? Lacking the mental means for making the necessary interdimensional computations, people are hard-pressed to produce reliable (less still, utility-maximizing) answers to trade-off questions. Within choice tasks, we often observe breakdowns in the transitivity of preferences as people choose A over B, B over C, and C over A. Across choice tasks, we often observe that the method of preference elicitation – for example, choice versus matching – determines which side of the issue people endorse. Intransitivities and preference reversals should simply never happen from the standpoint of rational-choice theory (Thaler 1991; Tversky and Thaler 1990). But these anomalies from a rational-choice point of view are readily explained by cognitive theories of choice that postulate widespread reliance on easy-to-execute heuristics. For instance, Tversky's (1972) elimination-by-aspects rule eliminates the cognitive strain of "compensatory" trade-off reasoning by allowing people to screen options "lexicographically," one value at a time, typically starting with the most important or salient value and eliminating all options that fail to pass some threshold, and then screening the remaining options on secondary values until only one remains. But there is no free lunch. The price of minimizing cognitive strain is susceptibility to error (in this case, intransitivities in preference). Ironically, the mental escape from trade-offs itself involves a trade-off – an effort-accuracy trade-off.

A second obstacle to trade-off reasoning is emotional. As Leon Festinger (1957) pointed out 40 years ago, most people find it dissonant to acknowledge to themselves that they have sacrificed one value for another. The more important the value, the greater the potential for anticipatory regret, in which people ponder what would have happened in the counterfactual world in which they chose the "other path." To avoid the cognitive dissonance of acknowledging that one is an incompetent or immoral decision maker, or to avoid sinking into depressive rumination about better possible worlds that could have been, people often "spread the alternatives." They exaggerate the importance of the chosen value and derogate the rejected value.

A third obstacle is fear of criticism. Critics can always accuse us of having chosen the wrong path, an especially tempting accusation given what prospect theory tells us about the psychophysical tendency for losses on the value we have sacrificed to loom larger than gains on the value we have chosen (Kahneman and Tversky 1979). Politicians quite rightly see early career changes in their future when they publicly endorse trade-offs that impose losses on key constituencies. The gratitude of the "winners" is rarely as intense or long-lived as the resentment of the losers.

The fourth obstacle is cultural. From a microeconomic perspective, it should be possible to reduce all values to a single utility metric. But cross-cultural analysis reveals that although people deem many trade-offs legitimate, they categorically reject others as contemptible and unworthy of any consideration. What accounts for the sharpness of this resistance? Tetlock et al. (1996) have argued that the resistance is not reducible to run-of-the-mill "incommensurability" – the cognitive difficulty of comparing proverbial apples and oranges. Such comparisons may be difficult, but we do them all the time when we balance our household budgets. Moreover, there is nothing embarrassing or shameful about admitting that we make trade-offs when we make decisions about the wine, meat, or leisure time we consume (unless in doing so, we reveal that we've violated some religious law or moral precept to which we supposedly adhere).

Rather, opposition to reducing diverse values to a single metric is rooted in "constitutive incommensurability." The guiding idea is that our commitments to other people forbid certain comparisons. To transgress these normative boundaries, to attach a monetary value to one's friendships or children or loyalty to a nation-state, is to disqualify oneself from certain social roles, to demonstrate that one just "doesn't get it" – one does not understand what it means to be a true friend or parent or citizen. We run into constitutive incommensurability whenever the treating of values as commensurable subverts one or both of the values in the trade-off calculus. To compare is to destroy. Even to think about certain trade-offs (less still, to make them) is to corrupt and degrade one's standing as a moral being in the larger community. In the words of the moral philosopher Joseph Raz (1986: 21): "It is impoverishing to compare the value of a marriage with an increase in salary. It diminishes one's potentiality as a human being to put a value on one's friendship in terms of improved living conditions." Durkheim (1973) expressed the same sentiment in sociological language when he observed that in both "primitive religious" and "advanced secular" societies, people ascribe a transcendental quality to fundamental values of their social order. Even sophisticated citizens of industrialized democracies tenaciously resist treating these sacred values as objects of market or political calculation. Their attitude is less one of utilitarian calculation than that of believers to their diety, a stance of absolute faith that imposes a mysterious barrier around social morality. Violations of sacred or ultimate values are not just cognitively perplexing; they are morally destabilizing. They shake the foundations of our social being, provoking both moral outrage and demands for punishment. And, as Daniel Bell (1980) argued, we should be none too sure that the inexorable advance of technical rationality will sweep such quasi-religious thinking away in the near future. Nineteenth-century predictions of the "end of religion" in the twentieth century have proven, at best, embarrassingly premature. We may be observing here a deeply human resistance to the homogenization of experience in the technically precise formulas of cost-benefit analysis. People resent the institutional pressures to conform to the "iron-cage" imperatives of functional rationality and economic efficiency. They want – and sometimes insist upon – more out of life.

When one adds up all of the obstacles to trade-off reasoning, one certainly does not have a logically tight case that explicit trade-off reasoning is impossible, but one does have a strong case that it is likely to be rather rare and painfully difficult. One should expect that people will often mismanage trade-offs and that, although elites may be more attuned to value conflicts, educational achievement and social standing will confer little protection against the powerful psychological forces arrayed against candid, self-conscious, and overtly compensatory weighing of conflicting values (Sniderman, Fletcher, Russell, and Tetlock 1996). One should also expect widespread reliance on lexicographic shortcuts, such as elimination by aspects (Tversky 1972), and cybernetic shortcuts (Steinbruner 1974), such as sequential adaptation in which people discover that they have had enough of any given value only after they have had more than enough. These shortcuts "solve" the incommensurability problem by eliminating the need for direct comparisons of conflicting values. People can make trade-offs without being at all conscious of having done so. When the trade-off is called to public attention, we should expect widespread recourse to the trilogy of decision-evasion tactics (Tetlock and Boettger 1994) – buck-passing (transfer responsibility to others), procrastination (delay the day of reckoning), and obfuscation (render opaque where one stands and, ideally, who wins and who loses as a result). And when the trade-off is public knowledge, and so too is one's responsibility for making the final call, we should expect widespread resort to the dual dissonance-reduction strategies of denial and bolstering, playing down the strengths of the to-be-slighted value and playing up the strengths of the to-be-rejected value, thereby producing the classic "spreading-of-the-alternatives" effect.

How serious a threat do these trade-off avoidance strategies pose to political rationality? Much hinges on subtle issues of governance beyond the province of this chapter. But insofar as one believes, pace Berlin (1969), that trade-offs are a defining feature of any pluralistic polity in which competing groups can never get everything they want and claim to deserve, often as a matter of "right," there are ample grounds for concern. Once an issue has been successfully framed (in the Gamson, not the Kahneman, sense) as implicating a right, it becomes a taboo trade-off that is exempted from the logrolling give-and-take of normal politics and ceases to be an openly negotiable item. And insofar as one believes that trade-off avoidance carries a steep price tag by inhibiting candid discussion of opportunity costs and looming threats, those grounds for concern are further reinforced. The more adroit interest groups become in framing their claims on collective resources as entitlements and rights, the more reluctant rational vote-maximizing politicians will be to make trade-offs that openly challenge the demosclerotic stranglehold those groups gradually acquire over national policy (cf. Olson 1982; Rauch 1995).

THE VALUE PLURALISM MODEL

Psychological arguments that stress the difficulty of trade-off reasoning inevitably collide with the arguments advanced by both evolutionary and economic theorists that trade-off reasoning is an indispensable and therefore universal skill. Coping with scarcity – of time, physical energy, emotional energy, and material resources – has been a fundamental feature of human existence for millions of years (cf. Cosmides and Tooby 1992). Coping with scarcity is also a defining feature of minimal competence for citizens in a free-market society in which all self-supporting adults are expected to set spending priorities within limited budgets (cf. Becker 1981). An apparent paradox thus arises: How do people cope as effectively with scarcity as they do if they are as inept as psychologists say at trade-off reasoning?

The value pluralism model – presented in detail in Tetlock et al. (1996) – strikes an uneasy compromise between the functionalist imperatives of survival in a world of scarcity and the psychological constraints on trade-off reasoning revealed by the laboratory literature. This model asserts that although some people and ideological factions are more open to the possibility that core values clash than are others (a political personality postulate of the model), virtually everybody can be motivated to engage in trade-off reasoning when the optimal conditions hold, including that: (a) scarcity compels people to acknowledge that values conflict (transparency); (b) the values in conflict are both important and approximately equally important (equal activation/salience of competing values); (c) people believe that it is culturally acceptable to consider the trade-offs in question; (d) people see no socially acceptable way of avoiding taking a stand by invoking one of the trilogy of decision-evasion tactics – buckpassing, procrastination, and obfuscation; and (e) people believe that they are accountable to an audience that magnifies motives for self-critical policy analysis and vigilance.

When all conditions are satisfied, we should expect a relatively rare pattern of cognitive processing to become quite common: namely, explicitly compensatory trade-off reasoning in which people acknowledge the legitimacy of conflicting values and propose integration rules for generating compromises that give some weight to each conflicting value, with the weighting often varying with the context.

A host of hypotheses follow from the general logic of the value pluralism model. This section summarizes the key predictions and empirical results over the last 15 years:

(a) The model assumes that underlying all political belief systems are ultimate or terminal values (Lane 1973; Rokeach 1973) that specify the end-state goals of public policy. These values – which may take such diverse forms as economic efficiency, social equality, individual freedom, crime control, national security, and racial purity – function as the back-stops of belief systems. When we press people to justify their policy preferences, all inquiry ultimately terminates in values that people find it ridiculous to justify any further. Antiabortion partisans consider "because life is sacred" a self-explanatory justification for their position just, as pro-choice partisans consider "women's liberty" to be a self-justifying justification for their position.

Political ideologies do vary dramatically, however, in the degree to which they acknowledge conflicts among terminal values. Some belief systems are self-consciously pluralistic, accepting the pervasiveness of value conflict and the necessity of trade-offs; others are self-consciously monistic, depicting core values as perfectly harmonious, all pointing in one policy direction (Berlin 1969). From a value pluralism perspective, advocates of pluralistic (usually centrist) ideologies should be more prac-ticed in complex trade-off reasoning than advocates of monistic (usually extremist) ideologies. Here we can report a rather reliable cross-national effect from content and structural analysis of intra-elite political debate: The point of maximum "integrative complexity" in elite political debate often peaks at the center or slightly to the left of center in legislative bodies, such as the U.S. Senate (Tetlock, Hannum and Micheletti 1984), the British House of Commons (Tetlock 1984), the Italian Chamber of Deputies (diRenzo 1967; Putnam 1971), and the Israeli Knesset (Maoz and Shayer 1987).

(b) The value pluralism model warns us, however, not to expect certain ideological groups to be always more prone to complex trade-off reasoning than other groups. Rather, the general expectation is for ideology-by-issue interactions in which the point of maximum complex-ity of trade-off reasoning shifts from one topical domain to another across ideological groups as a function of whether important and approximately equally important values have been brought into conflict by the framing of the issue. For instance, Tetlock (1986) found that liberals were most likely to reason in integratively complex trade-off terms when the issue frame brought economic efficiency into conflict with social equality (Okun's, 1975, "big trade-off"), whereas conservatives engaged in the most overtly compensatory trade-off reasoning when the issue frame brought national defense and fiscal prudence into conflict.

(c) The value pluralism model also warns us not to treat explicit trade-off reasoning as inherently cognitively or morally superior to categorical rejection of trade-offs. It is not difficult to identify historical contexts within which contemporary sympathies overwhelmingly favor those factions that vociferously denied trade-offs: Churchillian opponents of British appeasement of Nazi Germany in the 1930s who denounced Chamberlain's effort to strike a subtle balance between deterrence and reassurance (Tetlock and Tyler 1996); and abolitionists in the slavery debates of antebellum America who denounced free-soil Republicans who sought integratively complex compromises that would avert war and preserve the Union, but indefinitely preserve slavery in southern states (Tetlock, Armor, and Peterson 1994). It is also not difficult to identify historical contexts within which contemporary observers deplore not just one but both of the values that complex trade-off reasoners attempted to balance against each other. Pragmatic Nazis were quick in World War II to recognize the gruesome trade-off between their goals of mobilizing military resources to win the war and devoting resources to the extermination of Jews. There is nothing intrinsically morally meritorious about trade-off reasoning.

(d) The value pluralism model stresses the importance of political accountability as a moderator of how people deal with value conflict (Tetlock 1992). Complex trade-off reasoning should be more common in the rhetoric of governing parties that have responsibility for coping with scarcity than it should be among opposition parties (whose primary role is to incite resentment among those who feel they are getting the short end of the trade-off stick from the governing party). In line with this reasoning, Tetlock, Hannum, and Micheletti (1984) found that when control of both Congress and the presidency shifted from liberals to conservatives, there was a decline in trade-off reasoning in liberal rhetoric and a corresponding increase in conservative rhetoric. Indeed, Gruenfeld (1995) has shown that this "minority-majority" effect even holds up among decision makers who are not subject to electoral accountability, namely, justices of the U.S. Supreme Court. Majority opinions – which often require delicate coalition building and have the force of law – contain more explicit trade-off reasoning than do minority opinions, which offer authors the moral luxury of waxing indignant about the shortcomings of the majority opinion.

(e) Given the limited capacity of the mass public to process complex political messages, the value pluralism model predicts that imminent accountability to the electorate should reduce complex trade-off reasoning, at least in public statements. In the competitive heat of campaigns, political parties should find it advantageous to simplify their messages and downplay trade-offs, thereby minimizing opportunities for critics to highlight trade-offs that impose losses on identifiable, perhaps electorally decisive, constituencies. This prediction holds up well for most presidents of the twentieth century (Tetlock 1981a). But there may well be historical and political-cultural boundary conditions on this hypothesis: How people respond to rhetoric of varying complexity hinges on the evaluative schemata that are most readily accessible for information processing.

Shifting from past to ongoing work, we turn now to two exploratory lines of research. One examines the possibility that there is a large class of trade-offs to which the value pluralism model does not apply – taboo trade-offs to which people are incapable of responding strategically and can only give a gut or visceral response. The other line of work is more in the spirit of the value pluralism model: It examines the possibility that people intuitively appreciate both the strengths and drawbacks of complex trade-off reasoning but must be primed by salient situational cues to apply this knowledge to the evaluation of political candidates and arguments.

TABOO TRADE-OFFS: LIMITS ON THE MENTAL FLEXIBILITY OF COGNITIVE MANAGERS

Research on trade-off reasoning has been so completely dominated by utilitarian models of choice that little attention has been given to the possibility that people simply refuse to contemplate – at least consciously – certain trade-offs. Research on taboo trade-offs (in utilitarian terms, values that people stubbornly insist must be assigned infinite value) must therefore grapple with foundational issues. Accordingly, we begin with the definitional problems of what exactly constitutes a taboo trade-off and of which operational indicators might be used to ascertain whether we have stumbled upon a taboo. Conceptual and operational preliminaries to the side, we pose three additional questions: (1) How broad a consensus is there within American political culture on what is a taboo trade-off? (2) Are taboos absolute and unreasoned prohibitions, or is it possible to talk people out of their aversions by presenting arguments that address concerns they may have about the consequences of violating the taboo? (3) Do violations of taboos have the power to contaminate perpetrators and policy proposals associated with them? The second and third issues raise the question of whether taboo trade-offs are taboo in the original anthropological sense of the term. If so, it should be extraordinarily difficult to persuade people to abandon their aversions, and it should be extraordinarily easy for violations of taboos to taint, perhaps ruin, political careers.

Moral Outrage as a Defining Property of Taboo Trade-Offs

Our working definition of a taboo trade-off was any comparison that people deemed illegitimate because the comparison subverted or destroyed a culturally cherished value. Drawing on several lines of inquiry, including attribution theory, cognitive appraisal theories of emotion, and Durkeim's (1973) classic characterization of how people react to violations of the collective conscience, Tetlock et al. (1996) developed a moral outrage index to gauge reactions to "illegitimate" trade-offs. The index consisted of three components that corresponded to the traditional tripartite definition of attitudes (McGuire 1968). The cognitive component consisted of dispositional attributions to anyone who would seriously consider making a taboo trade-off or to anyone who would seriously consider permitting such conduct. Observers often rate advocates of such policy proposals as auctioning babies for adoption or buying and selling human organs for medical transplants as immoral, depraved, and even insane. The affective component consisted of the emotional reactions to transgressors: anger, contempt, and even disgust. Finally, the behavioral-intentional component consisted of support for punishing transgressors and of a desire to ostracize people who are unwilling to punish and perhaps even willing to tolerate such conduct. When respondents judged a series of transactions requiring trade-offs that intuitively varied from the uncontroversial to the contested to the taboo in mainstream political culture, the cognitive, affective, and behavioral components of the outrage index intercorrelate sufficiently to define a scale that passes the usual psychometric standards for internal consistency, with alphas between 0.7 and 0.85, depending on the exact items included in the scale.

Ideological Subcultures

With an index of moral outrage for gauging reactions to taboo status in hand, it is reasonable to ask how much consensus exists on what constitutes a taboo trade-off. Tetlock et al. (1996) found substantial consensus within mainstream political culture, with only a few pockets of sharp disagreement, but that the consensus fades quickly toward ideological fringes of society. They asked college student activists with a wide ideological range to report their reactions to three a priori types of trade-off transactions: relatively uncontroversial secular-secular (buying and selling goods and services that American citizens are normally permitted, even encouraged, to exchange); theoretically taboo secular-sacred (buying and selling goods and services that the American legal system attempts to insulate from the "universal solvent of money"); and sacred-sacred (trade-offs that pit against each other two values both of which are normally insulated from the universal solvent of money).

Several noteworthy results emerged. Most politically consequential, there was substantial agreement between conservative Republicans and liberal Democrats that a wide range of "blocked exchanges" (Andre 1992; Walzer 1983) should indeed remain blocked. In the broadly defined center of the political spectrum – ranging, say, from Ted Kennedy to Jesse Helms – most people concur that moral outrage is the appropriate response to proposals to permit the auctioning of unwanted babies for adoption, competitive markets for transplant organs, and the buying and selling of basic rights and obligations of citizenship, such as draft deferments, eligibility for citizenship, and votes. But the consensus is imperfect. Flash points of disagreement emerge even within the mainstream. Liberals view the buying and selling of conventional medical services and, to some degree, legal services as suspect categories – people seem to be buying health, life, and justice – whereas conservatives are not bothered by such transactions. And these disagreements become extremely pronounced as we move to the libertarian right and the Marxist left. Many transactions that mainstream political culture condemns libertarians accept and even enthusiastically endorse (such as market mechanisms for the placement of unwanted babies and for ensuring an adequate supply of human organs for medical transplants). Only a few conventionally taboo trade-offs elicit moral outrage from libertarians (e.g., paying someone to go to jail in one's place); by and large, they reserve their outrage for the censorious busybodies who invent "moral externalities" that prevent consenting adults from entering into mutually beneficial pacts, thereby thwarting society's movement toward the Pareto frontier. By contrast, it is difficult to find transactions that do not elicit at least some outrage from Marxists. Our Marxist respondents were prototypical "censorious busybodies." Even routine market transactions – hiring someone to clean one's house and, indeed, the buying and selling of one's house – provoke a measure of moral condemnation from Marxists, who view labor and commodity markets as inherently exploitative.

But our analysis thus far has been both ethnographically and psychologically thin. We have essentially rediscovered normative prohibitions on value trade-offs that thoughtful citizens already knew existed. And we have rediscovered ideological cleavages that will come as no surprise to political philosophers. Indeed, if the results had come out otherwise, our first reaction would have been to question whether the self-avowed Marxists and libertarians from undergraduate clubs truly understood the creeds that they ostensibly espoused. It is possible, however, to pose deeper questions about the psychocultural status of "taboo" trade-offs – questions with greater potential to yield surprising answers.

Taboo Trade-Offs: Unreasoned Aversion or Thoughtful Ideological Stands?

Imagine that someone proposes to permit a regulated market for buying and selling human organs – hearts, lungs, kidneys, livers, corneas – for medical transplants. Or imagine that someone proposes to allow all "qualified parents" (who pass the regular standards for adopting children) to bid for the right to adopt particular children in need of loving and supportive families. If you are like the overwhelming majority of our sample of 155 undergraduates, your first response is likely to be moral outrage – a composite of emotional and cognitive reactions and punitiveness. These policy proposals elicit such a powerful negative response because they breach taboos; they allow people to affix dollar values to something – human bodies and babies – that well-socialized beings are supposed to regard as sacred. But are taboo trade-offs "taboos" in the Malinowskian meaning of the term, absolute prohibitions, like that on incest, that require no further explanation? Or is there a cognitive component to these aversions? Is it possible to elicit reasons that people object to markets for babies and body organs? And by addressing those reasons in revised policy proposals, is it possible to overcome the resistance?

Approximately 60% of those who object to "marketizing" babies and body organs saw no need for a reason – even when held accountable and pressed for one – beyond the blanket condemnation that "the policy is degrading, dehumanizing, and unacceptable." We take this assertion to be simply a reassertion of the taboo – an "ugh" reaction that people find odd to be asked to justify. It is as though we had reached the backstop of these belief systems – the *de gustibus* line of defense where people find further queries to be absurd. But what about the 40% of respondents who offer rather specific reasons for considering the proposal unacceptable? Informal content analysis of these reasons revealed that many objections had an egalitarian character. One common concern about medical transplants is the fear that the poor will be driven into deals of desperation. They will need money so badly that they will feel compelled to submit to dangerous surgical interventions – donating part of one's liver or a kidney – that the well-off would never seriously consider. A widely held fear about baby auctions was that only healthy and attractive babies would draw bidders. A related concern is that the price of organs and babies will skyrocket and the market will cater only to the well-off. Another class of objection is more pragmatic or instrumental. Some people are not convinced that all other options have been investigated for increasing the supply of body organs for desperately needed transplants or the supply of parents for babies in need of families. These respondents suspect that "more civilized" solutions to the shortage of organs and parents can be found.

Our research on the "cognitive substrate" of taboo trade-offs assessed how much people change their minds about markets for body organs when we revised the policy proposal to address substantive objections that people raised. One series of questions included the following:

Would you still object to markets for body organs: (a) if you lived in a society that had generous social welfare policies and never allowed the income for a family of four to fall below $32,000 per year (explaining the concept of inflation-adjusted 1996 dollars)?; (b) if society provided the less well-off with generous "organ-purchase vouchers" that increased in value as recipient income decreased (the poorer the recipient, the larger the voucher)?; (c) if it could be shown that all other methods of encouraging organ donation had failed to produce enough organs and that the only way to save large numbers of lives was to implement a market for body organs?

Another series of questions probed reactions to permitting all qualified parents to bid for adoption rights. In one scenario, subjects were assured that if only attractive and healthy babies attracted high bids, then the money raised through the auction would go to create incentives to encourage other parents to adopt less attractive and less healthy babies, as well as to improve the current conditions of institutionalized life for these children. In another scenario, respondents were assured that poor people would not be prevented from adopting children because the program would provide generous vouchers to all poor people who want to adopt children, thereby permitting them to compete with the affluent would-be adopters (again, explaining the concept of vouchers). In a third scenario, subjects were assured that all less-radical possible solutions to the problem of nonadopted children had been explored and proven inadequate.

How successful were we in eroding the taboo through this series of counterfactual thought experiments? Whereas nearly 90% of respondents initially objected to each proposal, opposition fell to approximately 60% in the hypothetical worlds with protection for the poor and unattractive and a guarantee that all other options had been thoroughly explored. For nearly half of the population, the term *taboo* is apparently too strong. They are willing to consider – in a quasi-utilitarian manner

– conditions under which the benefits of the proposal might conceivably outweigh the costs. For the other half of respondents, though, the term *taboo* still seems apt. They are prepared to ban exchanges that both donors and recipients believe would leave them better off and that, arguably, would leave many third parties better off as well. In their eyes, taboo trade-offs remain an affront to the collective conscience, a kind of moral externality. As one female respondent protested, "What kind of people are we becoming?" Consequentialist arguments – whether they invoked egalitarian or efficiency concerns – missed the point: This woman's sense of personhood required categorically rejecting the taboo trade-offs. In March and Olson's (1989) terminology, the logic of obligatory, not anticipatory, action governed her choices. She knew with existential certainty who she was, and she knew that she did not fit into a social world that countenanced such transactions. Her decision process is perhaps better modeled as pattern matching than as utility maximizing.

Taboo Trade-Offs as Sources of Political Contamination

Imagine that someone confronts you with what initially looks like a standard OMB-style cost-benefit analysis that makes the case for reducing funding for an inefficient program designed to achieve a worthy goal, such as building hospitals in underserved rural areas, cleaning up toxic waste dumps to the point of zero risk, or eliminating all carcinogens from new food additives. If you are like most respondents – about 75% of them – your first response will be annoyance with government waste and gratitude for those who are trying to stem the hemorrhaging of taxpayer dollars into ineffective programs. Let's say, however, that the cost-benefit analysis includes an explicit dollar valuation of human life. Support for the would-be reformers should now plummet, and they should be pilloried as callous, arrogant, and inhumane.

Operationally, the taboo-contamination experiment takes the following form. In one condition, the taboo trade-off is covert. It is masked by a "deontic" justification that vaguely declares that "morally, it is the right thing to do." The specific scenario was inspired by the Superfund Act:

> A government program cleans up toxic waste sites to the point where they pose zero risk to public health. Last year, the program saved an estimated 200 lives at a cost of $200 million. The Danner Commission – whose mandate is to improve the efficiency of government – investigated the program and recommended a set of reforms that were implemented. As a result, this year the program could save an estimated 200 lives – just as many as before – but at a

cost of only $100 million, a saving of $100 million. If the government kept funding the program at last year's budget level of $200 million, the program could save an estimated 400 lives.

Now the Danner Commission recommends redirecting the saving of $100 million to other uses, including reducing the deficit, increased funding for programs to stimulate economic growth, and lowering taxes. Based on its analysis of these options, the commission concludes that "morally this is the right thing to do." What do you think? Should the government keep funding the program at $200 million or should it redirect the $100 million saved to other priorities?

After ensuring that all subjects fully comprehended the policy choice confronting them (via a knowledge test), subjects voted on this proposal, rated their agreement on scales ranging from "strongly favor keeping funding at $200 million" to "strongly favor redirecting the $100 million to other priorities," and rated the Danner Commission on a host of identity dimensions (moral, competent, and so on).

By contrast, in another experimental condition, subjects learned that

based on its analysis of the options, the Danner Commission has concluded that the cost of saving the additional 200 lives is about $500,000 per life – a cost that it still considers too high and one that cannot be justified, given other needs and priorities. The Commission therefore recommends redirecting the saving of $100 million to other uses, including reducing the deficit, increased funding for programs to stimulate economic growth, and lowering taxes.

Support for the Danner Commission recommendation hovers at 72% when the trade-off is masked by a deontic rationale, but falls to approximately 35% when the trade-off explicitly violates the normative injunction against dollar valuations of human life.

Additional experimental conditions address alternative interpretations. One argument is that people object not to attaching a dollar value to human life but rather to the particular cost estimate that the Danner Commission endorsed. There is nothing inherently wrong about pricing human life, but one should get the price right. To explore this possibility, subjects reacted to a commission that engaged in cost-benefit reasoning and concluded that funding should remain at $200 million because $500,000 per human life is a cost worth bearing. In still other conditions, $500,000 is a bargain; the commission would have been willing to pay either $1 million or $10 million. Although people judge the commission more favorably when it places a higher dollar value on human life, they still judge it less favorably, and substantially so, than when the commission offers a deontic rationale either for keeping funding at the $200 million level or for redirecting spending to other priorities.[1]

Another possibility is that people object to utilitarian reasoning in general and not just to the violation of this specific taboo trade-off. To test this possibility, subjects reacted to a Danner Commission that either redirected funding or kept funding constant and did so "after weighing all the relevant costs and benefits." Interestingly, vague utilitarian reasoning was every bit as effective in providing political cover as vague deontic reasoning. Tragic choices are best cloaked (Calabresi and Bobbit 1978), and either Kantian or utilitarian cloaks will do the job. People objected to the explicit spelling out of the trade-off. Doing so tarnished the image of a previously well-regarded reformist commission, rendering suspect its entire policy agenda.

These experiments show that previously popular politicians and acceptable policies can be transformed into objects of scorn by revealing that the politicians performed taboo mental calculations in reaching their conclusions. The damage to one's political identity can be so severe that even possessing an otherwise winning utilitarian argument is not sufficient to prevail in the court of public opinion. The "contamination" findings have important implications. Ambitious proposals to reform budget-busting entitlement programs – Medicare, Social Security – or more modest efforts to cap programmatic budgets can become politically poisonous as soon as defenders successfully frame the issue (in the Gamsonian sense) so that the budget cutters appear guilty of a taboo trade-off. The breaches of taboos might take diverse forms: "breaking faith with the elderly" (what price a promise to our grandparents?), "placing a dollar value on the health of the poor or elderly" (what price a life?), "betraying veterans who risked their lives for our country" (what price a sacred trust?), and "short changing the education and care of the young" (what price a child's dreams?). Big-ticket spending items are not, moreover, the only issues that implicate taboos. Defenders of the Superfund effort to reduce the risk posed by toxic waste dumps to zero, or of the Delaney Clause to ban new food additives that are at all carcinogenic, can always accuse opponents of acting as fronts for business groups who put profits over the lives of children who might eat contaminated dirt or artificially sweetened cereal. In a similar vein, advocates of campaign finance reform can stigmatize opponents as "holding up American democracy for sale"; proponents of state-financed health insurance and legal care can warn of devaluing the lives of the poor and decreasing their access to justice; oppo-

---

[1] The dollar valuation of $10 million per life is fantastically high; it would quickly exhaust American economic resources as of 1996. The entire U.S. federal budget could save only approximately 170,000 lives.

256

nents of capital punishment can argue that it is only a matter of time before an innocent man or woman is executed in a state-sanctioned murder and that, surely, any moral person would pay any price to avoid complicity in such an atrocity.

At this juncture, rational-choice theorists might argue that savvy politicians do not really believe taboo issue framings; they use such rhetoric to cudgel their opponents into submission. Psychological theorists might respond in three ways. First, the presumed efficacy of taboo rhetoric hinges at least on a receptive public, thus conceding the argument at the mass level. Second, the line between rhetoric and reality, public posturing and private thought, is often a fine one. Even accomplished politicians sometimes come to believe what they say via the processes of dissonance reduction and self-perception. Third, there is always the danger of rhetorical blowback (Snyder 1991). Once one announces that Social Security or Jerusalem or Kashmir is sacred and therefore nonnegotiable, one may convince others who, in turn, will hold one accountable for any deviation from that declaratory principle. Politicians thus become prisoners of their own rhetoric.

A more compelling rational-choice rejoinder is the game-theoretic observation that both sides are continually searching for taboo trump cards to play in the rhetorical competition for public support. Thus, we should expect a public dialogue of the deaf, as each side wraps itself in the mantle of a sacred value. But there is hope here for trade-off reasoning inasmuch as our data reveal people to be much more tolerant of sacred-sacred trade-offs than they are of secular-sacred trade-offs. Putting contending values on an equal, moral playing field can be a contribution in itself. As the late Aaron Wildavsky was fond of arguing, environmental programs that claim to save lives need to be weighed not against a dollar metric (opportunity costs of foregone growth) but against another life metric by invoking the causal argument that wealthier is healthier. But this example also illustrates another point: It is rhetorically easier to "sacralize" some issue stands than others. The two-step Wildavskian argument for economic growth requires more cognitive sophistication of the audience than the one-step environmentalist argument: Stop poisoning us!

PRIMING POLITICAL SCRIPTS: DEMAGOGIC OR PRINCIPLED? THOUGHTFUL OR CONFUSED?

The second line of work swings the pendulum partly back toward the rational end of the theoretical continuum on public opinion: It explores whether people have a deeper understanding of trade-off reasoning than the psychological literature has given them credit for possessing. The key idea is simple: An integral part of folk knowledge in our political culture is that it is possible to attach either positive or negative value spins to either complex trade-off acceptance or simple trade-off denial. Most people can readily imagine circumstances under which they would approve of complex trade-off reasoning – indeed, see it as a prerequisite for any mature, balanced, and thoughtful leadership. Let's label these mental scenarios the "thoughtful statesman script." But most people can also readily imagine circumstances under which they might view trade-off reasoning to be morally suspect – as prima facie evidence of a lack of principles, indecisiveness, and a tendency to straddle the fence, vacillate, and obfuscate. There are some things we should not even think of compromising. Let's call this set of mental scenarios the "opportunistic vacillator script." Conversely, looking at simple trade-off denial, many people can imagine circumstances under which they would deplore this style of thinking as evidence that the decision maker is rigid, self-righteous, and perhaps flat-out incapable of understanding other points of view – what we will call the "demagogue script." But many people can also imagine circumstances under which they might applaud trade-off deniers as courageous, resolute, and decisive souls who resist the temptation to try to be everything to everybody – what we will call the "principled leader script."

If we postulate that most people have internalized schemata or scripts that portray simple and complex trade-off reasoning in both flattering and unflattering lights, then drawing on the extensive literature on priming of knowledge structures (Higgins 1996), we should be able to increase the likelihood of positive or negative responses to trade-off reasoning by affecting the mental accessibility of these knowledge structures.[2] Consider the following experiment that adapts standard priming methods for manipulating cognitive availability to the study of perceptions of political leaders. In the first phase of the study (ostensibly concerned with memory), subjects receive biographical information about a politician and expect to be tested for the accuracy of their recall. In one condition, this biographical portrait primes people to think of negative stereotypes of complex trade-off thinkers (the opportunistic vacillator) and of positive stereotypes of simple thinkers (the principled leader); in a second condition, people are primed to think of the opposite stereo-

---

[2] Note that this psychological approach does not give people as much credit for a self-conscious capacity to shift from simple to complex modes of thinking as does the cognitive-manager position at the heart of the value pluralism model. Rather, it portrays the shift in evaluative standards (anti to pro complexity) as an automatic reaction to a priming cue, a function of the spreading activation laws of associative memory that determine the ease of retrieving particular cognitions and, hence, the likelihood of those cognitions influencing judgment.

types in which complexity connotes thoughtfulness and balance (the thoughtful statesman) and simplicity connotes rigidity, intolerance, and self-righteousness (the demagogue); in a third (control) condition, people receive no prime whatsoever.

Here is part of the prime designed to activate the thoughtful statesman script:

Abercrombie is really different from most politicians. He does not shy away from complex problems that have no clear right answers. He tries to understand all points of view (not just those of his campaign donors), to weigh conflicting perspectives carefully in the balance, and to arrive at an integrative judgment only after all the relevant evidence has been thoroughly investigated. He understands that responsible policy must involve trade-offs and compromises among competing groups and constituencies that have legitimate interests at stake. And he is willing to change his mind later should new evidence arise. Even his worst critics have to admire his balanced and thoughtful approach to public policy.

The other prime was designed to activate the evaluative script for the principled leader:

Abercrombie is really different from most politicians. He does not hold up his finger to figure out which way the wind is blowing. He sizes up situations quickly and decisively and makes his positions unmistakably clear, with no attempt to confuse people about where he stands with talk about "on the one hand" and "on the other hand." He also does not suffer fools gladly. When he thinks someone is spouting nonsense, he lets them know it. And once he does take a stand, you can count on him to stay the course and to be loyal to his convictions. Even his worst critics have to admire his courageous and principled approach to public policy.

After recall tests to ensure that subjects had attended to the "primes," all subjects moved to a different room under the guidance of a different experimenter to participate in a supposedly unrelated study of attitudes toward controversial issues. Subjects then listened to excerpts from two political speeches: one on the balanced budget amendment and the second on school vouchers. The experimental design is rather complex. Each speech took one of six forms. The speaker either supported or rejected the policy proposal and engaged in either no trade-off reasoning or moderately or extremely complex trade-off reasoning in reaching this policy conclusion.

The "trade-off denial" anti-voucher speech warned of "the destruction of public education and the creation of deep and divisive inequities in access to quality education, inequities far worse than currently exist." In the pro-voucher condition, the trade-off-denying speaker urged "the introduction of badly needed competition in a public school system that only the relatively wealthy can now escape. Only by vigorously stimulating competition can we improve the quality of education for the entire population and ensure that schools are run for the benefit of the children, not public service employees' unions and overpaid administrators." The moderately complex trade-off acceptance speech conceded the legitimacy of the arguments invoked by the other side but then proceeded to take exactly the same side as before. The highly complex trade-off acceptance speech not only conceded some legitimacy to the other side's concerns but noted that which position you take depends on balancing competing risks, as well as on which factual claims you believe. The speaker conceded that there were good grounds for being suspicious of public monopolies but also good grounds for believing that education is a legitimate and central function of government (ensuring that all citizens have some common experiences in growing up). The speaker also conceded that there were good grounds for believing in markets (that they deliver goods and services more efficiently) but went on to acknowledge good grounds for expecting markets to amplify inequality. The speaker concluded by noting that where one comes out on this issue hinges partly on judgments of which consequences one considers more likely (issues of fact), and partly on which consequences one deems more important (issues of moral valuation). The speaker then came down on one side or the other (always as emphatically as in the simple speech so as to hold the perceived issue position of the speaker as constant as possible across conditions).

The trade-off denial speech in support of the balanced budget amendment declared that

our federal government has demonstrated, beyond a reasonable doubt, that it was incapable of living within its means. Our elected representatives will always give in to special interests that demand just one more tax loophole, one more subsidy, one more low-interest loan, one more pork-barrel project. . . . Without the discipline of a binding, no-loophole constitutional amendment, the country will inexorably continue on a path of rising indebtedness – that, to our collective shame, we will bequeath to future generations.

The antiamendment trade-off-denial speech depicted the balanced budget amendment as yet

one more ploy by antigovernment forces to strangle popular spending programs that these politicians do not dare attack directly. The balanced budget amendment would prevent flexible government responses to economic recessions and national emergencies. The balanced budget amendment is also profoundly unfair and inefficient. It is unfair to ask people in the present to pay out of pocket for all long-term improvements that they make to the education, transportation, and health-care systems that will be available to people of the future. And it is inefficient because it will stifle initiative in areas where government can make an important long-term difference, such as promoting economic growth and scientific and technological innovation.

In the moderately complex trade-off statement, the speaker concedes the legitimacy of both perspectives and then comes down emphatically on one side. In the high complexity trade-off statement, the speaker not only acknowledges the legitimacy of the competing perspectives but specifies that the positions which one takes hinge, in part, on how skeptical one is about the American political system and, in part, on how effectively one believes government can direct resources to programs that will lay the basis for long-term prosperity. Does one believe, for example, that the government can intervene – in hard times – to reinvigorate the economy by creating jobs and guaranteeing everyone a minimal standard of living? The speaker then announces that based on his answers to these questions, he has come out solidly in opposition or support of the balanced budget amendment (in an effort once again to hold the perceived issue position constant across experimental conditions).

Three results merit special mention. First, priming or making accessible widely held stereotypes of trade-off reasoning had a big effect. Subjects primed by the thoughtful statesman script became increasingly positive toward complex trade-off arguments (rating the speaker as balanced, thoughtful, and even wise), and increasingly negative toward simple arguments that denied or minimized trade-offs (rating the speaker as simplistic, rigid, and intolerant). Second, subjects primed by the script for the principled leader moved in exactly the opposite directions. They responded more positively to the speaker who denied trade-offs (rating the speaker as strong and decisive), and less positively to the speaker who depicted the choice process as balancing conflicting legitimate concerns (rating the speaker as confused, uncertain, and indecisive). This pattern of trait attributions fits neatly into a 2×2 Peabody (1967) plot that allows us to sort out the positive and negative connotative meanings that people attach to the denotative dimension of simplicity complexity reasoning (Tetlock, Berry, and Peterson 1993). Third, control subjects who were not primed resembled subjects who had been exposed to the anticomplexity prime – a result that held especially strongly for subjects who scored highly on a self-report measure of dogmatism and intolerance of ambiguity. This pattern suggests that the principled leader script may be more spontaneously accessible than is the thoughtful statesman script. As a result, speakers who simply deny trade-offs may often have an advantage over their more complex counterparts.

A final study explored reactions to simple or complex trade-off reasoning in arguably the most polarized of all political debates in the last few decades, namely, abortion. Using a brief questionnaire to classify undergraduates in a large subject pool as either unequivocally pro-life, unequivocally pro-choice, or deeply ambivalent, this study assessed the reactions of subjects with strong "priors" to a political figure who took a pro or anti abortion stand and who did so in one of three ways: by denying that any trade-off was involved whatsoever and declaring that there was an unambiguous correct answer; by acknowledging that trade-offs existed and that there was uncertainty about the right answer (there was a risk of compromising one or another sacred value, e.g., life versus liberty); or by acknowledging the highly complex nature of the trade-offs involved by noting not only the legitimacy of conflicting sentiments but by specifying philosophical perspectives that should incline us to judge one or the other risk to be more or less acceptable.

Three findings again merit mention. First, the more complex the trade-off rationale that a politician offers for a pro-life or pro-choice stand, the less trusted and respected that politician is by those on the politician's side. We call this the "traitor" effect. The politician is, in the eyes of supporters, guilty of treasonous thoughts by failing to reject the other side's perspective categorically. Second, offering a complex trade-off rationale for a policy position on abortion does not gain the politician much approval from the other side, even though the politician acknowledges the legitimacy of their perspective. If anything, there is a trend in the opposite direction. Political partisans find it galling that someone can recognize the legitimacy of their point of view but not agree with it. Third, practitioners of complex trade-off rhetoric do at least enjoy an advantage among people who are "deeply ambivalent" on the issue of abortion. This group does indeed respond more positively to complex trade-off rhetoric.

CONCLUDING COMMENTS

It is useful to be explicit about the implications of these initial results for both our image of human nature and for democratic political theory. With respect to human nature, people appear neither to be hopelessly muddled incompetents when it comes to trade-offs (as a caricature of the cognitive literature might suggest) nor to be adroit practitioners of multivariate calculus who can perform conditional optimization problems in their sleep. That said, however, there is a lot of room in between. The emerging portrait of the trade-off reasoner is mixed. Many people believe that their core values do not conflict and they need to be prodded, sometimes poked pretty hard, into acknowledging that these values do conflict. But once primed to believe that trade-offs are a pervasive feature of political life, they become quite skeptical of rhetorical claims to have identified a dominant solution, often dismissing them as implausible, shrill, manipulative, and even demagogic.

With respect to democratic political theory, if we take sensitivity to trade-offs to be a necessary condition for thoughtful participation in a pluralistic polity, the current results offer grounds for both optimism and pessimism. Those inclined to see the glass a quarter full can point to ways of activating our latent potential to recognize value trade-offs and generate integrative solutions. They can also point to ways of stimulating skepticism toward politicians who bear trade-off-free policy packages and receptiveness toward politicians who tell us "painful truths" about conflicts between core values. But those inclined to see the glass three-quarters empty can point to the low frequency of trade-off reasoning in general; to the high frequency with which people deny even obvious trade-offs; to the great difficulty most people have in generating integrative solutions to those trade-offs they do recognize; to the far more enthusiastic response most people have to simple rhetoric that denies trade-offs than to complex trade-off rhetoric that acknowledges trade-offs; and to the ease with which taboo trade-offs can contaminate otherwise reasonable policy proposals, forcing politicians to retreat into simplistic cant or obfuscatory ruses. In short, the current findings hardly demonstrate that deliberative democracy is psychologically impossible, but they do highlight the opportunities that our judgmental weaknesses create for skillful political manipulators.

12

Backstage Cognition in Reason and Choice
MARK TURNER

Understanding how people reason and choose – the mechanisms, the biases, the constraints, the possibilities, the limits – is like understanding how people see. We have complicated and detailed folk theories of vision that are implicitly repeated throughout the culture. These theories seem so commonsensical and inevitably right that they form an unquestioned set of assumptions for most of us. About vision, we expect science to fill in technical details but not to surprise us. Yet cognitive science and neuroscience have shown conclusively that these folk theories of vision are very deeply wrong. For the most part, it is only these researchers who ever have the opportunity to question the folk theories of human vision, and even they must remain vigilant against the folk theories' influence. Someone who follows the folk theories of vision will think that anyone blind has no knowledge of the visual field and that the perceived color of an object is determined by the light it reflects. But these and other commonsensical expectations are demonstrably wrong. Someone who holds the folk theories will give wrong stories about the operations of vision, wrong predictions about what people will see under specified conditions, and wrong explanations of why people see as they do.

Just so, we have complicated and detailed folk theories, implicitly repeated everywhere, of how people reason and choose. They seem so inevitably right as to have come to form an unquestioned set of assumptions. They have had exceptionally strong influence on even the most advanced social scientific analyses. But cognitive science has begun to demonstrate how mistaken these folk theories may be. If we want to understand political reasoning and political choosing, their biases, constraints, limits, and possibilities, we need to reconsider our assumptions.

This study was conducted while the author was Agnes Gund Member of the School of Social Science, Institute for Advanced Study, Princeton, in 1996 and 1997. He is grateful for support provided by the Institute, the School, and Agnes Gund.

The central insight cognitive science offers to social science is that reason and choice operate, indispensably and inescapably, through what Gilles Fauconnier (1995) calls "backstage cognition." Backstage cognition is the integrated activity of intricate, systematic, powerful, and complex mental operations of interpretation and inference. Crucially, the backstage cognition that constitutes most of reason and choice takes place outside of consciousness, and so we do not even recognize that it is happening. Its operations skirt our notice even when we hunt for them, and they submit to being hauled into view only through scientific dedication, experiment, and luck. Just as we do not notice how we compute color constancy in the visual field, so we do not notice the backstage cognition of reason and choice.

If cognitive scientific claims about invisible, backstage cognition in reason and choice are even partially true, the consequences for political science are large, since they would imply that scholars who hope to analyze and make predictions about patterns of decision, judgment, preference, voting, negotiation, delegation, alliance, competition, confrontation, persuasion, or nearly any other political phenomenon will need to reconsider some of their most basic working assumptions about the nature of reason and choice.

Here, I hope to give a demonstration, or at least an illustration, of the way in which everyday political reasoning and choice, as well as sophisticated political scientific methods for analyzing them, depend upon backstage cognition. The kind of backstage cognition I have selected for my illustration is what Gilles Fauconnier and I have analyzed as "conceptual blending."[1] Conceptual blending is the mental operation of integrating two concepts to create a third concept, where the third concept is more than just a composition of the first two – it is a distinct concept with emergent meaning.

I will explore the operation of conceptual blending in two methods of explaining political behavior – counterfactual reasoning and the theory of rational choice. I will try to demonstrate that conceptual blending, which plays a central role in the backstage cognition of political reason and choice, conforms to neither folk theories nor the expectations of many political scientists. It has sources of invention and bias to which

---

[1] The theoretical work on conceptual blending has been done jointly by Gilles Fauconnier and me, and presented in various publications: Fauconnier (1997); Fauconnier and Turner (1994, 1996, 1998a, and 1998b); Turner (1996a and 1996b); and Turner and Fauconnier (1995, 1998, and 1999). The model we offer – the "network model of conceptual integration" – has additionally played a role in Collier and Levitsky (1997); Coulson (1995, 1996, and 1997); Grush and Mandelblit (1997); Mandelblit (1995a, 1995b, 1996, 1997, and in press); Mandelblit and Zachar (1998); Oakley (1995); Robert (1996); Veale (1996); Zbikowski (1997); and the work of many other scholars.

political science seems blind, and those sources of invention and bias have substantial effect in actual political reasoning and choice. Moreover, it can lead to substantial revisions of whatever concepts we use to construct a blend. Thus, blending is not just a process for simulating new scenarios but also a process for altering our old concepts – irrespective of the choices we make.

I introduce the theory of conceptual blending by means of an everyday example of reasoning and choice that involved a major corporation, an advertising agency, a lot of money, an audience of at least several million consumers, and an article in the *New York Times* that surveyed the damage. I have chosen this example because its aggressive and pyrotechnic presentation of conceptual blending makes the phenomenon, if not its principles, unmistakable. I then show the identical principles at work in counterfactual reasoning and the theory of rational choice. I conclude with some comments on how to construct an integrated theory of reasoning.

COME FLY WITH ME

In 1996, and at a cost of $15 million, British Airways presented a suite of printed advertisements in newspapers and magazines. Each had a big background photograph, a small inset photograph, and a few words to help us integrate the two photographs. The big photograph in one of these ads depicted a dove in a bird bath, and its small inset photograph depicted the head of a grinning man in a shower. Its text announced that British Airways provides private showers for its customers at its arrival lounges at London airports.

The inset photograph in these ads is always an intrusion. Like the big photograph, it has sharp rectangular boundaries. The two photographs are distinguished by technical features of photography and have content taken from different conceptual domains. But the ads typically suggest some morphological continuity between key elements of the inset photograph and key elements of the big photograph. For example, the head of the man in the shower rests on the body of the dove.

The ad I want to talk about presents a big black-and-white photograph printed in a technical style taken from the 1940s. It has low contrast, ambient lighting, and a hint of brownish coloring. It depicts an attractive young mother with neck-length hair, a simple string of pearls around her neck. She wears a short-sleeve knit top and a woven skirt, and sits cradling her infant in her arms as it reclines on its back, its head elevated and its knees slightly elevated, its legs sprawled in enviable comfort over her forearm, its outer thigh additionally supported by her left hand, on which she wears a set of wedding bands. She smiles at the face of her sleeping child, who wears a cloth diaper in a period style.

But the head of the infant is occluded by an inset photograph. The inset photograph is in color, with relatively high contrast and strong directional lighting. The photo depictings a smiling, sleeping businessman who is balding slightly. He is reclined in an airline seat. The scale of the photographs makes the shoulders of the businessman fit the shoulders of the infant and locates the businessman's head where the infant's head would be if his weren't in the way. The text above the photograph reads, "The new Club World cradle seat. Lullaby not included." The text beneath reads, "Introducing the unique new business class cradle seat. It doesn't simply recline but tilts as a whole, raising your knees and relieving your body of stress and pressure. Pity you may not be awake to enjoy all the other changes on new Club World."

Obviously, even obtrusively, the ad represents a blended scene that the reader of the ad is expected to *unpack*. We feel immediately and intuitively that the blended scene is combining two different "things" – which might be given many names, like notions, ideas, mental scenarios, or conceptual packets, but which I will call "mental spaces." *Mental space* is a term invented by Gilles Fauconnier (1994) for a cohesive bundle of meaning we assemble during thought, discourse, and action. For example, we make sense of the sentence "Skip Lupia will live in Palo Alto during 1999" by putting together a "mental space" in which Skip Lupia resides in Palo Alto during 1999. This mental space will undoubtedly be organized by recruiting from our general conceptual frame of what it means for someone to reside in a city for a period, and, depending on who is doing the understanding, it may also be organized by the general conceptual frame in which a researcher visits a research environment for a specified period of time. Thinking and talking always involve the construction of such mental spaces for purposes of local understanding and action. They are interconnected, and can be modified as thought and discourse unfold. Conceptual blending – of the sort we see in the British Airways ad – is an operation over mental spaces.

In the case of the British Airways ad, we feel that unpacking it involves setting up two "mental spaces": one mental space that has a baby being cradled in its mother's arms, and another that has a businessman flying business class in a British Airways airplane. We view these two mental spaces as somehow contributing structure to the blended scene. I will call such contributing mental spaces the "inputs" to the blend. In the case of the British Airways ad, I will call the first input the "business flight" space, and the second input the "mother-child" space.

The reader of the ad is meant to construct a *counterpart mapping* between some elements of the two spaces, the business flight space and the mother-child space: The cradle seat is the counterpart of the mother's cradling arms, and the businessman is the counterpart of the infant. These counterparts are projected to the blend: In the blend, the man is the baby and the seat is mother's arms. Counterparts can be established in many ways. The identical element in two separate spaces can be counterparts, as when we put together two mental spaces for "Three years ago, I was in Paris" where the "I" in the space with Paris three years ago is the counterpart of the "I" in the space of the person speaking. When two spaces have the identical role, those roles and their values can be counterparts, as when we say "Alan Greenspan is the new Paul Volcker" because one succeeded the other as chairman of the Federal Reserve Board. "He is a snake" asks us to construct a metaphoric counterpart mapping between "him" in one space and "snake" in another. And so on.

In conceptual blending, there is always *selective projection* from the inputs to the blend. Simply, this means that some structure from each input is replicated in the blended space. From the mother-child space in the British Airways ad, we project comfort and happiness but not the baby's incompetence at business, speech, and dining; from the business flight space we project the businessman's reclining position but not our certainty that he would prefer to be someplace else.

There is *emergent structure* in the blend. Emergent structure is new meaning in the blend that is not available in either of the inputs. For example, in the British Airways blend, the person in the seat can have the power, benefits, and responsibilities of advanced professional maturity and yet the comforts of infant dependency and irresponsibility.

There is also, often, *projection back to the inputs*. Structure and inferences that develop in the blend can lead us to modify the inputs. For example, in the British Airways blend, the unruffled comfort of the man-baby projects back to the business flight space: Regardless of our prejudices about airplane travel, the passenger in business class on British Airways is blissfully content.

Considerable work has been done to make it possible for the reader of the ad to establish even more elaborate connections between the two conceptual inputs, thereby increasing the fit between the blended space and its inputs. The posture of the baby in the mother's arms looks entirely natural but has been carefully posed to emphasize the raising of the knees and the tilting of the body to make the baby's posture blend more easily with the posture of the businessman in the cradle seat. The disparity in period styles of the photographs can be read as signifying temporal distance between the two input spaces – the business flight space and the mother-child space – inviting the reader to frame the businessman as the grown-up infant. This makes the woman in the blend his actual mother as she appeared and as she nurtured him when he was an infant. Projecting these identities to the blend gives features of happiness and comfort that come from being cradled not only like an infant but also by one's own mother, who adores her child and cares for it. The mother-child input can now be further framed as something remembered fondly, if unconsciously, by the businessman as he reclines. His comfort in the cradle seat brings back to him effectively, if indistinctly, the pleasure of being in his mother's arms.

Actually, in the business flight space, the businessman's mother may be dead or otherwise incapable of holding him in this way, and if she is living and tried it, the result would be uncomfortable and possibly injurious. The businessman cannot have in reality what he remembers so fondly. But in the blend, the businessman can have again what he can no longer have; he can have it both ways – he can be an adult who is a sleeping infant cradled in his mother's arms. Who would not want to fly with British Airways, on these terms?

The advertising agency that developed this ad presented it to focus groups, whose members reassured the agency that its meaning was unmistakable.

But as the *New York Times* reported in an article that reproduced the advertisement and analyzed it, actual readers often objected to it (Bryant 1996): "Many have written the airline to say they think the ad is Freudian, sexist, and even demeaning to flight attendants, who in the eyes of some beholders are represented by the mother in the ads."

The ad agency should not have been surprised. Conceptual blending is a quick, powerful, and inventive cognitive operation. A reader who conceives a blend and its inputs typically regards the interpretation of the representation as natural and inevitable, hardly an "interpretation" at all. In the case of the British Airways ad, whether we like the fact or not, we all possess the cultural frame in which an attractive young stewardess attends gently to the physical and psychological comfort of the older businessman. In this publicly shared conceptual frame, it is understood that part of what the airline is selling is the attention of such a woman. Despite the elimination of the most suggestive uses of this conceptual frame in airline advertising ("Coffee, Tea, or Me?"), it is still routinely used in print and video advertisements, in which an attractive stewardess – no longer wearing a short skirt, stockings, and pumps, and now additionally sharing the screen in alternation with an attractive steward – nonetheless gazes at the potential customer with an altogether attentive and pleasing look as if to suggest the prospect of her personal service. Once we have a young, attractive woman in the blend taking care of the businessman, it is straightforward for readers to recruit the frame of a stewardess and use it to structure both the blend and the business flight space, forming a connection between the stewardess in the business flight space and the woman in the blend. In the blend, the stewardess is a young, attractive, attentive mother, and the inference projected back to the business flight–influencing space is that on British Airways, you can expect a stewardess who treats you in a similar fashion.

According to the *New York Times,* the ad agency tried to dismiss these complaints by explaining that "people thought way too much about this," but that seems unlikely: People did not think they were "interpreting" at all; they thought they were responding to what was "there." In the blend, the woman is attractive, however proper. She caresses the businessman intimately, holding him against her full bosom, gazing down at him lovingly. Readers know the standard cultural frame of Oedipal sexual attachment to the mother, and the father is conveniently out of the picture. Given the ways in which conceptual blending operates, it is natural for readers to interpret these features of the blend as prompts to create corresponding elements in the business flight space.

It is true that the ad reads, "Lullaby not included," which, it can be argued, makes the woman in the ad a mother and not a stewardess, but of course it is just as easy to read the phrase in the opposite direction: On British Airways, the businessman enjoys the woman's intimate physical and personal attention, with full sexual connotations, but not the lullaby because the woman in the business flight input is, after all, technically a stewardess rather than a mother; mothers sing lullabies but stewardesses must draw the line somewhere.

Conceptual blending is path dependent: Blends are put together and unpacked using what the understander already has in his conceptual structures. Highly charged conceptual structures have a lower threshold for activation. Readers typically bring their politically and ideologically charged conceptual structures to bear whenever possible. When they do, they will not imagine that they are "reading in" to the blend any more than will the biophysical engineer who sees this ad and interprets it as principally displaying the posture achieved in the new cradle seat on British Airways.

For many readers of the ad, recruiting these politically and ideologically charged conceptual structures had a basic effect on their choice: The ad, which was intended to offer them incentives of personal comfort that would lead them to reason toward a commercial choice, led them to align commercial choice with ideological choice and so to refuse to patronize a corporation they judged to be sexist.

This example suggests two points about political persuasion. First, the British Airways ad suggests an answer to the abiding question, why do politicians stick with hackneyed presentations of their positions and policies – new bridge, new deal, rebuilding the infrastructure, land of opportunity, new day, dawn in America, drawing us together, closer to the people, a stronger America – despite pleas in every forum that they offer something new? Perhaps the politicians lack invention, but alternatively, perhaps they know intuitively that offering a new blend runs the risk that members of their audience will bring to its interpretation highly charged conceptual frames, leading some of them to interpret it in a way that will hurt the politician, who will then have to backpedal. In a climate of negative political attack, where a politician's utterances are read by opponents with an eye toward making them sound evil, the prudent politician will prefer clichés.

Second, it's nice to have your cake and eat it, too. I would not suggest that the ad agency (or anyone else) behind the British Airways blend thought this way, but imagine that market research had shown that the important audience for these ads is senior male businessmen and that they love the sensual, Oedipal connotations of the ad. In such a situation, a marketing executive, calculating over payoffs and costs in different audiences, might conclude that the payoff from stimulating the businessmen far outweighs the cost of angering those who will find the ad both sexist and offensive ("All the letter writers have been women," reports the *New York Times*), provided the accusation of sexism can be plausibly denied. The marketing executive would then have incentive to approve a blend that prompts for a persuasive interpretation strongly enough to induce it but tangentially enough, or with enough distraction, to make it deniable. This ploy is a standard weapon in the everyday political arsenal: Offer a presentation sufficiently new and sufficiently nuanced to suggest a persuasive interpretation that the politician can then ignore, neglect, or disavow. But this is risky business.

BACKSTAGE COGNITION

The British Airways ad shows us a basic cognitive operation, conceptual blending. The inventors of the ad used conceptual blending as a tool for guiding readers to reason toward a commercial choice. To the surprise and regret of British Airways, some readers connected that commercial choice to an ideological choice. The ad is specific evidence of my general claim in this chapter, a claim directed to social scientists who do qualitative research on the way human beings reason, judge, and choose in political, social, and economic situations:

• Reason and choice depend upon "backstage cognition."

The British Airways ad helps me drag some backstage cognition onstage since, quite exceptionally, the inventors of the blend recognize that it is a blend, mean the audience to recognize that it is a blend, and succeed in that intention. It is good as an introduction, bad as a prototype.

Fleshing out the claim that reason and choice depend on backstage cognition yields the following more specific claims:

- Basic cognitive operations like conceptual blending are the basis of reasoning and choice.
- Basic cognitive operations like conceptual blending are systematic and highly intricate.
- We rarely notice these basic cognitive operations or the details of their operation.

Operations of backstage cognition, like conceptual blending, typically operate

- Below the horizon of observation;
- Too intricately for consciousness to handle;
- Interactively with each other;
- On-line;
- Quickly;
- With powers of access and recognition not otherwise available.

This combination of features is partly responsible for the power of backstage cognition. It is also partly responsible for the difficulty – notorious in cognitive science – of recognizing the existence of these cognitive operations, or the greater difficulty of noticing them as they operate, or the yet greater difficulty of analyzing what it is they do when they operate.

The automatic ease and power of these basic cognitive operations makes it natural for the social scientist to skip over analyzing the way they work, their biases, and their effects. Nonetheless, they form the basis of reason, not only for the kind of people social scientists study but also for the social scientists doing the studying.

COUNTERFACTUAL REASONING

The blend in the British Airways ad could have been suggested, approximately, by a counterfactual statement: "Our British Airways cradle seat could not be more comfortable if it were your mother's arms." In the counterfactual blend, the seat is your mother's arms. The input spaces to this counterfactual blend are (1) "you" as an adult in the airplane seat; (2) "you" as an infant in your mother's arms. Actually, discovering the input spaces in this case can be quite complicated. The input spaces could differ even across readers who all achieve essentially the same blend. For example, people never historically cradled by their mothers could still construct the intended counterfactual blend by using a generic "Mother Cradling Child" input space. The blend would, in that case, take a specific "you" and a specific "mother" from the specific input space, but it would take cradling from the generic input space. In the blend, the specific "you" would be cradled in a way that had no biographical referent. Since few readers can remember being cradled in diapers by Mom, perhaps we all need this generic space as an input to the blend. It is even possible for a reader to interpret the two "you"s in the two input spaces as entirely generic and to construct a blend that applies generically to most people but not to the reader – perhaps the reader has some medical condition that prevents cradling or reclining in seats. Such a reader could even resent the blend.

A moment's thought shows that considerable emergent structure develops even in the relatively uncomplicated interpretation. For example, we do not interpret the counterfactual assertion as meaning that the seat is as short as your mother's arms, or that your mother could hold you comfortably for 12 hours. We do not interpret it as meaning that a passenger in a British Airways cradle seat must wear a diaper, or that infants are in fact permitted to use these cradle seats.

Counterfactual reasoning, which arises by virtue of conceptual blending, is an indispensable element of political reasoning. Consider a prototypical counterfactual assertion of the sort much relied upon in qualitative research:

- If Churchill had been prime minister in 1938 instead of Neville Chamberlain, Hitler would have been deposed and World War II averted.

This counterfactual assertion asks us to blend conceptual structure from different mental spaces to create a separate, counterfactual mental space. In Figure 12.1, the input spaces include (1) Churchill in 1938 as outspoken opponent of Germany; and (2) Neville Chamberlain in 1938 as prime minister facing the threat from Germany. To construct the blend, we project parts of each of these spaces to it, and develop emergent structure there.

From the first mental space, the blend takes Churchill. From the second mental space, the blend takes the role prime minister. In the blend, Churchill is prime minister by 1938. The blend is contrary to fact with respect to both of its input spaces.

Because the process of blending is largely unconscious, it seems easy, but it is in fact complex. It has many standard features that can be illustrated from the Churchill example:

Blends Exploit and Develop Counterpart Connections between Input Spaces. The space with Churchill and the space with Chamberlain

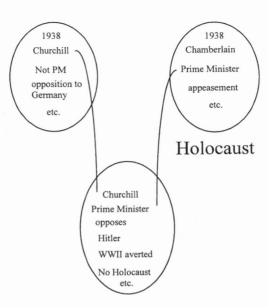

Figure 12.1. The "NO WWII" blend.

share many identity-counterparts, such as date, England, Germany, Hitler, and tension. Churchill and Chamberlain are, additionally, frame-counterparts: Each is an English political figure, holding a certain political office, with views about Germany.

Counterparts May or May Not Both Be Brought into the Blend, and May or May Not Be Fused in the Blend. Many paired counterparts are brought into the blend as fused units: Hitler in the blend is a single fused entity corresponding to Hitler in each of the inputs, but not equal to them – the Hitler in the blend has a different life. Churchill is brought into the blend but not fused with his frame-counterpart, Chamberlain. Chamberlain's political office is brought in but not fused with its frame-counterpart.

The Projection from the Input Spaces Is Selective. The blend takes from the space with Churchill his opposition to Germany but not his political office or his reputation as having poor judgment of the sort that would prevent him from obtaining a position of leadership. The blend takes from the space with Chamberlain the role *prime minister* and the situation faced by the prime minister in 1938, but not Chamberlain himself or the default knowledge attached to *prime minister* that world leaders facing aggression are concerned greatly with avoiding unnecessary war. We frame Chamberlain according to this default knowledge but keep it out of the blend, where we need a prime minister who views conflict as inevitable.

Blends Recruit a Great Range of Conceptual Structure and Knowledge without Our Recognizing It. Very little of the structure needed for the contrary-to-fact blended space is mentioned. The Churchill blend recruits conceptual frames of world leaders, political aggression, and wars. It recruits the relevant history of Germany and England. These recruitments are needed for the reasoning to work properly in the blend.

Blending Is a Process That Can Be Applied Repeatedly, and Blends Themselves Can Be Inputs to Other Blends. Someone might respond to the Churchill counterfactual, "That's only because Hitler was irrational: A more rational Hitler would have seen that his strategic chances were still excellent, and would not have backed down." This new counterfactual blend takes part but not all of the original Churchill blend, and additionally takes part but not all of the characteristics of Hitler from spaces that refer to actual situations. In the new counterfactual hyper-blend, World War II is not averted.

Former Prime Minister Margaret Thatcher created just such a hyper-blend (depicted in Figure 12.2) when she argued that as leaders of Britain, France, and the United States should have refused to appease Hitler, so Western leaders should refuse to appease aggressors in the war in Bosnia. Thatcher asked members of her audience to take two spaces – the space referring to the situation in Bosnia and the counterfactual space in which Hitler was opposed and the atrocities were averted – as inputs to the construction of a third, blended space in which the Western leaders oppose the aggressors in Bosnia and atrocities are thereby averted. Her policy – "Not Again!" – is anchored in what she takes to be the persuasiveness of the original counterfactual.

Of course, Thatcher implicitly invited her audience to imagine the counterfactual blend in which Margaret Thatcher is still prime minister during the period in which war breaks out in Bosnia, and the further counterfactual blend in which Margaret Thatcher is prime minister in 1938 and opposes Hitler. In both of these counterfactual blends, the aggressors back down and the atrocities are averted or ended. These two counterfactual blends can be made stronger if they receive projections from the space that contains (one view of) the "Falklands" war, in which Margaret Thatcher is prime minister, "The Iron Lady," war victor, courageous adversary of aggressors, enforcer of Britain's policy over vast geo-

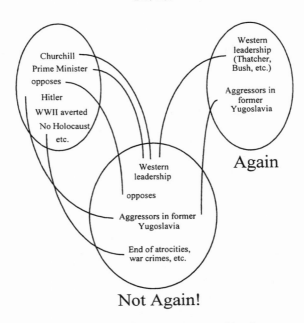

Figure 12.2. The "Not Again!" blend.

graphical distances, staunch in her defense of honor regardless of the considerable practical difficulties. Thatcher need not refer to the "Falklands" space; her identity evokes it, perhaps more effectively than any mention could.

The "Falklands" space and the two counterfactual blends, in which Thatcher faces down (a) Hitler and (b) the aggressors in Bosnia, are available to serve as reinforcing inputs to the "Not Again!" space, which represents Thatcher's policy toward Bosnia. Projections of this sort demonstrate the remarkable way in which character – once it has been connected to a specific actor in a space that has reference – can be projected to blends in which that specific actor faces past or hypothetical situations. In fact, character can be projected to *other* counterfactual blends having to do with what *other* actors might do or might have done if they possessed that character:

Blends Develop Structure Not Provided by the Inputs. Typically, the blend is not a simple cut-and-paste reassembly of elements to be found in the input spaces but instead resembles what Kahneman (1995) calls a "mental simulation," in which it develops considerable emergent structure. Usually, we focus on this additional emergent structure. For example, in the blend, but not in any of its inputs, Hitler backs down and World War II is averted.

Inferences, Arguments, and Ideas Developed in the Blend Can Have Effect in Cognition, Leading Us to Modify the Initial Inputs and to Change Our View of the Corresponding Situations. A student of historicist patterns that led to World War II might know Churchill's personality well but not have brought what she knows to bear on her conception of appeasement in 1938. The Churchill blend might challenge her to reconsider the causal weight of personality. Thatcher's blend might lead someone to rethink the situation in Bosnia and even to choose to intervene.

Selectivity of Projection and Variability of Recruitment Can Lead to Different Constructions and Inferences. We saw in the British Airways blend a classic case in which the activation of different input spaces for the blend led to different reasoning and different choices. Many people hearing the "Not Again!" blend proposed by Thatcher, which asks us to compose a scene in which Western powers intervene in a distant country, will complete that blend with structure from a "Vietnam" frame. Thatcher's blend will then include disaster for the intervening Western powers.[2] Thatcher's blend is meant to lead people to reason toward a political choice, but it can lead them to reason toward the opposite political choice if it is completed and elaborated differently.

How does structure develop in a counterfactual blend? How does structure developed in a blend lead us to reconsider input spaces?

Blends develop by three mechanisms: *composition, completion,* and *elaboration.* We selectively *compose* structure from input spaces into the blend. To do so, we exploit counterpart connections between the input spaces. *Completion* provides additional structure once a few elements have been brought in. A minimal framing of Churchill and Hitler as adversarial heads of state invites us to complete that structure by recruiting any amount of specific or general knowledge we have about personal opposition, international relations, negotiation, and so on. *Elaboration* develops the blend through imaginative mental simulation according to principles and logic in the blend.

Composition and completion often draw together conceptual structures usually kept apart. As a consequence, the blend can reveal latent contradictions and coherences between previously separated elements. It can show us problems and lacunae in what we had previously taken for

---

[2] I thank Mat McCubbins for this observation.

granted. It can equally show us unrecognized strengths and complementarity. In this way, blends yield insight into the conceptual structures from which they arise.

Composition, completion, and elaboration all recruit selectively from our most favored patterns of knowing and thinking. Consequently, blending is very powerful, but also highly subject to bias. It is hard to evaluate bias in blends, for two reasons. First, composition, completion, and elaboration operate, for the most part, automatically and below the horizon of conscious observation. Therefore, we rarely detect consciously the infrastructure in the blend that makes it effective. Second, since the emergent structure in the blend comes from our favored patterns of knowing and thinking, we are likely to regard biased infrastructure in the blend as unobjectionable, even if we somehow manage to detect it.

For example, in trying to reason about a blend only on the basis of its proper historical structure, we may unwittingly complete the blend with evidence from a later historical moment. In the Churchill counterfactual, we use what we know of 1938. But once we have Churchill as prime minister in the blend, it is impossible to prevent completion from another (covert) input space – Churchill as prime minister later in time. The counterfactual blend in which Churchill opposes Hitler in 1938 is plausible only because we can recruit to it Churchill's great determination in opposing Hitler during World War II, and we can know of that determination only because World War II was not averted. Our reasoning in the blend – that World War II might have been averted – depends, therefore, on the nonoccurrence of World War II: The blend makes sense to us only because it did not happen. In this way, our *ex post* knowledge can affect our supposed *ex ante* reasoning in ways detectable only on analysis. Even the selection of objects of ex ante reasoning can be influenced by ex post knowledge: Had Churchill never been prime minister, it is unlikely that we would think of constructing a blend in which he was prime minister in 1938.[3] Ex post input spaces seep into ex ante counterfactual blended spaces, and in fact prompt us covertly to construct them.

RATIONAL CHOICE

The study of rational choice has various names – game theory, rational play, theory of rational expectations, positive political theory, the new institutionalism, theory of interdependent decision making, economic theory of politics, and so on. It attempts to extract formal aspects of how

[3] I thank Bruce Bueno de Mesquita for conversation on this point.

actors make reasoned, strategic decisions given the goal of maximizing their profit, or, more accurately, their subjective expected utility.

A standard example of rational choice is "The Battle of the Bismarck Sea." An admiral must transport troops by ship. He can select the shorter northern route or the longer southern route. An enemy admiral must try to bomb them. He can send his planes either north or south to look for the targets. (Many restrictions are quietly assumed; we are not to ask whether the enemy admiral might send half of his planes in each direction, and so on.) There are exactly four sets of possible choices, since each player has two choices. Values are assigned for each player for each of the four outcomes. We then inspect the mathematics of the game tree to see which choice is better for each player.

This extremely simple example already has most of the features of rational choice. The decision making is interdependent and the decision makers act on their decisions. Various hypothetical sequences of actions have various outcomes, and these outcomes are assigned values for each player. In simple examples of this sort, these values might be given in dollar amounts or percentages of market share or years in jail or number of fatalities or some other unit, but in principle, all such values are really subjective values assigned by the players to the outcomes, relative to other outcomes. Players are always trying to enhance what they perceive to be their welfare by achieving higher subjective relative utilities. Game theory is the study of arithmetic conditions that arise in the tree of nodes leading to the outcome numbers, on the view that the arithmetic drives or should drive decision making at each node.

Inevitably, the theory of rational choice has sustained attack for making simplistic assumptions. For the most part, its theorists appear to be well aware that these games are cartoons of reality – "parsimonious models" rather than "thick descriptions." Not without reason, they are proud that their mathematically encrypted but conceptually simple analyses nonetheless show something about interdependent decision making. Something is already a lot in the analysis of reason and choice.

What I offer is not an attack on theory of rational choice but a demonstration of how it might be made less implausible and more adequate by being integrated with cognitive science. I follow Herbert Simon, but to say so is almost certainly misleading, since Simon's work has come unfortunately to be summarized by the slogan "bounded rationality," which is interpreted to mean that human reason, dragged down by cognitive limits and mental dispositions toward illusion, is a collapsed and partial version of an ideal rationality the principles of which we already understand. "Bounded rationality" means "what theorists of rational choice already work with, but adulterated." Economists and political scientists have, it seems, heard about as much talk on the subject of bounded rationality as they can stomach, and the phrase leads anyway to the conclusion that they can proceed with all legitimacy as they have done, so long as, at the end of the day, they concede that actual human beings have a specific handicap.

My subject here is not bounded rationality. My subject is, instead, how human beings actually do reason and choose. I propose, first, that some of the most important mental work they do is not a bounded form of what has come to be modeled as rational choice but, instead, brilliant backstage cognition that operates by principles at once more interesting, more complicated, and more evolutionarily sound than those of rational choice. Second, I propose that human political performance is often very good, indeed much better than it would be if play were merely rational, as that term is understood in game theory.

Herbert Simon's original comment on the interaction of cognitive science, political science, and economics stressed the general indispensability of cognitive science to economics and political science. His remarkable 1986 essay, "Rationality in Psychology and Economics," began with an inspiring assumption – "economic actors use the same basic processes in making their decisions as have been observed in other human cognitive activities . . ." (39); a crucial perspective – "The emerging laws of procedural rationality have much more the complexity of molecular biology than the simplicity of classical mechanics. As a consequence, they call for a very high ratio of empirical investigation to theory building. They require painstaking factual study of the decision-making process itself" (39); and an invaluable prescription:

Economics without psychological and sociological research to determine the givens of the decision-making situation, the focus of attention, the problem representation [i.e., the framing of the problem in context], and the processes used to identify alternatives, estimate consequences, and choose among possibilities – such economics is a one-bladed scissors. Let us replace it with an instrument capable of cutting through our ignorance about rational human behavior (39–40).

There are many avenues that could be taken to a "cognitive scientific theory of rational choice." I begin with a few that I will not pursue:

- In the typical situation, actors are engaged in simultaneous games that overlap. Any action is a move in many different games. Strategies to maximize expected utility over all these games are typically nonlinear. In principle, the output of any subgame of any game can be input to any subgame of any other game.
- In the typical situation, actors are adaptive: their first and strongest disposition is often not to play the game but to change it.

- Strategies for doing well in these simultaneous games include leaving some of them and relinquishing hope of gain from them.
- In the typical situation, actors work at conceptual reinterpretation of the history of play, so that other actors can be persuaded that the value and status of a past action must be changed, which entails that it lead to nodes different from those to which it was once thought to lead. Conceptually, which is what counts, the history of the game is not fixed.
- Actors must operate in general without knowing what game they are in, and the question always arises, who has the authority to recognize and establish the game being played? Actors attempt to influence other actors' thoughts about the game being played.

Actual human choice typically requires elaborate and complex cognitive work of the sorts that theory of rational choice does not at present recognize or treat. Attempts to introduce cognitive research to economics and political science include not only Simon's work but also Kahneman, Slovic, and Tversky (1982), Kahneman and Tversky (1979), and Richard Thaler (1991). Reviews of the divide between economics and cognitive science can be found in Hogarth and Reder (1987), Lewin (1996), and Smith (1991). Game theory has made rudimentary attempts to acknowledge some of this complexity. For example, a preliminary attempt has been made to recognize some gross distinctions in the extent and kinds of knowledge about the game possessed by the players (games of perfect, certain, symmetric, or complete information). An attempt has also been made to recognize the role of conceptual focal points (e.g., the number 100 rather than 99) in decision making. Nonetheless, as Lewin (1996: 1295) summarizes, "the 'declaration of independence' from psychology remain[s], and it haunts economics to this day."

It turns out that conceptual blending is a basic instrument of rational choice, as off-the-equilibrium-path arguments and Figure 12.3 demonstrate. Suppose that actor A believes that, for the past, present, or future, if A does P, actor B responds by doing Q; desiring to avoid Q, A has never done P and plans never to do P. The node S at which A does P and B does Q is put together cognitively by conceptual blending. It must be assembled in this fashion since it does not refer to any actual situation, and no one has any memory of it. To arrive at a conception of that space, we must blend together concepts of real actors (A and B), real characteristics of those actors, unreal actions (P), hypothetical responses (Q), and models of behavior. Importantly, this blended space is *causal* for the space of A's *actual* behavior.[4]

[4] I thank Bruce Bueno de Mesquita and Barry Weingast for illumination on this point.

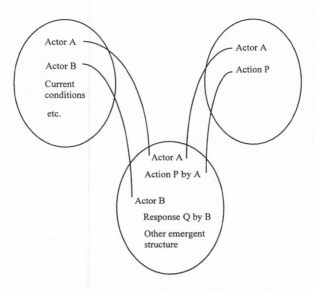

Figure 12.3. A node off the equilibrium path.

In fact, all nodes in a game must be constructed cognitively by conceptual integration, which is easiest to do for very simple games with two players, each of whom has a single move, where the outcomes are relatively clear and where some external agency imposes or provides payoffs in a single, monolithic, publicly recognized unit (yen, years in jail) and at a level that overshadows all other payoffs. It becomes harder to do the requisite conceptual blending as the game becomes more complicated.

Values must be assigned to these outcomes. This assignment of values also arises through conceptual blending. Rational choice analysis begins by taking those values as *given*. In this way, the theorist of rational choice takes the payoff matrix as an *oracle,* in the technical sense: In mathematics, one way to attack a problem is to try to show that if there were an oracle that could supply the answer to some part of the problem, we could solve the entire problem; this shows that the larger problem reduces to the problem solved by the oracle.

But in reality, the payoff matrix does not come from an oracle. Values attached to outcomes are not something outside of decision making; they come exactly from decision making, and the assignment of values is typically dynamic and shifting during action.

The player must assign the comprehensive value of an outcome by conceptual blending over all the relevant values, and this blending is unlikely to be linear. Suppose, for example, that Sue believes that if she has a chance to tell a certain story in casual conversation in a group that includes Max, it will prompt Max to begin to court her. She believes the same of Joe. She welcomes the courtship in either case. The chance arises, but Sue stays silent, because Max and Joe are both present, and she prefers not to induce known rivalry between them. The value of having Max and Joe court her is then not the sum of having each court her. There is essential emergent structure in this blend, and it includes an emergent value that is not the linear sum of the values of its inputs.

But now suppose that Todd is also present. Sue thinks Todd's reaction to seeing others court her will be, first, painful brooding, and, second, a determination to court her, which she welcomes highly. Then the high positive value of being courted by Max and Joe is unrelated to the positive values of being courted by Max or Joe.

The theorist of rational choice takes the conceptual content of the nodes and the matrix of values as given, and begins the analysis after this point. But from the cognitive perspective, these things are not given; they are instead constructed mentally by conceptual blending and other operations of backstage cognition.

The theorist of rational choice proceeds in the sequence: (1) Chart, or if that is impractical, characterize formally the tree of decisions and actions; (2) assign values; (3) analyze the resulting arithmetic of the game tree. There may be a few cases of decision making, like the Battle of the Bismarck Sea, where this procedure fits actual decision making. But in actual decision making, conceptual blending to assemble the nodes and values is permanently active. The contents and values of all the nodes are always under construction.

Conceptual blending is additionally indispensable to rational choice in a quite different way. It is the basis of deciding, at the specific level, what game one is playing, and, at the general level, whether or not one is playing a game at all.

First, the specific level. We use conceptual frames in understanding specific situations (e.g., seduction, debate). The conceptual frame is part of the blending network that constitutes our understanding of the specific situation. Since conceptual frames carry default inferences, it is natural to assume that decision making in any specific situation will depend on which frames are used by the decision maker. Yet Von Neumann and Morgenstern's *Theory of Games and Economic Behavior* (1944), which launched the application of game theory to economic behavior, offered as one of its great insights that certain essential mathematical regularities can be found in the formal structure of decision making that are independent of specific conceptual frames. Some cognitive scientists have argued that at least in certain specific cases, this assumption is demonstrably wrong (Kahneman and Tversky 1979; Simon 1978, 1982; Tversky and Kahneman 1986). If it is wrong as a general principle, then it follows that conceptual blending (of frames and specific situations) is indispensable to decision making. "Positive" social science depends on cognitive mechanisms of framing and blending.

Second, the general level. Conceptual integration is involved in deciding whether or not one is playing a game at all. *Rational choice on the goal of maximizing my utility* is itself a (very general) conceptual frame, which brings with it pressures on decision making. Certainly, people seem to try to reason toward welfare-enhancing decisions when they frame themselves that way – especially if they use a specific frame that carries *maximizing utility* as part of its stipulated goal structure (as in "Matching Pennies" or "poker," two of Von Neumann and Morgenstern's examples). But it is not easy for the cognitive scientist to swallow the assumption that people have no choice but to blend that abstract frame of *rational choice* with their current specific situation, all of the time, and always to act on the central inference of that blend.

There appears to be a feeling that evolutionary pressure by itself (succeed rather than fail) must ensure that actors try to enhance their welfare by maximizing their expected utility, but the mechanisms of evolutionary pressure are not simple. For example, curiosity and routine action to satisfy it are apparently adaptive for our species, but curiosity killed the cat. Acting on curiosity may be unrelated to any local or recognizable rational choice, game, or utility, and the details of its downstream utility may be, for the most part, unimaginable to the actor and beyond his evaluation. The benefit of curious behavior may be absolute but not resident within anything that looks like a strip of rational choice. Acting on curiosity does not have to be *reasoned,* it does not have to involve *decision,* and it does not have to be connected to any utility that is recognizable to the actor or that is imaginable by the actor. It can be *impulsive.* Yet much of our action – even our action in explicitly political, financial, or legislative contests – could in principle be driven by curiosity. It would be inappropriate to respond that in this case, the actor has placed a high value on satisfying curiosity and is making reasoned decisions accordingly. That claim merely reasserts that the curious actor is reasoning – to both values and decisions, is making decisions, and understands the connections among the decisions, the actions, and the values, when in fact it is unclear that the curious actor is reasoning toward values, is making reasoned decisions at all, or has any model relating these decision to these utilities.

The assumption of rational choice is, like the assumption that outcome values are supplied by oracle, a black box, one that a cognitive scientist, at least, would like to see filled.

TOWARD AN INTEGRATED THEORY OF REASONING

As we have seen, political scientists and economists often approach the analysis of human reasoning, such as counterfactual reasoning and rational choice, as if it were a species of implication. Implication is a deductive operation of formal logic, a matter of deriving propositions from other propositions by using principles (e.g., either p or *not* p) that are themselves simple, commonsensical, and supposedly invariant over all conceptual domains, and in such a way that the system of propositions remains consistent, the derivation runs legitimately over all possibilities, and the newly achieved propositions never invalidate the old. Implication is familiar from logic and mathematics, and it carries cultural prestige, and so naturally it provided some of the first models of reasoning.

But cognitive science has shown that human reasoning should not be expected to take the form of an implication-based logic. Evolution has standards for fitness, cultures have standards for success, and it is these standards, not the formal requirements of implication, that have mattered in our evolutionary past. People must predict, plan, imagine, explain, and act on the fly, and their fitness and welfare depend upon whether they have mechanisms for reasoning that are in fact effective under these conditions and for these purposes. In evolutionary terms, there is negligible benefit from, for example, scrutinizing our reasoning in unrelated situations to see whether we can discover any in-principle inconsistencies, or evaluating logically possible but clearly implausible contingencies, or constructing long-distance sequences of implications, or trying to discover principles of reasoning invariant over all conceptual domains. Human beings are not even typically motivated to optimal performance because even complete failure in any particular strip of endeavor has little evolutionary consequence unless it kills you at a young age. What does have consequence for evolution is whether, in total, over decades, you manage, sometime, to make certain things happen. On that requirement, human reasoning needs to be inventive, creative, reliable, strategic, opportunistic, social, natural, effective, and nonfatal, but it does not need to be especially good at cascading implication.

This does not suggest that analyses of reasoning as implication are to be rejected or discarded. On the contrary, sophisticated implication is highly useful in human reasoning as a test of what we have achieved through other, more basic operations. Even the mathematician and the physicist may use implication for the most part in this way, as a test of hypotheses that backstage cognition offers. And in politics and economics, certainly there are many important situations – currency arbitrage, for example – where legal and institutional authorities have established known and stable rules that govern more or less encapsulated strips of play; where other, faceless players can be assumed to operate out of specific and quantifiable self-interest; and where, therefore, applying sophisticated principles of implication to our reasoning can bring correction, improvement, and benefit. But advanced implication still remains dependent on the structures and biases of backstage cognition, and a view of reasoning that skips over the analysis of backstage cognition will inevitably miss much of what is going on.

What we all miss at the moment is an integrated theory of reasoning that combines the interest of the cognitive scientist in backstage cognition – complex, intricate, systematic, biased, nearly invisible mental operations executed in brains – with the interest of the political scientist and the economist in how people do reason or should reason inside special advanced contexts, such as delegative assemblies, voting booths, diplomatic negotiations, and markets. Human reasoning is integrated, but the study of it is dismembered in the university by the particular lines of division we have historically drawn among certain areas of study and research. From the cognitive perspective, the particular partition of departments typical of an American university – biology, psychology, political science, anthropology, literature, linguistics – is poorly chosen. Yet the faculty and its research are managed through incentive structures that keep the partition sharp. The good of integrating our studies of reasoning is evident, but how to change the university so they become integrated is much less clear.

13

Constructing a Theory of Reasoning: Choice, Constraints, and Context
ARTHUR LUPIA, MATHEW D. MCCUBBINS, AND SAMUEL L. POPKIN

The contributions to this volume, taken together, represent a synthesis of three approaches to the study of human behavior: rational choice, psychology, and cognitive science. Each essay presents an element of political reasoning, which, taken together, begins to create a single unified approach to modeling human behavior. Such a synthesis could not have taken place for the better part of this century.

For most of the history of rational choice theory, proponents were too wedded to deductive theory and *homo economicus* to deal with the broad array of emotions, interests, and "biases" that other scientists discovered in their research. In recent years, rational choice theorists have started to change. Compelled by the empirical challenges of such scholars as Simon, Kahneman, and Tversky, rational choice economists and political scientists have paid greater attention to empirical matters and have spent more time in experimental laboratories. Others have attempted to create new rational choice theories that have a more refined appreciation for a wide range of social scientific discoveries about human reason.

For most of the history of psychology, moreover, psychologists chose not to take choice or cognition seriously. As Robin Dawes has noted, much of the early research in psychology did not regard individuals as "decision-making units that weighed the consequences of various courses of action and then chose from among them." In recent years, the same criticism cannot be made. Some of the most important contributions of modern psychology, such as the general explanations of attitude formation and change offered by Eagly and Chaiken (1993) and Petty and Cacioppo (1986a), cannot be explained without assuming the presence of an active, hypothesis-testing mind. As Dawes again notes (1988: 19), "It is now legitimate for psychologists to talk about thinking, choice, mental representations, plans, goals, mental hypothesis-testing, and 'cognitive' biases."

The newest of the three disciplines, cognitive science, is not old enough

287

to have participated in the long-running standoff between rational choice theorists and psychologists. Its progress, however, forces a new perspective on scholars who wish to explain behavior (e.g., Clark 1997; Damasio 1994; Holland, Holyoak, Nisbett, and Thagard 1986). These studies show us that it is possible to craft explanations of behavior from an integrated foundation of premises about the thinking process (now central to psychology) and premises about goal-driven adaptation (the central tenet of rational choice theories).

Our current beliefs about the character of political reason have been informed by the contributions to this volume. Although what we have assembled here does not constitute a complete theory of political reason or behavior, it does clarify the path to better social scientific explanations of such phenomena. A sketch of the path is as follows:

Its first premise would borrow, from neoclassical economics, the assumption that human behavior involves *choice*. Scarcity is ubiquitous and forces people to make numerous choices. They must choose between turning left and turning right; they must choose whether to work with others or to kill whoever disagrees with them; they must choose whether to speak or remain silent; they must choose between Coke, Pepsi, and water; they must choose between Democrat and Republican. They must choose their answers to ballot initiatives and survey questions. To explain why people do what they do, we must first understand that behavior is a function of choice.

This first premise would also draw from the cognitive science paradigm called *connectionism*. Connectionism reveals that the choices people make depend on beliefs about causality in the environment. Connectionists argue that the evolution of beliefs is structured by the interaction among the external environment, the human ability to feel pain and pleasure, and the cognitive operation of the brain (see, e.g., Churchland and Sejnowski 1991 and Clark 1993 for reviews). An important lesson from cognitive science is that few of the behaviors that we recognize as political should be treated as if they are automatic – even if a response to a stimulus appears automatic, it was likely determined by choices made and feedback received at a previous time. This and other lessons from cognitive science reinforce the assumption that political behavior involves choice.

Our second premise is that uncertainty clouds all human choice. Systematic and universal physical limitations *constrain* human information processing. Our third premise is that a cognition-independent concept of expected utility maximization is *not sufficient* to describe uncertainty's effects. An advantage of current research in psychology and cognitive science, regarding both premises, is that it identifies concrete examples of the ways in which uncertainty affects reason and choice (see, e.g.,

Kahneman and Tversky 1984). The chapters by Turner and Tetlock, for example, reveal regular tendencies in the concepts that people will and will not relate to each other, while the chapters by Rahn, and by Lodge and Taber, reveal how affect shapes the manner in which adaptations to uncertainty occur.

The fourth premise, drawn equally from the positive study of political institutions and social psychology, is that each choice *context* can guide and constrain reason and choice. Through extensive observation and experimentation, psychologists have developed canons of human behavior that help to explain and to predict choice in a wide variety of contexts. Frohlich and Oppenheimer's experiments demonstrate that the framing of opportunities for altruism has systematic effects on the nature of altruistic behavior, while Denzau and North's, Lupia and McCubbins's, and Sniderman's chapters each show how political institutions frame fundamental aspects of the choices that political decision makers face.

CONCLUSION

Rational choice scholars in economics and political science are often quite critical of psychological and cognitive approaches to understanding human behavior; they point out that neither approach presents a single, simple, generalizable model of human behavior. At the same time, psychologists and cognitive scientists are often critical of rational choice theories, arguing that they generally fail to generate accurate predictions of human behavior. Although social scientists disagree about many things, we can all agree that these paradigm debates are often little more than scholars talking past each other.

In this volume, by contrast, scholars from different approaches attempt a synthesis that was not possible for most of this century. Instead of focusing on the shortcomings of competing approaches, each of our contributors integrates some of the competition's virtues into his or her favored ways of doing research. Each contributor brings to the debate the shared sense that understanding reason is the key to crafting better explanations of choice. And though each scholar contributes but an element of reason, collectively they lay the foundation for something of far greater value.

References

Abelson, R. 1959. "Modes of Resolution of Belief Dilemmas." *Journal of Conflict Resolution* 3: 343–352.

Abelson, R. 1963. "Computer Simulation of 'Hot' Cognition." In S. S. Tomkins and S. Messick, eds., *Computer Simulation of Personality*. New York: Wiley, 277–298.

Abelson, R. 1973. "The Structure of Belief Systems." In R. Schank and K. Colby, eds., *Computer Models of Thought and Language*. New York: Freeman, 287–339.

Abelson, R. 1987. "Conviction." *American Psychologist* 43: 267–275.

Abelson, R., E. Aronson, W. McGuire, T. Newcomb, T. Rosenberg, and P. Tannenbaum. 1968. *Theories of Cognitive Consistency: A Source Book*. Chicago: Rand McNally.

Abelson, R., and D. Prentice. 1989. "Beliefs as Possessions: A Functional Perspective." In A. Pratkanis, S. Brecker, and A. Greenwald, eds., *Attitude Structure and Function*. Hillsdale, NJ: Lawrence Erlbaum, 361–382.

Adorno, T., E. Frenkel-Brunswick, D. Levinson, and N. Sanford. 1950. *The Authoritarian Personality*. New York: Harper and Row.

Alchian, A. A. 1950. "Uncertainty, Evolution and Economic Theory." *Journal of Political Economy* 58: 211–221.

Aldrich, J. H. 1995. *Why Parties?* Chicago: University of Chicago Press.

Allwood, C. M., and H. Montgomery. 1987. "Response Selection Strategies and Realism of Confidence Judgments." *Organizational Behavior and Human Decision Processes* 39: 365–383.

Altemeyer, R. 1981. *Right-Wing Authoritarianism*. Winnipeg, Manitoba: University of Manitoba Press.

Althaus, S. L. 1996. *Who Speaks for the People? Political Knowledge, Representation, and the Use of Opinion Surveys in Democratic Politics*. Ph.D. dissertation, Northwestern University.

Anderson, J. 1983. *The Architecture of Cognition*. Cambridge, MA: Harvard University Press.

Anderson, N. 1991. *Contributions to Information Integration Theory*. Hillsdale, NJ: Lawrence Erlbaum.

References

Anderson, N., and S. Hubert. 1963. "Effects of Concomitant Recall on Order Effects in Personality Impression." *Journal of Verbal Learning and Verbal Behavior* 2: 379–391.

Andre, J. 1992. "Blocked Exchanges: A Taxonomy." *Ethics* 103: 29–47.

Ansolabehere, S., and S. Iyengar. 1994. "Riding the Wave and Exercising Ownership Over Issues." *Public Opinion Quarterly* 58: 335–357.

Ansolabehere, S., and S. Iyengar. 1995. *Going Negative: How Attack Ads Shrink and Polarize the Electorate.* New York: Free Press.

Aristotle. 1954. *Rhetoric.* New York: Modern Library.

Aronson, E. 1992. "The Return of the Repressed: Dissonance Theory Makes a Comeback." *Psychological Inquiry* 3: 303–311.

Arrow, K. J. 1973. "Formal Theories of Social Welfare." In P. Wiener, ed., *Dictionary of the History of Ideas,* 4: 276–284. New York: Scribner.

Arthur, W. B. 1988. "Self-reinforcing Mechanisms in Economics." In P. W. Anderson, D. Pines, and K. Arrow, eds., *The Economy as an Evolving Complex System.* Boston: Addison-Wesley, 33–48.

Arthur, W. B. 1990. "A Learning Algorithm that Mimics Human Learning." Santa Fe Institute Economics Research Program, Working Paper 90-026, Santa Fe, NM.

Arthur, W. B., 1992. "On Learning and Adaptation in the Economy." Institute for Economic Research Discussion Paper #854, Queen's University, Kingston, Ontario, Canada.

Aumann, R. J. 1981. "Survey of Repeated Games." In R. J. Aumann et al., eds., *Essays in Game Theory and Mathematical Economics in Honor of Oskar Morgenstern.* Zurich: Bibliographisches Institut, 11–42.

Axelrod, R. 1984. *The Evolution of Cooperation.* New York: Basic Books.

Bacon, F. 1621 and 1994. *Novum Organum.* Translated and edited by P. Urbach and J. Gibson. Chicago: Open Court.

Bargh, J. 1994. "The Four Horseman of Automaticity: Awareness, Intention, Efficiency, and Control in Social Cognition." In R. Wyer and T. Srull, eds., *Handbook of Social Cognition: Basic Processes,* Vol. I. Hillsdale, NJ: Lawrence Erlbaum Associates.

Bargh, J. 1997. "The Automaticity of Everyday Life." In R. Wyer, ed., *Advances in Social Cognition.* Vol. 10. Hillsdale, NJ: Lawrence Erlbaum Associates.

Bargh, J., S. Chaiken, R. Govender, and F. Pratto. 1992. "The Generality of the Automatic Attitude Activation Effect." *Journal of Personality and Social Psychology* 62: 893–912.

Barkow, J. H., L. Cosmides, and J. Tooby. 1992. *The Adapted Mind: Evolutionary Psychology and the Generation of Culture.* New York: Oxford University Press.

Baron, D. P. 1989. "A Noncooperative Theory of Legislative Coalitions." *American Journal of Political Science* 33: 1048–1084.

Baron, J. 1994. *Thinking and Deciding.* Cambridge: Cambridge University Press.

Baron, J., R. Gowda, and H. Kunreuther. 1993. "Attitudes Toward Managing Hazardous Waste: What Should Be Cleaned Up and Who Should Pay for It?" *Risk Analysis* 13: 183–192.

References

Barsalou, L. 1992. *Cognitive Psychology: An Overview for Cognitive Scientists.* Hillsdale, NJ: Lawrence Erlbaum Associates.

Bartels, L. M. 1995. "The American Public's Defense Spending Preferences in the Post–Cold War Era." *Public Opinion Quarterly* 58: 479–508.

Bartels, L. M. 1996. "Uninformed Voters: Information Effects in Presidential Elections." *American Journal of Political Science* 40: 194–230.

Bartlett, F. A. 1932. *Remembering: A Study in Experimental and Social Psychology.* New York: Cambridge University Press.

Bates, R. H. 1989. *Beyond the Miracle of the Market: The Political Economy of Agrarian Development in Kenya.* Cambridge: Cambridge University Press.

Batson, C. D., C. L. Turk, L. L. Shaw, and T. R. Klein. 1995. "Information Function of Empathetic Emotion: Learning That We Value the Other's Welfare." *Journal of Personality and Social Psychology* 68: 300–313.

Baumer, D. L., and H. J. Gold. 1995. "Party Images and the American Electorate." *American Politics Quarterly* 23: 33–61.

Baumol, W. J., and W. E. Oates. 1979. *Economics, Environmental Policy and the Quality of Life.* Englewood Cliffs, NJ: Prentice Hall.

Bechara, A., H. Damasio, D. Tranel, and A. R. Damasio. 1997. "Deciding Advantageously Before Knowing the Advantageous Strategy." *Science* 275: 1293–1294.

Becker, C. L. 1932. *The Heavenly City of the Eighteenth Century Philosophers.* New Haven: Yale University Press.

Becker, G. 1981. *A Treatise on the Family.* Cambridge, MA: Harvard University Press.

Bell, D. 1980. "The Return of the Sacred? The Argument on the Future of Religion." In D. Bell, ed., *The Winding Passage.* New York: Basic Books.

Bennett, W. L. 1988. *News: The Politics of Illusion.* New York: Longman.

Bennett, W. L. 1992. *The Governing Crisis: Media, Money, and Marketing in American Elections.* New York: St. Martin's Press.

Berelson, B. R., P. F. Lazarsfeld, and W. N. McPhee. 1954. *Voting: A Study of Opinion Formation in a Presidential Campaign.* Chicago: University of Chicago Press.

Berg, J., J. Dickhaut, and K. McCabe. 1995. "Trust, Reciprocity, and Social History." *Games and Economic Behavior* 10: 122–142.

Berlin, I. 1969. "Two Concepts of Liberty." In I. Berlin, *Four Essays on Liberty.* Oxford: Oxford University Press.

Bettelheim, B. 1989. *The Uses of Enchantment: The Meaning and Importance of Fairy Tales.* New York: Vintage.

Bikhchandani, S., D. Hirshleifer, and I. Welch. 1992. "Theory of Fads, Fashion, Custom, and Cultural Change as Informational Cascades." *Journal of Political Economy* 100: 992–1026.

Binmore, K. 1987 and 1988. "Modeling Rational Players: Parts I and II." *Economics and Philosophy* 3: 179–214; 4: 9–55.

Binmore, K. 1993. *Game Theory & the Social Contract 1: Playing Fair.* Ann Arbor: University of Michigan Press.

293

References

Bless, H., G. L. Clore, N. Schwarz, V. Golisano, C. Rabe, and M. Wölk. 1996. "Mood and the Use of Scripts: Does a Happy Mood Really Lead to Mindlessness?" *Journal of Personality and Social Psychology* 71: 665–679.

Bodenhausen, G. 1993. "Emotions, Arousal, and Stereotypic Judgments: A Heuristic Model of Affect and Stereotyping." In D. Mackie and D. Hamilton, eds., *Affect, Cognition, and Stereotyping: Interactive Processes in Group Perception*. San Diego: Academic Press, 13–37.

Bodenhausen, G. V., G. P. Kramer, and K. Süsser. 1994. "Happiness and Stereotypic Thinking in Social Judgments." *Journal of Personality and Social Psychology* 66: 621–632.

Bogdan, R. J. 1997. *Interpreting Minds: The Evolution of a Practice*. Cambridge, MA: MIT Press.

Boniger, D. S., J. A. Krosnick, and M. K. Berent. 1995. "Origins of Attitude Importance: Self-Interest, Social Identification, and Value Relevance." *Journal of Personality and Social Psychology* 68: 61–80.

Boynton, G. R., and M. Lodge. 1994. "Voter's Images of Candidates." In A. Miller and B. Gronbeck, eds., *Presidential Campaigns and American Self Images*. Boulder, CO: Westview Press, 159–175.

Boynton, G. R., and M. Lodge 1996. "J.Q.PUBLIC: A Computational Model of Candidate Evaluation." Paper presented at the annual meeting of the American Political Science Association, San Francisco.

Brady, H. E., and P. Sniderman. 1985. "Attitude Attribution: A Group Basis for Political Reasoning." *American Political Science Review* 79: 1061–1078.

Brehm, J., and W. M. Rahn. 1997. "Individual-Level Evidence for the Causes and Consequences of Social Capital." *American Journal of Political Science* 41: 999–1023.

Brewer, P. R., and M. R. Steenbergen. 1997. "All For One or One Against All? The Impact of Interpersonal Trust on Public Opinion." Paper presented at the annual meeting of the Southern Political Science Association, Nov. 5–8, Norfolk, VA.

Breyer, S. 1993. *Breaking the Vicious Circle: Toward Effective Risk Regulation*. Cambridge, MA: Harvard University Press.

Brody, R., and B. Page. 1972. "The Assessment of Policy Voting." *American Political Science Review* 66: 450–458.

Bruner, J. 1986. *Actual Minds, Possible Worlds*. Cambridge, MA: Harvard University Press.

Bryant, A. 1996. "Advertising." *New York Times*, June 6, sec. D.

Buchanan, B. 1991. *Electing a President: The Markle Commission's Report on Campaign '88*. Austin: University of Texas Press.

Budge, I., and D. Fairlie. 1983. *Explaining and Predicting Elections*. London: Allen and Unwin.

Bueno de Mesquita, B., and D. Lalman. 1992. *War and Reason: Domestic and International Imperatives*. New Haven: Yale University Press.

Burns, P. 1985. "Experience and Decision Making: A Comparison of Students and Businessmen in a Simulated Progressive Auction." *Research in Experimental Economics* 3: 139–157.

References

Cacioppo, J. T., and R. E. Petty. 1979. "Effects of Message Repetition and Position on Cognitive Response, Recall, and Persuasion." *Journal of Personality and Social Psychology* 37: 97–109.

Cacioppo, J. T., and R. E. Petty. 1985. "Central and Peripheral Routes to Persuasion: The Role of Message Repetition." In A. Mitchell and L. Alwitt, eds., *Psychological Processes and Advertising Effects*. Hillsdale, NJ: Lawrence Erlbaum.

Cain, B., J. Ferejohn, and M. P. Fiorina. 1987. *The Personal Vote: Constituency Service and Electoral Independence*. Cambridge, MA: Harvard University Press.

Cain, M. 1998. "An Experimental Investigation of Motives and Information in the Prisoners' Dilemma Game." *Advances in Group Processes* 15: 133–160.

Calabresi, G., and P. Bobbitt. 1978. *Tragic Choices*. New York: Norton.

Camerer, C. 1995. "Individual Decision Making." In J. H. Kagel and A. E. Roth, eds., *The Handbook of Experimental Economics*. Princeton: Princeton University Press.

Camerer, C. F., and H. Kunreuther. 1989. "Decision Processes for Low Probability Events: Policy Implications." *Journal of Policy Analysis and Management* 8: 565–592.

Campagna, A. S. 1994. *The Economy in the Reagan Years: The Economic Consequences of the Reagan Administration*. Westport, CT: Greenwood Press.

Campbell, A., P. Converse, W. Miller, and D. Stokes. 1960. *The American Voter*. New York: John Wiley and Sons.

Campbell, D. T. 1987. "Evolutionary Epistemology." In D. T. Campbell, G. Raditzky, and W. W. Bartley III, eds., *Evolutionary Epistemology, Rationality, and the Sociology of Knowledge*. La Salle, IL: Open Court, 47–90.

Carmines, E. G., and J. H. Kuklinski. 1990. "Incentives, Opportunities, and the Logic of Public Opinion in American Political Representation." In J. A. Ferejohn and J. H. Kuklinski, eds., *Information and Democratic Processes*. Urbana: University of Illinois Press.

Chandler, A. D., Jr. 1977. *The Visible Hand: The Managerial Revolution in American Business*. Cambridge, MA: Harvard University Press.

Cherniak, C. 1986. *Minimal Rationality*. Cambridge, MA: MIT Press.

Churchland, P. M. 1989. A *Neurocomputational Perspective: The Nature of Mind and the Structure of Science*. Cambridge, MA: MIT Press.

Churchland, P. M. 1995. *The Engine of Reason, the Seat of the Soul: A Philosophical Journey into the Brain*. Cambridge, MA: MIT Press.

Churchland, P. S., and T. J. Sejnowski. 1992. *The Computational Brain*. Cambridge, MA: MIT Press.

Clark, A. 1989. *Microcognition: Philosophy, Cognitive Science and Parallel Distributed Processing*. Cambridge, MA: MIT Press.

Clark, A. 1993. *Associative Engines: Connectionism, Concepts, and Representational Change*. Cambridge, MA: MIT Press.

Clark, A. 1997. *Being There: Putting Brain, Body, and World Together Again*. Cambridge, MA: MIT Press.

References

Clark, A., and A. Karmiloff-Smith. 1994. "The Cognizer's Innards: A Psychological and Philosophical Perspective on the Development of Thought." *Mind and Language* 8: 487–519.

Clore, G., and L. Isbell. 1999. "Emotion and Virtue and Vice," In James Kuklinski, ed., *Citizens and Politics: Perspectives from Political Psychology*. New York: Cambridge University Press.

Cobb, M. D., and J. H. Kuklinski. 1997. "Changing Minds: Political Arguments and Political Persuasion." *American Journal of Political Science* 41: 88–121.

Collier, D., and S. Levitsky. 1997. "Democracy with Adjectives: Conceptual Innovation in Comparative Research." *World Politics* 49: 430–451.

Collins, A., and E. Loftus. 1975. "A Spreading-Activation Theory of Semantic Processing." *Psychological Review* 82: 407–428.

Collins, A., and M. R. Quillian. 1968. "Retrieval Time from Semantic Memory." *Journal of Verbal Learning and Verbal Behavior* 8: 240–247.

Conover, P. J. 1984. "The Influence of Group Identifications on Political Perception and Evaluation." *Journal of Politics* 46: 760–785.

Converse, P. E. 1964. "The Nature of Belief Systems in Mass Publics." In D. E. Apter, ed., *Ideology and Discontent*. New York: Free Press.

Converse, P. E. 1970. "Attitudes and Nonattitudes: Continuation of a Dialogue." In D. Apter, ed., *Ideology and Discontent*. New York: Free Press, 206–261.

Converse, P. E. 1990. "Popular Representation and the Distribution of Information." In J. A. Ferejohn and J. H. Kuklinski, eds., *Information and Democratic Processes*. Urbana: University of Illinois Press.

Cosmides, L. 1989. "The Logic of Social Exchange: Has Natural Selection Shaped How Humans Reason? Studies with the Wason Selection Task." *Cognition* 31: 187–276.

Cosmides, L., and J. Tooby. 1992. "Cognitive Adaptations of Social Exchange." In J. H. Barkow, L. Cosmides, and J. Tooby, eds., *The Adapted Mind: Evolutionary Psychology and the Generation of Culture*. Oxford: Oxford University Press, 163–228.

Coulson, S. 1995. "Analogic and Metaphoric Mapping in Blended Spaces." *Center for Research in Language Newsletter* 9: 2–12.

Coulson, S. 1996. "The Menendez Brothers Virus: Analogical Mapping in Blended Spaces." In A. Goldberg, ed., *Conceptual Structure, Discourse, and Language*. Stanford, CA: Center for the Study of Language and Information.

Coulson, S. 1997. *Semantic Leaps: The Role of Frame-Shifting and Conceptual Blending in Meaning Construction*. Ph.D. dissertation, University of California, San Diego.

Coursey, D. L., and E. A. Dyl. 1990. "Price Limits, Trading Suspensions, and the Adjustment of Prices to New Information." Unpublished manuscript, Business School, Washington University, St. Louis, MO.

Coursey, D. L., and C. F. Mason. 1987. "Investigations Concerning the Dynamics of Consumer Behavior in Uncertain Environments." *Economic Inquiry* 25: 549–504.

References

Cox, G. W. 1997. *Making Votes Count: Strategic Coordination in the World's Electoral Systems.* Cambridge: Cambridge University Press.

Cox, G. W., and M. D. McCubbins. 1993. *Legislative Leviathan: Party Government in the House.* Berkeley and Los Angeles: University of California Press.

Crandall, R. W. 1997. "The Costly Pursuit of the Impossible." *Brookings Review* 15: 41–47.

Crick, F. 1994. *The Astonishing Hypothesis: The Scientific Search for the Soul.* New York: Charles Scribner's Sons.

Critical Review. 1995. "Rational Choice Theory and Politics." New Haven, CT: Critical Review Foundation.

Damasio, A. R. 1994. *Descartes' Error: Emotion, Reason, and the Human Brain.* New York: G. P. Putnam's Sons.

Dawes, R. M. 1988. *Rational Choice in an Uncertain World.* San Diego: Harcourt Brace Jovanovich.

Delli Carpini, M. X., and S. Keeter. 1991. "Stability and Change in the U.S. Public's Knowledge of Politics." *Public Opinion Quarterly* 55: 583–612.

Delli Carpini, M. X., and S. Keeter. 1996. *What Americans Know About Politics and Why It Matters.* New Haven: Yale University Press.

Delprato, D. J., and B. D. Midgley. 1992. "Some Fundamentals of B. F. Skinner's Behaviorism." *American Psychologist* 47: 1507–1520.

Denzau, A., and P. Grossman. 1993. "Punctuated Equilibria: A Model and Application of Evolutionary Economic Change." Unpublished manuscript, Economics Department, Washington University, St. Louis, MO.

Denzau, A. T., and D. C. North. 1994. "Shared Mental Models: Ideologies and Institutions." *Kyklos* 47: 3–31.

Derryberry, D., and D. M. Tucker. 1994. "Motivating the Focus of Attention." In P. M. Niedenthal and S. Kitayama, eds., *The Heart's Eye.* San Diego, CA: Academic Press, 167–196.

Devine, P. 1989. "Stereotypes and Prejudice: Their Automatic and Controlled Components." *Journal of Personality and Social Psychology* 56: 680–690.

Dimock, M. A. 1997. "Political Knowledge and Voter Strategies for Candidate Assessment in Congressional Elections." Paper presented at the annual meeting of the Western Political Science Association, March 13–15, Tucson, AZ.

Dimock, M. A. 1998. "Knowledge, Trust, Community and Public Policy Attitudes." Paper presented at the annual meeting of the American Political Science Association, Sept. 3–6, Boston, MA.

Dimock, M. A., and S. L. Popkin. 1995. "Knowledge, Trust and International Attitudes." Paper presented at the annual meeting of the American Political Science Association, Chicago, IL.

Dimock, M. A., and S. L. Popkin. 1997. "Political Knowledge in Comparative Perspective." In S. Iyengar and R. Reeves, eds., *Do the Media Govern: Politicians, Voters, and Reporters in America.* Thousand Oaks, CA: Sage Publications.

References

DiRenzo, G. J. 1967. *Personality, Power, and Politics: A Social Psychological Analysis of the Italian Deputy and His Parliamentary System*. Notre Dame, IN: University of Notre Dame Press.

Ditto, P. H., and D. F. Lopez. 1992. "Motivated Skepticism: Use of Differential Decision Criteria for Preferred and Nonpreferred Conclusions." *Journal of Personality and Social Psychology* 63: 568–584.

Downs, A. 1957. *An Economic Theory of Democracy*. New York: Harper and Row.

Durkheim, E. 1973. *Moral Education*. New York: Free Press.

Durkheim, E. 1976. *The Elementary Forms of the Religious Life*. 2d ed. London: Allen and Unwin.

Eagly, A., and S. Chaiken. 1984. "Cognitive Theories of Persuasion." In L. Berkowitz, ed., *Advances in Experimental Social Psychology*, 17: 267–359. New York: Academic Press.

Eagly, A., and S. Chaiken. 1993. *The Psychology of Attitudes*. Fort Worth, TX: Harcourt Brace Jovanovich.

Easley, D., and J. Ledyard. 1992. "Theories of Price Formation and Exchange in Double Oral Auctions." In D. Friedman and J. Rust, eds., *The Double Auction Market: Institutions, Theories and Evidence*. Redwood City, CA: Addison-Wesley.

Eavey, C. L. 1986. "Committee Games and Fairness Norms." Paper presented at the annual meetings of the APSA in Washington, D.C., September.

Eavey, C. L., and G. J. Miller. 1984. "Fairness in Majority Rule Games with Core." *American Journal of Political Science* 28: 570–586.

Eckel, C. C., and P. Grossman. 1996. "The Relative Price of Fairness: Gender Differences in a Punishment Game." *Journal of Economic Behavior and Organization* 30: 143–158.

Ehrenberg, R. G., and R. S. Smith. 1997. *Modern Labor Economics: Theory and Public Policy*. 6th ed. Reading, MA: Addison-Wesley.

Eldredge, N., and S. J. Gould. 1972. "Punctuated Equilibria: An Alternative to Phyletic Gradualism." In T. J. M. Schopf, ed., *Models in Paleobiology*. San Francisco: Freeman, Cooper and Co., 82–115.

Elster, J. 1989. *Nuts and Bolts for the Social Sciences*. Cambridge: Cambridge University Press.

Elster, J. 1999. *Alchemies of the Mind: Rationality and the Emotions*. Cambridge: Cambridge University Press.

Enelow, J. M., and M. J. Hinich. 1984. *The Spatial Theory of Voting*. Cambridge: Cambridge University Press.

Fauconnier, G. 1994. *Mental Spaces: Aspects of Meaning Construction in Natural Language*. 2d ed. Cambridge: Cambridge University Press, 1994. [1st ed. Cambridge, MA: MIT, 1985]

Fauconnier, G. 1997. *Mappings in Thought and Language*. Cambridge: Cambridge University Press.

Fauconnier, G., and M. Turner. 1994. "Conceptual Projection and Middle Spaces." UCSD Cognitive Science Technical Report 9401. San Diego. [Available from cogsci.ucsd.edu and from www.wam.umd.edu/~mturn]

References

Fauconnier, G., and M. Turner. 1996. "Blending as a Central Process of Grammar." In A. Goldberg, ed., *Conceptual Structure, Discourse, and Language*. Stanford, CA: Center for the Study of Language and Information, 113–130. [Expanded web version: www.wam.umd.edu/~mturn/WWW/ centralprocess.WWW/centralprocess.html]

Fauconnier, G., and M. Turner. 1998a. "Conceptual Integration Networks." *Cognitive Science* 22: 133–187.

Fauconnier, G., and M. Turner. 1998b. "Principles of Conceptual Integration." In J. P. Koenig, ed., *Conceptual Structure, Discourse, and Language, II*. Stanford, CA: Center for the Study of Language and Information.

Fazio, R. 1995. "Attitudes as Object-Evaluation Associations: Determinants, Consequences, and Correlates of Attitude Accessibility." In R. Petty and J. Krosnick, eds., *Attitude Strength: Antecedents and Consequences*. Hillsdale, NJ: Lawrence Erlbaum Associates, 247–282.

Fazio, R., D. Sanbonmatsu, M. Powell, and F. Kardes. 1986. "On the Automatic Activation of Attitudes." *Journal of Personality and Social Psychology* 50: 229–238.

Fazio, R., and C. Williams. 1986. "Attitude Accessibility as a Moderator of the Attitude-Perception and Attitude-Behavior Relations: An Investigation of the 1984 Presidential Election." *Journal of Personality and Social Psychology* 51: 505–514.

Feldman, J. 1959. *An Analysis of Predictive Behavior in a Two-Choice Situation*. Ph.D. dissertation, Carnegie Institute of Technology.

Feldman, S. 1988. "Structure and Consistency in Public Opinion: The Role of Core Beliefs and Values." *American Journal of Political Science* 32: 416–440.

Feldman, S. 1995. "The Survey Response." In M. Lodge and K. McGraw, eds., *Political Judgment: Structure and Process*. Ann Arbor: University of Michigan.

Ferejohn, J. A. 1990. "Information and the Electoral Process." In J. A. Ferejohn and J. H. Kuklinski, eds., *Information and Democratic Processes*. Urbana: University of Illinois Press.

Ferejohn, J. A., and M. Fiorina. 1974. "The Paradox of Nonvoting: A Decision-Theoretic Analysis." *American Political Science Review* 68: 525–536.

Ferejohn, J. A., and J. H. Kuklinski, eds. 1990. *Information and Democratic Processes*. Urbana: University of Illinois Press.

Festinger, L. 1957. *A Theory of Cognitive Dissonance*. Stanford, CA: Stanford University Press.

Festinger, L. 1964. *Conflict, Decision, and Dissonance*. Stanford, CA: Stanford University Press.

Fiorina, M. P. 1981. *Retrospective Voting in American National Elections*. New Haven: Yale University Press.

Fischhoff, B., P. Slovic, and S. Lichtenstein. 1977. "Knowing with Certainty: The Appropriateness of Extreme Confidence." *Journal of Experimental Psychology: Human Perception and Performance* 3: 552–564.

References

Fishbein, M., and I. Ajzen. 1975. *Belief, Attitude, Intention, and Behavior: An Introduction to Theory and Research.* Reading, MA: Addison-Wesley.

Fishkin, J. S. 1997. *The Voice of the People: Public Opinion and Democracy.* New Haven: Yale University Press.

Fiske, A., and P. E. Tetlock. 1997. "Taboo Trade-offs: Reactions to Transactions that Transgress Spheres of Justice." *Political Psychology* 18: 255–297.

Fiske, S. 1981. "Social Cognition and Affect." In J. Harvey, ed., *Cognition, Social Behavior, and the Environment.* Hillsdale, NJ: Lawrence Erlbaum Associates, 227–264.

Fiske, S. T., and S. E. Taylor. 1991. *Social Cognition,* 2d ed. New York: McGraw-Hill.

Flood, M. M. 1952. "Some Experimental Games." Rand Corporation Research Monograph, RM 789-1, June 20, Rand Corporation, Santa Monica, CA.

Flood, M. M. 1958. "Some Experimental Games." *Management Science* 5: 5–26.

Foucault, M. 1965. *Madness and Civilization.* Translated by Richard Howard. New York: Random House.

Freeman, M. 1997. "Grounded Spaces: Deictic -self Anaphors in the Poetry of Emily Dickinson." *Language and Literature* 6: 7–28.

Friedman, D., and J. Rust, eds. 1992. *The Double Auction Market: Institutions, Theories and Evidence.* Redwood City, CA: Addison-Wesley.

Friedman, M. 1953. *Essays in Positive Economics.* Chicago: University of Chicago Press.

Friedman, M. 1962. *Capitalism and Freedom.* Chicago: University of Chicago Press.

Frohlich, N. 1974. "Self Interest or Altruism, What Difference?" *Journal of Conflict Resolution* 18: 55–73.

Frohlich, N., and J. A. Oppenheimer. 1992. *Choosing Justice: An Experimental Approach to Ethical Theory.* Berkeley: California University Press.

Frohlich, N., [and J. A. Oppenheimer]. 1995. "The Incompatibility of Incentive Compatible Devices and Ethical Behavior: Some Experimental Results and Insights." *Public Choice Studies* 25: 24–51. [Incorrectly published without Oppenheimer's name.]

Frohlich, N., and J. A. Oppenheimer. 1996a. "Experiencing Impartiality to Invoke Fairness in the n-PD: Some Experimental Results." *Public Choice* 86: 117–135.

Frohlich, N., and J. A. Oppenheimer. 1996b. "On Measuring Self Interest through Dictator Experiments: Some Problems." Presented at the Southern Economics Association Meetings, Washington Hilton Hotel, Washington, DC, Nov. 15.

Frohlich, N., and J. A. Oppenheimer. 1997. "A Role for Structured Observation in Ethics." *Social Justice Research* 10: 1–21.

Frohlich, N., and J. A. Oppenheimer, with P. Bond and I. Boschman. 1984. "Beyond Economic Man." *Journal of Conflict Resolution* 28: 3–24.

Frohlich, N., J. A. Oppenheimer, T. Hunt, and H. Wagner. 1975. "Individual Contributions for Collective Goods: Alternative Models." *Journal of Conflict Resolution* 19: 310–329.

References

Fukuyama, F. 1995. *Trust: The Social Virtues and the Creation of Prosperity.* New York: Free Press.

Gambetta, D. 1988. "Can We Trust Trust?" In D. Gambetta, ed., *Trust: The Making and Breaking of Cooperative Relations.* Oxford: Basil Blackwell.

Geddes, B., and J. Zaller. 1989. "Sources of Popular Support for Authoritarian Regimes." *American Journal of Political Science* 33: 319–347.

Gilens, M. 1996. "Race Coding and White Opposition to Welfare." *American Political Science Review* 90: 593–604.

Gillette, C. P., and J. E. Krier. 1990. "Risk, Courts, and Agencies." *University of Pennsylvania Law Review* 138: 1027–1109.

Gode, D. K., and S. Sunder. 1992a. "Lower Bounds for Efficiency of Surplus Extraction in Double Auctions." In D. Friedman and J. Rust, eds., *The Double Auction Market: Institutions, Theories and Evidence.* Redwood City, CA: Addison-Wesley.

Gode, D. K., and S. Sunder. 1992b. "A Comparative Analysis of Efficiency of Economic Institutions with Zero Intelligence Traders." GSIA Working Paper 1992–23, Carnegie-Mellon University.

Gode, D. K., and S. Sunder. 1993. "Allocative Efficiency of Markets with Zero Intelligence (ZI) Traders: Market as a Partial Substitute for Individual Rationality." *Journal of Political Economy* 101: 119–137.

Goldstein, D. 1997. "Political Advertising and Political Persuasion in the 1996 Presidential Campaign." Paper presented at the annual meeting of the American Political Science Association, September.

Graber, D. 1984. *Processing the News: How People Tame the Information Flow.* New York: Longman.

Grabowski, H., and J. Vernon. 1983. *The Regulation of Pharmaceuticals.* Washington, DC: American Enterprise Institute.

Green, D. P. 1988. "On the Dimensionality of Public Sentiment toward Partisan and Ideological Groups." *American Journal of Political Science* 32: 758–780.

Green, D. P., and A. E. Gerken. 1989. "Self-Interest and Public Opinion toward Smoking Restrictions and Cigarette Taxes." *Public Opinion Quarterly* 53: 1–16.

Griffin, D., and A. Tversky. 1992. "The Weighing of Evidence and the Determinants of Confidence." *Cognitive Psychology* 24: 411–435.

Grossman, P., and C. C. Eckel. 1996. "Anonymity and Altruism in Dictator Games." *Games and Economic Behavior* 16: 181–191.

Gruenfeld, D. H. 1995. "Status, Ideology, and Integrative Complexity on the U.S. Supreme Court: Rethinking the Politics of Political Decision Making." *Journal of Personality and Social Psychology* 68: 5–20.

Grush, R., and N. Mandelblit. 1997. "Blending in Language, Conceptual Structure, and the Cerebral Cortex." In P. A. Brandt, F. Gregersen, F. Stjernfelt, and M. Skov, eds., *The Roman Jakobson Centennial Symposium: International Journal of Linguistics Acta Linguistica Hafniensia,* 29: 221–237. Copenhagen: C. A. Reitzel.

References

Hadfield, G. K. 1992. "Bias in the Evolution of Legal Rules." *Georgetown Law Journal* 80: 583–616.

Hahn, F. H. 1987. "Information, Dynamics and Equilibrium." *Scottish Journal of Political Economy* 34: 321–334.

Hammond, J. S., R. L. Keeney, and H. Raiffa. 1998. "The Hidden Traps in Decision Making." *Harvard Business Review* 5: 47–58.

Hardin, R. 1971. "Collective Action as an Agreeable N-Prisoners' Dilemma." *Behavioral Science* 16: 472–479.

Hardin, R. 1982. *Collective Action*. Baltimore, MD: Johns Hopkins University Press.

Hardin, R. 1993. "The Street-Level Epistemology of Trust." *Politics & Society* 21: 505–529.

Harsanyi, J. 1967. "Games with Incomplete Information Played by 'Bayesian' Players, I: The Basic Model." *Management Science* 14: 159–182.

Harsanyi, J. 1968a. "Games with Incomplete Information Played by 'Bayesian' Players, II: Bayesian Equilibrium Points." *Management Science* 14: 320–334.

Harsanyi, J. 1968b. "Games with Incomplete Information Played by 'Bayesian' Players, III: The Basic Probability Distribution of the Game." *Management Science* 14: 486–502.

Haskell, T. L. 1985. "Capitalism and the Origins of the Humanitarian Sensibilities." *American Historical Review* 90: 339–361, 547–566.

Hastie, R., and B. Park. 1986. "The Relationship Between Memory and Judgment Depends on Whether the Task Is Memory-Based or On-line." *Psychological Review* 93: 258–268.

Hastie, R., and N. Pennington. 1989. "Notes on the Distinction Between Memory-Based Versus On-line Judgments." In J. Bassili, ed., *On-line Cognition in Person Perception*. Hillsdale, NJ: Lawrence Erlbaum, 1–18.

Hauser, M. D. 1996. *The Evolution of Communication: An Introduction to Evolutionary Psychology*. Cambridge, MA: Harvard University Press.

Heider, F. 1958. *The Psychology of Interpersonal Relations*. New York: Wiley.

Heiner R. 1983. "The Origins of Predictable Behavior." *American Economic Review* 73: 560–595.

Hibbs, D. 1987. *The American Political Economy: Macroeconomics and Electoral Politics*. Cambridge, MA: Harvard University Press.

Higgins, E. T. 1996. "Knowledge Activation: Accessibility, Applicability and Salience." In E. T. Higgins and A. Kruglanski, eds., *Social Psychology: Handbook of Basic Principles*. New York: Guilford Press, 133–168.

Higgs, R. 1987. *Crisis and Leviathan: Critical Episodes in the Growth of American Government*. New York: Oxford University Press.

Hilts, P. J. 1992. "'Hole' in Tumor Patient's Memory Reveals Brain's Odd Filing System." *New York Times*, Sept. 15, sec. B.

Hinich, M. J., and M. C. Munger. 1992. "Ideology and the Theory of Political Choice." Unpublished manuscript, Department of Political Science, University of North Carolina.

References

Hinich, M. J., and M. C. Munger. 1994. *Ideology and the Theory of Political Choice*. Ann Arbor: University of Michigan Press.

Hoffman, E., K. McCabe, and V. L. Smith. 1996. "Social Distance and Other-Regarding Behavior in Dictator Games." *American Economic Review* 86: 653–660.

Hoffman, E., and M. Spitzer. 1985. "Entitlements Rights and Fairness: An Experimental Examination of Subjects' Concepts of Distributive Justice." *Journal of Legal Studies* 15: 254–297.

Hogarth, R. M., and M. Reder. 1987. *Rational Choice: The Contrast between Economics and Psychology*. Chicago: University of Chicago Press.

Holland, J. H. 1975. *Adaptation in Natural and Artificial Systems: An Introductory Analysis with Applications to Biology, Control, and Artificial Intelligence*. Ann Arbor: University of Michigan Press.

Holland, J. H. 1988. "The Global Economy as an Adaptive Process." In P. W. Anderson, D. Pines, and K. Arrow, eds., *The Economy as an Evolving Complex System*. Boston: Addison-Wesley, 117–124.

Holland, J. H., K. J. Holyoak, R. E. Nisbett, and P. R. Thagard. 1986. *Induction: Processes of Inference, Learning, and Discovery*. Cambridge, MA: MIT Press.

Holland, P. W. 1986. "Statistics and Causal Inference." *Journal of the American Statistical Association* 81: 945–960.

Holyoak, K., and P. Thagard. 1995. *Mental Leaps: Analogy in Creative Thought*. Cambridge, MA: MIT Press.

Houston, D. A., and S. J. Sherman. 1995. "Cancellation and Focus: The Role of Shared and Unique Features in the Choice Process." *Journal of Experimental Social Psychology* 31: 357–378.

Houston, D. A., S. J. Sherman, and S. M. Baker. 1991. "Feature Matching, Unique Features, and the Dynamics of the Choice Process: Predecision Conflict and Postdecision Satisfaction." *Journal of Experimental Social Psychology* 27: 411–430.

Hovland, C. I. 1959. "Reconciling Conflicting Results from Experimental and Survey Studies of Attitude Change." *American Psychologist* 14: 8–17.

Hovland, C. I., I. L. Janis, and H. H. Kelley. 1953. *Communication and Persuasion: Psychological Studies of Opinion Change*. New Haven: Yale University Press.

Huckfeldt, R., and J. Sprague. 1995. *Citizens, Politics, and Social Communication*. New York: Cambridge University Press.

Hull, D. L. 1988. *Science as a Process: An Evolutionary Account of the Social and Conceptual Development of Science*. Chicago: University of Chicago Press.

Hurwitz, J., and M. Peffley. 1987. "How Are Foreign Policy Attitudes Structured?" *American Political Science Review* 81: 1099–1120.

Hutchins, E., and B. Hazlehurst. 1992. "Learning in the Culture Process." In C. G. Langton, C. Taylor, J. D. Farmer, and S. Rasmussen, eds., *Artificial Life 11*, Redwood City, CA: Addison-Wesley, 689–706.

References

Isaacs, H. R. 1958. *Scratches on Our Minds: American Images of China and India*. New York: John Day.

Isen, A. M. 1987. "Positive Affect, Cognitive Processes, and Social Behavior." In L. Berkowitz, ed., *Advances in Experimental Social Psychology* Vol. 21. New York: Academic Press.

Iwakura, N., and T. Saijo. 1992. "Payoff Information Effects of Public Good Provision in the Voluntary Contribution Mechanism: An Experimental Approach." Paper presented at the Annual Public Choice Meetings, March: New Orleans.

Iyengar, S. 1996. "The Case of the Vanishing Footprints: A Review of Research on Political Campaigns." Paper presented at the annual meeting of the Association for Education in Journalism, St. Petersburg, FL, September.

Iyengar, S., and D. R. Kinder. 1987. *News That Matters: Television and American Opinion*. Chicago: University of Chicago Press.

Iyengar, S., N. Valentino, S. Ansolabehere, and A. Simon. 1996. "Running as a Woman: Gender Stereotyping in Women's Campaigns." In P. Norris, ed., *Women, Media, and Politics*. New York: Oxford University Press.

Jackendoff, R. 1980. *Consciousness and the Computational Mind*. Cambridge, MA: MIT Press.

Jackson, M., and P. Hill. 1995. "A Fair Share." *Journal of Theoretical Politics* 7: 169–179.

Jacobson, G. C. 1990. "The Effects of Campaign Spending in House Elections: New Evidence for Old Arguments." *American Journal of Political Science* 34: 334–362.

Jacobson, G. C. 1992. *The Politics of Congressional Elections*. 3d ed. New York: HarperCollins.

Jacoby, W. G. 1988. "The Impact of Party Identification on Issue Attitudes." *American Journal of Political Science* 32: 643–661.

Jamal, K., and S. Sunder. 1988. "Money vs. Gaming: Effects of Salient Monetary Payments in Double Oral Auctions." Working Paper, No. 16-88-89, Carnegie-Mellon University.

Janis, I. L., and L. Mann. 1977. *Decision Making: A Psychological Analysis of Conflict, Choice, and Commitment*. New York: Free Press.

Jennings, M. K., and R. G. Niemi. 1981. *Generations and Politics: A Panel Study of Young Adults and Their Parents*. Princeton, NJ: Princeton University Press.

Jensen, M. C., and W. H. Meckling. 1976. "Theory of the Firm: Managerial Behavior, Agency Costs, and Ownership Structure." *Journal of Financial Economics* 3: 305–360.

Johnson, H. T., and R. S. Kaplan. 1987. *Relevance Lost: The Rise and Fall of Management Accounting*. Boston: Harvard Business School Press.

Johnston, R., A. Blais, E. Gidengil, and N. Nevitte. 1996. *The Challenge of Direct Democracy*. Montreal, Quebec: McGill-Queens University Press.

Jones, B. 1994. *Reconceiving Decision-Making in Democratic Politics: Attention, Choice, and Public Policy*. Chicago: University of Chicago Press.

References

Judd, C. M., and J. W. Downing. 1995. "Stereotypic Accuracy in Judgments of the Political Positions of Groups and Individuals." In M. Lodge and K. McGraw, eds., *Political Judgment: Structure and Process.* Ann Arbor: University of Michigan Press.

Judd, C. M., and J. Krosnick. 1989. "The Structural Basis of Consistency among Political Attitudes: Effects of Political Expertise and Attitude Importance." In A. Pratkanis, S. Becker, and A. Greenwald, eds., *Attitude Structure and Function.* Hillsdale, NJ: Lawrence Erlbaum Associates, 99–128.

Kahneman, D. 1995. "Varieties of Counterfactual Thinking." In N. J. Roese and J. M. Olson, eds., *What Might Have Been: The Social Psychology of Counterfactual Thinking.* Hillsdale, NJ: Lawrence Erlbaum.

Kahneman, D., J. L. Knetsch, and R. Thaler. 1986. "Fairness as a Constraint on Profit Seeking: Entitlements in the Market." *American Economic Review* 76: 728–741.

Kahneman, D., and D. Miller. 1986. "Norm Theory: Comparing Reality to Its Alternatives." *Psychological Review* 93: 136–153.

Kahneman, D., P. Slovic, and A. Tversky, eds. 1982. *Judgment under Uncertainty: Heuristics and Biases.* New York: Cambridge University Press.

Kahneman, D., and A. Tversky. 1979. "Prospect Theory: An Analysis of Decision under Risk." *Econometrica* 47: 263–291.

Kahneman, D., and A. Tversky. 1984. "Choices, Values, and Frames." *American Psychologist* 39: 341–350.

Kalai, E., and E. Lehrer. 1990. "Bayesian Learning and Nash Equilibrium." Unpublished manuscript, Department of Managerial Economics and Decision Sciences, Northwestern University.

Kandel, E. R., J. H. Schwartz, and T. M. Jessel. 1995. *Essentials of Neural Science and Behavior.* Norwalk, CT: Appleton & Lange.

Kaplan, R. S. 1984. "The Evolution of Management Accounting." *Accounting Review* 59: 390–418.

Kaplan, R. S. 1988. "One Cost System Isn't Enough." *Harvard Business Review* 66: 61–66.

Kernell, Samuel. 1993. *Going Public: New Strategies of Presidential Leadership.* Washington, DC: CQ Press.

Kettl, D. 1992. *Deficit Politics: Public Budgeting in its Institutional and Historical Context.* New York: Macmillan.

Key, V. O., Jr. 1966. *The Responsible Electorate: Rationality in Presidential Voting, 1936–1960.* Cambridge, MA: Harvard University Press.

Khong, Y. F. 1992. *Analogies at War: Korea, Munich, Dien Bien Phu, and the Vietnam Decisions of 1965.* Princeton, NJ: Princeton University Press.

Kiewiet D. R. 1983. *Macroeconomics and Micropolitics.* Chicago: University of Chicago Press.

Kiewiet, D. R., and M. D. McCubbins. 1991. *The Logic of Delegation: Congressional Parties and the Appropriations Process.* Chicago: University of Chicago Press.

Kinder, D. R. 1983. "Diversity and Complexity in American Public Opinion."

References

In A. Finifter, ed., *Political Science: The State of the Discipline.* Washington, DC: American Political Science Association.

Kinder, D. R. 1986. "Presidential Character Revisited." In R. Lau and D. Sears, eds., *Political Cognition.* Hillsdale, NJ: Lawrence Erlbaum Associates.

Kinder, D. R., G. Adams, and P. Gronke. 1989. "Economics and Politics in the 1984 American Presidential Election." *American Journal of Political Science* 33: 491–515.

Kinder, D. R., and D. R. Kiewiet. 1981. "Sociotropic Politics: The American Case." *British Journal of Political Science* 11: 129–161.

Kinder, D. R., and D. Sears. 1985. "Public Opinion and Political Action." In G. Lindzey and E. Aronson, eds., *The Handbook of Social Psychology.* Vol. 1. New York: Random House.

Kite, C. M., and W. M. Rahn. 1997. "Political Community and Public Mood: A Comparison of the U.S. and Swedish Cases." Typescript, University of Umeä, Sweden.

Klayman, J., and Y. W. Ha. 1987. "Confirmation, Disconfirmation, and Information in Hypothesis Testing." *Psychological Review* 94: 211–228.

Kleinnijenhuis, J., and J. de Ridder. 1997. "Effects of Issue Priorities in the News on Voting Preferences." In C. W. Aarts and B. Steenge, eds., *Setting Priorities in the Public Sector.* Dordrecht, Netherlands: Kluwer.

Knight, F. H. 1921. *Risk, Uncertainty, and Profit.* Boston: Houghton Mifflin Co. Reprinted 1971. Chicago: University of Chicago Press.

Konow, J. 1994. *A Positive Theory of Economic Fairness.* Working Paper 94081. Los Angeles: Loyola Marymount University.

Konow, J. 1995. "Which is the Fairest one of All?: Some Evidence on Theories of Fairness." Working paper (mimeo), Dept. of Economics, Loyola Marymount University, Los Angeles.

Kramer, R. M., M. B. Brewer, and B. A. Hanna. 1995. "Collective Trust and Collective Action: The Decision to Trust as a Social Decision." In R. Kramer and T. R. Tyler, eds., *Trust in Organizations.* Thousand Oaks, CA: Sage Publications.

Krehbiel, K. 1991. *Information and Legislative Organization.* Ann Arbor: University of Michigan Press.

Kreps, D. M. 1990a. *A Course in Microeconomic Theory.* Princeton, NJ: Princeton University Press.

Kreps, D. M. 1990b. "Corporate Culture and Economic Theory." In J. E. Alt and K. A. Shepsle, eds., *Perspectives on Positive Political Economy.* Cambridge: Cambridge University Press, 90–143.

Kreps, D. M., P. Milgrom, J. Roberts, and R. Wilson. 1982. "Rational Cooperation in the Finitely Repeated Prisoners' Dilemma." *Journal of Economic Theory* 27: 245–252.

Krosnick, J. A. 1988. "The Role of Attitude Importance in Social Evaluation: A Study of Policy Preferences, Presidential Candidate Evaluations, and Voting Behavior." *Journal of Personality and Social Psychology* 55: 196–210.

References

Krosnick, J. A. 1989. "Attitude Importance and Attitude Accessibility." *Personality and Social Psychology Bulletin* 15: 297–308.

Krosnick, J., and R. Petty. 1995. "Attitude Strength: An Overview." In R. Petty and J. Krosnick, eds., *Attitude Strength: Antecedents and Consequences.* Hillsdale, NJ: Lawrence Erlbaum Associates, 1–24.

Kruglanski, A. 1980. "Lay Epistemology Process and Contents." *Psychological Review* 87: 70–87.

Kruglanski, A., and I. Ajzen. 1983. "Bias and Error in Human Judgment." *European Journal of Social Psychology* 13: 1–44.

Kruglanski, A., and T. Freund. 1983. "The Freezing and Unfreezing of Lay Inferences: Effects on Impressional Primacy, Ethnic Stereotyping, and Numerical Anchoring." *Journal of Experimental Social Psychology* 19: 448–468.

Kruglanski, A., and D. Webster. 1996. "Motivated Closing of the Mind: 'Seizing' and 'Freezing.'" *Journal of Personality and Social Psychology* 103: 263–283.

Kuhn, T. S. 1970. *The Structure of Scientific Revolutions.* 2d ed. Chicago: University of Chicago Press.

Kuklinski, J. H., and N. L. Hurley. 1994. "On Hearing and Interpreting Political Messages: A Cautionary Tale of Citizen Cue-Taking." *Journal of Politics* 56: 729–751.

Kuklinski, J. H., and N. L. Hurley. 1996. "It's a Matter of Interpretation." In D. M. Mutz, P. M. Sniderman, and R. Brody, eds., *Political Persuasion and Attitude Change.* Ann Arbor: University of Michigan Press.

Kuklinski, J. H., P. J. Quirk, D. Schwieder, and R. Rich. 1997. "Misinformation and the Currency of Citizenship." Paper presented at the annual meeting of the American Political Science Association, San Francisco.

Kunda, Z. 1987. "Motivation and Inference: Self-Serving Generation and Evaluation of Evidence." *Journal of Personality and Social Psychology* 53: 636–647.

Kunda, Z. 1990. "The Case for Motivated Reasoning." *Psychological Bulletin* 1083: 480–498.

Lacroix, S. J. 1989. "Homogenous Middleman Groups: What Determines the Homogeneity?" *Journal of Law, Economics, and Organization* 5: 211–222.

Lakoff, G. 1987. *Women, Fire and Dangerous Things.* Chicago: University of Chicago Press.

Lakoff, G. 1991. "Metaphors and War." Electronic message on the Internet, January 3.

Landy, M., M. Roberts, and S. Thomas. 1990. *The Environmental Protection Agency: Asking the Wrong Questions.* New York: Oxford University Press.

Lane, R. 1973. "Patterns of Political Beliefs." In J. Knutson, ed., *Handbook of Political Psychology.* San Francisco: Jossey-Bass.

Lane, R. E. 1995. "What Rational Choice Explains." *Critical Review* 9: 107–126.

Larrick, R. P. 1993. "Motivational Factors in Decision Theories: The Role of Self-Protection." *Psychological Bulletin* 113: 430–440.

References

Lascher, E. L., and M. R. Powers. 1997. "Expert Opinion and Automobile Insurance Reform: An Empirical Assessment." *Journal of Insurance Regulation* 16(2): 197–222.

Lau, R. 1985. "Two Explanations for Negativity Effects in Political Behavior." *American Journal of Political Science* 29: 119–138.

Lau, R. 1989. "Construct Accessibility and Electoral Choice." *Political Behavior* 20: 5–32.

Lau, R., and D. Redlawsk. 1997. "Voting Correctly." *American Political Science Review* 91: 585–598.

Lau, R., and D. Redlawsk. 1999. "An Experimental Study of Information Search, Memory, and Decision Making during a Political Campaign." In J. Kuklinski, ed., *Citizens and Politics: Perspectives from Political Psychology*. New York: Cambridge University Press.

Laver, M., and N. Schofield. 1990. *Multiparty Government: The Politics of Coalition in Europe*. Oxford: Oxford University Press.

Laver, M., and K. Shepsle. 1996. *Making and Breaking Governments: Cabinets and Legislatures in Parliamentary Democracies*. Cambridge, MA: Cambridge University Press.

Leake, D. B. 1991. "Goal-Based Explanation Evaluation." *Cognitive Science* 15: 509–545.

Leamer, E. E. 1987. *Specification Searches: Ad Hoc Inference with Nonexperimental Data*. New York: Wiley.

LeDoux, J. 1996. *The Emotional Brain: The Mysterious Underpinnings of Emotional Life*. New York: Simon and Schuster.

Ledyard, J. O. 1995. "Public Goods: A Survey of Experimental Research." In J. H. Kagel and A. E. Roth, eds., *The Handbook of Experimental Economics*. Princeton, NJ: Princeton University Press, 111–194.

Levi, M. 1996. "Social and Unsocial Capital: A Review of Putnam's *Making Democracy Work*." *Politics & Society* 24: 45–55.

Levitin, T. E., and W. E. Miller. 1979. "Ideological Interpretations of Presidential Elections." *American Political Science Review* 73: 751–771.

Levy, F., and R. Murnane. 1992. "Earnings Levels and Earnings Inequality: A Review of Recent Trends and Proposed Explanations." *Journal of Economic Literature* 30: 1333–1381.

Lewin, K. 1933. "Environmental Forces." In C. Murchison, ed., *A Handbook of Child Psychology*. Worcester, MA: Clark University Press, 590–625.

Lewin, K. 1951. *Field Theory in Social Science*. New York: Harper.

Lewin, S. 1996. "Economics and Psychology: Lessons for Our Own Day from the Early Twentieth Century." *Journal of Economic Literature* 34: 1293–1323.

Liberman, A., and S. Chaiken. 1991. "Value Conflict and Thought-Induced Attitude Change." *Journal of Experimental Social Psychology* 27: 203–216.

Lichtenstein, M., and T. Srull. 1987. "Objectives as Determinant of the Relationship between Recall and Judgment." *Journal of Experimental Social Psychology* 23: 93–118.

Liebling, A. J. 1961. *The Press*. New York: Ballantine Books.

References

Lindgren, K. 1992. "Evolutionary Phenomena in a Simple Dynamics." In C. G. Langton, C. Taylor, J. D. Farmer, and S. Rasmussen, eds., *Artificial Life 11*. Redwood City, CA: Addison-Wesley, 295–312.

Lodge, M. 1995. "Toward a Procedural Model of Candidate Evaluation." In M. Lodge and K. M. McGraw, eds., *Political Judgment: Structure and Process*. Ann Arbor: University of Michigan Press.

Lodge, M., K. McGraw, and P. Stroh. 1989. "An Impression-Driven Model of Candidate Evaluation." *American Political Science Review* 83: 399–419.

Lodge, M., M. Steenbergen, and S. Brau. 1995. "The Responsive Voter: Campaign Information and the Dynamics of Candidate Evaluation." *American Political Science Review* 89: 309–326.

Lodge, M., and P. Stroh. 1993. "Inside the Mental Voting Booth: An Impression-Driven Model." In S. Iyengar and W. McGuire, eds., *Explorations in Political Psychology*. Durham, NC: Duke University Press.

Lodge, M., and C. Taber. 2000. "Three Steps toward a Theory of Motivated Political Reasoning." In A. Lupia, M. D. McCubbins, and S. L. Popkin, eds., *Elements of Reason: Understanding and Expanding the Limits of Political Rationality*. New York: Cambridge University Press.

Loomes, G., and R. Sugden. 1982. "Regret Theory: An Alternative Theory of Rational Choice under Uncertainty." *Economic Journal* 92: 805–824.

Lord, C., M. Lepper, and E. Preston. 1984. "Considering the Opposite: a Corrective Strategy for Social Judgment." *Journal of Personality and Social Psychology* 47: 1231–1243.

Lord, C., M. Ross, and M. Lepper. 1979. "Biased Assimilation and Attitude Polarization: The Effects of Prior Theories on Subsequently Considered Evidence." *Journal of Personality and Social Psychology* 27: 2098–2109.

Lupia, A. 1994. "Shortcuts versus Encyclopedias: Information and Voting Behavior in California Insurance Reform Elections." *American Political Science Review* 88: 63–76.

Lupia, A. 2000. "Who Can Persuade Whom? How Simple Cues Affect Political Attitudes." In J. H. Kuklinski, ed., *Thinking about Political Psychology*. New York: Cambridge University Press.

Lupia, A., and M. D. McCubbins. 1998. *The Democratic Dilemma: Can Citizens Learn What They Need to Know?* Cambridge: Cambridge University Press.

Luskin, R. C. 1987. "Measuring Political Sophistication." *American Journal of Political Science* 31: 856–899.

Luskin, R. C. 2000. "From Denial to Extenuation (and Finally Beyond): Political Sophistication and Citizen Performance." In J. H. Kuklinski, ed., *Thinking about Political Psychology*. New York: Cambridge University Press.

Mandelblit, N. 1995a. "The Theory of Blending as Part of the General Epistemological Developments in Cognitive Science." Unpublished manuscript.

Mandelblit, N. 1995b. "Beyond Lexical Semantics: Mapping and Blending of Conceptual and Linguistic Structures in Machine Translation." *Proceedings of the Fourth International Conference on the Cognitive Science of Natural Language Processing*, Dublin.

Mandelblit, N. 1996. "Formal and Conceptual Blending in the Hebrew Verbal System: A Cognitive Basis for Morphological Verbal Pattern Alternations." Unpublished manuscript.

Mandelblit, N. 1997. *Grammatical Blending: Creative and Schematic Aspects in Sentence Processing and Translation*. Ph.D. dissertation, University of California, San Diego.

Mandelblit, N. In press. "Blends in Hebrew Causatives." *Proceedings of the Fourth Conference of the International Cognitive Linguistics Association*, Albuquerque, NM.

Mandelblit, N., and O. Zachar. 1998. "The Notion of Dynamic Unit: Conceptual Developments in Cognitive Science." *Cognitive Science* 22: 229–268.

Maoz, Z., and A. Shayer. 1987. "The Cognitive Structure of Peace and War Argumentation: Israeli Prime Ministers versus the Knesset." *Political Psychology* 8: 575–604.

March, J. G., and J. P. Olson. 1989. *Rediscovering Institutions: The Organizational Basis of Politics*. New York: Free Press.

Marcus, G. E., and M. B. MacKuen. 1993. "Anxiety, Enthusiasm and the Vote: On the Emotional Underpinnings of Learning and Involvement during Presidential Campaigns." *American Political Science Review* 87: 672–685.

Marks, R. 1992. "Repeated Gains and Finite Automata." In J. Creedy, J. Borland, and J. Eichberger, eds., *Recent Developments in Game Theory*. Brookfield, VT: Edward Elgar.

Markus, H., and R. Zajonc. 1985. "The Cognitive Perspective in Social Psychology." In G. Lindzey and E. Aronson, eds., *The Handbook of Social Psychology*. Vol. 1. New York: Random House.

Martin, L., and M. Tesser, eds. 1992. *Construction of Social Judgments*. Hillsdale, NJ: Lawrence Erlbaum Associates.

Martin, L. L., D. W. Ward, J. W. Achee, and R. S. Wyer, Jr. 1993. "Mood as Input: People Have to Interpret the Motivational Implications of Their Moods." *Journal of Personality and Social Psychology* 64: 317–326.

Mayer, J. D., and E. Hanson. 1995. "Mood-Congruent Judgment Over Time." *Personality and Social Psychology Bulletin* 21: 237–244.

Mayseless, O., and A. Kruglanski. 1987. "What Makes You So Sure? Effects of Epistemic Motivations on Judgmental Confidence." *Organizational Behavior and Human Decision Processes* 39: 162–183.

McCaleb, T. S., and R. E. Wagner. 1985. "The Experimental Search for Free Riders: Some Reflections and Observations." *Public Choice* 47: 479–490.

McCauley, R. N., ed. 1996. *The Churchlands and Their Critics*. Cambridge, MA: Blackwell Publishers Inc.

McClosky, H., P. J. Hoffman, and R. O'Hara. 1960. "Issue Conflict and Consensus among Party Leaders and Followers." *American Political Science Review* 54: 406–427.

McDermott, M. 1997. "Voting Cues in Low-Information Elections: Candidate

References

Gender as a Social Information Variable in Contemporary U.S. Elections." *American Journal of Political Science* 41: 270–283.

McEachern, W. A. 1994. *Macroeconomics: A Contemporary Introduction.* 3d ed. Cincinnati, OH: College Division, South-Western Publishing Co.

McGraw, K., M. Lodge, and P. Stroh. 1990. "Candidate Evaluation: The Effect of Salience, Order, and Sophistication." *Political Behavior* 12: 41–58.

McGraw, K., and N. Pinney. 1990. "The Effects of General and Domain-Specific Expertise on Political Memory." *Social Cognition* 8: 9–30.

McGuire, W. J. 1968. "The Structure of Human Thought." In R. Abelson, E. Aronson, W. McGuire, T. Newcomb, M. Rosenberg, and P. Tannenbaum, eds., *Theories of Cognitive Consistency: A Sourcebook.* Chicago: Rand McNally.

McGuire, W. J. 1969. "Nature of Attitudes and Attitude Change." In G. Lindzey and E. Aronson, eds., *Handbook of Social Psychology.* Reading, MA: Addison-Wesley.

McGuire, W. J. 1985. "Attitudes and Attitude Change." In G. Lindzey and E. Aronson, eds., *Handbook of Social Psychology.* New York: Random House.

McKelvey, R. D., and P. C. Ordeshook. 1986. "Information, Electoral Equilibria, and the Democratic Ideal." *Journal of Politics* 8: 909–937.

McKelvey, R. D., and P. C. Ordeshook. 1990. "Information and Elections: Retrospective Voting and Rational Expectations." In J. A. Ferejohn and J. H. Kuklinski, eds., *Information and Democratic Processes.* Urbana: University of Illinois Press.

Merelman, R. D. 1986. "Cultural Displays: An Illustration from American Immigration." *Qualitative Sociology* 11: 335–352.

Merrill, R. A. 1988. "FDA's Implementation of the Delaney Clause: Repudiation of Congressional Choice or Reasoned Adaptation to Scientific Progress." *Yale Journal on Regulation* 5: 1–88.

Miller, D. T., and M. Ross. 1975. "Self-Serving Biases in the Attribution of Causality: Fact or Fiction?" *Psychological Bulletin* 82: 213–225.

Miller, G. J., and J. A. Oppenheimer. 1982. "Universalism in Experimental Committees." *American Political Science Review* 76: 561–574.

Miller, N. E. 1944. "Experimental Studies of Conflict." In J. M. Hunt, ed., *Personality and the Behavior Disorders*: Vol. 1. New York: Roland Press, 431–465.

Mitchell, R. C., and R. T. Carson. 1989. *Using Surveys to Value Public Goods: The Contingent Valuation Method.* Baltimore, MD: Johns Hopkins University Press.

Mondak, J. 1993. "Source Cues and Policy Approval: The Cognitive Dynamics of Public Support for the Reagan Agenda." *American Journal of Political Science* 37: 186–212.

Mondak, J. 1994. "Cognitive Heuristics, Heuristic Processing, and Efficiency in Political Decision-Making." In M. Delli Carpini, L. Huddy, and R. Y. Shapiro, eds., *Research in Micropolitics.* Vol. 4. Greenwich, CT: JAI Press.

Morris, D. 1967. *The Naked Ape.* New York: McGraw-Hill.

References

Morrow, J. 1994. *Game Theory for Political Scientists*. Princeton, NJ: Princeton University Press.

Mroz, J. E. 1993. "Russia and Eastern Europe: Will the West Let Them Fail?" *Foreign Affairs* 72: 44–57.

Mutz, D. 1992. "Impersonal Influence: Effects of Representations of Public Opinion on Political Attitudes." *Political Behavior* 14: 89–122.

Myerson, R. B. 1983. "Mechanism Design by an Informed Principal." *Econometrica* 51: 1767–1797.

Myerson, R. B. 1989. "Credible Negotiation Statements and Coherent Plans." *Journal of Economic Theory* 48: 264–303.

Neely, J. 1977. "Semantic Priming and the Retrieval of Lexical Memory: Roles of Inhibitionless Spreading Activation and Limited-Capacity Attention." *Journal of Experimental Psychology: General* 106: 226–254.

Neuberg, S. 1989. "The Goal of Forming Accurate Impressions during Social Interactions: Attenuating the Impact of Negative Expectancies." *Journal of Personality and Social Psychology* 56: 431–444.

Neuberg, S., and S. Fiske. 1987. "Motivational Influences on Impression Formation: Dependence, Accuracy-Driven Attention, and Individuating Information." *Journal of Personality and Social Psychology* 53: 431–444.

Neuman, W. R. 1986. *The Paradox of Mass Politics: Knowledge and Opinion in the American Electorate*. Cambridge, MA: Harvard University Press.

Neuman, W. R., M. Just, and A. Crigler. 1992. *Common Knowledge: News and the Construction of Political Meaning*. Chicago: University of Chicago Press.

Newell, A. 1990. *Unified Theories of Cognition*. Cambridge, MA: Harvard University Press.

Nie, N. H., S. Verba, and J. R. Petrocik. 1976. *The Changing American Voter*. Cambridge, MA: Harvard University Press.

Niedenthal, P. M., and M. Setterlund. 1994. "Emotional Congruence in Perception." *Personality and Social Psychology Bulletin* 20: 401–411.

Nisbett, R. E., and L. Ross. 1980. *Human Inference: Strategies and Shortcomings of Social Judgment*. Englewood Cliffs, NJ: Prentice-Hall.

Noll, R. G., and J. E. Krier. 1990. "Some Implications of Cognitive Psychology for Risk Regulation." *Journal of Legal Studies* 19: 747–779.

Nordhaus, W. 1975. "The Political Business Cycle." *Review of Economic Studies* 42: 169–190.

North, D. C. 1990. *Institutions, Institutional Change and Economic Performance*. Cambridge: Cambridge University Press.

Nozick, R. 1974. *Anarchy, State and Utopia*. New York: Basic Books.

Oakley, T. 1995. *Presence: The Conceptual Basis of Rhetorical Effect*. Ph.D. dissertation, University of Maryland.

O'Flaherty, B. 1985. *Rational Commitment: A Foundation for Macroeconomics*. Durham, NC: Duke University Press.

Okun, A. M. 1975. *Equality and Efficiency: The Big Trade-off*. Washington, DC: Brookings Institution.

Olson, M. 1965. *The Logic of Collective Action: Public Goods and the Theory of Groups*. Cambridge, MA: Harvard University Press.

References

Olson, M. 1982. *The Rise and Decline of Nations.* New Haven: Yale University Press.

Olson, R. G. 1967. "Deontological Ethics." In *Encyclopedia of Philosophy*, 2: 343. New York: Collier Macmillan & Free Press.

Oppenheimer, J. A. 1985. "Public Choice and Three Ethical Properties of Politics." *Public Choice* 45: 241–255.

Orbell, J., and R. M. Dawes. 1991. "A 'Cognitive Miser' Theory of Cooperators' Advantage." *American Political Science Review* 85: 515–528.

Ordeshook, P. C. 1986. *Game Theory and Political Theory: An Introduction.* New York: Cambridge University Press.

Ostrom, E. 1990. *Governing the Commons: The Evolution of Institutions for Collective Action.* Cambridge: Cambridge University Press.

Ottati, V., and R. S. Wyer, Jr. 1990. "The Cognitive Mediators of Political Choice: Toward a Comprehensive Model of Political Information Processing." In J. Ferejohn and J. Kuklinski, eds., *Information and Democratic Processes.* Urbana: University of Illinois Press.

Page, B. I., and R. Y. Shapiro. 1992. *The Rational Public: Fifty Years of Trends in Americans' Policy Preferences.* Chicago: University of Chicago Press.

Park, B. 1989. "Trait Attributes as On-Line Organizers in Person Impressions." In J. Bassilli, ed., *On-Line Cognition in Person Perception.* Hillsdale, NJ: Lawrence Erlbaum Associates, 39–60.

Parkinson, B., R. B. Briner, S. Reynolds, and P. Totterdell. 1995. "Time Frames for Mood: Relationships between Momentary and Generalized Ratings of Affect." *Personality and Social Psychology Bulletin* 21: 331–339.

Payne, J. W., J. R. Bettman, and E. J. Johnson. 1992. "Behavioral Decision Research: A Constructive Processing Perspective." *Annual Review of Psychology* 43: 87–131.

Peabody, D. 1967. "Trait Inferences: Evaluative and Descriptive Aspects." *Journal of Personality and Social Psychology* 7: 1–18.

Pennington, N., and R. Hastie. 1986. "Evidence Evaluation in Complex Decision Making." *Journal of Personality and Social Psychology* 51: 242–258.

Pennington, N., and R. Hastie. 1988. "Explanation-Based Decision Making: Effects of Memory Structure on Judgment." *Journal of Experimental Psychology: Learning, Memory, and Cognition* 14: 521–533.

Petrocik, J. 1996. "Issue Ownership in Presidential Elections with a 1980 Case Study." *American Journal of Political Science* 40: 825–850.

Petty, R., and J. Cacioppo. 1984. *Attitudes and Persuasion: Classic and Contemporary Approaches.* Dubuque, IA: W. C. Brown.

Petty, R., and J. Cacioppo. 1986a. *Communication and Persuasion: Central and Peripheral Routes to Attitude Change.* New York: Springer-Verlag.

Petty, R., and J. Cacioppo. 1986b. "The Elaboration Likelihood Model of Persuasion." In L. Berkowitz, ed., *Advances in Experimental Social Psychology.* Vol. 19. New York: Academic Press, 123–205.

Piattelli-Palamarini, M. 1994. *Inevitable Illusions: How Mistakes of Reason Rule Our Minds.* New York: John Wiley.

References

Pinker, S. 1997. *How the Mind Works*. New York: W. W. Norton & Company.

Plotkin, H. C. 1998. *Evolution in Mind: An Introduction to Evolutionary Psychology*. Cambridge, MA: Harvard University Press.

Plott, C. R. 1983. "Externalities and Corrective Policies in Experimental Markets." *Economic Journal* 93: 106–127.

Plutchik, R. 1994. *The Psychology and Biology of Emotion*. New York: Harper-Collins.

Polanyi, Michael. 1983. *The Tacit Dimension*. Gloucester, MA: Peter Smith.

Popkin, S. L. 1991. *The Reasoning Voter: Communication and Persuasion in Presidential Campaigns*. Chicago: University of Chicago Press.

Popkin, S. L. 1994. *The Reasoning Voter: Communication and Persuasion in Presidential Campaigns*. 2d ed. Chicago: University of Chicago Press.

Powell, R. 1990. *Nuclear Deterrence Theory: The Search for Credibility*. New York: Cambridge University Press.

Pratkanis, A. 1989. "The Cognitive Representation of Attitudes." In A. Pratkanis, S. Breckler, and A. Greenwald, eds., *Attitude Structure and Function*. Hillsdale, NJ: Lawrence Erlbaum Associates.

Price, V., and P. Neijens. 1997. "Opinion Quality in Public Opinion Research." *International Journal of Public Opinion Research* 9: 336–360.

Price, V., and J. Zaller. 1993. "Who Gets the News: Alternative Measures of News Reception and Their Implications for Research." *Public Opinion Quarterly* 57: 133–164.

Prior A. N. 1967. "Logic, Deontic." In *Encyclopedia of Philosophy*, 4: 509–512. New York: Collier Macmillan & Free Press.

Przeworski, A. 1991. *Democracy and the Market: Political and Economic Reforms in Eastern Europe and Latin America*. Cambridge: Cambridge University Press.

Putnam, R. 1971. "Studying Elite Culture: The Case of Ideology." *American Political Science Review* 65: 651–681.

Putnam, R. 1993. *Making Democracy Work*. Princeton, NJ: Princeton University Press.

Putnam, R. 1995. "Bowling Alone: America's Declining Social Capital." *Journal of Democracy* 6: 65–78.

Pyszczynski, T., and J. Greenberg. 1987. "Toward an Integration of Cognitive and Motivational Perspectives on Social Inference: A Biased Hypothesis-Testing Model." In L. Berkowitz, ed., *Advances in Social Psychology*. Vol. 20. New York: Academic Press, 297–340.

Pyszczynski, T., J. Greenberg, and K. Holt. 1985. "Maintaining Consistency between Self-Serving Beliefs and Available Data: A Bias in Information Evaluation." *Personality and Social Psychology Bulletin* 11: 179–190.

Quattrone, G., and A. Tversky. 1988. "Contrasting Rational and Psychological Analyses of Political Choice." *American Political Science Review* 82: 719–735.

Rae, D. 1981. *Equalities*. New Haven: Yale University Press.

Rahn, W., J. Aldrich, and E. Borgida. 1994. "Individual and Contextual Variations in Political Candidate Appraisal." *American Political Science Review* 88: 193–199.

Rahn, W. M., J. Brehm, and N. Carlson. 1997. "National Elections as Institutions for Creating Social Capital." Paper presented at the annual meeting of the American Political Science Association, Washington, DC.

Rahn, W. M., and R. Hirshorn. 1997. "Political Advertising and Public Mood." Unpublished manuscript, University of Minnesota.

Rahn, W. M., B. Kroeger, and C. M. Kite. 1996. "A Framework for the Study of Public Mood." *Political Psychology* 17: 29–58.

Rahn, W. M., and J. Transue. 1997. "The Decline of Social Trust among American Youth: The American Economy, Value Change, and Social Capital." Unpublished manuscript, University of Minnesota.

Ram, A., and D. B. Leake, eds. 1995. *Goal-Driven Learning*. Cambridge, MA: MIT Press.

Rauch, J. 1995. *Demosclerosis: The Silent Killer of American Government*. New York: Times Books.

Rawls, J. 1971. *A Theory of Justice*. Cambridge, MA: Harvard University Press.

Raz, J. 1986. *The Morality of Freedom*. New York: Clarendon Press, Oxford University Press.

Riker, W., and P. Ordeshook. 1968. "A Theory of the Calculus of Voting." *American Political Science Review* 62: 24–42.

Robert, A. 1996. "Blending in the Interpretation of Mathematical Proofs." Paper presented at the Second Conference on Conceptual Structure, Discourse, and Language, Buffalo, NY.

Rohde, D. 1991. *Parties and Leaders in the Post-Reform House*. Chicago: University of Chicago Press.

Rokeach, M. 1973. *The Nature of Human Values*. New York: Free Press.

Ross, L. 1977. "The Intuitive Psychologist and His Shortcomings: Distortions in the Attribution Process." In L. Berkowitz, ed., *Advances in Experimental Social Psychology*, 10: 174–221. New York: Academic Press.

Ross, L., and C. A. Anderson. 1982. "Shortcoming in the Attribution Process: On the Origins and Maintenance of Erroneous Assessments." In D. Kahneman, P. Slovic, and A. Tversky, eds., *Judgment under Uncertainty: Heuristics and Biases*. Cambridge: Cambridge University Press.

Roth, A. E. 1988. "Laboratory Experimentation in Economics: A Methodological Overview." *Economic Journal* 98: 974–1031.

Roth, A. E. 1995. "Bargaining Experiments." In J. H. Kagel and A. E. Roth, eds., *The Handbook of Experimental Economics*. Princeton, NJ: Princeton University Press, 253–342.

Rozin, P., and C. Nemeroff. 1995. "The Borders of the Self: Contamination Sensitivity and Potency of the Body Apertures and Other Body Parts." *Journal of Research in Personality* 29: 318–340.

Rubenstein, A. 1998. *Modeling Bounded Rationality*. Cambridge, MA: MIT Press.

Rumelhart, D., and A. Ortony. 1977. "The Representation of Knowledge in

Memory." In R. Anderson, R. J. Spiro, and W. E. Montague, eds., *Schooling and the Acquisition of Knowledge*. Hillsdale, NJ: Lawrence Erlbaum.

Saijo, T., S. Takahashi, and S. Turnbull. 1996. "Justice in Income Distribution: An Experimental Approach." Presented at annual meetings of the International Studies Association, San Diego, April 18.

Saijo, T., and T. Yamaguchi. 1992. "The Spite Dilemma in Voluntary Contribution Mechanism Experiments." Paper presented at the annual Public Choice Meetings, New Orleans, March.

Samuelson, W., and R. Zeckhauser. 1988. "Status Quo Bias in Decision Making." *Journal of Risk and Uncertainty* 1: 7–59.

Sanbonmatsu, D., and R. Fazio. 1990. "The Role of Attitudes in Memory-Based Decision Making." *Journal of Personality and Social Psychology* 59: 614–622.

Sanford, A. 1986. *The Mind of Man: Models of Human Understanding*. New Haven: Yale University Press.

Sanitioso, R., and Z. Kunda. 1991. "Ducking the Collection of Costly Evidence: Motivated Use of Statistical Heuristics." *Journal of Behavioral Decision Making* 4: 177–178.

Schank, R., and R. Abelson. 1977. *Scripts, Plans, Goals, and Understanding*. Hillsdale, NJ: Lawrence Erlbaum.

Schelling, T. C. 1973. "Hockey Helmets, Concealed Weapons, and Daylight Savings: A Study of Binary Choices with Externalities." *Journal of Conflict Resolution* 17: 381–428.

Schwarz, N., H. Bless, and G. Bohner. 1991. "Mood and Persuasion: Affective States Influence the Processing of Persuasive Communications." In M. P. Zanna, ed., *Advances in Experimental Social Psychology*, 24: 161–199. New York: Academic Press.

Schwarz, N., and G. Clore. 1983. "Mood, Misattribution, and Judgments of Well-Being: Informative and Directional Functions of Affective States." *Journal of Personality and Social Psychology* 45: 513–523.

Schwarz, N., and G. Clore. 1988. "How Do I Feel About It? The Informative Functions of Affective States." In K. Fiedler and J. Forgas, eds., *Affect, Cognition, and Social Behavior*. Toronto: Hogrefe International, 44–62.

Sears, D. O. 1983. "The Persistence of Early Political Predispositions: The Roles of Attitude Object and Life Stage." In L. Wheeler and W. J. McGuire, eds., *Political Socialization, Citizenship Education, and Democracy*. New York: Teachers College Press.

Sears, D. O., L. Huddy, and L. Schaffer. 1986. "A Schematic Variant of Symbolic Politics Theory, as Applied to Racial and Gender Equality." In R. Lau and D. Sears, eds., *Political Cognition*. Hillsdale, NJ: Lawrence Erlbaum Associates, 159–202.

Seligman, A. B. 1997. *The Problem of Trust*. Princeton, NJ: Princeton University Press.

Shaw, D. 1997. "Candidate Appearances and Television Advertising in the 1988–1996 Presidential Elections." Paper presented at the annual meeting of the American Political Science Association, Washington, DC, September.

References

Shepsle, K. 1978. *The Giant Jigsaw Puzzle: Democratic Committee Assignments in the Modern House.* Chicago: University of Chicago Press.

Shepsle, K. 1979. "Institutional Arrangements and Equilibrium in Multidimensional Voting Models." *American Journal of Political Science* 23: 27–60.

Shepsle, K., and B. R. Weingast. 1981. "Structure Induced Equilibrium and Legislative Choice." *Public Choice* 37: 503–519.

Shepsle, K., and B. R. Weingast, eds. 1995. *Positive Theories of Congressional Institutions.* Ann Arbor: University of Michigan Press.

Simon, A. 1997. *The Winning Message.* Ph.D. dissertation, University of California, Los Angeles.

Simon, H. A. 1957. *Models of Man.* New York: John Wiley.

Simon, H. A. 1959. "Theories of Decision Making in Economics and Behavioral Science." *American Economic Review:* 253–283.

Simon, H. A. 1967. "Motivational and Emotional Controls of Cognition." *Psychological Review* 74: 29–39.

Simon, H. A. 1978. "Rationality as Process and Product of Thought." *American Economic Review: Proceedings* 68: 1–16. Reprinted in Simon 1982.

Simon, H. A. 1982. *Models of Bounded Rationality.* 2 vols. Cambridge, MA: MIT Press.

Simon, H. A. 1985. "Human Nature in Politics: The Dialogue of Psychology with Political Science." *American Political Science Review* 79: 293–304.

Simon, H. A. 1986. "Rationality in Economics and Psychology." *Journal of Business* 59; reprinted in Hogarth and Reder 1987, 25–40.

Simon, H. A. 1995. "Rationality in Political Behavior." *Political Psychology* 16: 45–61.

Slovic, P., D. Griffin, and A. Tversky. 1990. "Compatibility Effects in Judgment and Choice." In R. M. Hogarth, ed., *Insights in Decision-Making: Theory and Applications.* Chicago: University of Chicago Press.

Smith, A. 1991. *National Identity.* Reno: University of Nevada Press.

Smith, E. R. 1993. "Social Identity and Social Emotion: Toward a New Conceptualization of Prejudice." In D. M. Mackie and D. L. Hamilton, eds., *Affect, Cognition, and Stereotyping: Interactive Processes in Group Perception.* New York: Academic Press.

Smith, E. R., and S. Henry. 1996. "The In-Group Becomes Part of the Self: Response Time Evidence." *Personality and Social Psychology Bulletin* 22: 635–642.

Smith, V. L. 1991. "Rational Choice: The Contrast between Economics and Psychology." *Journal of Political Economy* 99: 877–897.

Smith, V. L., and J. M. Walker. 1990. "Monetary Rewards and Decision Cost in Experimental Economics." Unpublished manuscript, Economic Science Laboratory, University of Arizona.

Sniderman, P. M. 1993. "The New Look in Public Opinion Research." In A. Finifter, ed., *Political Science: The State of the Discipline II.* Washington, DC: American Political Science Association.

Sniderman, P. M., R. A. Brody, and P. E. Tetlock. 1991. *Reasoning and Choice:*

References

Explorations in Political Psychology. New York: Cambridge University Press.

Sniderman, P. M., J. F. Fletcher, P. H. Russell, and P. E. Tetlock. 1996. *The Clash of Rights: Liberty, Equality, and Legitimacy in Pluralist Democracy.* New Haven: Yale University Press.

Sniderman, P. M., J. M. Glaser, and R. Griffin. 1990. "Information and Electoral Choice." In J. Ferejohn and J. Kuklinski, eds., *Information and Democratic Processes.* Urbana: University of Illinois Press.

Sniderman, P. M., P. Peri, R. DeFiguredo, and T. Piazza. 2000. *The Outsider: Prejudice and Politics in Modern Italy.* Princeton, NJ: Princeton University Press.

Snyder, J. 1991. *Myths of Empires: Domestic Politics and International Ambition.* Ithaca, NY: Cornell University Press.

Snyder, J. 1996. "Military Force and Regional Order." In E. A. Kolodziej and R. Kanet, eds., *Coping With Conflict After the Cold War.* Baltimore, MD: Johns Hopkins University Press.

Sowell, T. 1980. *Knowledge and Decisions.* New York: Basic Books.

Spellman, B. A., and K. Holyoak. 1992. "If Saddam is Hitler Then Who is George Bush? Analogical Mapping Between Systems of Social Roles." *Journal of Personality and Social Psychology* 6: 913–933.

Spence, M. 1973. "Job Market Signaling." *Quarterly Journal of Economics* 87: 355–374.

Spillman, L. 1997. *Nation and Commemoration: Creating National Identities in the United States and Australia.* New York: Cambridge University Press.

Stein, Herbert. 1984. *Presidential Economics: The Making of Economic Policy from Roosevelt to Reagan and Beyond.* New York: Simon and Schuster.

Steinbruner, J. D. 1974. *The Cybernetic Theory of Decision.* Princeton, NJ: Princeton University Press.

Stevens, L., and S. Fiske. 1995. "Motivation and Cognition in Social Life: A Social Survival Guide." *Social Cognition* 13: 189–214.

Stimson, J. A. 1991. *Public Opinion in America: Moods, Cycles, and Swings.* Boulder, CO: Westview.

Stimson, J. A., M. B. MacKuen, and R. S. Erikson. 1995. "Dynamic Representation." *American Political Science Review* 89: 543–565.

Stonier, A. W., and D. C. Hague. 1973. *A Textbook of Economic Theory,* 4th ed. New York: John Wiley & Sons.

Suedfeld, P. 1985. "Cognitive Managers and Their Critics." *Political Psychology* 13: 435–454.

Suedfeld, P., S. Bluck, L. Loewen, and D. Elkins. 1994. "Sociopolitical Values and Integrative Complexity of Members of Student Political Groups." *Canadian Journal of Political Science* 26: 121–141.

Suedfeld, P., and A. B. C. Walbaum. 1992. "Altering Integrative Complexity in Political Thought: Value Conflict and Audience Agreement." *InterAmerican Journal of Psychology* 26: 19–36.

318

References

Sunstein, C. R. 1990. "Paradoxes of the Regulatory State." *University of Chicago Law Review* 57: 407–441.

Sunstein, C. R. 1993. "Endogenous Preferences, Environmental Law." *Journal of Legal Studies* 22: 217–254.

Sweeney, P., and K. Gruber. 1984. "Selective Exposure: Voter Information Preferences and the Watergate Affair." *Journal of Personality and Social Psychology* 46: 1208–1221.

Taber, C. S. In press. "The Interpretation of Foreign Policy Events: A Cognitive Process Theory." In D. A. Sylvan, and J. F. Voss, eds., *Problem Representation in Political Decision Making*. London: Cambridge University Press.

Taber, C. S., M. Lodge, and J. Glather. 2000. "The Motivated Construction of Political Judgements." In J. H. Kuklinski, ed., *Thinking About Political Psychology*. New York: Cambridge University Press.

Taber, C. S., and M. Steenbergen. 1995. "Computational Experiments in Candidate Evaluation." In M. Lodge and K. McGraw, eds., *Political Judgment: Structure and Process*. Ann Arbor: University of Michigan.

Taber, C. S., and R. Timpone. 1996. *Computational Modeling*. Sage University Paper Series on Quantitative Applications in the Social Sciences, 07-113. Newbury Park, CA: Sage.

Tesser, A. 1986. "Some Effects of Self-evaluation Maintenance on Cognition and Action." In R. Sorrentino and E. T. Higgins, eds., *The Handbook of Motivation and Cognition: Foundations of Social Behavior*. New York: Guilford Press, 435–464.

Tetlock, P. E. 1981a. "Pre- to Post-Election Shifts in Presidential Rhetoric: Impression Management or Cognitive Adjustment?" *Journal of Personality and Social Psychology* 41: 207–212.

Tetlock, P. E. 1981b. "Personality and Isolationism: Content Analysis of Senatorial Speeches." *Journal of Personality and Social Psychology* 41: 737–743.

Tetlock, P. E. 1983. "Cognitive Style and Political Ideology." *Journal of Personality and Social Psychology* 45: 118–126.

Tetlock, P. E. 1984. "Cognitive Style and Political Belief Systems in the British House of Commons." *Journal of Personality and Social Psychology* 46: 365–375.

Tetlock, P. E. 1985. "Accountability: A Social Check on the Fundamental Attribution Error." *Social Psychology Quarterly* 48: 227–238.

Tetlock, P. E. 1986. "A Value Pluralism Model of Ideological Reasoning." *Journal of Personality and Social Psychology* 50: 819–827.

Tetlock, P. E. 1989. "Structure and Function in Political Belief Systems." In A. R. Pratkanis, S. J. Breckler, and A. G. Greenwald, eds., *Attitude Structure and Function*. Hillsdale, NJ: Lawrence Erlbaum, 129–151.

Tetlock, P. E. 1991. "An Alternative Model of Judgment and Choice: People as Politicians." *Theory and Psychology* 1: 451–477.

Tetlock, P. E. 1992. "The Impact of Accountability on Judgment and Choice: Toward a Social Contingency Model." In M. Zanna, ed., *Advances in*

Experimental Social Psychology, 25: 331–376. San Diego, CA: Academic Press.

Tetlock, P. E., D. Armor, and R. S. Peterson. 1994. "The Slavery Debate in Antebellum America: Cognitive Style, Value Conflict, and the Limits of Compromise." *Journal of Personality and Social Psychology* 66: 115–126.

Tetlock, P. E., and A. Belkin, eds. 1996. *Counterfactual Thought Experiments in World Politics.* Princeton, NJ: Princeton University Press.

Tetlock, P. E., and R. Boettger. 1994. "Accountability Amplifies the Status Quo Effect When Change Creates Victims." *Journal of Behavioral Decision Making* 7: 1–23.

Tetlock, P. E., and J. I. Kim. 1987. "Accountability and Judgment Processes in a Personality Prediction Task." *Journal of Personality and Social Psychology* 52: 700–709.

Tetlock, P. E., P. Micheletti, and K. Hannum. 1984. "Stability and Change in Senatorial Debate: Testing the Cognitive versus Rhetorical Style Hypothesis." *Journal of Personality and Social Psychology* 46: 979–990.

Tetlock, P. E., R. Peterson, and J. Berry. 1993. "Flattering and Unflattering Personality Portraits of Integratively Simple and Complex Managers." *Journal of Personality and Social Psychology* 64: 500–511.

Tetlock, P. E., R. Peterson, and J. Lerner. 1996. "Revising the Value Pluralism Model: Incorporating Social Content and Context Postulates." In C. Seligman, J. Olson, and M. Zanna, eds., *Ontario Symposium on Social and Personality Psychology: Values.* Hillsdale, NJ: Lawrence Erlbaum.

Tetlock, P. E., L. Skitka, and R. Boettger. 1989. "Social and Cognitive Strategies of Coping with Accountability: Conformity, Complexity, and Bolstering." *Journal of Personality and Social Psychology* 57: 632–641.

Tetlock, P. E., and A. Tyler. In press. "Winston Churchill's Cognitive Style: The Debate over Appeasement of Nazi Germany and Self-Governance for India." *Political Psychology* 17: 149–170.

Thaler, R. 1991. *Quasi Rational Economics.* New York: Russell Sage Foundation.

Tufte, E. 1978. *Political Control of the Economy.* Princeton, NJ: Princeton University Press.

Turner, M. 1987. *Death is the Mother of Beauty: Mind, Metaphor, Criticism.* Chicago: University of Chicago Press.

Turner, M. 1989. "Categories and Analogies." In D. Helman, ed., *Analogical Reasoning: Perspectives of Artificial Intelligence, Cognitive Science, and Philosophy.* Dordrecht Netherlands: Kluwer, 3–24.

Turner, M. 1991. *Reading Minds: The Study of English in the Age of Cognitive Science.* Princeton, NJ: Princeton University Press.

Turner, M. 1996a. "Conceptual Blending and Counterfactual Argument in the Social and Behavioral Sciences." In P. Tetlock and A. Belkin, eds., *Counterfactual Thought Experiments in World Politics.* Princeton, NJ: Princeton University Press, 291–295.

Turner, M. 1996b. *The Literary Mind: The Origins of Thought and Language.* New York: Oxford University Press.

References

Turner, M., and G. Fauconnier. 1995. "Conceptual Integration and Formal Expression." *Metaphor and Symbolic Activity* 10: 183–203.

Turner, M., and G. Fauconnier. 1998. "Conceptual Integration in Counterfactuals." In J. P. Koenig, ed., *Conceptual Structure, Discourse, and Language, II.* Stanford, CA: Center for the Study of Language and Information.

Turner, M., and G. Fauconnier. 1999. "A Mechanism of Creativity." *Poetics Today* 20: 397–418.

Tversky, A. 1972. "Elimination by Aspects: A Theory of Choice." *Psychological Review* 79: 281–299.

Tversky, A. 1977. "Features of Similarity." *Psychological Review* 84: 327–352.

Tversky, A., and D. Kahneman. 1974. "Judgment Under Uncertainty: Heuristics and Biases." *Science* 185: 1124–1131.

Tversky, A., and D. Kahneman. 1981. "The Framing of Decisions and the Psychology of Choice." *Science* 211: 453–458.

Tversky, A., and D. Kahneman. 1986. "Rational Choice and the Framing of Decisions." *Journal of Business* 59: 251–278; reprinted in Hogarth and Reder 1987, 67–94.

Tversky, A., S. Sattath, and P. Slovic. 1988. "Contingent Weighting in Judgment and Choice." *Psychological Review* 95: 371–384.

Tversky, A., and R. H. Thaler. 1990. "Preference Reversals." *Journal of Economic Perspectives* 4: 201–211.

Uleman, J., and J. Bargh. 1989. *Unintended Thought.* New York: Guilford Press.

Uslaner, E. M. 1996. "Faith, Hope, and Charity: Social Capital, Trust, and Collective Action." Unpublished manuscript, University of Maryland.

Valavanis, S. 1958. "The Resolution of Conflict When Utilities Interact." *Journal of Conflict Resolution* 2: 156–169.

Vallone, R., L. Ross, and M. Lepper. 1985. "The Hostile Media Phenomenon: Biased Perception and Perceptions of Media Bias in Coverage of the Beirut Massacre." *Journal of Personality and Social Psychology* 49: 577–585.

Veale, T. 1996. "Pastiche: A Metaphor-Centred Computational Model of Conceptual Blending, with Special Reference to Cinematic Borrowing." Manuscript available from http://www.wam.umd.edu/~mturn/WWW/blending.html.

Viscusi, W. K. 1992. *Fatal Trade-offs: Public and Private Responsibilities for Risk.* New York: Oxford University Press.

Von Neumann, J., and O. Morganstern. 1944. *Theory of Games and Economic Behavior.* Princeton, NJ: Princeton University Press.

Walsh, V. 1996. *Rationality, Allocation, and Reproduction.* Oxford: Clarendon Press.

Walzer, M. 1983. *Spheres of Justice.* New York: Basic Books.

Wason, P. 1966. "Reasoning." In B. M. Foss, ed., *New Horizons in Psychology.* London: Penguin.

Wegener, D. T., and R. E. Petty. 1995. "Flexible Correction Processes in Social

References

Judgment: The Role of Naive Theories in Corrections for Perceived Bias." *Journal of Personality and Social Psychology* 68: 36–51.

Wilcox, C., L. Sigelman, and E. Cook. 1989. "Some Like It Hot: Individual Differences in Response to Group Feeling Thermometers." *Public Opinion Quarterly* 53: 246–257.

Wildavsky, A. 1988. *Searching for Safety*. New Brunswick, NJ: Transaction Publishers.

Wildavsky, A., and K. Dake. 1990. "Theories of Risk Perception: Who Fears What and Why?" *Daedalus: Journal of the American Academy of Arts and Sciences* 119: 41–60.

Williamson, O. E. 1975. *Markets and Hierarchies, Analysis and Antitrust Implications: A Study in the Economics of Internal Organization*. New York: Free Press.

Wilson, T., and S. Hodges. 1992. "Attitudes as Temporary Constructs." In L. Martin and A. Tesser, eds., *Construction of Social Judgments*. Hillsdale, NJ: Lawrence Erlbaum, 37–65.

Wittman, D. 1995. *The Myth of Democratic Failure: Why Political Institutions Are Efficient*. Chicago: University of Chicago Press.

Woolley, J. T. 1998. "Exorcising Inflation-Mindedness: The Transformation of Economic Management in the 1970s." *Journal of Policy History* 10: 130–152.

Wrong, D. H. 1994. *The Problem of Order: What Unites and Divides Society*. Cambridge, MA: Harvard University Press.

Wyer, R., and T. Srull. 1989. *Memory and Cognition in Its Social Context*. Hillsdale, NJ: Lawrence Erlbaum Associates.

Zajonc, R. 1980. "Preferences Need No Inferences." *American Psychologist* 35: 151–175.

Zajonc, R. 1984. "On the Primacy of Affect." *American Psychologist* 39: 117–123.

Zaller, J. R. 1992. *The Nature and Origins of Mass Opinion*. New York: Cambridge University Press.

Zaller, J. R. 1998. "Monica Lewinsky's Contribution to Political Science." *P.S.: Political Science and Politics* 31: 182–189.

Zaller, J. R., and S. Feldman. 1992. "A Simple Theory of the Survey Response." *American Journal of Political Science* 36: 579–616.

Zanna, M. 1990. "Attitude Function: Is it Related to Attitude Structure?" *Advances in Consumer Research* 17: 98–100.

Zbikowski, L. 1997. "Conceptual Blending and Song." Unpublished manuscript, University of Chicago.

Zeckhauser, R. J., and W. K. Viscusi. 1995. "Risk within Reason." In J. Simon, ed., *The State of Humanity*. Oxford: Basil Blackwell, 628–637.

Author Index

Author Index

Author Index

Author Index

Mason, C. F., 29
Mayer, J. D., 150
Mayseless, O., 172, 178
McCabe, K., 94, 107
McCauley, R. N., 12
McClosky, H., 67, 75, 75n
McCubbins, M. D., i, xi, 3n, 13, 14, 47n, 52, 54n, 56, 154, 156, 156n, 161, 185, 188, 289
McDermott, M., 110, 129
McEachern, W. A., 6n
McGraw, K., 133n, 184, 186
McGuire, W. J., 109, 166, 250
McKelvey, R. D., 55n, 57n, 153n, 156
McPhee, W. N., 3, 190
Meckling, W. H., 9
Merelman, R. D., 132n
Micheletti, P., 247
Midgley, B. D., 12
Milgrom, P., 30
Miller, G. J., 100, 100n
Miller, W. E., 67, 71, 136n, 155, 190, 216, 230
Mondak, J., 154, 155, 158, 159, 189
Montgomery, H., 172, 178
Morganstern, O., 25, 283
Morris, D., 132
Morrow, J., 185, 188
Mroz, J. E., 180
Munger, M. C., 35, 45
Murnane, R., 217
Mutz, D., 189
Myerson, R. B., 57n

Neely, J., 190, 196n, 198, 200
Neijens, P., 157
Neuman, W. R., 50
Nevitte, N., 72n
Newell, A., 51n, 52n
Nie, N. H., 69
Niedenthal, P. M., 212
Niemi, R. G., 110
Nisbett, R. E., 24, 29, 31, 33, 36, 51n, 160, 166, 185, 288
Nordhaus, W., 158
North, D. C., 13, 14, 24, 42, 57n, 289
Nozick, R., 102n

Oakley, T., 265n
Oates, W. E., 103
O'Hara, R., 75, 75n
Okun, A. M., 247
Olson, J. P., 80n, 234
Olson, M., 3n, 102, 246
Olson, R. G., 99

Oppenheimer, J. A., 15, 84, 87, 90, 93n, 95, 96, 96n, 98, 100, 101, 102, 103n, 104, 106, 106n, 107, 289
Orbell, J., 141
Ordeshook, P. C., 7n, 55n, 57n, 153n, 156, 212
Ostrom, E., 3n
Ottati, V., 215

Page, B. I., 153, 154, 160n, 161
Park, B., 183, 186
Parkinson, B., 135n
Peabody, D., 261
Peffley, M., 136
Peterson, R. S., 240, 244, 246, 248, 250, 261
Petrocik, J. R., 69, 110
Petty, R. E., 109, 148, 166, 169, 185, 188, 195, 287
Pinker, S., 162, 162n, 164, 165
Plotkin, H. C., 162n
Plott, C. R., 103n
Plutchik, R., 132, 133
Polanyi, M., 38
Popkin, S. L., i, 3, 18, 47, 54n, 109, 130, 136, 153, 155, 157n, 158, 215, 216, 218, 219n
Powell, M., 183
Powell, R., 3n
Powers, M. R., 158
Pratkanis, A., 189
Pratto, F., 195, 198, 200, 201n
Price, V., 157, 214
Prior, A. N., 99
Przeworski, A., 44
Putnam, R., 140, 141, 218, 247
Pyszczynski, T., 188, 207

Quattrone, G., 76, 77
Quillian, M. R., 198
Quirk, P. J., 17, 170, 171

Rabe, C., 131n
Rae, D., 67
Rahn, W. M., 15, 16, 18, 131, 132, 132n, 135, 141, 142, 218, 228
Raiffa, H., 167
Ram, A., 208
Rauch, J., 246
Rawls, J., 100
Raz, J., 244
Reder, M., 281
Redlawsk, D., 159, 189
Reynolds, S., 135n
Rich, R., 170, 171

326

Subject Index